SOCIAL WELFARE AND RELIGION IN THE MIDDLE EAST

A Lebanese perspective

Rana Jawad

This edition published in Great Britain in 2009 by

The Policy Press
University of Bristol
Fourth Floor
Beacon House
Queen's Road
Bristol BS8 1QU
UK

Tel +44 (0)117 331 4054
Fax +44 (0)117 331 4093
e-mail tpp-info@bristol.ac.uk
www.policypress.org.uk

North American office:
The Policy Press
c/o International Specialized Books Services (ISBS)
920 NE 58th Avenue, Suite 300
Portland, OR 97213-3786, USA
Tel +1 503 287 3093
Fax +1 503 280 8832
e-mail info@isbs.com

British Library Cataloguing in Publication Data
A catalogue record for this book is available from the British Library.

Library of Congress Cataloging-in-Publication Data
A catalog record for this book has been requested.

ISBN 978 1 86134 953 8 hardcover

Cover design by The Policy Press
Front cover: image kindly supplied by www.panos.co.uk
Printed and bound in Great Britain by MPG Books Group

Contents

List of tables and figures

Tables

Figures

Acknowledgements

Thank you to:

My family first and foremost.

The Policy Press for supporting this book project.

The Economic and Social Research Council (ESRC) for funding the development of my research on the Middle East.

In the UK: Robert Walker, Tony Fitzpatrick and the University of Nottingham for supervising and funding the initial PhD dissertation; Bob Deacon for his subsequent timely guidance; Katie Anders for her assistance with the Bibliography.

In Turkey: Professor Ayse Bugra and all colleagues at the Social Policy Forum (Bogazici University), Burcu Yakut-Cakar, Selmin Kaska and Ahmet Icduygu, the officials who met with me in the various government agencies, the United Nations Development Programme (UNDP), the welfare organisations and the families who received me in their homes.

In Iran: Professor Ali Saeidi, Saeed Sadequi, Dr Hassan Zare, Neda Shoar and all colleagues at the Social Welfare Research Institute (Tehran), Azade, Mr Hamid Nazari, Mr Ali Farahani and all colleagues at Emdad, the Ministry of Welfare and the Social Security Organisation.

In Egypt: my dear friend Nadine Moussa, Ehaab Abdou, Hania Sholkhamy, Heba Raouf, all colleagues at the UNDP-Egypt Office, the Arab Medical Council and the Ministry for Social Solidarity.

In Lebanon: Ms Nada Fawaz, Mr Yakoub Kassir, Ms Wafa Baba, Ms Joelle Dib, Sister Benoit, Sheik Sami, the Ministries of Social Affairs and Finance and the National Social Security Fund, colleagues in the United Nations agencies, and all the welfare organisations who have taken part in my research over the years. Thanks also to my colleagues at the American University of Beirut, Jocelyn Dejong and Mona Harb.

Last but not least, thank you also to the service users of all the participating organisations in this research who are – always – the litmus test of social welfare services and have been the most critical group in the kind of research undertaken here. Many others deserve my thanks and I am unable to list them all here.

List of Arabic words with English translations[1]

Al Hala Al Ijtima`iya	The social case
Al Hala Al Islamiya	The Islamic case
Fitra	Human nature: predisposed to do good (Islamic)
Harakat Al Mahruumin	Movement of the oppressed
Istid`aaf	Oppression, disempowerment (Islamic)
Iwaa	Shelter
Mahsuubiya	Patronage
Mustad`af	Oppressed, disempowered (Islamic)
Ramadan	Muslim fasting month
Saddaqah	Charitable handout (Islamic)
Takaaful (Ijtima`i)	Financial sponsorship, social solidarity
Takleef Shar`i	Legal Islamic duty
Waqf (pl. Awkaaf)	Religious endowments
Wasta	Personal intermediation/favour
Zakat	Islamic tax (equivalent to 2.5% of assets)

[1] Translations adapted from Baalbaki (2001).

List of abbreviations

DfID	Department for International Development (UK)
ESRC	Economic and Social Research Council
EU	European Union
FBO	Faith-based organisation
GDP	Gross Domestic Product
GNI	Gross National Income
GNP	Gross National Product
ILO	International Labour Organization
IMF	International Monetary Fund
IRFED	International Institute for Research and Training for Standardised Development
MENA	Middle East and North Africa
MSA	Ministry of Social Affairs (Lebanon)
NGO	Non-governmental organisation
NSSF	National Social Security Fund (Lebanon)
PRWORA	Personal Responsibility and Work Opportunity Reconciliation Act (US)
RWO	Religious welfare organisation
SEWP	Social ethics–welfare particularism
UN	United Nations
UN-DESA	United Nations Department of Economic and Social Affairs
UNDP	United Nations Development Programme
UN-ESCWA	United Nations Economic and Social Council for Western Asia
UNICEF	United Nations International Children's Emergency Fund
UNRISD	United Nations Research Institute for Social Development
USAID	United States Agency for International Development

Map of the Middle East

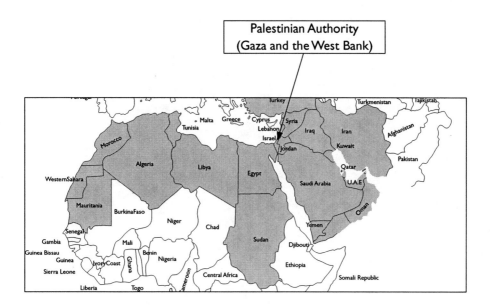

Palestinian Authority
(Gaza and the West Bank)

ONE

Introduction: religion and social policy – an "old–new" partnership

One wonders whether the greater willingness of social scientists to consider religious factors in Third World cases might be the result of a strange marriage of positivism and post-modernism in which cultural relativism serves as cover for a deep-seated modernism that still sees religion as a symptom of backwardness. (Gorski, 2005, p 187)

[R]eligious faith is a good thing in itself, ... far from being a reactionary force, it has a major part to play in shaping the values which guide the modern world, and can and should be a force for progress ... I see Faith and Reason, Faith and Progress, as in alliance not contention.... We can think of the great humanitarian enterprises which bring relief to those who are suffering – the Red Cross, the Red Crescent or Islamic Relief, CAFOD and Christian Aid, Hindu Aid and SEWA International, World Jewish Relief and Khalsa Aid – all the charities which draw inspiration from the teachings of the different faiths.... And in the West, for example, we owe an incalculable debt to the Judaeo-Christian tradition in terms of our concepts of human worth and dignity, law and democracy. (Blair, 2008, p 9)

Once the muse of the founding fathers of the modern social sciences, today religion has mostly become associated with a regressive or self-deluding impulse; or at best it is regarded as a cultural artefact. By the 1970s, few scholars would have imagined the centrality of religion on the world stage in the new millennium, but the last three decades have indeed been marked by the prominence of religiously inspired social and political mobilisation worldwide, as highlighted by a variety of publications that consider evidence on all the world religions (Antoun and Hegland, 1987; Moyser, 1991; Esposito, 2000; Mitsuo, 2001; Haynes, 2003; Madeley and Enyedi, 2003; Sutton and Vertigans, 2005; Bacon, 2006; Freston, 2007; Thomas, 2007; Delibas, 2009).

Is Tony Blair, previous leader of one of the most advanced and secular nations of the world, now a global development protagonist, lecturing on faith and globalisation at Yale University and seeking to broker Middle East peace, blowing the trumpet of neoliberalism and pointing us in the direction of things to come? Can religious identity be party to the making of the good society of the future? Or is this merely a sign of desperation and a loss of creative thinking about the state of what some sociologists (see Beckford, 1989; Gorski, 2005) have hailed as the post-materialist world?

This book is an enquiry into the relevance of religion to modern social welfare. It focuses on the region of the Middle East, arguably the religious capital of the world, and seeks to open up a broader debate on the contribution of religiously inspired social welfare to the study and practice of contemporary social policy. In examining the role of religious welfare, particularly of Islam in the Middle East, this book seeks not only to contribute to our understanding of social welfare practices and institutions in the Islamic tradition, but also to explain how social welfare provision constitutes the comparative advantage that major Islamic social movements like Hizbullah (Lebanon), Hamas (Palestinian Territories), the Justice and Development Party (Turkey) and the Muslim Brotherhood (Egypt) have over their respective governing state bodies. Delibas (2009) provides one of the most recent contributions to the growing body of literature on Islamic social movements in this regard – albeit from a political science perspective.

Thus, the study of religious welfare in this region can offer a unique and innovative perspective on the political dynamics there. Moreover, it can shed light on new possibilities of positive public action in the region against social injustice and human deprivation (Jawad, 2008).

The most common term used by commentators to describe the apparent comeback of religion in the public sphere is *resurgence* (Antoun and Hegland, 1987; Haynes, 2003; Sutton and Vertigans, 2005; Thomas, 2007), with its concomitant undertones of a previously outlawed uprising. To this end, Gorski (2005) speaks of the *return of the repressed*, denoting the return of religion to academic debate after a period of political and theoretical repression. Madeley and Enyedi (2003) take a more tempered view, questioning the factual basis of the religious neutrality of Western modern nation-states and arguing that the influence of religion in politics has never totally disappeared, even in Europe. To this end, Madeley (2003a) speaks of a "new-old" phenomenon to describe the ongoing role of religion in European politics.

In this book, I place these two words (old and new) in the sequential order that is more common in the Arabic usage, as can often be heard in Lebanon during street demonstrations when protestors reiterate in front of the filming news crew their "old–new" demands for better public services or a minimum wage that matches the rising cost of living. Thus, I shall endeavour to show that the relationship between religion and social welfare is indeed an "old–new" partnership, bearing both intellectual and practical implications.

Much of the renewed interest of scholars in the public role of religion was inspired by the 1979 Iranian revolution at a time when Europe and North America had been experiencing a growth in New Age religious movements (Introvigne, 2004; Bainbridge, 2007; Robbins and Lucas, 2007). These events would attest to the dynamic capacity of religion to speak to successive generations of human society, prompting the prominent American sociologist Robert Bellah (1970) to rekindle the torch of Max Weber and revive the sociological study of religion by redefining modern religion in the symbolic terms of faith (as opposed to cognitive belief), giving it an innate home in the human self.

> [R]eligion is part of the species life of man, as central to his self-identification as speech ... religion, as that symbolic form through which man comes to terms with the antinomies of his being, has not declined, indeed, cannot decline unless man's nature ceases to be problematic to him. (Bellah, 1970, pp 223, 227)

Bellah (1970) is particularly famous for popularising the notion of an American civil religion, drawing on the ideas of the revolutionary French thinker Jean-Jacques Rousseau's *Social Contract*. To this end, Gorski (2005, p 173) makes the highly convincing argument, reciting Emile Durkheim's original thesis, that:

> [R]eligion in the broader sense of 'the sacred' and the 'collective conscience' was a functional necessity of life ... old religions would have to be replaced by new religions, meaning civil religions and with other sources of 'mechanical solidarity', such as occupational associations.

Thus, far from God being dead, as Nietzsche famously proclaimed in the 19th century, it was the secularisation precept of modernisation theory that had collapsed (Gorski, 2005), with José Casanova's (2008) coining of the term the "*deprivatisation* of religion".

In the present international political order in which we live, Muslim populations and Muslim organisations have emerged as key objects of scrutiny, which sees most recent texts with an Islamic theme centred around discussion of the implications of September 11 (for example, Wickham, 2002; Sutton and Vertigans, 2005; Tal, 2005) and the "exceptionalism" of Islam – the Middle East in particular – to an otherwise globally integrating and democratising world (Clark, 2004; Esposito and Mogahed, 2007; Salamey and Pearson, 2007).[1] This has emphasised the scant attention paid to Islam within the social science literature (Ernst, 2004; Sutton and Vertigans, 2005), a situation that is even more deficient in the subject area of social policy (Deacon, 1997; Midgley, 1997; Gough and Wood, 2004; Hall and Midgley, 2004; Hill, 2006), although it should be noted that the *International Encyclopaedia of Social Policy* (Fitzpatrick et al, 2006) does redress some of the gaps in knowledge about Middle Eastern social policy.

But, this book argues that, ironically, it is the very study of social policy in the Middle East that can bear the most fruits in understanding the micro level of public action in the region and in exploring new avenues for positive future action towards the formulation of a potentially more just social order in the region. A major impetus behind this would be the need to recognise the field of the "social" (Orloff, 2005; Karshenas and Moghadam, 2006a) in the formulation of public policy.

Consequently, in examining the dynamics of social welfare and religion in the Middle East, this book uses the language and tools of enquiry that are commonly associated with the subject of social policy. This rather trivial statement is of tremendous symbolic significance: it echoes the argument made by Sutton and Vertigans (2005) that dispassionate social scientific study is necessary for helping us better understand controversial religious phenomena. Thus, regardless of the various arguments that have pitched the development of social scientific knowledge or indeed the rise of the welfare state itself against religion (Wuthnow, 1988; Iannaccone et al, 1997; Kahl, 2005) the stance taken in this book is that social policy can in fact offer a new and potentially transformative understanding of the political and social dynamics of the Middle East, indeed that religion and social policy can work together in positive symbiosis (Bullis, 1996).

An "old–new" partnership: religion in social policy scholarship

An arduous task faces this book: in bringing together religion, social policy and the Middle East, it is necessary to address both real and imagined obstacles to a constructive discussion around these topics. The obstacles I refer to have as much to do with how scholars, the media and decision makers have thought about the key subjects of this book, as they have with the contemporary conjuncture of Middle Eastern countries themselves and the track records of both state intervention and religious activities there.

There are thus some prevailing stereotypes, stigmas, myths and indeed two to four hundred years of major social transformations that have relegated religious identity to the idiosyncratic realm of personal preference or even delusion. Indeed, it is also possible to argue, as Bullis (1996) does for the case of social work, that social policy and religion are concerned with two irreconcilable and competing subjects: the former being concerned with justice, the latter with truth (Levinas and Guwy, 2008). It is useful to outline briefly some of these real and imagined obstacles that make religion and social policy unlikely bedfellows.

Religion is usually concerned with supernatural and idealistic issues such as belief in a higher being, correct moral behaviour, personal redemption, salvation and worship in order to secure a better place for oneself in the afterlife (Wuthnow, 1988; Zrinščak, 2006). Therefore, religion has less to do with the practical concerns of human life on earth, namely economic and technological progress, social equality, political freedom, justice or social solidarity (Tyndale, 2000). In terms of social order, religion is generally considered as a conservative force favouring tradition and control (Smith, 1996) at a time when social policy is a highly applied field concerned with evolving social rights and therefore must respond to changing social needs. Thus, far from being amenable to the promotion of tolerance and pluralism, religion has a long history of inciting fundamentalism and social conflict (Tyndale, 2000).

The French revolution put an end to centuries of religious domination and upheaval in Europe. In contrast, it is fair to say that in the geographical contexts around the world today where religion continues to hold public sway, religiously based violence continues to flourish and in many cases to hijack political power. There has been sufficient media coverage of Shi'as against Sunnis, Protestants against Catholics, Serbs against Albanians and, in the US, bombings of abortion clinics, to attest to the violent nature of religiously inspired hatred (Esposito and Mogahed, 2007).

It is not surprising, then, that the mainstream social policy literature should also attest to the marginalisation of religion in the study of the good society, and the nature of human well-being – not least perhaps, because social policy became the dominion of the secular nation-state after the Second World War. Today, it is common in contemporary historical accounts of social policy (for example, in Page and Silburn, 1999; Offer, 2006) and in public speeches such as that by Tony Blair cited at the beginning of this chapter to mention or pay passing tribute to the role of the various religious traditions in the world in teaching about or struggling for human well-being and social progress. In the British context, for example, Page and Silburn (1999) remark that Christian Socialism may have provided the preconditions for the post-war welfare settlement but this remark ends in the same sentence that introduces the notion of the debt of the British welfare state to Protestant Christianity.

We are more likely to find discussion of religion in accounts of the role of the voluntary sector in social welfare. Bacon (2006) offers relevant examples in North America and Northern Ireland while Valins (2006) offers discussion of Jewish social care in the UK. Chapter Two will engage more fully with this discussion. Thus, it remains the case that in the mainstream social policy literature, systematic studies of the role of religion in social policy remain few and far between. Very modestly, this book will refer to all the relevant sources on religion and social policy written in the last three decades, which include among them sources on the Middle East. It will become evident that scholarship in this area has progressed very slowly, with very few relevant publications published in the last 10 years.

Like the UK, the rest of Northern Europe, arguably the home of secularisation and of modern social policy, where the social democratic tradition has been able to flourish, has little place for discussion of religion as a serious contender in the world of welfare. Indeed, some have argued that the purpose and nature of the welfare state has replaced those human needs traditionally filled by religious belief, not least because the welfare state was supposed to recreate the social bonds that had been dominated by the pre-existing religious order. The "gift relationship" that Titmuss (1970) defended as the core philosophy of the welfare state was an innately ethical concept, which he argued paralleled the primordial ties that bound traditional religious societies (Titmuss, 1970, p 210). Indeed, it is noteworthy that Titmuss (1970) argued that what Marx failed to do was to develop a moral theory for socialism. Yet today, discussion of morality, ethics or religion is marginal in the social policy literature, with few exceptions such as

Donnison (1989), Dean (2006) and Fitzpatrick (2008). In the North American context, it is perhaps more usual to adopt a moral stance in discussion of social welfare. To this end, Skocpol (2000) argues strongly that biblical (religious) beliefs and motivations provide the most powerful engine yet for reviving the ideals and practical commitment to social justice. Celebrating what she sees as the great debt of modern American democracy to the cross-class religio-social movements of the 19th century, Skocpol (2000) pitches conservatives against liberals, neatly summarising the state of social policy in our times thus:

> In recent years, the academic literature on 'social welfare policy' has been so dominated by leftist secularists that it has written out of the record positive contributions from religiously inspired services to the poor. If noted at all, such ministry has transmuted into Machiavellian acts of class of racial domination. This is unfortunate, because much of redeeming value has been accomplished by religiously committed individuals and congregations delivering spiritual along with material aid to fellow members or needy persons beyond the existing congregation. (Skocpol, 2000, p 24)

Thus, within the European context, those social policy professionals who take the big step towards considering the connections between religion and social welfare are a very rare breed, and when they do this they feel impelled to begin their arguments with the usual disclaimers, devoting several paragraphs in their prefaces and acknowledgements to arguing that one does not have to be religious to want to explore the connections between religion and social policy, just like "you do not have to be a fool to study madness". These are the words of Van Kersbergen (1995, p viii), a previous student of Gøsta Esping-Andersen, and one of the first contemporary social policy academics in Northern Europe to seriously consider the role of religion in the welfare state. Van Kersbergen (1995) looks at the specific case of Christian Democracy in Germany, Italy and the Netherlands to make the case for the possibility of a welfare regime called social capitalism. Wilber and Jameson (1980), Higgins (1981), Hornsby-Smith (1999) and Nesbitt (2001) are among the earliest works in the US and the UK to pay attention to the role of religion in social policy, while some of the most recent publications on the subject are penned by Kahl (2005) and Opielka (2008), with a new edited volume on the religious origins of European social policy by Kees Van Kersbergen and Philip Manow (2009). It has also often been the case that social scientists have more willingly recognised the role of religion in public policy in the Third World than they have in the Western context (for good critiques, see Wilber and Jameson, 1980; Gorski, 2005).

Thus, as already suggested above, there are some variations within Northern Europe and North America on academic debate about the role of religion in social policy. The US and continental Europe tend to stand apart from the UK because of the better-established recognition of the roles of the voluntary sector and the churches in public service provision (Esping-Andersen, 1999; Skocpol, 2000). This also includes recognition of the role of spirituality in health and social welfare, especially in the North American context (Tangenberg, 2004). By contrast, in the UK, it is only recent publications such as Spalek and Imtoual (2008) that have begun to take a fresh look at the implications of spirituality for the study of the social sciences. Like the US case, authors on non-Western contexts have also long acknowledged the critical role of spirituality in public action there (see, for example, Ver Beek, 2000). The question of religion thus contributes to the challenge of holism in that it appeals precisely to the moral, spiritual and emotional dimensions of human experience in a way we are only just beginning to appreciate in the social sciences. The rejection of dualism made here advocates an ontology of the social actor as a *whole*. Linked to this is the importance of religion in stimulating associational life and providing the moral energy behind the ideals and the pursuit of social justice. For Skocpol (2000), the two are inextricably linked in historical terms and she argues forcefully that US democracy would not be what it is were it not for the 19th-century federations, charities, voluntary associations and citizens' groups that were led by individuals with deep religious values, but not actually under 'clerical control' (Skocpol, 2000, p 37).

It is important to note here the key role that the cultural turn in the social sciences is playing in introducing religion (back) into the social policy agenda. Opielka's (2008) chapter is part of an edited volume on the role of culture in the welfare state. Social policy observers (Midgley, 1997; Hall and Midgley, 2004; Hill, 2006) have been predicting, for some time now, the intensification of cultural considerations in the study of social policy as greater attention is paid to issues such as the politics of recognition, social exclusion, multiculturalism and the quality of life (Hornsby-Smith, 1999). In the West, this argument has gained more weight in light of the longer periods of economic security enjoyed by Western societies, otherwise denoted by the term 'post-materialism' (Beckford, 1989; Inglehart and Baker, 2000) . This means that consideration of spirituality and religion will need to be taken more seriously in the study of well-being and in the advancement of new avenues for policy making. Indeed, it is also possible to argue that the role of religious faith and the social services provided by religious and voluntary groups will experience increasing demand as a result of the current global economic downturn.

To summarise, based on a review of the contemporary relevant literature in the sociology of religion, social policy, historical sociology and political science, it is impossible not to enunciate the key question that arises from decades of scholarship on the condition of modernity and the quest for human happiness: does religion have a relevant public role to play in the pursuit of human well-being? Can religion offer as convincing a solution to social problems and human prosperity as the (welfare) capitalist state has?

This is the key problematic of this book. From this basic problematic, the argument now focuses on the geographical region of the Middle East, which forms the core concern of this book. The stereotypes and stigmas mentioned above become doubly heavy in the Middle East, because this is a region of political conflict, where some of the world's last remaining totalitarian regimes look set to stay. It is also a region of economic exceptionalism to global capitalist expansion (as explained at the beginning of this chapter) as well as being a highly conservative and gendered society.

Beyond the Rentier state: religion and social policy in the Middle East

The Middle East is a black hole in social policy, both as an academic subject and as a tool of public policy. Scholars, both East and West of the globe, have hardly approached the subject, and Middle Eastern governments are vague and slow in their social policy announcements. Only international development agencies, specifically the United Nations (UN), appear to engage with the study of social policy in the region and have commissioned studies on poverty, social development and social security such as a recent edited volume released by the United Nations Research Institute for Social Development (UNRISD) entitled Social Policy in the Middle East (Karshenas and Moghadam, 2006b) and various reports on social policy by the United Nations Economic and Social Council for Western Asia (UN-ESCWA) (2004, 2005) and the United Nations Department of Economic and Social Affairs (UN-DESA) (see Ortiz, 2007). Is this silence on the region of the Middle East in the social policy literature due to deliberate neglect or lack of capacity? The answer is a combination of both.

It appears, then, of little wonder that for a region that usually occupies media headlines and academic enquiry with concerns over global security and the supply of petroleum oil, the Middle East would indeed be inimical to any talk of progressive social policy. Indeed, if I have argued above that the social policy literature is fairly mute on religion, then it is near non-existent on the Middle East.

For clarity, the geography of the Middle East includes countries in the Middle East and North Africa (henceforth MENA), which according to Henry and Springborg (2001, p 8) extends "from Morocco to Turkey along the southern and eastern shores of the Mediterranean and as far East as Iran and south to Sudan, Saudi Arabia and Yemen". The region has a population of half a billion people, which is Muslim in the majority, but as it is home to the world's three largest monotheistic religions, it continues to have substantial Christian and Jewish populations.

In a recent publication (Jawad, 2008), I have reviewed the major recent English-language works on social policy in the Middle East. Only one of them actually has the words 'social policy' and 'Middle East' in the title (see Karshenas and Moghadam, 2006b), the remaining books (see El-Ghonemy, 1998; Henry and Springborg, 2001; Soroush, 2002; Clark, 2004; Heyneman, 2004; Wiktorowicz, 2004; Behdad and Nomani, 2006; Moghadam, 2006a) skirt in and out of an array of social welfare issues that connect Islamic theology, jurisprudence and institutions to public policy, to underdevelopment, to social movements, to charity, to globalisation, to wealth polarisation and to gender inequality. It is, therefore, not surprising that the conceptualisation of social policy in the region, which is based on the old and narrow wisdom of the Rentier state (Beblawi, 1990), appears to have outrun its course with very little in the way of new thinking as to what social policy means or how it works in the contemporary Middle East. This is happening at a time of increased interest in social welfare programmes by Middle Eastern states, primarily due to the initiatives of international development institutions such as the World Bank and the UN-ESCWA. It is crucial to note that the first Arab Human Development Report (UNDP, 2002) cited Islamic welfare as the central force behind the alleviation of poverty in the Arab region. Subsequent country-specific Human Development Reports continue to refer to the central role of faith-based welfare in society, which can account for over 50% of the civil society sector (see, for example, the 2008 Human Development Report for Egypt: UNDP and Institute of National Planning, Egypt, 2008).

The first Poor Laws to be documented in human history were written in Ancient Egypt and Mesopotamia (modern-day Iraq) (Ellor et al, 1999) and are, therefore, a historical precursor to the ethical teachings of the three Abrahamic faiths. Such milestone historical documents, which formally expressed the importance of charity towards the poor and less fortunate in society, began with the Code of Hammurabi (1792–1750 BC), the Egyptian Poor Law (from 3000 BC), the Israelite covenant with God and the Mosaic Code (circa 2112–2004 BC) and Islamic Law (from 6th century AD) (Bullis, 1996, pp 70, 71). There have also been laws on charity towards the poor found in Ancient Phoenicia (circa 1500 BC), which is now modern Lebanon.

The dust of European (de)colonisation has settled, and media headlines are as much about entertainment as they are about critical enquiry (Ernst, 2005), but what has happened to social policy in the Middle East in the decades since mid-20th-century independence? Indeed, what do local Middle Eastern populations today think of social welfare, equality, justice and solidarity? As Ernst (2005, p 28) argues: "Islam is a subject ... most ... experienced ... through negative images and stereotypes ... the time has come to go beyond those images and encounter real human beings".

Very modestly, this book will seek to redress some imbalances in the study of the Middle East as a region, and in the study of social policy as a secular utilitarian tradition of how human society can best be organised and experienced.

Conventionally, the study of social policy in the Middle East rests on the conceptual framework of the Rentier state, coined in the 1970s as a result of the discovery of oil in Latin America and the Middle East and first used by Beblawi (1990) to refer to social policy in the Middle East, and more recently, referred to again by Karshenas and Moghadam (2006b) in their consultancy work for the UNRISD. As Beblawi (1990) argued, the Rentier state denotes the almost exclusive dependence of Middle Eastern states on revenues from natural resources (hydrocarbon gas and petroleum oil) to finance social and public services. This dependency has hampered the development of citizenship or social rights as the bases of any social contract between state and society.

'Rent' is a category of revenue first used by classical economists as originating from land ownership. Its meaning has, however, expanded to include all other revenues aside from the standard methods of remuneration for labour or capital. It also includes the difference between marginal cost and sale price. Rents can therefore be generated through the exercise of monopolistic behaviour or imperfect information, which produce imbalances in market conditions (Destramau, 2000, p 321).

The Rentier state refers primarily to the oil-producing countries of the Middle East (the Gulf states, Iraq, Iran and Algeria) while generally excluding a number of other countries in the region. It has also been applied to Latin American oil-producing countries. It excludes other civil society actors (such as the family, community and international actors) and a considerable number of historical, cultural and political forces that have influenced human well-being directly (Jawad, 2008). Beblawi (1990) even went as far as arguing that even the non-oil-producing nations of the Middle East such as the countries along the Mediterranean coast (including those of North Africa (such as Egypt and Morocco)) were influenced by a Rentier mentality whereby the allocation of resources and the organisation of political relationships were dominated by favours and personal contacts.

Yet, by focusing entirely on the characteristic of oil-rich countries, which draw on oil revenues to finance social and public services, the Rentier state excludes a host of independent variables in the analysis of Middle Eastern social policy, namely the cases of non-oil-producing countries (which make up almost two thirds of the total 23 nations in the region), factors such as history and culture, a long line of local civil society and global actors and, crucially, the role of the two largest religions of the region, Islam and Christianity.

The inadequacy of the concept of the Rentier state arises not just from the need to appreciate the more complex array of historical, cultural and religious forces that are actually working at national, international and local level in the Middle East. The need for new thinking also arises from the very conceptualisation of the changing landscape of social policy studies, its scope and objectives. This is not dissimilar to the rethinking of social policy that has been occurring within the Western context since the 1980s (Lewis, 2000). For, by focusing analysis on how social welfare programmes are financed by oil-producing Middle Eastern states, and how this has undermined the development of citizenship, a very static image of social and political dynamics is produced, which leads to a status quo of passive citizens facing a coercive and corrupt state. In this scenario, democracy and socially inclusive development are put forward by global development institutions as the main tools for effective social policy (Karshenas and Moghadam, 2006a).

It is useful at this point to consider the importance of a cultural perspective on social policy analysis that has been put forward by some authors such as Clarke (2004), Pfau-Effinger (2004) and Van Oorschot et al (2008) in order to develop the argument for the need to think about religious welfare works in the Middle

East, or indeed in other contexts around the world. Clarke (2004) argues that the way we think about the welfare state matters a great deal for what the welfare state can actually do. This emphasises the useful analytical import of a cultural perspective.

According to Clarke (2004, p 154), the welfare state is a combination of "institutionalised formations (apparatuses, policies, practices) and political-cultural imaginaries (symbolizing unities, solidarities and exclusions)". Thus, the history of the welfare state cannot be understood in a linear form that imposes a rational and objectivist approach to the study of social policy. Instead, as Clarke (2004, p 5) argues, our reading of history needs to be "conjunctural", in that it should be sensitive to the variety of forces that come into play in order to produce a particular event or definition of a concept. This implies that at the heart of the conflict over welfare and its meaning is the definition of nationhood and the construction of the "people" in a nation as citizens. These views are also echoed by Pfau-Effinger (2004, 2008), who argues that values, ideals and knowledge exercise an important influence on the dynamics of social policy. For our present purpose, this would mean supplementing the historical account of social policy from the point of view of the state, which is portrayed in the books reviewed through an analysis of the multiplicity of social actors and the polysemy of the concept of welfare itself. This is based on recognising social policy as a discourse and as an anthropological phenomenon.

Thus, while the political-economic analysis offered by the Rentier state conceptualisation can help us understand how some Middle Eastern states might have succeeded or failed to redistribute wealth in their countries, it misses the way in which the social order was itself negotiated and how the state also exercised influence on the formation of national identity and its symbols. Indeed, a cultural analysis would suggest that political conflict over welfare and its association with nation-building in the Middle East is part and parcel of the nature of social policy, since a social settlement is a particular negotiation arrived at by various conflicting groups.

A cultural perspective on social policy analysis provides ample reason to consider the role of religion in social welfare. Religious identity has long constituted a major driving force behind many of the most enduring political, social and pro-poor movements around the world, and not just in the Middle East (Smith, 1996; Esposito, 2000): from the church-led liberation movements of the 1970s in Latin America (Montgomery, 1982), to the Buddhist Sarvodaya Movement in Sri Lanka (Brazier, 2001), to the Catholic-inspired Solidarity Trade Union Movement in Poland (Hruby, 1982), stretching further back to the Christian Socialist movements of the 18th and 19th centuries in the UK. Indeed, Collins (2007) notes that in Medieval Europe, sporadic popular uprisings by the poor against feudal elites were always energised by religious symbolism, and that Franciscan monks are the precursors to modern-day leftist movements. In Medieval Japan, Buddhist monasteries were centres of economic development and military prowess (Collins, 2007). The examples abound across human history and geographical location.

In the modern Middle East, some well-known examples of such movements include the Muslim Brotherhood in Egypt, the Justice and Development Party (AK Parti) in Turkey, Hamas in the Occupied Palestinian Territories and Hizbullah in Lebanon (Shadid, 2001). Indeed, there is a growing literature on faith-based welfare around the world, which is establishing firm ground for religious identity to be an active force in the public sphere (Bacon, 2006; Tyndale, 2006; Clarke and Jennings, 2008). So far, this literature remains largely descriptive in nature. In development studies, Tyndale (2006), Clarke and Jennings (2008) and Tomalin (2008) offer a particular view of the achievements of faith groups with regard to the UN's Millennium Development Goals. In the West, faith-based welfare is located within the broader literature on the voluntary sector (Bacon, 2006), while some authors have also demonstrated the historical links between Christianity and social policy (Kahl, 2005; Hollinger et al, 2007). Authors from the last two decades such as Higgins (1981) and Nesbitt (2001a) offer descriptive works on the role of the established churches in dealing with the problems of modern capitalism. Higgins (1981) emphasises how religious beliefs have provided the ideological backdrops for most social policy systems around the world, with 8th-century Buddhism in particular providing some of the earliest orphanages and social care services. Opielka's (2008) recent addition to this literature provides an overview of classical sociological theory on religious welfare and extends this to include a broader definition of religion that encompasses political ideologies such as Marxism and New Age spiritual movements.

In terms of Islamic welfare practices, the literature is primarily focused on Islamic Law in relation to *zakat* (obligatory almsgiving) and the historical role of the *waqf* (religious endowments) (Benthall and Bellion-Jourdan, 2003; Dallal, 2004; Richardson, 2004). Weiss (2002) considers Islamic voluntarism in Africa in line with the other main focus in the literature on Islamic economics (Tripp, 2006). Clarke (2004) considers Islamic social institutions in Egypt, Jordan and Yemen in relation to social movement theory. Benthall and Bellion-Jourdan (2003) provide a legal-political discussion of Islamic charity in the context of international human relief agencies, suggesting that Islamic welfare primarily seeks to promote Islamic political interests. No comprehensive analysis that brings together service users and service providers yet exists of religious welfare in its natural disciplinary home: social policy.

Further, there are important developments in the field of social policy and in the international community that make this book timely, namely the increasingly international character of social policy studies (spearheaded by globalisation and an interest in East Asian welfare regimes), new partnerships between the state and faith groups in the UK and the US following welfare reform legislation (Bacon, 2006; Farnsley, 2007) and the increasing attention of global actors (such as the World Bank and the UK's Department for International Development: DfID) on faith-based activity (Clarke and Jennings, 2008). This is exemplified by the establishment in recent years of the DfID-funded Religion and Development programme at Birmingham University and the Berkley Center for Religion,

Peace and World Affairs at Georgetown University in Washington, DC. Thus, as religion regains its centrality in academic and policy debates, it is apt that this book is focused on the study of faith-based welfare in the region where much of religious history has been written: the Middle East.

Aims and scope of the book

This book will present a new and systematic analysis of social welfare in the Middle East through the lens of religion, arguably the longest and most dynamic surviving force of social and political action in the region (and perhaps also the world). Based on an in-depth study of the Lebanon, and drawing on supplementary research conducted in Egypt, Iran and Turkey, the book argues that religion – whether through the state apparatus, or civil society organisations or populist religious movements – is providing sophisticated solutions to the major social and economic problems of the Middle East. This argument, as I have stated elsewhere (Jawad, 2008) is driven not by an ideological affiliation to Islam or the Middle East, nor by nostalgia for a happier Islamic past.

Rather, the primary aim of this book is deeply pragmatic, following on from the questions mentioned in the previous section, which seek the local experience of Middle Eastern populations on the key dimensions of social welfare. This pragmatic aim entails seeking out and trying to understand what positive examples of public action there are in the Middle East, what motivates ordinary people to act in the interest of the public good and thus to critically analyse these as potential building blocks for social policy in the future. This follows a long line of scholarly work in development studies that argues that developing countries need to be able to elaborate policies that suit their societies, which in many ways are qualitatively different from those of advanced capitalist democracies where development theorising has traditionally taken place (Cowen and Shenton, 1995). As Cornwall and Gaventa (2000) argue, it is time that the literature considered how social policy works in poorer countries of the South and not just in Northern or transitional economies.

Moreover, at a time when global processes of economic liberalisation and democratisation are challenging the nature and role of the state in the lower-income countries to sustain basic standards of public and social provisioning, it is incumbent that alternative means by which to ensure human welfare be found (Kabeer and Cook, 2000). This book thus supports the view that locally relevant alternatives and indeed 'home-grown' solutions to social problems deserve to be considered as a means of providing sustainable policy measures. Indeed, local survival strategies in low-income countries could offer possibly generalisable lessons for the treatment of poverty. A notable observation is made in the literature of the increasingly important institutional role played by community-level organisations in social welfare provision:

> In many parts of the world, informal popular and community associations, self-help groups and networks are actively involved in bridging the service provision gap. These include religious bodies.... A failure to consider them in discussions of social policy contributes to and reinforces their marginalisation. (Cornwall and Gaventa, 2000, p 57)

Thus, this book will open up analysis of how social policy works in the Middle East beyond the notion of the Rentier state. This means taking into account a much more complex and broader set of actors within and beyond the state, as well seeking out the values, meanings, ideals and knowledge of both service providers and service users on the ground in the Middle East. In this sense, the perspective of this book is rooted in the lived experience of social policy in the Middle East and, in order to understand the social fabric that underpins social welfare in the region, it is imperative to consider the role of religion in the Middle East. The emphasis of this book on finding positive local public action hints at the history of such policy making, which has not been fully responsive to local social realities and has often been 'hijacked' by local structures of power (Destramau, 2000; Thompson, 2000; Kabeer, 2004).

Thus, the book will highlight how human well-being in contexts like Lebanon is not synonymous with social policy as a set of social measures in public administration. The path to human well-being is more complex since it draws on different concepts and resources to those traditionally known in the West. The crux of the argument will be to unpack the world of religious welfare in the Middle East, using the examples of the countries focused on in this study by looking at how social actors use religion to inform their conceptualisation and implementation of key concepts such as social welfare, solidarity, justice and equality. The emphasis will be on drawing out the key issues of policy elaboration both in terms of policy content and the power processes through which policy discourse is constructed.

The ultimate aim of this conceptual discussion is to advance two key proposals, one theoretical and the other practical:

- the final analysis in this book will present a welfare model based on the Lebanese case, which has been verified to some extent by the cases of Egypt, Iran and Turkey;
- a social policy 'agenda' or the practical ramifications of the empirical research on which this book is based for the future development of social policy both in Lebanon and in the Middle East will be presented.

To summarise, the central questions that structure the argument in this book are:

(1) What do the major world religions say about social welfare and how have religion and social policy interacted in various national welfare settings?

(2) How does religious affiliation inform social action and shape the conceptualisation of human well-being in Lebanon and the wider Middle East?

(3) How is this conceptualisation packaged, implemented, delivered and evaluated in practice through social actors, welfare institutions and policy tools?

(4) What are the key issues raised about the configuration of social policy in Lebanon and the region?

(5) How does religious affiliation shape the conceptualisation of social cohesion and solidarity in the region?

(6) Is there a model of social welfare for the region emanating from the Lebanese case?

(7) What are the theoretical and practical implications of the Lebanese case for the future prospects of social policy in the Middle East?

These questions form the platform on which this book will seek primarily to describe what service providers and service users in the countries studied think about social welfare and, subsequently, to understand the reasons or explanations they give for their thoughts. This will entail mapping out the subjective meanings, motives, perceptions, emotional and moral experiences that welfare providers and users in the region have about the role of religious affiliation in social welfare.

Definition of terms

It is useful to begin with a working definition of religion, borrowed from the eminent American sociologist Robert Wuthnow (1988, p 308, emphasis added), which also expresses the core substance of this book:

> [R]eligion cannot be understood very well if attention is limited only to arguments about disembodied ideas (symbols) or even abstract conceptions of organizations and actions. Religion has an organic quality, a communal and moral dimension, that binds people to one another and creates close dependencies between them and their environments.... Religions become embodied as moral communities – as networks of deeply felt obligation to one another and to collective rituals and beliefs, all of which provide a sense of belonging, even security, to the participants. *The very beliefs and ideas of which any religion is comprised reflect and dramatize these moral obligations; thus, even a focus on belief requires more than abstract consideration of ideas.*

The above definition of religion signals the way in which religion is part of lived experience and not just a symbolic set of abstract beliefs. This supports the logic of this book's discussion. Moreover, it recognises that religion is a concept that is dynamic and extends beyond the traditional world religions such as Christianity, Hinduism, Islam or Judaism to include other 'isms' such as Marxism and new movements such as Jehovah Witnesses and the Moonies (Opielka, 2008). What all these religious orientations have in common is that they represent three key issues for their adherents, which are: ultimate values, sacredness and transcendence. These are borrowed from Durkheim, Weber and Marx (Opielka, 2008).

Since this book is focused on the Middle East, the religions that have been chosen for study are the main religions of the region: Christian, Druze and Muslim. However, it should be noted that these communities are not internally homogenous and that none of the religious welfare organisations that were eventually selected for the research were representative of their whole communities. Likewise, it should be noted that in Lebanon, there is a fine line between religion and sect or ethnicity since social actors may be staunch Shi'as or Christian Orthodox politically or culturally without being religiously observant.

Moreover, the definition of religion provided here has sought to incorporate an understanding based on explicit rules and practices as much as the basic moral values that were subsumed by the dominant culture. Thus, the religious character of the organisations researched was not necessarily determined by the presence of clerics within them. All these factors merely reinforce the wide spectrum of religious identity incorporated into this book.

To this extent, the literature on religious welfare distinguishes between spirituality, religiosity and religion (Bullis, 1996; Gilliat-Ray, 2003), as it does between faith-based and religious organisations. The religious organisations researched in Lebanon for this book were religious in the sense that they not only employed clerical staff and belonged to Christian or Muslim ideological orders but they also actively used religious teachings and spiritual acts of worship in their social welfare work. However, two of them fell on the fringes of this conceptualisation of religion, which reinforced how religion can act as ethnicity/sectarianism or underlie secular/lay value systems. Finally, it is important to note that this book finds the term 'faith-based welfare' ill suited for the study of religion-based welfare in the Middle East. Thus, the terms 'religious welfare' and 'religious welfare organisations' (RWOs) as opposed to 'faith-based welfare' will be used. This distinction will be discussed in the next chapter since it forms the crux of the argument in this book and the reasons for this will be demonstrated through the research reported here.

Sociologists commenting on the social structure of lower-income countries have tended to be guided by structural functionalism, indeed theorists of social exclusion and cohesion from the classics such as Emile Durkheim to the post-moderns such as Serge Paugam have emphasised the statutory nature of roles in so-called 'traditional' societies. The latter authors have gone as far as suggesting that each social role is also a level in the social hierarchy and, by the same token, social exclusion is in fact only tolerated in 'traditional' societies. On the other hand, their view of social roles in advanced modern societies has been much more dialectal where the self is a social being. The position advocated in this book is that social roles are profoundly dynamic although it is accepted that in the context of the Middle East, the research reported in the book points to the contrary in some cases.

Social welfare is conceptualised in three main ways in this book: as a vision of social well-being, as a system of social provision and as a measure of outcomes. Philosophically, the concept hinges on three essential dichotomies: subjective/ objective, universal/relative and individual/collective (Fitzpatrick, 2001, pp 8-10). The discussion in subsequent chapters will explore how service providers and service users eventually defined social welfare themselves. In the theoretical literature, many definitions have been put forth for welfare, which include happiness, security, preferences, needs and desert (Fitzpatrick, 2001, p 5). The research reported in this book does not always converge with these definitions. From the religious perspective, it is also necessary to consider the spiritual or metaphysical dimensions of welfare or indeed that the issue may not even be about material welfare but about other metaphysical criteria in that individuals may forgo material well-being for spiritual redemption in the afterlife. To this extent, the book takes on board the implications of the increasing importance of culture in political philosophy, which has put forward the case that social justice is just as much a matter of cultural recognition and identity politics as it is of wealth redistribution (Fraser, 1997).

Social welfare thus includes the narrower definition of social administration inherent in the provision of vital social services such as health and education as well as the broader definition that is directly linked to social development and encompasses a concern for the elimination of social inequalities or the advancement of equity.

In terms of social policy, this is conceptualised as a key axis of public policy or indeed a set of purposive actions in the public sphere aimed at ensuring human well-being in the widest sense through a variety of actors and tools. The definition of social policy adopted in the book is informed by Davis (2001) and Kabeer (2004). This definition neither assumes a direct relationship between social policy and social development nor assumes that social policy is separate from economic policy. Spicker (2000) provides a useful classification of the different purposes of social policy, which basically demarcate between personal and collective welfare. I used these during the research for this book and they serve to organise the book's argument. They are:

- needs provision;
- remedying disadvantage;
- behavioural change;
- potential development;
- maintaining circumstances;
- producing disadvantage.

Spicker (2000) defines social policy as a pre-eminently moral act, an assertion that is supported in this book.

While the concept of social policy may be most meaningful to the Western European context where the welfare state has had a much richer history (Kabeer, 2004), social policy does reflect the orientation in this book towards a set of policies and purposive social actions that are aimed at safeguarding and advancing human well-being and social justice in the broadest sense. My emphasis has perhaps eventually fallen on purposive social action and the recognition that although there may not be social policy as such in Lebanon, there is a policy regime. I have not assumed that the state is the central leading actor in this endeavour and, as such, the scope and nature of social policy as presented in the data reflect the context-specific circumstance of the country case studies researched for this book.

The concept of poverty is understood first and foremost as a state of socioeconomic deprivation that is manifested in a variety of material ways such as a low level of income, a limited ability to access basic social services or limited capabilities. This reflects the dominant understanding of poverty in the context of the Middle East. Poverty also carries within its definition the more spiritual connotations of moral humility often associated with religious faith (Rahnema, 1997).

Finally, the concept of power forms a key platform for discussing the nature and purpose of social policy in this book. Fitzpatrick (2001, pp 85-90) offers a useful overview on the definition of power as:

- *quantitative capacity*, which can be accumulated, producing a dualistic understanding of the concept. Pluralism, elitism and radicalism are three axes around which this notion of power exists;
- *legitimate authority*, which offers a qualitative definition of power whereby it is based on moral authority that is consented to and abided by, by the social actors on whom such power is exercised;
- *power as production*, which is based on Foucault's ideas on practices and discourses of normalisation.

The book will illustrate how power was defined in the particular context of Lebanon and how far it was corroborated by the other national welfare settings I researched.

Organisation of the book

The book has two thematic parts which serve the dual purpose of (a) describing religious welfare in the context-specific case of Lebanon, with supporting examples from Egypt, Iran and Turkey, and (b) synthesising the implications of this description in subsequent chapters. Thus, the book also has a more analytical and theoretically oriented dimension.

The general structure of the book is as follows. Chapter Two provides a platform on which the key problematic of the book is set out. It draws on the experiences of both Northern and Southern contexts of social policy in order to highlight what the major world religions teach about social welfare and how social policy has interacted with religion in various national welfare settings around the world. The chapter will focus on the five major world faiths – Hinduism, Buddhism, Judaism, Christianity and Islam – in their general and local forms since these are the faiths that have had the most direct influence on national politics and social welfare. The chapter will consider examples from other worldviews such as Confucianism and Zoroastrianism. Thus, the chapter will highlight points of divergence and convergence across world religions and national welfare settings. The chapter also refers to the development studies literature since this is the academic discipline that has traditionally been devoted to so-called 'Third World' social science. The key claim made in the chapter is that concern with human morality fundamentally unites secular and religious welfare initiatives. Indeed, religious influences can be found in social policy for many countries around the world. Authors such as Van Kersbergen (1995) and Kahl (2005) argue that in Western Europe particular Christian traditions have had a direct impact on the configuration and structure of social policy in various countries.

Chapter Three contextualises the discussion in the book by providing a country profile of Lebanon and an in-depth view of the political and welfare institutions there. This includes a historical look at the development of social policy in Lebanon, which flourished in the post-independence era and floundered around the time the 1975 civil war broke out. In this respect, the experience of Lebanon is representative of the rest of the region, where spending on public and social services peaked during the oil boom era.

Chapter Four is the first of the three empirical chapters in the book. It reports direct evidence on the lived experience of social welfare in the Middle East, based primarily on Lebanese case studies and drawing on supplementary examples from Egypt, Iran and Turkey. Thus, the chapter fulfils the call made in this book to move beyond old stereotypes and misconceptions about the region and to seek the human experience there. The chapter considers the motivations and basic philosophy underpinning religious welfare in Lebanon. It sets the scene by describing how social welfare in Lebanon is conceived, motivated and conceptualised as policy. To this end, the chapter provides profiles of five prominent religious organisations in Lebanon and the Ministry of Social Affairs. The chapter seeks to explore social welfare as a philosophy of social service, the aim being to present conclusions about the nature and role of social welfare in Lebanon. The extent to which social policy targets transformational social change as opposed to merely offering palliative relief assistance forms the crux of the chapter. The chapter incorporates perspectives from the cases of Egypt, Iran and Turkey in order to explore the generalisability of the Lebanese case.

Chapter Five progresses to explore social welfare as a system of provision and a measure of outcomes in Lebanon, again with supplementary evidence from the other countries. Here, the focus is on two types of social programmes: social care and micro-credit/cash benefits. The concern is to consider the mechanics and dynamics of service delivery and consumption. The chapter asks key questions about how religious welfare defines the object of its interventions and, therefore, how appropriately it responds to the causes of social problems instead of their symptoms. This will include consideration of the mechanisms of service evaluation used by the religious welfare organisations to assess the impact of their work. These are supplemented with my own empirical observations.

Chapter Six looks at how solidarity and social cohesion are understood and experienced in the Middle East. In particular, it allows in-depth analysis of the power dynamics underpinning social policy in Lebanon, which tend to point towards an elitist and paternalist approach to policy making. The chapter draws out the key characteristics of social cohesion in Lebanon and the basis on which the social order is maintained. The place of solidarity and the role of RWOs in modifying or sustaining the social order are central to the chapter.

Chapter Seven synthesises the empirical discussion of social welfare in the preceding chapters by presenting a welfare model based on the Lebanese case. This will be denoted as social ethics–welfare particularism (SEWP). References will be made to the existing literature on welfare regimes and social reproduction in order to explore the theoretical implications of the Lebanese case for the wider study of social policy in the region. The strength of the SEWP model is that it is validated by the preliminary research reported in this book on the welfare situations of Egypt, Iran and Turkey. The chapter falls short of offering an in-depth historical analysis of social policy in the region although it does give an analysis of the Lebanese situation. The historical analysis of social welfare for the region is a topic for another book on this subject.

Chapter Eight considers the practical implications of religious welfare as highlighted in the book for social policy more broadly in the Middle East. The chapter advances some policy recommendations for Lebanon but also considers the prospects for religious welfare gaining more formal status in the social policy literature and having a more effective role in public policy in the Middle East. The extent to which religion is already a negative force in public policy in the region, or is viewed as a threat to global security, will also be addressed. Thus, the chapter will seek to clarify what value religion holds for social policy. It will base its argument for the Middle East on key examples from the literature on the politics of North America and Western Europe where religious associations have played a central role in the development of democracy, and in the heritage of the welfare state. While there are varying arguments as to whether or not the Middle East needs or indeed has already gone through its own Reformation (Tripp, 2006), the chapter notes that, regardless of global politics and the agendas of global actors like the DfID, UN and World Bank, religious organisations in the Middle East will continue to do their work and serve their populations.

A key dimension of this chapter will be to consider the traditional disjunction between private religion and public policy (Trigg, 2007). The chapter will suggest that faith-based organisations (FBOs) need to be considered as valid partners in civil society. They have already played a key part in the democratic history of major countries around the world (Skocpol, 2000; Demerath, 2007a). As Demerath (2007b) argues, there is a difference between religious dogma controlling political institutions and religious-inspired individuals entering the political sphere.

The question for governments and international development institutions is: are they willing to engage on an equal footing with such religious groups and to see them as valid public actors? The question for academic observers is: can they engage rationally with the contribution of RWOs to human well-being? The challenge for RWOs is to put their message across in such a way that they are not misunderstood.

The Conclusion summarises the main arguments of the book.

A note about the research reported in the book

Almost a decade's-worth of primary research and first-hand experience of social and development policies in the Middle East, beginning in 1999, went into this book – most of which is reported here for the first time.

I shall first explain the Lebanon part of the research, which occurred between 2000 and 2005, and then the second phase of fieldwork, which included Egypt, Iran and Turkey and took place in 2007 and 2008. Lebanon is an illustrative example of the Middle Eastern experience of religious welfare and social policy to the extent that it has dynamic secular and religious welfare sectors. However, Lebanon is atypical of the region in terms of its political structure, which is based on the proportional representation of the sects in government. Lebanon is also exceptional in that it has the oldest liberal market system in the region.

My fieldwork in Lebanon began with my PhD thesis (2000–05) and was further developed in 2007–08 thanks to a grant from the Economic and Social Research Council (ESRC), which allowed me to return to Lebanon to update my research and conduct a dissemination workshop with the religious groups, policy makers and experts who had been part of my original PhD research. During this fieldtrip, I met again with senior officials in the Ministry of Social Affairs (MSA).

The organisations that were researched in Lebanon (and which are discussed in this book) were six in number: the MSA and five of the most prominent RWOs, which were chosen from the main religious denominations in Lebanon. The RWOs chosen were also the largest in terms of the variety of services they offered and their extensive presence throughout Lebanon. The newest of the organisations are roughly 25 years old (these are the Hizbullah organisations) and the oldest is over 80 years old (the Dar Al Aytam, mentioned below). The RWOs chosen enjoy very high social standing within their communities and have links to political figures in the Lebanese political establishment. They also have varying degrees of religiosity – not all of them have clerical staff, for example. The Lebanese RWOs are:

- Dar Al Aytam (Muslim Sunni) – www.daralaytam.org/;
- Emdad and Al-Qard Al-Hassan (Muslim Shi'a – affiliated to Hizbullah) – http://almashriq.hiof.no/lebanon/300/320/324/324.2/hizballah/emdad/ [no web address available for Al-Qard Al-Hassan];
- Al Urfan Al Tawhidiya (Druze) [no web address available];
- Soeurs Antonines (Christian Maronite) – www.cmdsa.edu.lb/2008/homepage.aspx [web address of an affiliated school];
- Caritas (Christian – Roman Catholic) – www.caritas.org/worldmap/mona/lebanon.html

In addition to the MSA proper, two local development centres acting as service providers and community outposts for the MSA were included in the Lebanon research. These were located in a Muslim and a Christian area respectively.

The social services that were studied were social care (both family and institution based) and all types of financial assistance such as cash handouts and micro-credit. Social care was chosen because it is at the heart of the MSA's work and is a problematic issue for the whole of MENA. It is also the primary preoccupation of religious worldviews, which are very concerned with protecting the family. Financial assistance is much less common due to the lack of resources and a particular aversion to promoting laziness.

The target population was mainly drawn from the Greater Beirut area, which included Mount Lebanon but also extended to the Chouf (pronounced 'shoof') Mountain region in the Bekaa and Southern Lebanon. Due to the breadth of the study and my objective of engaging key policy makers, the research eventually focused on the headquarters of the RWOs and the MSA, which were located in Beirut, Mount Lebanon and the Chouf Mountain depending on the sect of the organisation (except for the MSA, of course, which was in central Beirut). These regions are primarily urban settings except for the Chouf Mountain and Southern Lebanon. The sample population thus included the poorest urban communities in Lebanon, which were in the southern suburbs of Beirut, but also some of the poorer rural areas in the Chouf Mountain and Southern Lebanon.

In Lebanon, 114 interviews were conducted with government ministers, managing directors, religious leaders, policy makers and consultants, programme managers and administrators, application officers, field and social workers, service users and beneficiaries.

With regards to the inclusion of Egypt, Iran and Turkey in this book, these will supplement the Lebanon case study and provide important depth to the analysis. These three countries reflect the diverse historical, political, religious and cultural forces shaping social policy in the Middle East. They represent a range of implicit and explicit relationships between religion and the state, ranging from collaboration, as in the case of Iran, to resistance, as in the cases of Egypt and Turkey, although even in the latter two countries, the tide may be changing.

Politically, Turkey is a strong secular republic where there is increasing visibility of Islamic public action through the rise of the ruling Justice and Development

Party (AK Parti). Iran is an Islamic state where the clerical establishment has the ultimate say over public policy. In terms of social policy, all four countries have a contribution-based system with uneven or, indeed, incomplete levels of coverage. It is interesting to note that for Egypt, Iran and Turkey, social policy has become a particularly important issue in the last three years. Egypt is revising its social policy plan and attempting to coordinate activities more. Iran has established a Ministry of Social Welfare for the first time to coordinate its disparate welfare institutions. And Turkey is in the midst of a reform process in order to gain accession to the European Union (EU). This has seen the creation of new government bodies to manage the reform of social policy.

Socially, Iran and Turkey are the two major non-Arab countries of the region in contrast to Lebanon and Egypt. Neither was colonised by European powers. Economically, Iran is the only oil-producing nation of the four countries and it has also had much less contact with the political agendas of international development institutions as a result of the sanctions it is enduring. With regards to primary research, the following organisations were researched:

- Insani Yardim Vakfi (Istanbul, Turkey) – www.ihh.org.tr/;
- Deniz Feneri Denergi (Istanbul, Turkey) – www.denizfeneri.org.tr/afet_cin_ deprem.aspx;
- two state-run local community centres in Istanbul (Turkey);
- the Social Planning Organisation (Ankara, Turkey);
- in Iran, the state controls all major social welfare initiatives, making them "para-state organisations" (Saeidi, 2004). I visited (a) two provincial branches of the Imam Khomeini Relief Foundation (Comité Emdad), one in Tehran and one in the city of Mashhad – www.emdad.ir; (b) the Social Welfare Ministry, Government of Iran; and (c) the Social Security Organisation;
- the Ministry of Social Solidarity (Cairo, Egypt);
- the Muslim Brotherhood (Cairo, Egypt) (a meeting was held with a senior member).

In addition, I conducted interviews with social policy experts, all of whom have been involved in major consultancy works for their respective governments or for international bodies such as the UN on social policy and poverty in the countries involved. These social policy experts are all academics and based at the American University of Cairo (Egypt), Tehran University (Iran) and Bogazici University (Turkey). In both Egypt and Turkey, I also met with the representatives of the United Nations Development Programme (UNDP), which gave me further insight into how far each of the countries in question was being advised by the UN on social policy, and how far they had integrated civil society and RWOs in their new social policy plans.

The primary research that is reported in this book thus rests on very solid grounds, benefiting as it does from data from four major countries of the Middle East, with the Lebanese data having been both updated and verified with research participants. I also made use of official policy documents and grey literature from the organisations that I studied, including confidential internal reports at the MSA in Lebanon. In all, what this book offers is a robust analysis of the variety of forms in which religious welfare is expressed in the Middle East.

Moreover, the countries included in this analysis are a diverse mix, and encompass major non-Arab populations of the Muslim world. The strength of the data reported in this book is that it cuts across both Muslim and Christian welfare organisations. All research participants remain anonymous when they are quoted in the book but they are denoted by acronyms, which refer to the organisation they belong to and a number.

Note

[1] One view of exceptionalism argues that North American and European concerns for oil, the Russian threat, and the pressures of the Arab–Israeli conflict have led them to support the authoritarian regimes that exist in the region (Esposito and Mogahed, 2007), thus facing accusations of double standards. Other commentators on global terrorism who take a socioeconomic perspective argue that the rise of Islamic fundamentalism (read as exceptionalism) is directly connected to poverty. Religious demagogues use a populist version of Islam to gain the allegiance of deprived Muslim populations (see, for example, Wickham, 2002; Salamey and Pearson, 2007). The solution, according to this view of Islamic terrorism, is that counterterrorist foreign policy must seek to promote social welfare services in Muslim countries in order to counter the appeal of Islamic fundamentalism. A contrasting perspective argues that those in abject poverty are not politically driven to join Islamic insurgencies; rather, it is those populations that have achieved some modicum of well-being that are attracted by extreme political Islam. The US promotion of the 'New Middle East' is seen to be one means of promoting democratic rule and liberal values in the region that are supposed to lift it out of politically vulnerable poverty (Salamey and Pearson, 2007). This argument is refuted by Esposito and Mogahed (2007), who cite new survey data from the World Gallup Poll and other studies, which show that radical terrorists are affluent, well educated and not very religious. In offering an in-depth analysis of Shi'a, Sunni, Druze, Maronite and Roman Catholic welfare in Lebanon, this book suggests that Hizbullah is no different in its social welfare strategies than the other sects in Lebanon. It is the patron–client logic of the political structure in Lebanon that dictates that the ruling faction(s) of the Lebanese sect should offer welfare support to its communities. These arguments are expanded further throughout the book, with supporting data from other countries.

TWO

Religion and the foundations of social policy

Introduction

This chapter sets the scene for the discussion of this book by reviewing the literature on the relationship between religion, human well-being and social policy. In Chapter One, I suggested that the relationship between religion and social policy is not new and in many ways is mutually constitutive: world religions are not just belief systems, they are also social systems with strong impulses to be active in the public sphere (Haynes, 2003). Concurrently, their public role and standing on issues of social welfare, justice and human dignity have been shaped by their interaction with the various social and political ideologies that have come into place throughout human history (Higgins, 1981; Chan and Lap-Yan, 2000; Tyndale, 2003).

This has meant that religiously inspired welfare has been championed not just by the clerical establishments of the major world faiths but also, and indeed more significantly, by lay individuals who in many cases have been prominent intellectuals and social reformers as in the cases of Christian Socialism (Atherton, 1994), modern Hindu thinkers such as Ghandi and Rammohan Roy (Richards, 1985), Muslim reformist thinkers such as the Egyptian Seyyed Qutub and the Iranian Abdolkarim Soroush (Tripp, 2006) and the Christian Democratic movement in the Catholic countries of Europe (Van Kersbergen, 1995). In all cases, religiously inspired ideals have been at the forefront of public action, with many finding their way directly into the machinery of modern governments.

The engagement of the Catholic Church in the 1980s Solidarity Movement of Poland or with Christian Democracy in Western Europe, the development of socialist strands of Protestantism and Sunni Islam from the 19th century, and the proliferation of the Hindu *gram seva* (village service) in India under the leadership of Gandhi in the early 1900s, are all illustrations of an ongoing historical engagement between religion and social welfare action. It is also the case that world religions have been influenced by each other, such as the influence of socially conscious Christianity on Hinduism through India's contact with Britain (Klostermaier, 1994). It is, therefore, very much the case that the interpretation of religious teaching is itself historically contingent: the same teachings are read differently by different human generations. The ethical social teachings that are described, therefore, in this chapter are generic teachings that are more or less common within the faiths discussed. The way in which these teachings have been used and interpreted by various denominations within these faiths will also be explored.

I will focus on the five major world faiths – Hinduism, Buddhism, Judaism, Christianity and Islam – which together command adherents from over half of the world's six billion people. This is primarily due to the need to focus the discussion although reference will be made to the welfare-related teachings and practices of smaller faiths such as Baha'i and Sikhism, as well as worldviews that are not quite religions but more philosophies such as Confucianism. New Age spiritualist movements will also be referred to although the activities of such movements in terms of material welfare (such as poverty reduction and healthcare) are not very advanced. Max Weber's (1930) study of religion also focused on these five religions, although he did not live to conduct a full study of Islam (Sutton and Vertigans, 2005).

What is noteworthy about these main five religions is that they have some of the most elaborate enunciations on public social welfare that can be found in any of the world faiths. These five religions are also the only ones to have penetrated formal state apparatus around the world: from India and Sri Lanka, to Iran, Saudi Arabia and Israel, to the UK, Germany, Greece and the US (although Confucianism has played its part in Far Eastern public policy). Already, then, this chapter is beginning to say something about the connection between religion and social policy in the modern world. Established state religions have continued to exist and defy the drive of secularisation, even in the supposed heartland of secularity: Western Europe (see Madeley's excellent critique of state neutrality in Western Europe; Madeley, 2003a, 2003b).

In contrast to Hinduism and Judaism, Buddhism, Christianity and Islam have become truly transnational in character (Freston, 2007), mutating into a variety of localised forms, such as Pentecostalism in Latin American, Africa and the Far East, Western Buddhism in Europe and European-based Islam as a result of burgeoning immigrant populations outside the traditional lands of Islam. This chapter will devote special attention to the understanding of social welfare and social justice in Islam, as this is the main religion of interest in this book.

The relevance of religious teachings to human life has been framed in a variety of ways by modern scholars, all of which flow into an overarching concern with *ethics* (the rules that govern correct social relationships). The well-known progressive Muslim thinker credited with instigating Islam's equivalent to the Christian Reformation (who is of Iranian origin and also a trained cleric, although currently residing as an academic in the US), Abdolkarim Soroush (2002), talks about the religious social order that governed the world until a few centuries ago when European Enlightenment permeated the remaining regions of the world. This religious world order, according to Soroush (2002), was characterised by the centrality of God in human society and the dedication of all human activities to Him. As the basis of social order, religious institutions naturally dominated the spheres of law, education, healthcare and economic activity. Stark (2005) attests to this by situating the first stirrings of capitalist investment and entrepreneurship in the mercantile expansion of 9th-century monastic orders in Europe, led by (Saint) Augustine, who countered previous church teachings by ruling that there was no evil in commerce.

But by the time of the European Enlightenment (18th century), together with the newly flourishing ideas around science, reason and freedom, God was removed from the centre of the universe, and was replaced with humankind. It is fair to say that, since the 17th century, it is the centrality of the human being as master of their own destiny and of the universe that has come to define the new world order. The key question for Soroush (2002), who grapples with showing the democratic capacities of Islam and reconciling it with the modern values of freedom and reason, is about ethics: to what extent does the Muslim (in the modern world) have the sanctioned capacity to devise laws that can regulate society in a just way and which can nevertheless remain true to the spirit of Islamic worship and the centrality of God in human life? In response, Soroush (2002) rejects what he calls "ethics of the Gods" for a human-mediated version of rule of social conduct. From Soroush's Shi'a standpoint, it is possible and wholly reasonable that the Qur'an may be reinterpreted to suit the circumstances of the day. In this he does not differ from the 19th-century Muslim reformist thinkers (Tripp, 2006).

Other scholars of religion such as Gwynne (2009) express the relevance of religion by attributing to it qualities of temporality and geographical locality. For while it is true that religion ultimately relates to questions that are beyond physical time and space, it also has a dimension that relates to the here and now and is expressed first and foremost through the clear enunciations made in the major world faiths on the good and moral life. Gwynne (2009, p 87) links this directly to the way in which religion represents "a comprehensive socio-cultural framework that provides members with ultimate meaning and purpose". The ethics of the major world faiths link the transcendental with the transient, the ideal with the material. From a religious perspective, the material world is of innate value.

This relates to a final key dimension in which the relevance of religion is discussed for contemporary social welfare issues. This is expressed in the more mundane language of caring, compassion, dignity, autonomy, solidarity and justice (Higgins, 1981; Chan and Lap-Yan, 2000; Nesbitt, 2001b, 2001c; Tyndale, 2003). In this respect, religious worldviews incite human beings to recognise each other's innate worth. The sacred worldview is not distant in this respect from secular inclinations towards equality, solidarity and social progress. Observers of the work of international development institutions such as Cowen and Shenton (1996), Tyndale (2003, 2006), Clarke and Jennings (2008) and Thomas (2007) are among a growing chorus of voices who highlight the prophetic and quasi-religious character of modern-day development with its faith in social progress and its promises of prosperity. Manji and O'Coill (2002) give an insightful historical analysis of how the concept and practice of what we today call "development" itself emerged from the early 19th-century Christian missionary work around the world. The secular and the sacred worldviews thus share a common concern for morality, which is rooted in their common focus on the human being, their welfare and their ultimate destiny.

This chapter is made up of two broad sections, a third shorter section and finally a conclusion. The first section considers the teachings of the five major world faiths on social welfare. How are human well-being, social justice, social welfare, equality and solidarity understood according to these major faiths? To this end, the section considers the dynamic nature of religious interpretations and the way in which lay people and major social reformers have used religious teachings to bring out progressive social change. The second section considers the theoretical literature on religion and social policy. It explores examples of how religion has actively interacted with social policy in a variety of national settings, and throughout human history. This is linked to the way in which social analysts have conceptualised the role of religion in social welfare, with most relegating it to the voluntary sphere of charity and philanthropy. The third section sets the tone for the empirical chapters of the book (Chapters Four, Five and Six) by scrutinising the term 'faith-based' welfare (and organisations) as an adequate signifier of religiously inspired social welfare action. To this extent, I shall argue in favour of the terms 'religious welfare' and 'RWOs', which denote the particular understanding of religion advanced in this book and the comprehensive ethical import of the world's main religions to issues of social welfare and social policy.

Human well-being and social ethics in the five major world faiths

As many authors argue (see Nesbitt, 2001b, 2001c; Tyndale, 2006; Gwynne, 2009), there are basic values about human life, dignity, equality, social justice, property, honest communication, law and order that are professed by the five major faiths discussed in this chapter: Hinduism, Buddhism, Judaism, Christianity and Islam. Similar values about how to live an ethical life are also professed by the smaller faiths such as Sikhism, Zoroastrianism and Baha'i, as well as other culturally specific philosophies such as Confucianism, which is tightly tied to Far Eastern national identities and socioeconomic development, from China to Vietnam (Walker and Wong, 2005).

For many of these sacred worldviews, it is apt to note that the ethical prescriptions they make are directed primarily at the individual. World religions do not immediately seek to prescribe what types of social structures and public institutions are needed for the good society. What they offer are moral standards for correct social relations (Nesbitt, 2001c). They want to win over the minds and hearts of human beings first, and through this to establish a just social order that is pleasing to God and beneficial to humankind.

We can take as a basic example the Ten Commandments or Decalogue, which are reported to be the first laws revealed to the prophet Moses (Gwynne, 2009). These Ten Commandments (or 'ten words' in traditional Hebrew terminology) appear in modified forms in both Christianity and Islam, which are the other two

Abrahamic faiths. They involve directives that need to be fulfilled by the human being as a moral individual, such as belief in one God or the Trinity, prohibition from killing and paying an obligatory alms tax.

Similarly, in the oriental faiths of Hinduism and Buddhism, the core teaching is about how to live one's life according to the *dharma*. This has no exact English translation but, from the Buddhist perspective, it denotes 'the way things are in reality' and involves following the Four Noble Truths related to suffering (the renunciation of material wants and desires), which a Buddhist needs to succeed at in order to attain self-knowledge and reach *nirvana/nirbana*. In Hinduism, *dharma* also denotes the essence of things, and is usually translated into English as 'religion', 'law', 'duty' or 'righteousness'. By following *dharma*, a Hindu is able to fulfil the ultimate goal, which is liberation from the endless wheel of reincarnation (Multi-Faith Centre, 2007). Hinduism has a functional equivalent to the Ten Commandments in the form of the *yamas* and *niyamas*, which are also a set of moral guidance rules for human beings (Gwynne, 2009).

To a certain extent, then, it is possible to argue that the world religions focus on getting the human being right first, and through the correct and morally enlightened human being, establishing the good and just society. The same is true of the smaller faiths such as Sikhism, Zoroastrianism and the moral philosophy of Confucianism, all of which incite believers to seek union with God through a virtuous life (Sikhism), or to seek to have a clear and rational mind that can lead to a true faith (Zoroastrianism) or to knowing one's place in society in order to reach the goal of social harmony (Confucianism) (Walker and Wong, 2005; Multi-Faith Centre, 2007).

Gwynne (2009, p 111) further argues that what unites all of these major faiths is one "golden rule of ethics": do unto others as you would have them do to you. By this injunction, society can be established on the basic premise of selfless inter-subjectivity. The private righteousness of the human being is meant to translate automatically into a public social order. This mixture of private welfare and public action finds expression in many world religions, as in the case of family-based social care in Hong Kong, which was promoted by the chief executive of the Hong Kong Special Administrative region in the 1990s (Chiu and Wong, 2005).

The world faiths, as will be illustrated by the empirical research reported in Chapters Four to Six, attest to the supremacy of human nature as the basis of the good society. In this sense, they diverge from our mainstream understanding of modern social policy, which seeks to regulate the social institutions of society and to place the human being as a dependent variable of larger structural forces, be they the market, the state or the family. This contrast will be taken up in the discussion of this book.

The purpose of this section is to outline what the major world faiths say about human well-being, social justice, equality and social solidarity. It will show that while the world faiths have clear injunctions about social and material well-being, the primary condition of welfare is found at the level of the human being's personal spiritual wellness – which is nevertheless connected to their social interaction with society at large. The section will also show that many of the world faiths do not like big government: they caution against the evils of earthly politics and the control of elite minorities over the popular masses. This seems to relate to a mistrust of the welfare state, leading to a situation of welfare residualism as is commonly referred to in the social policy literature for welfare conditions where the state has a minimal role in social welfare (Titmuss, 1976).

To a certain extent, therefore, there is a tension as to how far to embrace or detach oneself from the material concerns of earthly life. In this regard, Gorski (2005, p 180) cites Weber's distinction between "world-affirming" and "world-rejecting" religions whereby the major faiths discussed in this book would all fall under the latter category. This tension of affirming/rejecting earthly life is further discussed in the next section, which looks at the way in which social policy has interacted/or not with the various world faiths.

Hinduism

One of the three "cosmocentric" religions, as classified by Weber (Hinduism is grouped here with Buddhism and Confucianism) (Gorski, 2005, p 181), Hinduism teaches that the primary goal of the human being is to follow the *dharma* in order to liberate themselves from the endless cycle of rebirth into the earthly world. It is a religion that is more likely than others to promote detachment or at the very least indifference to the material world. The importance of ritual and contemplation in Hinduism is the key means by which to achieve this escapism.

There are four central aims (*puruchartas*) for human existence according to Hinduism (Multi-Faith Centre, 2007, p 178):

- *dharma* (religious life) as the basic foundation and duty for virtuous living;
- *artha* (economic development) as the basic necessity of life;
- *kama* (sense gratification) by which sensual pleasures are enjoyed in moderation in order to maintain a healthy body and mind;
- *moksha* (liberation and salvation) relating to the ultimate escape from the endless wheel of reincarnation.

Hinduism is particularly known for its emphasis on *varna ashrama dharma*, meaning the duty that must be upheld by the human being in respecting their social class (*varna*) and traditional life stages (*ashrama*) (Gwynne, 2009).

Respecting one's place in society, which also entails a position of subordination in a hierarchy of social statuses (such as sisters towards brothers, students towards teachers, as expressed in the tying of threads ritual of *Rakshabandhan*) is central to the maintenance of social order and harmony. Hinduism and Confucianism are alike in this respect.

The *dharma* as a source of religious inspiration to help the poor and deprived was especially prominent in the thinking of the 19th-century spiritual leader Sahajanand Swami, who established a reform branch of Hinduism known as

Bochasanwasi Shri Akshar Purushottam Swaminarayan Sanstha (BAPS) (Martin et al, 2007). Together with his followers, Sahajanand Swami established almshouses and dug ponds in times of famine and drought. Although he did not abolish the caste system, he saw his fight as being against social injustice, calling for a restoration of *dharma* in the Gujarat state as the only way to bring about prosperity and well-being (Martin et al, 2007).

Hinduism, like the other world faiths, transmits its teachings about moral life and the purpose of human existence through accounts of the lives of the Hindu deities. These can be found in the sacred Hindu texts known as the *Vedas* (meaning knowledge). It is believed that the *Vedas* are divided into four parts, each of which deals with a specific dimension of human life such as worship, curing diseases, physics and astronomy (Multi-Faith Centre, 2007). In some Hindu traditions, the *Vedas* are further divided into five *Upavedas* (sub-branches), which deal with a whole array of social issues, one of the most significant for our purposes being the practice of government as found in the *Artharva veda*.

The ideas of Vinoba Bhave (1895–1983), one of the last of a long line of modern Hindu reformist thinkers stretching back to Rammohan Roy in the 18th century, have been highly influential on the understanding of government based on the Hindu tradition, both in India and for various other religio-political movements in the South Asian continent (Richards, 1985). Based on the Hindu precept of non-violence, Bhave argued in favour of a form of popular rule (*lok-niti*), which is suspicious of "government by politicians", and indeed of the welfare state, which Bhave regarded as a means by which an elite minority controls the popular masses. From here comes the name of the famous Sir Lankan Sarvodaya Movement (which also claims Buddhist roots). Related to this, Bhave is quoted as saying the following:

> The moral and material welfare of the country will only be assured by the establishment of a band of workers who will keep clear of the whirligig of office, who will be alert and watchful, conscientious in their study of facts, and ready for sacrifice. To such a group we have given the name Sarvodaya Samaj. *Sarvodaya is not a sect; it has not compulsory practices, no rigid discipline, Sarvodaya depends on service through understanding in a spirit of love.* (Bhave, cited in Richards, 1985, p 200, emphasis added)

Selfless service is indeed a central tenet in Hinduism. It relates to a key precept of *dharma*, which is to fulfil one's duties without selfishness. In this regard, Hinduism has a very important concept known as *seva*, meaning sacrifice and selfless service towards the deity.

In the citation above, Bhave has interpreted the notion of selfless service as a sentiment shared by human beings towards each other, in a spirit of suspicion of any form of representative rule, including democracy. The non-violent and inclusive ideas of Bhave stand in stark contrast to those of Vir Savarkar

(1883–1966), who argued for a violent liberation of India from all non-Hindu influence (Klostermaier, 1994). Vir Savarkar is one of the most inspirational figures behind various forms of Hindu fundamentalism today. He distinguished between *Hindu-dharma*, or Hinduism as a world religion, and *Hindudom*, which is the unifying sociocultural heritage of all Hindus (Klostermaier, 1994). In this thinking, formal government rule is a natural path for Hindu nationalism.

Major new developments in Hindu thinking on social and political ethics can be traced back to the writings of the most famous of all modern Hindu reformist thinkers – Rammohan Roy (1772–1833). Roy has been described as the "father of modern India" and one of the greatest "benefactors of mankind" (Richards, 1985, p 1). He believed in the need for religious and political reform and actively critiqued cruel Hindu customs and beliefs such as infanticide and the burning of widows on the funeral pyres of their deceased husbands (*sati*). Through his contact with the Christian social gospel in the 18th century, Roy developed a new understanding of the "path of works", which sought to bring about a Hindu revival and a new concern with social ethics (Klostermaier, 1994).

Roy reinterpreted Lord Krisna's call as one to rid Hindu society of its social ills. His ideas were to influence later generations of Hindu reformers such as B. G. Tilak (1856–1920) and, of course, Mahatma Gandhi (1869–1948). In Tilak's commentary on the *Bhagavad Gita*, the most sacred and influential Hindu text recounting the spiritual awakening of Lord Krisna, the *Gita* is considered as "the gospel of action". Here Tilak, like his fellow reformist thinkers, stressed the importance of selfless action (*karma*) rather than devotional prayer (*bhakti*) or renunciation as the central teaching of the *Gita*. This move towards a more secular form of Hindu political identity was to influence the later ideas of Mahatma Gandhi, who was deeply concerned with the economic development of India and envisioned a nation made up of hundreds of thousands of small, self-sufficient villages that were not overburdened by an overpowering centralised state. For Gandhi, who was not averse to being called a Socialist (Richards, 1985), the motors of his political thinking were grounded in the Hindu concepts of *ahimsa* (love), which he likened to St Paul's notion of love and of doing good in society, and of *Satyagraha* (truth-force, search for truth), which underpinned the belief in non-violence for which Gandhi was famous for. These two concepts gave a religiously inspired basis for Gandhi's sociopolitical vision of a prosperous and just India.

Buddhism

The second of Weber's 'cosmocentric' faiths, Buddhism is often regarded as the 'daughter of Hinduism', sharing with it similar texts like the *Bhagavad Gita* and concepts like the *dharma* and *sarvodaya* (Gywnne, 2009). There are no deities or canonical life of the Buddha in Buddhism, which underlines the basic Buddhist philosophy of personal responsibility for one's own life and actions. Five basic moral principles (*Pancasila*) underpin the *dharma*, which are similar to the Abrahamic Decalogue in that they are negative sanctions against various immoral acts such as destruction of other living creatures, sexual misconduct, theft and false speech. *Dharma* itself is encapsulated in what Buddhism calls the Four Noble Truths (Multi-Faith Centre, 2007; Gwynne, 2009):

- *Duhkha* (suffering or 'unsatisfactoriness' as a result of basic human experiences such as birth, pain and ageing);
- *Samudaya* (origin of suffering, meaning that it is basic human desires such as greed, hatred, jealousy and ignorance that cause human beings to become attached to the material pleasures of life and therefore to suffer when they lose them);
- *Nirvana* (cessation of suffering, which relates to the ability to transcend the sources of material suffering or *duhkha*);
- *Magga* (The Way – to cessation of suffering, which entails the actual human practices, or 'skills' as Buddhism calls them, which will lead out of suffering).

Magga entails the Holy Eightfold Path: right view, right intention, right speech, right action, right livelihood, right effort, right mindfulness and right concentration. These lead to *Nirvana* (Harvey, 1990). Like Hinduism, Buddhism also has as the final human goal, liberation from reincarnation. But unlike Hinduism, in Buddhism there is no belief in a caste system or life–cycle rituals. Furthermore, Buddhism attaches particular importance to the ethical dimension of life in attaining liberation.

The life of Buddha Sakayamuni is often held as a model to follow by practising Buddhists (Gwynne, 2009). There are many positive values that are promoted such as loving-kindness (*metta*), compassion, generosity and almsgiving for the monastic community by the lay people. Detachment from physical possessions is also encouraged (Gwynne, 2009). These teachings are especially prominent in the second of the moral principles, which says: "I refrain from taking that which is not given".

The emphasis in Buddhism on personal skill and practice to attain *Nirvana*, meditation and the monastic life, epitomised by the community of the *sangha*, has earned Buddhism accusations of escapism, selfishness and disengagement from society and material demands of survival and prosperity (Harvey, 1990, p 127; Zadek, 1993). Some Buddhist experts have even argued that the Buddha did not think that such a thing as society was possible (Zadek, 1993). Instead, the Buddhist belief is that the true spiritual life whereby a person is able to conquer feelings such as greed, ignorance and hatred can only be achieved by a solitary existence where the nun or monk can focus on their inner selves only. However, this does not mean that there is no place for communal living or commercial activity.

Brazier (2001) explains that the ideal Buddhist life is one of small communities where commercial activity is at a small scale and work is both salutary and necessary. These communities would have an active spiritual life and people would have diverse occupations and not be enslaved to waged work and principles of efficiency.

What Buddhism warns against is material independence, where a person seeks to have their own material resources by which they can survive independently of the community. In this respect, Buddhism stands in sharp opposition to the engines of modern capitalism (Brazier, 2001, p 180). It is not uncommon for Buddhist monks to go hungry since their existence depends on donations from the lay people.

However, this does not mean that Buddhism is devoid of a vision for the social life. Brazier (2001) argues that new forms of Buddhism are very socially engaged. According to him, the Buddha started a social movement that is democratic and socialist in character although it is not directly aligned with any of these modern secular forms of thinking. Buddhism does not advocate a particular system of political rule but it does advocate the empowerment of ordinary people through their potential for spiritual greatness. Like some Hindu traditions, Buddhism also cautions against centralised forms of political rule and teaches that social status must be based on wisdom as opposed to popular vote. The Buddha is often recounted as having favoured deprived people. By advocating the Middle Way through the Four Noble Truths, Buddhism rejects the belief of socialism that material benefits bring human well-being. It agrees more with the capitalist notion of private property, but it also rejects the capitalist orientation towards capital accumulation and consumerism, favouring minimalism as the path to freedom (Brazier, 2001).

Brazier (2001) also argues that there is a socially transformational dimension to Buddhism that has its seeds in the original teachings of the Buddha. There have been many examples of Buddhist uprising and protest against war and political oppression as in Burma and Vietnam. On another level, modern-day socially engaged Buddhists are faced with important dilemmas about how far to engage with modern-day secular institutions. The Buddha is presented as a socially engaged actor who, after gaining enlightenment, set forth into the city to spread his teachings and transform society (Brazier, 2001).

Linked to this is the key concept of *sangha* (the orders of the monks), which Zadek (1993) argues more commonly reflects Buddhism's emphasis on community-based social action. In this sense, Zadek argues that Buddhism incites believers to act to improve the world, which is considered imperfect. The extent to which this can lead to economic development has been hotly debated in Buddhism, with many arguing that the economic dependence of the elite Buddhist monks on the laity for their very survival means that there is little scope left for capital accumulation and entrepreneurship (Ariyaratne, 1980; Ling, 1980; Zadek, 1993).

Nevertheless, Sarvodaya is the most famous example of a Buddhist community organisation (Zadek, 1993; Brazier, 2001) and will be discussed in the next section as well as in Chapter Six.

Judaism

This is the first of the 'theocentric', world-rejecting religions, as classified by Weber (Gorski, 2005, p 181). Like Islam, and in contrast to Christianity, Judaism is very concerned with correct application of the law and correct practice (Orthopraxy), as opposed to the nature of faith and correct belief (Orthodoxy) (Benthall and Bellion-Jourdan, 2003). Focused on the personal worship of the creator God, and on the sole pursuit of personal salvation, Judaism (like the other Abrahamic faiths) teaches that redemption in the afterlife can only be achieved through engagement and struggle with the material world and its temptations (Gorski, 2005). Thus, the human being in Judaism is meant to enjoy the material world and to recognise that it is God who has created all good things in it. But with benefit from the world also comes responsibility for protecting and preserving creation (Lifshitz, 2007).

Like Islam, and unlike Christianity, Judaism thus has a substantial body of canonical law and, as mentioned above, is more deeply concerned with ethico-legal matters affecting the life of the community than the spiritual experience of religious life (Wuthnow, 1988; Novak, 1992). Like Christianity, Judaism teaches that humankind was created in the 'image of God'. This underlines the dual nature of humanity: it is both spiritual and material (Lifshitz, 2007).

There are numerous Jewish biblical passages calling on human beings to be just and righteous (Gwynne, 2009). To this end, Judaism teaches that God does not ask human beings for external religious formalities, but ethical integrity in both thought and action (Gwynne, 2009, p 96). Thus, it is a core belief of Judaism, whether orthodox or reform, that there is no point worshipping God through prayer and ritual while day-to-day activities pervert justice and oppress others. The human being in Judaism must therefore strive to be wise (*hakham*), righteous (*tzaddik*) and upright (*yashar*) (Gwynne, 2009).

The Talmud has much legal and non-legal discussion of moral issues, particularly in the *Tractate Pirkei Avoth* (Ethics of the Fathers) where it is noted that "The world stands on three things: Torah, divine service and acts of loving-kindness". Loving-kindness is a key dimension of all branches of Judaism, and Rabbi Julia Neuberger (2008) sees it as a cornerstone of welfare from the Jewish perspective, arguing for the simple precept of the importance of giving to others. Rabbi Neuberger (2008) places an emphasis on the term *g'millut chassadim*, which denotes all acts of selfless kindness and service to others beyond the obligatory 10% almsgiving in Judaism known as *tzedakah* (not far off semantically from the Islamic sister term *saddaqah*).

The moral foundations of Jewish moral teachings are found in the Torah's extensive legal codes, which total 613 commandments and are aimed ultimately at reinforcing the faith of the believer of God. These 613 commandments have been distilled throughout the tradition of Jewish teachings to be summaries by key psalms such as "Act justly, love mercy and walk humbly with God" (the prophet Micah), "Keep justice and do righteousness" (the prophet Isaiah) and

"The just man lives by his faithfulness" (the prophet Habakkuk). These teachings are underpinned by the core Hebrew concept of *tikkum olam* (repair the world), which Rabbi Neuberger (2008) argues shows the primacy attached to social responsibility within Jewish belief.

Like Christianity and Islam, belief in God and the divine will is for Judaism the compass of human morality and is what allows human beings to distinguish between right and wrong (Gwynne, 2009). To this end, the Ten Commandments are the central moral principles guiding an ethical Jewish life. According to Jewish belief, there are seven moral principles that were given to the prophet Noah by God before the flood and which form the moral basis for all humanity. The seven principles know as the Noahide Laws are similar to the Ten Commandments and include prohibitions against false gods, murder, theft, sexual immorality, blasphemy, cruelty to animals and corruption of the justice system (Gwynne, 2009). Loving one's neighbour, whatever their religion, is thus a founding principle of Jewish morality (Multi-Faith Centre, 2007).

Romain (1991), a British reform Jewish Rabbi, also argues that it is not in the teachings of Judaism to divorce religious convictions from social and political engagement with the injustices of wider society. Romain cites several legal injunctions by Amos, Isaiah and Micah that incite the faithful to stand up to corruption, oppressive political hierarchies and abuses of power. These prophets were very clear that Judaism covered not just private affairs but also public ones. This view connected secular activity to spiritual matters and is in the spirit of the famous injunction by Amos to "let justice roll down like water and righteousness like an everlasting stream" (Romain, 1991, p 234).

Another key tenet of Jewish belief that is relevant to consider for our purposes relates to probity in commercial activity (Romain, 1991). There are many injunctions in Leviticus, Deuteronomy and Exodus that relate to dealing fairly with business customers, not having a large profit margin and not concealing the truth about the items being sold. Numerous other detailed injunctions exist regarding fair competition, paying employees fair wages and earning profits ethically. Private property is acceptable in Judaism but there are strict laws surrounding its possession and how it is used (Lifshitz, 2007). Indeed, property should be used to help those who are worse off.

We now come to the discussion of poverty and wealth in Judaism. Like its sister theocentric faiths, Judaism has special injunctions on charity and helping those in need. In the *Ethics of the Fathers* 3.21, it is said: "Where there is no bread, there is no Torah, and where there is no Torah, there is no bread" (cited in Tyndale, 2000, p 9). Material prosperity is thus tightly linked to spiritual development in Judaism. The special alms tax (referred to above) that is paid to poor families – known as *tzedakah* – is usually translated as charity, but can also mean social justice and righteousness (Tyndale, 2000; Neuberger, 2008). Interpretations vary as to what proportion of personal income should be paid in as *tzedakah* but this is between 10% and 20% (Lifshitz, 2007; Neuberger, 2008). Lifshitz (2007) argues that in spite of *tzedakah*, wealth accumulation is still not frowned upon in Judaism and there are no clear rules about economic equality since the accumulation of wealth is not seen as coming at the expense of the poor.

To this end, Lifshitz (2007) notes that private property is a central tenet of Judaism, citing the numerous injunctions in the Torah and the Ten Commandments against 'coveting' and stealing. The story of King Ahab who steals the vineyard of Naboth and murders him, and is then punished by the prophet Elijah, is held as an important parable of the sanctity of private property in Judaism. Indeed, this right is almost absolute and there are no ceilings on its limits in Judaism. In this, Judaism is similar to early Protestantism (Calvinism) but contrasts with Catholicism, for example, where the fall of man has stripped him of an absolute claim to private property (Lifshitz, 2007). This reaches extreme forms as in the Talmudic assertion that "To rob a fellow man even of the value of a penny is like taking away his life from him".

The importance of private property in Judaism relates to the notion of man's dominion over God's creation and his ability not just to enjoy it but also to use his creative powers to improve it (Lifshitz, 2007). It is man's ability to enjoy fully the fruits of the material world that allows him to exercise his full dominion and creative powers over creation. Lifshitz (2007) thus concludes that Judaism has a bias towards wealth, and its accumulation, with sympathy for those living in poverty: "One who enjoys the fruits of his own labour is greater than one who fears heaven". This view is aimed at encouraging human creativity in this world, as an expression of the godly nature of humankind. Indeed, this wealth must be derived from honest means. However, it stands in sharp contrast to Christian teachings where wealth is frowned on and Jesus is famously known for saying: "It is easier for a camel to go through the eye of a needle, than for a rich man to enter into Kingdom of God" (Matthew, 19:24).

Poverty is not generally associated with righteousness in Judaism, according to Lifshitz (2007). Rather, it is a burden to be avoided at all cost: "One who must weigh every penny – it is as though he bears all the suffering of the world upon his shoulders, and as though all the curses of Deuteronomy have descended upon him" (Exodus Rabba, 31:14, cited in Lifshitz, 2007, p 75). Human beings are taught that they must not be burdens on their community and that poverty should be avoided and the poor have no legal claim on the wealth of the rich.

In Judaism, therefore, concern with the welfare of others is more a matter of showing them compassion and sympathy than giving them financial aid. Welfare is often described in the ancient socio-agricultural terms of the Land of Israel. According to Lifshitz (2007), a section of the cultivated land always had to be reserved for the needs of the poor as well as the fixing of tithes for specific periods of time in order to help the poor. Although the Torah does make some clear injunctions on helping the poor such as:

> If there is a poor man amongst you, one of your brothers within your gates in your land that the Lord your God gives you, do not harden your heart, nor close your hand to your poor brother. But open your

hand wide and surely lend him enough for his needs. (Deuteronomy, 15:7–8, cited in Lifshitz, 2007, p 75),

these are much less than the injunctions affirming the importance of private property, argues Lifshitz.

As the Hellenistic period approached, Jewish charity became more urban based and institutionalised to the extent that charitable funds became a prevalent feature of all Jewish communities in the Middle Ages. But voluntary private charity continued to exist side by side with the institutionalised forms of charity. Very often the private form of charity was dedicated to close family relatives who were in need. Thus, there is some tension in the Talmud with regards to private and public charity and how far the individual should prioritise their next of kin and others close to them, as opposed to strangers (Lifshitz, 2007).

To conclude, Judaism, like Islam, is unclear about how imperative the obligation of charity is: how far should private property take precedence over the coercion of charity and collection of taxes for the benefit of the poor (Lifshitz, 2007; Makris, 2007)? In the Jewish case, Lifshitz (2007) cites major Medieval Rabbis who saw charity as a communal obligation that had to be fulfilled at all costs. However, these interpretations are not justified by the Torah teachings, according to Lifshitz, for even though charity in Judaism is a religious obligation on the Jewish community enforceable by coercion, it does not automatically translate into limiting the rights of private property or the structural redistribution of wealth. The coercion to pay charity is not legally enforceable, and it is intrinsic to the understanding of justice in Judaism that private property rights should be respected. This leaves essential room for human freedom to use its creative powers to solve social problems, independently of Talmudic teachings (Lifshitz, 2007).

Christianity

For over a thousand years, Christianity has been tightly associated with the European continent. But this is no longer the case: with over 2.1 billion Christians worldwide, the centre of Christianity is now shifting elsewhere to Africa, Latin America and the Far East (Freston, 2007). Together with Islam, Christianity is one of the largest faiths of the non-Western world.

Like Judaism, Christianity was also erected upon the main principles of the Ten Commandments, although Jesus went further in his Sermon on the Mount later recorded in the gospel of Matthew, by adding further injunctions that have given Christianity its particular character (Gwynne, 2009, p 103). For example, Jesus went beyond the basic Jewish commandment of "do not murder", adding that one must not get angry with a brother or sister, or insult them. Jesus taught that the human being was obliged not merely to avoid vice but to actively embrace virtue. St Paul added the precept of faith in Jesus as the spiritual motivation to adhere by the Decalogue. Indeed, the centrality of the person of Jesus in Christian faith parallels that of Sakayamuni in Buddhism, giving Christianity its monastic character and detachment from the material world (Gwynne, 2009).

Arguably the central message of Jesus Christ was the injunction of 'love'. The New Testament uses the Greek term '*agape*', which is a higher form of love and relates more to God's divine love for humanity, expressed through his incarnate Son. This became Jesus's new, eleventh commandment: "I give you a new commandment, that you love one another. Just as I have loved you, you also should love one another" (Gwynne, 2009, p 104).

Christian beliefs and practices rest on three essential sources:

- *the Creeds*, which are the summary statements of Orthodox beliefs although Quakers and Baptists tend to reject these;
- *tradition*, which relates to the authoritative understandings and interpretations of basic Christian beliefs, as found in the Creeds and scriptures;
- *reason, conscience and experience*, whereby it is possible to interpret the Bible on the basis of human faculties according to the demands of the day.

Some controversy surrounds the validity of human reason for interpreting the Bible and this is a particular feature of Methodism (Multi-Faith Centre, 2007, pp 132-3). A linked point is that, like Judaism, Christianity also accepts the existence of innate human morality, which is separate from belief in Christ's message. Catholicism, in particular, under the influence of Augustine, developed the doctrine of 'natural law', which is based on secular reasoning (Stark, 2005).

However, the three major branches of Christianity have differed in the bases on which they have interpreted the teachings and life of Christ and where they place the authority for such interpretation: Catholic morality is based on papal teaching and the famous encyclicals such as the *Rerum Novarum* (1891), Orthodox morality is based on the church fathers, and Protestant morality stems from a close reading of the Bible. These various traditions have had a direct impact on the way in which ideas about poverty and social welfare have been formulated in the countries with Christian populations and even how social policy has been structured (Hornsby-Smith, 1999; Kahl, 2005).

Some general points first about the place of poverty in Christianity: as is well known, concern for poverty is a major dimension of righteousness in Christianity and directly relates to the rewards of the afterlife (Martin et al, 2007). Jesus is famously reported as advising a young man to sell all his property and give it to the poor in order to inherit eternal life (Martin et al, 2007). The Roman Catholic Church is perhaps the most stringent in its articulation of the just redistribution of resources and the fact that, to please God, humanity must live in equality (Tyndale, 2000). Other authors point to the parable of the Good Samaritan (Pemberton, 1990) as a key lesson about caring for the plight of fellow humans. Pemberton (1990) links this to the Catholic notion of the "preferential option for the poor". Even though Jesus admitted that the poverty could never be abolished, he also taught that it was harder for the rich to enter heaven, as the famous saying about the "eye of the needle" cited above attests. Thus, to help the poor was an expression of personal faith.

Christianity, particularly the Roman Catholic branch, advocates near-veneration of the condition of poverty, with many medieval well-to-do Christians giving up their material possessions to live a life of frugality (Tynedale, 2000; Kahl, 2005). In Christian teaching, detachment from material goods is considered to lead to higher levels of spirituality and virtue (Kahl, 2005; Martin et al, 2007). The collection of charitable alms, known as the tithe, was also a key fixture of Christian practice in the Medieval Ages although this has dwindled in modern times (Midwinter, 1994). Today, Western Christian groups carry their missions into developing countries where they are known to set up hospitals, income-generating projects and schools (Martin et al, 2007; Clarke and Jennings, 2008).

The political and social engagement of the Christian churches in matters of social justice, equality and solidarity is, thus, centuries old and well documented throughout medieval and early modern Europe (Atherton, 1994; Midwinter, 1994; Innes, 1998; Fehler, 1999; Kahl, 2005). This literature is tremendously large and it is not possible to review here all the forms of Christian-inspired social welfare that have come into existence. A useful summative argument is, however, provided by Higgins (1981), who reminds us that even some of the most prominent modern figures in Western social policy such as Seebohm Rowntree and William Beveridge were either inspired by their religious beliefs or had advisors who were religious. Thus, the task of explaining the eventual secularisation of social policy in Europe from the 16th century onwards is not straightforward.

According to Higgins (1981), this transition to a secular form of social welfare provision was, in part, due to the lack of administrative capacity on the part of the churches to continue to act as effective social controllers and social welfare providers as society became urbanised and pauperisation increased. Moreover, the 'self-help' ideology that came to characterise the churches in the 19th century (such as the ideas of Samuel Smiles and the Charity Organisation Society) coincided with the rise of the liberal ideas propagated by emerging social thinkers such as Thomas Malthus, John Stuart Mill and David Ricardo.

What I shall offer here, then, is a broad-brush review of the most influential currents of thinking on poverty and social welfare in Christianity. I will consider the understanding of poverty and poor relief that crystallised around the period of the 16th-century Reformation in the main branches of Catholicism, Lutheranism and Protestantism (Innes, 1998; Fehler, 1999; Kahl, 2005). I will then consider the formal elaboration of modern Christian social teachings that crystallised in the 19th century:

- In the case of Catholicism, these relate to the social teachings of the Catholic Church which are generally agreed to be founded on the encyclical letter written by Pope Leo XIII in 1891 called *Rerum Novarum* in which he addressed universal social issues such as human dignity and worth, the rights and responsibilities of society, the preferential option for the poor and solidarity (Van Kersbergen, 1995).

- In the case of Protestantism, modern social teachings on poverty and social welfare gained a formal status as a result of the 19th-century Social Gospel Movement, which spread particularly in Britain and the US where it continues to be quite influential (Atherton, 1994). The British Labour government, and (former Prime Minister) Tony Blair in particular, have a strong affiliation to the Christian Socialist Movement, which is directly inspired by the Social Gospel Movement. This movement sought actively to go beyond simple Christian notions of love, justice and honesty by engaging with economic and social issues in a direct way in order to seek to provide real solutions to the modern problems of urban degradation, squalor, inequality, crime, racial tensions and poor schools (Atherton, 1994).

Finally, I will briefly consider the newer Christian religion of Pentecostalism, which is sweeping Africa, Latin America and the Far East and is more directly associated with poor communities around the world (Freston, 2007), although it continues to boast a substantial following among the middle-class elites in the US.

The shift of political and religious power from ecclesiastical to lay control that occurred in 16th-century Europe and the accompanying desire to separate out the deserving from the undeserving poor masses has come to be known as the Reformation (Cunningham, 1998). It is a turning point in the history of Western European Christianity and a sharpening of the contours around the two main Christian denominations of Catholicism and Protestantism. Although Innes (1998) warns that the distinctions between social welfare practice in the 17th and 18th centuries were not so sharp between Catholic and Protestant poor relief, Kahl (2005) shows that the conceptualisation of poverty among the Christian denominations did bear significant distinctions. Further, Kahl argues that both Catholic and Lutheran understandings of social welfare are engrained to this day in modern-day social policy. This explains the key divide between Lutheran countries such as Germany, which oblige welfare recipients to seek work, and Catholic countries such as France, where the poor are not blamed for their condition.

To this extent, the conceptualisation of poverty and how to deal with the poor within the 16th-century Catholic, Lutheran and Reformed Protestant (Calvinist) traditions could be summed up as follows (Kahl, 2005):

- In Catholicism, poverty was sacred and helping the poor through private charity earned the benefactor salvation in the afterlife. In this view, the poor were blameless and were not to be forced to work or to take responsibility for their deprivation. During the counter-Reformation, the concept of *caritas* became popularised, attaching a notion of divine benevolence to those who helped the poor. Poverty was not banned, and it was certainly not secularised or institutionalised in the slowly forming early modern states (Kahl, 2005).

Instead, "the postulate of charity" was considered the "highest divine poor law" (Catholic historian Fösser, cited in Kahl, 2005, p 106). The conviction that poverty should continue to be a matter for private charity is one of the sharpest divisions between Catholicism and Protestantism and is one reason why in Catholic countries today (such as France, Italy and Spain), social welfare provision continues to be patchy and fragmented, with Catholic relief services occupying centre stage in social welfare. Like the preservation of personal wealth advocated in Judaism above, the concept of *caritas* in Catholicism obliged the rich to pay charity to the poor but did not give the poor an automatic right to claim charity from the rich (Kahl, 2005).

• In Lutheranism, the translation of the Bible into the vernacular led to the concept of work becoming elevated to a spiritual duty and taking centre stage in the post-Reformation thinking (Kahl, 2005). God's favour could only be gained by true faith as opposed to the Catholic practice of benevolence to the poor, which was no longer viewed in the Lutheran perspective as leading to salvation. Thus, poverty began to acquire negative connotations of laziness and undeservingness. The imperative of controlling and managing the poor in Lutheranism progressively translated into more centralised forms of outdoor poor relief. The 1522 Nuremberg Poor Law replaced the practice of almsgiving with the introduction of a municipal common fund to help the poor. By 1859, Lutheran social reformers devised a new policy whereby the state would protect the community from the undeserving poor and seek to help those truly in need. Both secular and religious authorities began to take responsibility for the poor, based on Luther's basic principle that "No one should live idle on the work of others" (Kahl, 2005, p 104). Thus, it is possible to argue that Lutheranism is the predecessor of the modern welfare state. The huge amount of legislation that was introduced by Lutheran countries to deal with poor relief stood in sharp contrast to the Catholic countries, which were opposed to the individualisation of faith in Protestantism, arguing that helping the poor was a religious duty of benevolence.

• In Calvinism, otherwise known as Reformed Protestantism, work reached ever-higher spiritual heights. Weber's infamous (1930) study of the origins of modern capitalism emphasises the notion of the 'calling' that a true Puritan felt towards work.[1] Calvin turned work into an absolute moral duty and placed discipline and rationality at the centre of the good Christian's life (Kahl, 2005). This eventually developed into the belief that poverty was a curse from God, an irreparable sin, while material wealth was a sign of God's blessing. Thus, Calvin developed two key ideas about the nature of poverty that led to its stigmatisation: these were the doctrines of predestination and the work ethic. In this view, the poor had to be punished and forced to work in what later became know as the workhouse system (Kahl, 2005). The poor became classified into different categories depending on their moral conduct and ability to work, as was the case in the 1601 English Poor Law. But Calvinism retained a feature similar to Catholicism in that poor relief was considered to be a matter for the church and not the state authorities. England and the Netherlands thus continued to have localised forms of poor relief. Private Christian charity continued to flourish well into the 19th century in these countries.

The 19th century did indeed see the consolidation of both Catholic and Protestant social teachings as has already been noted above. With regard to the Social Gospel Movement and the spread of socially engaged Christian movements in Britain and the US, influential thinkers behind this movement in Britain have included William Temple (1881–1944) and R.H. Tawney (1880–1962). In the US, major thinkers have been Walter Rauschenbusch (1861–1918) and John C. Bennet (1902–). Beyond Britain and the US, the movement of liberation theology that developed in Latin America was led by Ulrich Duchrow (1935–) and Gustavo Guiterrez (1928–). Other socially engaged Christian thinkers of a more conservative leaning include Michael Novak (1933–) and Brian Griffiths (1941–). The central preoccupation of these major social Christian thinkers is a critique of capitalism and a concern with the state of urban–industrial societies (Atherton, 1994, p 11). Some of the central tenets of Christian Socialism and the Social Gospel Movement may be summarised as follows (Atherton, 1994, pp 14-15):

(1) A fundamental concern for all humanity, based on the core belief of God's essential relationship to the human being.
(2) The imperative of addressing the social context within which human beings live.
(3) The need to collaborate in the fight for social justice with other social actors such as trade unions or socialists even where they were not Christians. Indeed, in the Social Gospel every human being was believed to have God's nature in him.
(4) The importance of social action and of actively providing programmes and services to improve the plight of the urban poor, such as education and producer co-operatives.
(5) A direct challenge to capitalism and the values of competition and accumulation which underpin it.
(6) A critique of the otherworldly evangelical belief of the church and the need to remain grounded in the realities of social action.
(7) Spirituality and worship continued to be the central driving force behind the movement.

To this day, committed Christian Socialists continue to critique social policy and to seek to influence the role of the state. Bayley (1989), an Anglican priest, makes a particularly strong argument against neoliberalism, arguing for a form of government rooted in romantic/pastoral/community/decentralised popular rule. He cites Richard Titmuss to argue that the welfare state intrinsically depends on there being a welfare society. This is not too far away from the vision of self-sufficient villages envisioned by Gandhi. Davis et al (2008) also critique the present Labour government over its lack of a moral vision for social welfare, arguing for a revival of such notions as gift, covenant, justice and advocacy. To a large extent, while the church is not in a position to write policy, Christian leaders do influence the moral standards according to which social policies are devised (Fischer, 2001; Nesbitt, 2001c). This is particularly evident in two major documents on urban poverty and social justice that appeared in the UK and Germany in the late 1990s: *Faith in the City* (by the Church of England) and *For a Future Founded on Solidarity and Justice* (a joint work by the Catholic Bishops and the Evangelical Church of Germany). Fischer (2001) describes how these reports signal landmark attempts by the religious establishment in both countries to directly engage with the social and economic policies of the times, arguing for a role for the church as a mediator between socially silenced populations and the government. Thus, Fischer (2001, p 161) concludes that "there is no doubt about the church's role in tweaking the national consciousness of British and German citizens and insisting upon the immediacy of the problem".

Like the Social Gospel Movement, Catholic social teaching has also entailed a critique of capitalism although questions may remain as to how far-reaching this critique is (Van Kersbergen, 1995; Hornsby-Smith, 1999). However, Adloff (2006) argues that social Catholicism had strong relations with the labour movement, unlike the Social Gospel reformers, especially in the US.

The central social teachings in social Catholicism are to be found in the 19th-century *Rerum Novarum*, followed by the *Quadragesimo Anno* (1931) (Van Kersbergen, 1995). Van Kersbergen (1995) argues that before the *Rerum Novarum*, the Catholic Church did not really engage with the 'social question' and was only impelled to do so in the 1880s due to the need for a prominent Vatican leader.

The *Rerum Novarum* thus entailed Pope Leo XIII's response to the social upheaval caused by capitalism and industrialisation. On a more critical note, Van Kersbergen (1995, p 219) argues that it symbolised more an attempt to "keep workers as Catholics in the church". Defending the pursuit of justice, the protection of social rights and the just wage, the Pope nevertheless continued to support the importance of private property rights, as in the other faiths discussed in this chapter. However, the Pope also called for the need to temper the free reign of market forces with moral considerations. The Catholic principle of "preferential option for the poor" was again reiterated in the *Rerum Novarum*. It also upheld the doctrine of subsidiary, which is central to Catholic social thinking, whereby responsibility for social welfare must not rest with the state but rather must begin with the family and local community. Most importantly, the *Rerum Novarum* continued to hold on to the central idea of charity and as such did not provide a substantial programme for action. The emphasis remained more on social obligations as opposed to rights, with the encyclical continuing to promote the importance of private property as the root out of poverty. This appeared to be the only real human right human that contradicted the Pope's call for justice (Van Kersbergen, 1995; Hornsby-Smith, 1999).

The social teachings of the Vatican are paralleled by the lay political movement of Christian Democracy, which flourished in the inter-war years in some key Catholic countries, namely Germany, Italy and the Netherlands (Van Kersbergen, 1995). The Christian Democratic movement, which was inspired by Catholicism, shared many of the core beliefs of the Vatican teachings, such as the organic nature of society, the centrality of the family, and the subsidiarity principle. Much of its success, according to Van Kersbergen (1995), was owed to its attempt to reconcile liberalism and socialism as a result of its ability and conviction in the politics of mediation between all social groups and social classes. Therefore the Christian Democratic Movement was able to draw upon a broad base of social support. Thus, in the post-war period, Christian Democratic governments all over Europe were at the forefront of the reconstruction effort and the formulation of generous social policies. The latter have been especially corporatist in nature, with generous family-oriented policies and employment-based insurance (Hornsby-Smith, 1999).

The final segment of this consideration of Christianity considers the rise of Pentecostalism or Evangelicalism in non-Western contexts (Freston, 2006). This is a popular form of Protestantism that has been spreading since the 1950s among poor populations in Africa, Asia and Latin America. Because of its highly voluntary and non-institutionalised nature, Evangelicalism has lost its links with normative church doctrine (Freston, 2007). The main drive behind this form of Christianity is conversion, and the revival of morality is portrayed as the main root to prosperity. There is a growing involvement in social projects as many Pentecostals have increasingly moved to the Left in their beliefs that government must provide for the basic social needs of the population. The immense developmental success of the Christian Base Communities in Latin America is one where Catholicism in the developing world has had a major impact on social and economic welfare (Bruneau, 1980).

Islam

Islam is the last of the 'divinely revealed' religions, and also the last and most central religion of this chapter. Also believing in the Decalogue first revealed to Moses, Muslims follow first and foremost the 'five pillars' of Islam:

- belief in the oneness of God (*shahada*);
- prayer (*salat*);
- obligatory almsgiving for the purification of one's wealth and soul and also for helping the poor and needy (*zakat*);
- fasting during the month of Ramadan (*saum*);
- pilgrimage to Mecca for those who can afford it (*hajj*) (Multi-Faith Centre, 2007).

A central tenet of Islam is *Tawhid*, which relates to the unity of God and the absolute veneration of all creation towards Him. The natural order of the universe is itself considered to be a way in which nature too worships God. Islam itself means submission to the will of God and, while Muslims believe in the absoluteness of the divine will, the human being is also believed to have free will, for which they are held accountable on the day of judgement. Human beings in Islam are born in an original state of purity.

Like Judaism, Islam is also intensely concerned with legal injunctions (Wuthnow, 1988). Several schools of Islamic jurisprudence exist in the Sunni denomination and much of the controversy surrounding the adaptability of Islam to modernity concerns who has the right to interpret the Islamic law and the Qur'an. Muslims derive their beliefs from three key sources:

- the *Qur'an*, which is believed to be the direct word of God transcribed by the companions of the prophet Mohamed during his lifetime;
- the *hadiths*, which are the holy sayings of the prophet Mohamed and are verified by witnesses;
- the *sunna*, which is a record of how Mohamed lived his life, and is supposed to be an example for all Muslims to follow.

Like the Noahide Laws in Judaism, *dharma* in Hinduism and natural law in Catholicism, Islam also teaches that morality is innate to human nature. This is called *Fitra* and is a running theme in my research in Lebanon, which is reported in the chapters that follow. Thus, religion is supposed to be a natural expression of the human condition; indeed various excerpts in the Qur'an state that religion is not meant to make human life difficult but to facilitate it.

It is thus often argued that Islam is a way of life (Ragab, 1980; Ernst, 2004), with God telling Muslims that the revelation of Islam marks the completion of humankind's religion on earth. Islamic injunctions thus deal with two dimensions of human existence: *ibadat* (worship) and *mu'amalat* (social relations). Shari'a law has very explicit rulings on family and social relations, sexual relations, eating, hygiene, economic activity, inheritance, warfare, dealing with non-Muslims, crime and punishment and to a certain degree Islamic government. These rulings vary in the degrees to which they are a duty towards God or they are prohibited by Him. Prayer, fasting and *zakat* are obligatory (*fard*), *saddaqah* or voluntary almsgiving is recommended (*mustahab*), eating pork is *haram* (forbidden/sinful) (Gwynne, 2009).

It is argued that Shari'a law is supposed to represent the public interest (*maslaha*) (Behdad, 2006; Tripp, 2006). In this sense, public interest means safeguarding religion, life, future of the society, sanity and property (Behdad, 2006, p 12). Thus, when a society is functioning well, the Islamic state will not intervene and will only supplement the Islamic practices of charity and almsgiving.

The interpretation of the Qur'an and the Shari'a varies between the two main Muslim denominations of Sunni and Shi'a, although it remains an activity reserved for the clergy. Sunni Islam is the more Orthodox version of Islam and uses the technique of *qiyas* or analogical reasoning to interpret/apply the law. Shi'a Islam practises *ijtihad*, which allows for new innovations in the interpretation of Islamic law according to the needs of the times (Makris, 2007). In practice, both Shi'a and Sunni forms of Islam remain quite doctrinal in their approach to Islamic teachings (Makris, 2007) and vastly new innovations in interpretation are few and far between. It is left up to Muslim intellectuals to seek to reinterpret the Qur'an in new ways, particularly in relation to gender issues, which can earn them the wrath of the clergy.

There are many injunctions in the Qur'an and in the sayings of the prophet that incite human beings towards justice, equality and love among fellow humans. The Qur'an teaches that "justice is closest to piety" and that "God loveth not such as are proud and boastful, who are avaricious and enjoin avarice on other, and conceal that which God has bestowed upon them of his bounty" (cited in Tyndale, 2000, p 12). Nevertheless, according to Behdad (2006), Islamic public policy generally favours the free running of the market. Prices should not be fixed by the state, and wages and the rights of workers should also be left to the workings of the market.

The world is considered as belonging to God, all creation is His wealth and all human beings are poor, as many excerpts in the Qur'an reiterate (Martin et al, 2007). There are also many injunctions about the importance of helping one's relatives who are in need, orphans and any passer-by who happens to ask for help. The key criterion is that the male breadwinner is absent. For, unlike in Christianity, poverty in Islam is a social ill (Martin et al, 2007). Ali, the nephew of Mohamed, and also the highly venerated Imam of the Shi'a denomination, is famously reported as saying: "If poverty were a man, I would have killed him". But although poverty is looked upon negatively in Islam, the latter has not appeared to incite the same level of veneration for work that is found in reformed versions of Protestantism.

There are three core practices in Islam that directly relate to wealth distribution and socioeconomic development:

- *zakat* (obligatory alms tax);
- *saddaqah* (voluntary almsgiving);
- *waqf* (religious endowments for use in the public interest) (Martin et al, 2007).

The last of these is not part of formal Islamic teachings in the Qur'an (Dallal, 2004), rather a meticulous legally sanctioned practice that reached its apex under the Ottoman Empire with the development of the city of Istanbul (Isin and Üstünda, 2008). I shall focus primarily on *zakat* and *waqf* here. Then, I will engage with the core debates in Islamic political economy that pitch an elitist, capitalist-oriented form of Islam with a more socially oriented form of Islam that stands on the side of the oppressed and the underdog (Behdad, 2006; Tripp, 2006).

The laws surrounding *zakat* are very complex (Makris, 2007) but it is basically agreed to be a tax of 2.5% on all assets (gold, silver and merchandise), which is spent primarily on Muslims (Heyneman, 2004; Richardson, 2004). This 2.5% rate was fixed by the Sunni schools of law during the era of the first Muslim Caliph, Abu Bakr, and not during the lifetime of the prophet (Ridgeon, 2003). Additionally, a 10% tax is levied on various products such as food. The poor are not obliged to pay *zakat*, and in practice many Muslims pay more than the stipulated 2.5%. Abu Bakr is famously reported as giving away all of his wealth, saying that he left God and messenger for his family (Ridgeon, 2003, p 258). Shi'as also have the principle of *khums*, which is a 5% levy on assets and is additional to *zakat*.

The Qur'an states: "those who spend their wealth in the way of God are like a grain [of wheat] that grows seven ears, each carrying a hundred grains. God multiplies further to whom he will" (cited in Ridgeon, 2003, p 257). It is indeed noteworthy that out of all the major world faiths discussed in this chapter, Islam is the only religion that places the disbursement of personal wealth as an article of true faith. Disagreement in practice exists as to who collects this tax – the state or the clergy. I have not found clear explanations of this in the literature but my research in the region appears to suggest a distinction between Shi'as and Sunnis in this regard, which Ridgeon (2003) touches on but does not explicitly address. In Sunni countries like Pakistan and Saudi Arabia (a theocratic state), *zakat* is an obligation collected by the state. It is also collected from companies whereas traditionally it would be collected from individuals (Ridgeon, 2003). In Iran, also a theocratic state, it is the clergy who collect *zakat* and the state is more of an administrative apparatus. Ridgeon (2003, p 259) argues that, contrary to Khomeini's pre-revolutionary injunctions during exile, Iran found the *zakat* to be insufficient to finance the modern Iranian state and had to seek recourse in other 'illegitimate' forms of taxation. Some countries like Malaysia have also changed the categories of industrial sectors on which *zakat* is levied (Ridgeon, 2003).

A fundamental feature of *zakat* is that it purifies the wealth and soul of the giver. Numerous injunctions in the Qur'an read to the effect of "Take of their wealth a free-will offering to purify them" (cited in Ridgeon, 2003, p 258). Dean and Khan (1997) argue further that there is a fundamental concern with social solidarity through the act of *zakat*. In paying *zakat*, the poor lay claim to the wealth of the rich, and the rich express their solidarity with the poor. The act itself of giving *zakat* and any kind of charitable donation is important in Islam. Muslims are meant to give in secret or at least not boast about their donations. Indeed, giving alms in Islam is considered as a loan that the Muslim pays to God and this is frequently contrasted with usury, which is prohibited in Islam (Ridgeon, 2003).

Zakat continued to be common practice in the Muslim lands well into the 19th and 20th centuries, at which point the modern Arab nations began to emerge and state action subsumed Islamic rule. It is argued that the practice of *zakat* gradually fed into the growing appeal of socialism in the Arab world (Ridgeon, 2003). The celebrated Arab nationalist leader Gamal Abdel Al-Nasser, who was President of Egypt from 1956 to 1970, argued for the compatibility of Islam with socialism based on the principle of *zakat*. Indeed, Islamic socialism became tightly interwoven with the state nationalist discourse in the Arab world of the 1960s as sweeping land redistribution reforms spread across the region (Tripp, 2006).

I now turn to the subject of *waqf*. It is quite likely that Muslims learnt about the practice of pious endowments dedicated to public benefit from the Byzantines and medieval Christians (Dallal, 2004). However, the complex legal system that came to rule the practice of *waqf* during the Muslim era was entirely Muslim in character (Dallal, 2004). Dallal (2004, p 13) defines *waqf* as:

> the only form of perpetuity known in Islam. The Arabic term means withholding or preventing ... *waqf* protects something by preventing it from becoming the property of a third person. The founding of a *waqf* means the extinction of a right of property without transferring this right to some other party.... The founder also surrenders the power of disposal of the returns or the usufruct that the *waqf* may yield, but he or she has the right to specify the use of the income ... on the condition that they fall within the Islamic limit of permitted good.

Waqf thus represents a social initiative in the interest of the public good. Its main use was to provide public funds and to fulfil many of the functions of the modern nation-state. *Waqf* included agricultural land, hotels, stables, hospitals, schools, baths and many more. Significantly, *waqf* depended on regular capital investments to ensure its longevity. In practice, *waqf* was also used to evade taxes or circumventing inheritance laws since, according to *waqf* law, an endowment could be set up for the specific benefit of one's family members (Dallal, 2004). This was a major reason why many *waqf* institutions were set up by Muslim women during the Ottoman Empire and throughout the Muslim world, becoming a tool of female empowerment. *Waqf* also served political purposes through the establishment of particular law schools, and it provided the clergy with an economic base. During Ottoman times, *waqf* was a key policy for political and territorial expansion (Dallal, 2004).

In modern times, *waqf* properties have become subsumed under ministries of *waqf*, with new legislation prohibiting family-based *waqf* following colonial influences that sought to spoil the image of *waqf*. The French, for example, plundered the fertile agricultural lands of Algeria by seeking to destroy the historical institution of *waqf* (Dallal, 2004). Thus, *waqf* in the Arab and Muslim worlds today is but a spectre of its former self in terms of its social orientation towards public benefit, although it is well known that Middle Eastern states are sitting on huge masses of *waqf* wealth (Dallal, 2004).

Where does Islam stand therefore in relation to wealth equality? It is fair to say that the various Muslim camps pull in a variety of directions, each justifying an interpretation of Islamic economics that is more capitalist in some respects and more socialist in others. Behdad (2006) argues that the Islamic revivalism we see today finds avid followers of free market entrepreneurship and wealth accumulation in such places as Afghanistan, the Gulf countries and Pakistan for example, as well as advocates of a radical Islamic socialist classless society as we might find among certain social movements in Egypt, Iran, Lebanon and Morocco. For Behdad (2006), there is a struggle between two forms of Islam: a rebellious Islam of the *mustada'fin* (the oppressed), which is based on the mass mobilisation of the poor, against a second, more elitist, Islam belonging to the era of empire (meaning Pax Islamicus in the era of the Ummayyads and later of the Abbasids in the 7th and 8th centuries), which is conservative in nature and seeks order and tradition. This confrontation, argues Behdad (2006), is fought at the level of Islamic jurisprudence. This pitches greed and corruption against selflessness and the pursuit of religious purity, much of which was largely lost after Mohamed died. The centuries following Mohamed's death and leading to the fall of the Ottoman Empire were marred by intense wealth accumulation and in many cases uncontrolled corruption.

The 19th century and the experience of colonialism witnessed a revival of Muslim socialist thinking as major Muslim reformists sought to redefine Muslim identity in the wake of anti-colonial movements (Behdad, 2006; Tripp, 2006). Major Muslim reformist thinkers such as Seyyed Jamal al-Din Afghani (d. 1897), Muhammad Abdu (d. 1905), Sayyid Qutb (d. 1966), Shariat-Sangalaji (d. 1944) and Ahmed Kasravi (d. 1946) sought in Islam the answer to the social ills of the day. Many advocated a reinterpretation of Islamic texts and a removal of power from the hands of the clergy (Hardie and Algar, 2000; Behdad, 2006; Tripp, 2006). The mood was very much one of political mobilisation based on an egalitarian understanding of Islam, which reached momentum in the 1920s as Islamic reformers began to express the grievances of the urban and rural underclass who were growing frustrated with secular forms of government and the social upheavals caused by industrialisation.

The view of Islam as a socialist classless society was to become epitomised in the writings of the Iranian political activist Ali Shariati, who died in 1977 just before the Iranian revolution. Shariati's view stood in sharp contrast to that of Abul Ala Maududi (d. 1979), who saw capitalism as a foundational element of Islamic society. This was underpinned by a fundamental commitment to individualism (Behdad, 2006). These varying currents of engagement with modern political ideologies have imbued state and society in the Middle East. Yet, Tripp (2006) argues that although Muslim reformist thinkers have presented a critique of capitalism, they have not succeeded in finding an alternative. Islamic states still resort to modern forms of taxation and trade, and the Muslim banking system still resorts to capitalist methods of business. Thus, Tripp (2006) argues, Islam needs to provide some kind of solution that allows Muslim societies to accommodate and embrace capitalism if it is to provide socially progressive solutions to Muslim societies.

The next section considers how the theoretical literature has considered the role of religion and social policy, and how social policy has actively engaged with religion around the world.

Contextualising religion in social policy theory and practice

There is an increasing role of religious welfare groups in the Middle East, Africa and South East Asia (Esposito, 2000). Even in the US and the UK, much debate has already surrounded the expansion of so-called faith-based initiatives (Bacon, 2006; Farnsley, 2007). This has spurred observations among many authors that the religious worldview is increasingly surpassing trades unions, political parties and other interest groups as a more relevant form of social organisation and identity.

Religious organisations are scattered from South East Asia to the Middle East, providing social protection and political representation for many of the poor and dispossessed (Esposito, 2000; Davis, 2001). As identity politics increasingly surpasses other forms of political negotiation that seek to promote the common good, what do we make of such movements? After all, do they not represent the mainstream of civil society in countries where states are contested for their legitimacy and responsibilities towards their citizens (Esposito, 2000)?

I argue that we should look historically at how such organisations have evolved in their societies as a response to state neglect or incapacity to deal with grave social inequalities. The Akhdams in Yemen and the Shi'as in Lebanon, Iraq and Bahrain are examples in this respect (Destramau, 2000). Where does the social policy literature stand on the subject of religion as a basis for social organisation and social justice? Where do the major world religions stand in relation to these same issues? This is the subject of this section.

The section considers the existing literature on the role of religion in social policy from an international perspective. This brings together the experiences of the Middle East with advanced capitalist democracies in order to consider the practical value of religion as a response to human welfare.

One of the main themes of this section will thus be that religious and secular forms of welfare are both bound by an equal concern for morality and human nature. Thus, religion remains of key relevance to the formulation of social policy. Since welfare actors in low-income settings are quite often working under the banner of development, indeed religious organisations often claim to be doing development work, the section will also include discussion of the relationship between religion and development. The section locates religion analytically within the field of social policy and asks why it is that as social policy is currently undergoing a process of reconstruction, religion is not part of this project.

The argument will contrast the role of religion in the Western European experience of social policy with that of the Middle East. As key issues are drawn out in the history of social policy in lower-income countries, so too will be shown the significance of social exclusion in Western European social policy. The discussion will examine various approaches that researchers have used to theorise social policy in lower-income contexts, with particular reference to the welfare regime literature that has increasingly attracted development theorists. The key argument I will make is that the line between the religious and the secular is not always clear, and that religious and secular forms of welfare are both fundamentally concerned with human morality.

Indeed, the development literature intricately supplements this discussion since theorisation of human well-being in poorer countries is most often done through the framework of development policy. In this section I present key questions about how far religion can play a complementary role in policies for the promotion of human welfare and socioeconomic development. The literature on development has addressed the role of religion more directly in relation to lower-income countries. I thus draw from authors on the anthropology of development to show how the very genealogy of key concepts in development studies, social exclusion included, is located within religious traditions particular to Western Europe. The distinction between the religious and the secular is thus depicted as rather tenuous, even in developed societies.

Indeed, the key argument I will make in favour of social policy's re-engagement with religion is the following: the marginalisation or indeed total disappearance of religion from the social policy arena in advanced capitalist societies does not signify a diminished concern with morality within those societies. Indeed, as Spicker (2000) states, social policy is a fundamentally moral act. Fitzpatrick (2001) too recognises that human nature is perhaps the most central idea of social policy, thus suggesting that metaphysical debate has direct practical significance. On philosophical grounds at the very least, I argue that human welfare would benefit from the engagement between social policy and religion. The argument will include the concept of social exclusion that has underscored the inherently moral crisis in the demise of the Western welfare state.

The discussion will draw attention to the fundamental and socially transformational role that religious affiliation has played in the Arab world in contrast to the more recent history of advanced capitalist democracies. But I will also argue that the distinction between religion and secularism can be misleading and much development and social policy thinking in modern or post-modern societies is imbued with religious morality. There is thus contrast and convergence in the experience of religion in social policy for both East and West.

Divergences in North–South experiences of religion in social policy

In industrialised societies, the relationship between religion and social welfare first began to be eclipsed around the 16th century with the advent of the Poor Laws in Britain and the political development of the state (Hill, 1997). The problematic of religion in Western social policy is predicated upon the separation between church and state, which stems from the Enlightenment era. As a result, religious welfare has tended to be considered under the banner of the informal, voluntary or charitable sector in advanced industrialised societies (Midgley, 1997; Page and Silburn, 1999; Valins, 2006). Their value has nevertheless remained. Midgley (1997) cites several studies where it is shown that people in need draw on non-formal services even alongside the statutory services that are made available to them.

However, this does not negate the fact that in Western scholarship, the role of the voluntary sector in social welfare has been looked down on as "unprogressive" (Offer, 2006, p 151), although the new literature on the mixed economy of welfare is increasingly paying attention to the role of the third sector, particularly in the area of informal social care (Arksey and Glendinning, 2007).

The advent of the concept of human rights and the way in which it has been developed by thinkers such as T.H. Marshall as a fundamental rationale for social development that structures the relationship and obligations between state and citizens has served to marginalise the role of religious welfare in advanced capitalist societies. Germany is one exception where the principle of *jus sanguinis* still informs citizenship legislation and Christianity has figured more prominently in mainstream politics (Davis, 1997). The Netherlands too has traditionally followed the system of pillarisation (Rodger, 2000), which has been considered to denote a specific understanding of human welfare rooted in society's capacity to feel compassion and solidarity.

Some authors such as Whelan (1996) lament the way in which the voluntary sector has been sidelined since the work of charities is now increasingly being done through contracts. Whelan (1996) sees this as seriously handicapping the innovative work of such organisations and even goes as far as saying that the contract culture is undermining the possibilities of moral renewal. The voluntary sector is indeed the broad title under which most faith-based initiatives are classified (Innes, 1998; Page and Silburn, 1999; Bacon, 2006).

But while Whelan (1996), speaking in the British context, depicts religious welfare as the victim of the welfare state, other religious groups have accused the welfare state of actually doing harm to society in terms of encouraging dependency and weakening the moral fibre (see, for example, Bayley, 1989). This has been the case also in the US where religious groups believe that it is the church's job to provide for the needy and that in fact social services should be contracted out and paid for by the government (Midgley, 1996).

This has been especially argued by neoconservatives and the New Christian Right, who believe that the welfare state undermines family values, is unsustainable and threatens the Christian character of the US (Midgley, 1996). Economic liberalism has thus tended to go hand in hand with religious social welfare, a case very similar to Lebanon. Indeed, the basic logic of the Protestant work ethic and the idea that people in need are held accountable by the principle of reciprocity when they receive social welfare has resurfaced in Britain in a more diluted version through workfare schemes. The Jewish communities have been very much in favour of the separation between religion and the state since this has allowed them to establish a highly sophisticated network of Jewish social services (Macarov, 1995).

But while formal state institutions have, relatively speaking, continued to ensure a substantial degree of social equality in advanced industrial societies, the case is different in other parts of the world like the Middle East. Here, the absence of effective democracy has meant that, in practice, religion (especially Islam) appears to be the only platform on which to mount effective opposition or indeed to access vital social services; indeed, religion has formed the basis for independence movements as well as processes of empowerment (Esposito, 2000). It may not substitute the state ultimately and the motives of religious organisations may not always be pure, but religion is providing feasible alternatives.

Indeed, contrary to the modernisation thesis, the flourishing of modern industrial societies has not been accompanied by an automatic decline in 'traditional' societies or religious affiliation (Esposito, 2000). As Esposito (2000) remarks, the last two decades of the 20th century saw a revival worldwide of religious fervour, especially among Islamic people and included some of the most modern of Muslim countries such as Algeria, Egypt, Lebanon, Tunisia and Turkey. The rise of religious nationalisms, whether they be Buddhist, Christian Maronite, Christian Orthodox, Hindu, Muslim or Serbian, has been characterised by the ability to legitimise governments, mobilise popular support and justify ethnic cleansing (Esposito, 2000, p 1).

So, instead of post-independence nation-states engaging in nation-building projects, there has been a spontaneous fusion between religion, nationalism, ethnicity and tribalism in global politics, leading to the effective handicapping of states in numerous countries such as Sudan, Rwanda, Somalia, Nigeria, Bosnia, Kosovo, India, Kashmir, Afghanistan, Indonesia, Pakistan, Sri Lanka and, of course, Lebanon.

What is especially interesting about the resurgence of Islam in these cases is the fact that it is not only a banner under which poor and dispossessed populations mobilised in the 1980s and 1990s, but it also includes in its ranks members of the elites as well as educated thinkers and professionals (Esposito, 2000). Hence, Islam is very much a channel of protest in mainstream society and in the absence of effective democracy in the Middle East, it acts as the only platform for political opposition that society can resort to (Esposito, 2000). Likewise, it is important to recognise that some of these organisations have supported the status quo and merely been a façade for the state and elites (Destramau, 2000; Esposito, 2000). The post-Enlightenment era relegated religion to the private sphere of life and reason to the public sphere (Esposito, 2000; Henkel and Stirrat, 2001). The influence of Enlightenment thinking not only seriously undermined our ability to appreciate the full scope of religious identity (with its implications for public life), it also meant that we totally ignored its dynamic character. Thus, human well-being became strictly a matter of material improvements (Tamimi, 2000, p 14).

The implications of this have perhaps been more serious for Islam than for Christianity, the two main religions that concern the present book. The connections between secularism and Islam as well as between development and Islam are much less tenuous. This is due, first, to the more overtly political content of the Islamic worldview and, second, to the fact that Islam is predominantly a religion among colonised peoples. Secularism can be considered a Christian invention to the extent that the separation between church and state was made clear in St Paul's injunction about rendering unto Caesar what was his. Indeed, the advent of secularism in Christian society brought an end to centuries of despotic rule (Tamimi, 2000, p 16).

In this sense, it is easier to appreciate why it is that serious theoretical consideration of the role of religion in human welfare in the Arab world should be addressed. For the Western context, debates on multiculturalism or ethnicity could also benefit from increased understanding of Islamic welfare and Muslim societies. Likewise, a focus on the way in which spirituality and emotional welfare are treated in religious welfare could be useful. The EU has only recently been grappling with the definition of European citizenship and has been actively engaging in debates about how to incorporate Muslim communities into this definition (Ramadan, 2001). Dean and Khan (1997) make similar comments about Muslims in Britain.

So, while the social policy literature as it stands has dealt with Christianity and Judaism in greater detail, much less is known about Islamic concepts of welfare. Indeed, the social policy literature has not sufficiently addressed the elaboration of social policy in the South. As Kabeer and Cook (2000) have argued, economic globalisation and political democratisation are posing serious challenges to the role of the state in social and public provisioning in countries of the South. For all these reasons, it is important to consider how theoretically adaptable the literature is to the understanding of social policy in lower-income countries.

Before the discussion progresses to considering how human welfare and social policy in lower-income countries have been conceptualised, I shall end this subsection by noting briefly here the intermingling of the religious with the secular in the social policy and development literature. The irony is, of course, that while development theory is to all intents and purposes secular, a genealogical analysis of its key concepts shows that it remains absolutely indebted to Christianity.

A continuum of the religious and secular: common moral concerns

Commentators locate the roots of development within 19th-century Europe among key thinkers such as Saint-Simon, Auguste Comte and John Stuart Mill (Cowen and Shenton, 1995; Pieterse, 2001). Radical critics of development discourse have been quick to denounce its religious metaphors as they have its dependency on religious doctrines.

> The idea of progress also had Christian origins stemming from the doctrine of divine revelation in which Providence through history maps out a design in advance of human efforts. Enlightenment thinkers constructed secular variants of this idea, giving autonomy to human purpose and proposing the prospect of unlimited improvement through unaided human effort. (Cowen and Shenton, 1995, p 31)

Kothari (1988, cited by Pieterse, 2001, p 25) has echoed these ideas by depicting development very much as a kind of process of redemption that operates with the same logic as Christianity albeit as a process of rationalisation.

Similar views have been expressed by Henkel and Stirrat (2001) in their critique of the concept of participation, which has been hailed as the *new orthodoxy* of development activity today. Taking an anthropological perspective on development, these authors argue that seemingly culturally neutral concepts such as 'development', 'science', 'reason' and 'participation' are in fact rooted in specific religious traditions that were secularised during the Enlightenment era.

In the case of the concept of 'participation', its more well-known historic roots go back to the 18th and 19th centuries, which witnessed Bourgeois emancipation in Europe (Henkel and Stirrat, 2001). But the less well-known religious roots go back even further – to the 16th-century Reformation era, which saw a kind of decentralisation of the administrative structures of Christian worship (Henkel and Stirrat, 2001, p 173). Thus, there was a strong populist move towards direct participation in the reading of the Bible (which meant the rejection of Latin) and indeed other changes in the liturgy. Participation effectively meant "participation of man in the infinite grace of God" (Henkel and Stirrat, 2001, p 173). The legacy of these reforms can be attested in modern Europe today, for example in the 'subsidiarity' principle (Catholic origin) of the EU and indeed the working-class non-conformity movements in Britain.

Unsurprisingly, the founders of key British development non-governmental organisations (NGOs) such as OXFAM, Save the Children Fund and Christian Aid were non-conformists (Henkel and Stirrat, 2001). Interestingly, Henkel and Stirrat (2001) note that personal salvation is very much a key facet of how the enthusiasm surrounding participation is being expounded by its key proponents today.

On a more secular although equally moral note, the concept of 'social exclusion' has recently emerged in the discourse of European social scientists as representing "a shift in the moral imagination of advanced capitalist democracies" (Silver, 1995, p 58). As rich societies awaken to the "broken promises of liberal democracy" in ensuring freedom and equality based on the "sovereignty of the individual" (Schwarzmantel, 1994, p 211), so they must contend with the prevailing realities of pluralism, elitism and the 'deep structures' of gender discrimination and class conflict that have exacerbated the incidences of exclusion from "political participation, economic security and state assistance" (Schwarzmantel, 1994, p 224).

In the European context, it is the concept of 'solidarity' that appears to capture the moral undertones of the concept of 'social exclusion'. The religious origin of the concept in French Catholic discourse is only one illustration of its moral reverberations. Commentators such as Byrne (1999) have argued for increased involvement of church-based organisations to combat social exclusion since such organisations are already involved with excluded social groups. Moreover, the conservative-corporatist or Christian Democratic stance on social welfare, which seeks to promote social cohesion, is very much the ethos of the International Labour Organization (ILO), one of the key actors in the social exclusion debate, as are the EU, International Monetary Fund (IMF) and World Bank (Deacon, 1997).

Even more significant is how religion was incorporated into the original sociological analysis of social cohesion in classical sociology. In researching the actual formation of the social bond, Durkheim reasoned that the social bond was totally absent in modern society but still existed in more primitive societies where it was manifested in the religious consensus (Xiberras, 1994). Thus, Durkheim equated the meaning of the sacred in religious communities with that of society in the modern context.

As Esposito (2000) argues, the significance of religion, especially in regions such as the Middle East, has been too hastily dismissed as stagnant. Our discussion thus moves to an appraisal of the way in which social policy has approached the theorisation of human welfare in the South.

Religion in the study of social policy and human welfare in the South

The discussion now moves to a consideration of where religion stands on the theorisation of social policy and human welfare in the South. I shall review the role of religion in both the social policy and development policy literatures in order to draw conclusions about their adequacy in explaining how human welfare is achieved there.

Factoring religion into social policy analysis

Lewis (2000, p 3) has stated that there is a need to rethink social policy in advanced Western democracies in order to respond to the "dislocation of social policy that has occurred over the last two or three decades in the context of wider social, political, economic, and cultural changes". The emergence of 'new' groups of welfare subjects, the spatial and economic reorganisation of production within nation–states due to globalisation, and the emerging influence of research on temporal, corporal and emotional factors on human behaviour, all pose challenges to social policy in rich countries.

In the context of what we call today developing countries, Kabeer and Cook (2000) similarly argue for a need to reconsider the role of social policy in the South. The difference though is that such an endeavour would be new since social policy has not existed in lower-income countries in the South as it has in Western Europe. The main challenges facing the state in these lower-income countries, according to Kabeer and Cook (2000), are economic globalisation and democratisation. Conceptualisation of the role of social policy in the Southern hemisphere is thus happening in the context of development policy. The case is similar for the consideration of the role of religion in human welfare in countries of the South.

Here, I shall review three key ways in which social policy and human welfare in the South are being approached theoretically. First, I will consider the development literature where some authors have argued for the need to redefine the social policy agenda in the South. Second, I will look at how other authors have considered the importance of religion in development. This will entail a brief overview of Islamic welfare. Finally, I will consider how welfare regime theory has gained in popularity among development theorists who seek to apply it to the developing world context.

Following Kabeer and Cook's (2000) vein of thinking, several authors (Cornwall and Gaventa, 2000; Deacon, 2000; Hong, 2000; Kabeer, 2000; Moore, 2000) have considered how to conceptualise social policy by focusing primarily on the promotion of active citizenship participation, human rights and an institutional approach to poverty that fights social exclusion. In this vein, Hong (2000, p 47) argues the following with regard to China:

> It would be completely irrelevant to take the European welfare models, or American, Japanese or Latin American models as the criteria for China. Each society has its own natural environment and political, economic, social, cultural and historical background, thus the basic needs of the people and the resource components are bound to be different.

A key proposal is thus made by Kabeer and Cook (2000) at the outset of the debate on how to approach the study of social policy in the South: this is that it is important first to redefine the very meaning of the social in the context of the South in order to adequately define the focus of social policy. This is especially problematic, according to Kabeer and Cook (2000), since delineating social policy from development in the context of the South is an issue yet to be resolved.

It is the recognition in development studies that the social content of policies, whether they relate to safety nets for economic growth or seeing the economic and the social as equally important, should be given more attention that aptly illustrates the importance of defining the social in the context of developing countries. This definition, Kabeer and Cook (2000) argue, is different to that of advanced capitalist democracies.

The focus on social institutions in the analysis on how to promote social policy recognises that meso-level social associations between the state and the individual play an important role in service provisioning and quite often form the basis of important social movements that entail sophisticated notions of citizenship as a social right with corresponding obligations from the state (Cornwall and Gaventa, 2000). Religious welfare is mentioned as important in this regard (Cornwall and Gaventa, 2000; Gough, 2000; Davis, 2001) although actual theorisation of the role of religion remains modest.

Where authors have considered the role of religion in human welfare in the Southern hemisphere, it has been as a way of reconceptualising development (Harcourt, 2003; Hope and Timmel, 2003; Kumar, 2003; Loy, 2003; Maheshvarananda, 2003; Swami, 2003; Tyndale, 2003) and, to a large extent, this has been accompanied by calls to disengage poorer countries from the development endeavour altogether (Muzaffar, 2003).

The focus of these authors is on promoting ethical human standards as the means by which to promote social justice. At the heart of this is the importance of developing human spirituality and religious faith. Thus, a religious perspective allows a moral debate about the nature of human life and makes vivid basic precepts of social solidarity, service to others, sharing and "collective compassion" (Loy, 2003). Religion is ultimately about self-knowledge and knowing one's humanity; as such it provides the basis on which socially transformational action can take place.

Several case studies are described in Africa and the Arab world (Balchin, 2003; Hope and Timmel, 2003; Maoulidi, 2003; Martínez, 2003) where faith is an intrinsic part of the spiritual and economic development endeavours of the NGOs described. Volunteering, human solidarity and the notion of sharing freely with others is a key dimension of these development NGOs. Citing David Korten, whose ideas on changing the culture of development have been influential at the World Bank, Hope and Timmel (2003, p 94) identify the comparative advantage of faith-based development as follows: "It is this shared social synergy and social vision that is often lacking in government and secular development work that is the basis of good development work undertaken by religious groups". Hope and Timmel (2003) cite well-known successful development projects such as the Sarvodaya Movement in Sri Lanka (Buddhist), the Bangladesh Rural Advancement Committee (Muslim) and the Basic Christian Communities of Brazil. The secret of the success of such organisations is their "inspiration, motivation and discipline", which they draw from their faith and which allows them to operate with accountability and mutual support (Hope and Timmel, 2003, p 94). Equally, Tyndale (2003) draws attention to the fact that it is the intrinsic values of religious faith such as human solidarity and social justice that are needed to make development successful.

What is striking, however, is that there is a sense in the literature in which there is both good and bad religion (Hope and Timmel, 2003; Swami, 2003). Good religion promotes spirituality, love of both fellow humans and the earth, while bad religion is about fundamentalism and discrimination. Thus, Swami (2003) and Tyndale (2003) suggest that dialogue among religions must be promoted first through an emphasis on shared spirituality, not on religious differences. Only in this way can religious organisations clarify their thinking on development and work more effectively.

To this extent, Tyndale (2003) considers the main criticisms made of religious organisations. The first concerns their idealistic vision of a fair society, which is difficult to apply, in her view, due to their lack of practical know-how to carry out development work effectively. The other major obstacle that Tyndale (2003) notes is that the work of religious organisations is too small-scale to make a major difference to living standards although their contact with the grassroots is very important. Moreover, she argues that development institutions have been hesitant to work with religious organisations since the latter are often associated with political conflict. This, paradoxically, is the same reason why religious organisations are perhaps the only ones who can successfully resolve conflicts, as occurred in Guatemala or Sierra Leone (Tyndale, 2003).

Nevertheless, Tyndale (2003) concludes with the recommendation that a joining of forces between development institutions that are more scientifically and technologically adept and faith-based organisations that have important spiritual insights as well as grassroots experience would allow a more successful development agenda.

The authors cited above offer an insightful debate about the role of religion in human welfare and make an ideological plea to promote human solidarity through shared spirituality and collective compassion. But they do not advance a theoretical approach for the study of social welfare from a religious perspective.

In the specific case of Islamic welfare, few authors have considered in detail how Islamic welfare works. Ahmad (1991) and Dean and Khan (1997) discuss how the obligatory almsgiving of *zakat* embodies a meaning of both social solidarity and social welfare. Translated from Arabic, *zakat* means growth or purity. It is a religious obligation that ensures the redistribution of wealth, not by coercion but through the acceptance of moral principles. To this extent, to give *zakat* becomes an act of faith or piety towards God as opposed to merely an act of altruism or mutuality. *Zakat* also has a fundamental economic function, which is to ensure the proper distribution and circulation of wealth in order to safeguard the social, economic and political body or structure of the *Umma* (Muslim nation) from deterioration.

Islam is not opposed to the accumulation of wealth but to its hoarding and to the exploitation of people for its accumulation (Ahmad, 1991). The Qur'an (51:19) states: "in their wealth is the right of him who asks, and him who is needy". Thus, *zakat* purifies the wealth out of which it is given and not the soul of the donor. It serves the cause, not of charity, but of social justice. And unlike the ordinary forms of taxation or insurance, *zakat* is supposed to cement the sense of fellow feeling between Muslims and to bind together the *Umma*. Ahmad (1991) argues that there are clear precepts for development and the just redistribution of wealth in Islam.

Thus, *zakat* provides very much a basis for social rights in Islam, which is as much a matter of social cohesion and personal identity as it is about equality and social justice (Ramadan, 2001). The vastness and complexity of this understanding of social justice is one that Western social policy has long grappled with, namely in its attempt to reconcile liberty with solidarity (Dean and Khan, 1997).

Conversely, Mehmet (1990) has argued that Islamic people have fallen short of successfully engaging with development discourse and indeed of articulating their own vision of development. Islam as it has been lived by Islamic peoples in our times has perhaps been too focused on personal spiritual salvation. It is important to note, however, that the understanding of development in Mehmet's (1990) mind is primarily about increasing productive capacities and economic growth. What Mehmet (1990) fails to recognise perhaps is that religious worldviews may not provide tools for development as we know it but they may provide alternative visions to it.

Tucker (1996) is acutely aware of this issue. He points out that in the Middle East, Islamic peoples felt threatened by the cultural hegemony of development discourse and actively sought to defend what they considered was their very identity and dignity:

> Development theories, whether of the conventional or radical types,
> have failed to come to terms with this phenomenon and have tended
> to dismiss it as a regrettable return to 'traditionalism' or a regressive
> form of sacralisation. (Tucker, 1996, p 5)

There is also consideration of religion in the gender and development literature. Hashim (1999), for example, looks at how it might be possible to reconcile feminism and Islam by finding supportive statements in Islamic teachings about women's rights and equality to men. To this extent, Hashim (1999) argues that development practitioners generally, and feminist activists in particular, would greatly enhance the effectiveness of their work by appealing to indigenous value systems since local people are much more likely to concede to the demands of social change if they are convinced culturally of the need for it: "Incorporating the study of rights accorded to women in Islam into the awareness-raising and educational components of development interventions could be very effective in improving women's lives" (Hashim, 1999, p 12).

Tripp (1999) also argues along similar lines from a Christian perspective and refers, of course, to the life and actions of Christ and his revolutionary message about women's equality. She argues that for the vast majority of people who her organisation works with, spiritual concerns are a key dimension of their everyday lives and it would be both impractical and unethical to approach them with a secular discourse. Tripp (1999) further comments that development is a holistic process and therefore requires attention to all facets of human life, including the spiritual.

Thus, religion and development inevitably share some common concerns about human welfare but they are rooted in distinct epistemological traditions. Many authors who advocate an alternative vision to development have expressed frustration with its lack of spiritual content. While they do not go as far as looking at the role of religion, what they have sought to revive are the vernacular knowledge systems of people around the world. Latouche (1997), Rahnema (1997), Sahlins (1997) and Pieterse (2001) are just some of the many authors who advocate a post-development era.

Many of these authors are staunch environmentalists and while their message may appear as slightly romantic, there is value in their critiques since they show that spiritual concerns can blend well and structure material concerns for survival and prosperity. These views are echoed by Tucker (1996, p 8) as he denounces the false tension that has been mounted between political economy and culture:

> But the economic and political transformation of society is inseparable from the production and reproduction of meaning, symbols and knowledge, that is cultural reproduction.... The material has no necessary priority over the perceptual. It is precisely because we assume that belief is efficacious only in 'traditional' societies while 'modern' societies are governed by science that we so assiduously delegitimise the myths of other societies while failing to deconstruct our own myths of development.

Tucker (1996) argues that culture necessarily steers our attention to the cognitive, emotional and moral facets of human experience that are so often ignored and yet are fundamental to human needs and human rights.

I therefore argue that the role of religion needs to be factored into the analysis of human welfare and social policy because of the turn towards culture and holism in the social sciences generally.[2] As Pieterse (2001) notes, if the project of holism is to be more effective, it must add spirituality and emotion to politico-economic analyses. This move towards holism means that all the disparate fragments of human knowledge need to be reassembled into a new totality.

The extent to which this culturally sensitive analysis has penetrated theoretical thinking about how social policy works in the South has led to affirmations of the importance of the role of religion but no actual analysis of how it interacts with human welfare. The most renowned approach to comparative social policy that has been pioneered by Esping-Andersen also falls short in this regard.

The welfare regime approach

Esping-Andersen's welfare regime approach has attracted enthusiasm from some development theorists (Davis, 2001; Gough and Wood, 2004). Lauded for being a middle-range analysis based on political economy but still sensitive to historical discrepancies (Gough, 2000), the approach has appeal in three main ways, according to Gough (1999). First, the approach magnifies the notion of 'welfare mix' since it concerns the relationship between state, market and household "in producing livelihood and distributing welfare" (Gough, 1999, p 2). Second, the focus on political economy allows an important analysis of power structures. Finally, the notion of 'regime' allows exploration of clusters of nations according to the norms and values underpinning the particular political settlements that produce a trajectory of social policy making in their particular contexts (Gough, 1999; Davis, 2001). Indeed, Kabeer (2004) rejects the transferability of the welfare regime approach to the South but still argues that the notion of a 'policy regime' is useful for analysis.

The most recent comprehensive study of the transferability of the welfare regime model to the non-Western world (Gough and Wood, 2004) omits from its analysis the region of the Middle East (including North Africa), with no attention to religious welfare actors. The discussion of informal security regimes fits primarily with agrarian peasant cultures, which does not characterise the Middle East. Barrientos' (2004) account of the segmented public–private provision of welfare in Latin America does bear relevance for Lebanon where the labour market and family are core providers of welfare. However, Barrientos omits the churches from his analysis, focusing instead on the state welfare reform and the role of the labour market.

Esping-Andersen's model has been the object of heated debate, raising criticisms on a number of counts: these have ranged from its lack of gender-sensitiveness, to its assumption of the homogeneity and internal coherency of policy regimes, to questioning of the accuracy of the clusters of nations (Bonoli, 1997; Arts and Gelissen, 2002; Kasza, 2002). Where developing country contexts are concerned, criticisms have been raised regarding the transferability of the model. The approach has been criticised for its path dependency since this assumes a false level of stability in the era of globalisation and structural adjustment programmes (Kabeer, 2004). Gough (1999) and Davis (2001) note that the concept fails to highlight the importance of health, education and housing programmes, which play a more important role in poor countries than do income-maintenance schemes.

Criticisms have also been raised about welfare outcomes. Needs satisfaction and self-sufficiency, it is argued, are more important in lower-income settings whereas Esping-Andersen's typology is built on decommodification (Gough, 2000; Davis, 2001). Stratification outcomes overemphasise class-based social structures at the expense of gender, religious, ethnic and clientelistic outcomes (Ferrera, 1996; Davis, 2001). Esping-Andersen's typology is criticised for not giving enough attention to the critical role of international development institutions without which policy analysis of social welfare in low-income settings would be very lacking (Gough, 1999; Davis, 2001). Finally, Gough (1999) points to the problem of terminology inherent in the concept of 'welfare', which in certain country contexts such as the Far East denotes charity and is contrasted with 'development', which implies more long-term notions of social investment. This also resonates with the situation in Lebanon.

One model of welfare proposed by Ferrera (1996) may, however, respond to some of the key characteristics of social policy in a region like the Arab world. Ferrera provides an analysis of four Southern European nations – Greece, Italy, Portugal and Spain – that are traditionally classified with other Latin countries into the *conservative-corporatist* category. Ferrera (1996) notes that while these countries may have a strong Catholic influence on welfare, they are not rudimentary systems since they have been heavily influenced by socialism or communism.

Ferrera (1996) identifies four distinctive traits of this cluster of welfare states:

- a fragmented and dualistic income maintenance system with high benefits for old-age pensions and relatively nothing for the young or unemployed;
- a departure from continental corporatism to universalism, particularly in health;
- low involvement of the state in social provision and a peculiar dependence on a public–private mix;
- prevalence of clientelism and patronage networks through the apparatus of the state as key channels of access to cash subsidies.

Such characteristics may exist in Lebanon.

Although the welfare regime approach may be a useful theoretical tool for understanding how social policy works in lower-income countries, it underestimates the importance of cultural analysis and this is a crucial point that I have raised in this section. If we were to consider human welfare from the perspective of religion, I would argue that perhaps the whole parameters of the analysis would change.

This book considers the case of Lebanon in comparison to the literature on welfare regime theory but it will suggest that the religious perspective necessarily draws attention to the importance of culture and subjective experience since it is an inherently actor-oriented approach to human welfare.

A working definition of religious welfare

The preceding discussion has explored a very broad view of religion as a system of belief and a system of practice. Social actors, whether lay or clerical, are motivated by their beliefs and faith in a particular worldview to act in the public interest or to influence human well-being and social development in some way. The actions of these social actors are translated into programmes, which affect the basic day-to-day living of ordinary people, their health, knowledge, income and broader environment.

In this view, I would argue that faith is a narrow definition of what this chapter has sought to explore. In the Australian context, Melville and McDonald (2006) offer an insightful critique of the term 'faith-based' when they argue that it is an imported US term that can be misleading because it does not adequately capture the nature of the relationship between charities and churches in the Australian welfare reform process, nor does it adequately describe the diversity of RWOs operating in Australia. There are many different types of religious welfare actors operating from churches, congregations and lay organisations, all of whom have different priorities and targets. Thus, noting how American Charitable Choice legislation acts in favour of service delivery at the level of religious congregations (instead of the more secularised mainstream churches), Melville and McDonald (2006, p 72) argue that:

the term faith-based in the context of American Charitable Choice and welfare reform is employed to signal a particular mode of service delivery in a reconfigured set of institutional relations with the state.... It represents a fundamental moralisation of welfare that significantly reconfigures the nature and trajectory of the American liberal welfare state.

In Australia, however, Melville and McDonald (2006) argue that the term 'faith-based' does not capture the lack of clear institutional boundaries between the churches and charities due to the longstanding involvement of the churches in Australian social welfare provision. Instead, they advocate the use of a typology of faith-based welfare based on the work of Sider and Unruh (cited in Melville and McDonald, 2006). There are five types of faith-based welfare where more attention is paid to the role of faith in social welfare provision:

- faith-permeated organisations;
- faith-centred organisations;
- faith-affiliated organisations;
- faith-background organisations;
- faith–secular partnerships.

In the context of the Middle East, which is the subject matter of this book, I would argue further that the focus on faith as the key dimension of religion is a particular Protestant view of what constitutes religious identity. As already explored above, the Reformation led to the development of new interpretations of the Bible, with Martin Luther emphasising personal faith as the sole prerequisite for salvation. Bellah (1970), in redefining religion in the terms of symbolic faith as opposed to cognitive belief, contradicts what most of the faiths discussed in this chapter are about. It certainly contradicts what Islam – the main religion of the Middle East – is about. While *Iman* (literal meaning of faith in Arabic) is a cornerstone of religious conviction for both Christians and Muslims in the countries discussed in this book, it is distinct from, constitutive of and, thus, can never replace *din* (religion). Thus, faith is only one facet of a broader religious identity, which belongs to a social order. Religion, as the following three chapters will illustrate, is about social order. It is a system for living.

   For these reasons, I shall not use the term 'faith-based' to denote the basic subject matter of this book. I shall instead refer to 'religious welfare' and RWOs.

Conclusion: the value of religion to social policy

This chapter has served to locate the position advocated in this book within the theoretical literature on the role of religion in social policy and human well-being. It first explored how the five major world religions – Hinduism, Buddhism, Judaism, Christianity and Islam – have understood social welfare and how various interpretations of these religions have come into being. To this end, the chapter has argued the following:

- Both clerical and lay actors have used religious teachings to act in the public interest and to define human well-being.
- The world faiths have interacted with modern secular ideologies such as capitalism and socialism and indeed have been influenced by each other. As such, they have shaped social policy as much as they have been shaped by their contact with the social problems of society and how to find solutions for them.
- The world religions described in this chapter speak first and foremost to the human being. By focusing on the moral nature of the human being, the world religions seek to institute the just society.
- Thus, human well-being is defined in deeply spiritual and moral terms, in a way that is pleasing to the divine creator God or to the ultimate truths of the faith involved.
- The world religions appear to advocate small government and free markets, except the socialist forms of Christianity, some of which advocate a return to romantic, communitarian society. In the case of Islam, there remains deep conflict in legal interpretations as to the extent to which Islam is a religion for the rich or for the poor.
- In spite of the warnings of some authors such as Frederick Powell (2007) about religious welfare taking society back to a socially conservative order, this chapter suggests that the world faiths in lower-income countries have often been sources of liberation from oppression and injustice. This is intrinsic to the history of lower-income countries as opposed to the West.

The chapter then examined the social policy and development policy literatures in order to show that religion remains a highly relevant although often marginalised issue of investigation. The development literature in particular offers important insights into social policy and religious welfare in the South since it is a discipline traditionally concerned with lower-income countries.

In considering the importance of religion in social policy in both Western and Arab experiences, I have argued that social policy remains intricately concerned with issues of human morality and human nature. As such, the place of religion in social policy remains relevant even to advanced capitalist democracies that are secular societies. Likewise, I have argued that the line between the secular and the religious is tenuous by demonstrating through the development policy literature how key concepts in Western thinking about development are genealogically rooted in Christian traditions.

The chapter has thus argued that the view of religious welfare as another form of voluntary action is insufficient for understanding the nature and dynamics of religious welfare particularly as there are many examples around the world that show how religiously inspired political parties and religious groups have played a prominent public role in shaping state social policy. In the Middle East, there also exist theocratic states where religion is at the heart of public policy.

In reviewing how social policy and religion have been theorised in relation to the South, I have considered the welfare regime approach, which has caught the attention of some development theorists who argue that the concept can benefit the understanding of social policy in the South. I have, nevertheless, drawn attention to how religious welfare allows us to explore human needs in a more holistic way as well as to look at human agency and subjective experience. Thus, religious welfare offers valuable insights into human welfare and social action in a way that the welfare regime approach cannot. Finally, the chapter has critiqued the term 'faith-based' in favour of the more comprehensive term 'religious welfare', which more adequately reflects the way in which religion is understood in the Middle East and by the five faiths described in this chapter. To this end, the chapter has advanced the term 'religious welfare organisation' (RWO).

To conclude, there is a strong basis for arguing that while the clerical establishment is not directly involved in the writing of social policy (except in theocratic states like Iran and Saudi Arabia), religious bodies do influence the moral standards by which policy making is set. Whether in the Middle East or in Europe, religious discourse has intermingled with ruling political ideologies in such a way as to produce social policy that, to all intents and purposes, is founded on religious ethics.

Notes

[1] It is not possible here to enter into more detailed discussion on the debate surrounding the Protestant work ethic. But it is useful to point out that this work has already been well critiqued. Giddens' introduction to the 1992 edition referenced here provides a comprehensive overview of the shortcomings of Weber's thesis, such as that post-medieval Catholicism also developed strong links to capitalist enterprise as referred to elsewhere in this book, and that other parts of 16th- and 17th-century Protestant Europe such as the Netherlands, the Rhineland and Switzerland, not considered by Weber, did not confirm to his thesis. The similarities between Catholicism and Protestantism are further discussed in Higgins (1981) and Innes (1998).

[2] For a fuller discussion of this debate, see Tucker (1996), Fraser (1997) and Pieterse (2001).

THREE

Lebanon: a profile of political and welfare institutions

Introduction

Lebanon is of both intrinsic and instrumental value in this book. It presents an interesting case for research because of the diversity of religious groups there and because of its weak state (Migdal, 1988). Lebanon has historically stood out among the remaining Arab nations of the region because of its liberal social and political systems, its dynamic laissez-faire economic sector, which has always been open to trade with the outside world, the relative freedom of its press and the high levels of education of its population. Lebanon has also hosted the wars of the Middle East, being vulnerable to international interference from both East and West. For all these reasons, observers have disagreed over the extent to which Lebanon is a microcosm of or an exception to the rest of the Middle East, and particularly the Arab states within it.

For the purposes of this book, which focuses on the role of religion in social policy, Lebanon provides the most active multi-faith civil society sector in the Middle East. In many ways, the history of social policy in Lebanon and its current configuration is representative of the more general experiences of its sister countries. Indeed, like the rest of the Arab states, there is a serious lack of statistical data on poverty and standards of living in Lebanon (UN-ESCWA, 2005). This partly reflects the neglect of Arab governments towards the study of social welfare. Hence, Lebanon forms the basis of an instructive case study for this book.

The purpose of this chapter is to paint a profile of Lebanon's political context and its welfare institutions in order to focus the discussion on religious welfare in the Middle East. Basic data on development and public social expenditure, which are provided in Appendix A, supplement this profile. First, I offer a description of Lebanon's religious demography and political economy. Then, I give a historical overview of social policy in Lebanon, the ideological and political forces that have led to the configuration of a partial and incomplete social security system today. Thus, the aim is to depict a nation-state where religious identity coupled with questions of social justice and human well-being have been at the crossroads of sporadic political strife throughout Lebanon's modern history.

Since the research for this book was first conducted in 2000–05, new developments have begun to occur at government level in Lebanon, particularly since 2007 with the launching of a major national survey of poverty and economic growth, commissioned by the UNDP office in Beirut and supported by the Lebanese government. I have also been given access to confidential grey literature on the MSA's new Social Strategy for Lebanon. These developments are still in their infancy, although they mark the increasing attention of the MSA in Lebanon to social policy. These new activities are also paralleled in Egypt, Iran and Turkey, as mentioned in Chapter One. There is, therefore, a concerted attempt in these major countries to get to grips with social problems and give more coherency to social policy. The extent to which religious welfare is seen as a source of problems or a solution will receive more detailed treatment in the final chapter of this book.

Lebanon's religious demography

Lebanon is a middle-income country (US$5,584 GDP per capita PPP [purchasing power parity]) with a population of just over four million (UNDP, 2008). No official government census has been conducted in Lebanon since 1932 when Lebanon was still under French mandate due to the precarious political structure of Lebanese politics, which is based on proportional representation of the Lebanese sects (Faour, 2007). Nevertheless, the country is home to the most concentrated mix of religious sects (totalling 18) living in close proximity in the Arab region (Choueiri, 1999; Faour, 2007).

Of these, an estimated 60-65% are Muslims, constituted of Sunnis, Shi'as and Druze (Choueiri, 1999; Faour, 2007). The last two of these sects have tended to inhabit rural areas. The Sunni hold on power has been upturned by rising Shi'a political revivalism ever since the 1975 civil war (Hagopian, 1989). Christians constitute 25% of the population and are mostly Maronites. There are other Catholic and Orthodox denominations. The Maronites have traditionally occupied Mount Lebanon. The sects in Lebanon are also geographically demarcated, a situation that crystallised in the civil war. A longstanding Armenian community, dating back to their persecution by the Ottomans, is based in East Beirut.

Lebanon's political economy – in and out of war

According to the constitution, the Lebanese state is secular. Nevertheless, sectarianism underpins the country's political system. Thus, the three highest government posts are reserved for the three largest sects: the President of the republic must be Maronite, the Prime Minister Sunni, the Leader of the Chamber of Deputies Shi'a.[1] Public sector posts too must be evenly distributed among the sects.

Lebanon is, in theory, a consociational democracy whose sociopolitical turmoil has been well documented (Salibi, 1988; Kedourie, 1994; Fisk, 2001). Harb (1999) qualifies it as a sectarian–capitalist state propelled by extremist confessional politics, which has concentrated power among ethnic elites – known also as 'spiritual families' – who have their own *Zuama*, or political leaders (Salibi, 1988, p 216) and a commercial/financial laissez-faire economy headed by a bourgeoisie with weak political power. The latter is unable to establish a genuinely capitalist state. Thus, feudal relations of production have subsisted simultaneously as the capitalist bourgeoisie has enjoyed free rein in economic activity (Harb, 1999).

Lebanon inherited a dependent capitalist economy from the French mandate in 1942, with the Beirut-based bourgeoisie at its helm. The traditional backbone of the economy has been the services and banking sector, accounting for over 70% of GDP (World Bank, 2008).

Until 1974, Lebanon enjoyed a period of prosperity and pluralist democracy (El-Khazen, 1993) and was often held up as a paragon of successful modernisation in the Arab world (Corm, 1998). Lebanon is now in the throngs of a deep economic crisis, with an increasing external debt now over US$40 billion, although its population still ranks among the most highly skilled in the region in terms of levels of educational attainment and has the greatest social/political freedoms.

Within this institutionalised non-meritocracy, an important cultural factor permeates economic and political life: *wasta*. This means 'intermediary' in Arabic (Cunningham and Sarayrah, 1993, p 1) and denotes special privileges in cases where an individual intercedes on behalf of someone else to help them benefit. *Wasta* emphasises the role of personal relationships like family and friends in decision-making processes.

Lebanese politics, El-Khazen (1993, 1994) argues, is now in a dubious position where the state is neither outright authoritarian nor coherently democratic. This was magnified by almost three decades of Syrian military and political dominance over Lebanon, which was marked by intensifying synchronicity in political and economic activity between both countries, and is part of the wider conflict over Lebanon's affiliation to the Arab nation. Although Syria was forced to withdraw its troops in 2005 under massive international and Lebanese pressure, following the shock assassination of previous Prime Minister Rafik Hariri, it is still the case that Lebanon's internal affairs play to the tune of regional politics. This has been the case ever since the late 1960s when the country became a battleground for the Palestinian–Israeli confrontations.

Today, Lebanon is a country striving to retrieve its status as the regional epicentre but continues to suffer major political setbacks – the most recent major war being between Hizbullah and Israel in 2006, after which Hizbullah promised to pay every family whose home was destroyed US$12,000 as rent for a new house until they were able to normalise their situation again.

The assassination of Mr Hariri on 14 February 2005 – who had been credited with raising Lebanon from the ashes of civil war through the expansion of his real-estate empire – shook Lebanon to the core, and unleashed a spiralling cycle of violence and political instability. A combination of social and political crises in the shape of demonstrations against the rising cost of living (unmatched by a monthly minimum wage of barely US$400) and a subsequent stand-off between the ruling and opposition parties over Hizbullah's satellite communication masts saw Lebanon skirting yet again on the brink of a second civil war in May 2008.

Today, Lebanese politics is no longer divided along lines of Christian versus Muslim. Rather, the key issue remains (as ever) about national sovereignty and nation-building. Two opposing political alliances are split along this line: the supporters of Mr Hariri's family, otherwise known as the Future Movement (now headed by the late Prime Minister's son and sister), have joined forces with elements of the Maronite Lebanese Forces and the Druze Progressive Socialist Party in support of a pro-US policy at the heart of which is the disarmament of Hizbullah. Hizbullah, together with the other major Shi'a faction of Lebanon, Amal, have joined forces with the Maronite Christian Free Patriotic Movement led by General Michel Aoun. For this camp, Lebanon needs to protect the resistance movement and maintain its relations with Syria. A government of national unity was formed in the summer of 2008 following over six months of political vacuum when ministers could not agree on a new President for the republic. Until when this new government will hold, no one can tell. The threat of a new war between Israel and Hizbullah also remains on the table.

It is argued that the roots of the Lebanese civil conflict lie in an extreme reliance on a laissez-faire economy, which, coupled with a confessional political regime, failed to institute appropriate mechanisms for social justice and equity (Harb, 1999). To this extent, ever since its inception as a state in 1920, Lebanon – unlike its regional neighbours – never embarked on a nation-building project (Nauphal, 1996). This has been confirmed by the effective cantonisation of the country, which, at the height of the 1975 civil war (around 1988), was on the verge of becoming divided into federal states. Others have argued that Lebanon fared well as a pluralist democracy but has always been highly vulnerable to regional squabbles and thus been forced to host proxy wars.

Historical overview of social policy in Lebanon

This section gives a historical overview of the development of social policy in Lebanon by considering the official policy approaches to poverty and social problems. Accordingly, I review the government stance on these issues as well as the role of other welfare institutions operating in Lebanon.

The year 2007 marked an important shift in thinking within the Lebanese government, with the publication of the first national survey report on inequality, poverty and economic growth (Laithy et al, 2008), commissioned by UNDP-Lebanon, the MSA and the Central Statistical Administration, since the landmark study on living conditions that came out in 1998 (UNDP and MSA, 1998). Both reports were carried out under the auspices of the UNDP's Beirut office but while the 1998 report was just beginning to cover basic survey work on household consumption following the end of the civil war, the 2007 report marked the formulation of a 'Social Action Plan' aimed at tackling poverty, social justice and equity (Laithy et al, 2008), and built on the reform process initiated at the Paris III donor conference for Lebanon in January 2007 (see MSA, 2006).

Thus, this section considers what various poverty studies have said about the phenomenon of poverty in Lebanon and raises questions about the historical incapacity in the Lebanese government to devise adequate social policies to deal with the issue. This leads to another key theme of the section, which looks at the actual nature of the state in Lebanon and how close it is to the ideal of the welfare state. This analysis considers the experience of citizenship in Lebanon and its achievements for social development. The section challenges the traditionally state-centric focus of social policy by illustrating how social policy in Lebanon combines formal/public with private/informal institutions. This will allow exploration of the NGO sector in the Lebanese social arena, particularly religious organisations.

'Productivist' state: post-war development and reconstruction

Social policy in Lebanon is overshadowed by concern with economic development and reconstruction – partly due to the endless cycle of conflict and destruction that Lebanon is unable to escape. This denotes the 'productivist' character of the state (Luciani, 1990b; Gough, 2000). The 1975–89 civil war inevitably shifted attention away from sustainable human development to immediate infrastructural repair (Findlay, 1994). Lebanon continues to come under sporadic fire either from the direction of Israel or internally when the Lebanese factions take up arms against each other. After 1990, the new government of National Unity sought to build an economic alliance between well-to-do Lebanese contractors and the newly wealthy political establishment. These actors are now the key decision makers in the post-war development initiative (Corm, 1998). Leading them was the, now assassinated, Prime Minister Rafik Hariri. Critics have been quick to warn against the policy soundness and indeed social justice of a post-war development strategy focused on boosting private sector investment and building infrastructure (Nehme, 1997b; Corm, 1998; Khalidi-Beyhum, 1999). Since the Hizbullah–Israeli war in August 2006, it is the reconstruction wing of Hizbullah (Jihad Al Binaa), along with support from the Gulf countries, that has taken responsibility for rebuilding the South and the Southern Shi'a suburb of Beirut.

According to Laithy et al (2008, pp 2, 3), the new Social Action Plan, which will steer the reform process,

> focuses on pursuing an inter-ministerial approach to improving efficiency, cost effectiveness and coverage in the delivery of services, including better targeted safety nets for the most deprived and vulnerable population groups.... The plan calls for the elaboration of a comprehensive and longer-term Social Development Strategy.... This effort would be part of the broader strategy for attaining inclusive and sustained economic growth, social equity and social justice.

This is an important improvement on Lebanon's social policy statement at the 1995 World Summit on Social Development in Copenhagen:

> Lebanon has a liberal economic system, where the role of the state is limited to formulating the legal, institutional, and infrastructural framework necessary for economic growth. The state also provides some intervention in the social and developmental sphere through a number of public institutions and ministries, in particular the Ministry of Social Affairs. Therefore, plans to combat poverty and unemployment do not appear as stand-alone plans, but form part of the overall comprehensive framework of the reconstruction and development plans, which place priority on ensuring the demands of economic growth. This policy considers that improving wages, and fighting unemployment and poverty are natural by-products of this growth. Economic growth is the key to official social policy. (cited by Khalidi-Beyhum, 1999, p 43)

Today, the World Bank and UNDP are playing a lead role in Lebanon's social policy agenda through a restructuring of the MSA and the various national poverty surveys mentioned above. The United Nations International Children's Emergency Fund (UNICEF) also plays a lead role in the social care sector and is set to launch, together with the MSA, a major study on the status of children in care.

There are several formal state institutions that make up the social security regime in Lebanon. Some commentators are quite optimistic about the efforts that these institutions are investing in reinventing themselves although it is recognised that the institutions are not coordinated in their anti-poverty strategies. This is emphasised by the lack of a comprehensive government policy (Melki, 2000).

Most important are the Ministries of Social Affairs, Public Health, Education and the Displaced, as well as the National Social Security Fund (NSSF), which falls under the Ministry of Labour. Even though the prevailing economic policies in the country limit the MSA's mandate to providing basic social safety nets, it is nevertheless able to extend vital services to traditionally vulnerable groups such as orphans, widows, older people and disabled people (Nehme, 1997a; Khalidi-Beyhum, 1999). The ministry is also especially active in rural areas, offering alleviation for urgent needs, and runs basic preventative and curative health programmes throughout the country.

Other government agencies include the Council for the South and the High Relief Agency, which also provide a wide range of services including direct cash payments and construction work. There are also several employment-based social insurance institutions, a breakdown of which is provided in Appendix B. The social security system will be considered in more detail in Chapter Seven. At this point, I shall mention that state social security coverage hinges not on citizenship membership of the nation but on active membership of the workforce (Melki, 2000). It is also particularly generous for civil servants and the military.

The special status accorded to military personnel and the lack of commitment to poverty reduction is evident in public expenditure. As Table A2 in Appendix A illustrates, in comparison to military expenditure, which occupies 4.5% of GDP, health and education account for 3.2% and 2.6% respectively (UNDP, 2008). The share of the private sector in health and education is double that of the public sector (UNDP, 2008). In stark contrast, debt servicing takes up 16.1% of GDP (UNDP, 2008). Paradoxically, Lebanon is among the highest-spending countries on healthcare in the world but suffers from strategic and administrative mismanagement (Melki, 2000). In view of the marginal role that state social policy has in Lebanon, the next subsection considers how poverty has been understood in Lebanon.

Recognising the problem of poverty: social inequality and war

It is commonly accepted that the 1975 civil war has been the most important cause of poverty and human deprivation in the country: there was an estimated two thirds decline in GDP between 1975 and 1990; hyperinflation reached 400% in 1987; per capita income fell to less than US$1,000; and there were sharp increases in unemployment (Khalidi-Beyhum, 1999, p 45). The official death toll was 65,000, with thousands more permanently disabled (Khalidi-Beyhum, 1999, p 39). Hundreds of thousands of people were either internally displaced[2] or forced to emigrate and the misery belts that now fringe urban centres in Lebanon are an unfortunate legacy of the conflict. The Hizbullah–Israeli war in 2006 also led to around 1,000 deaths in Lebanon, and sporadic clashes between the various Lebanese factions add to the casualties. But apart from the impact of the war, it is also Lebanon's historically unregulated sectarian–capitalist orientation that commentators argue fuels the engines of civil unrest (Beydoun, 1994a, 1994b; Haddad, 1996; Nehme, 1997b; El-Ghonemy, 1998; Harb, 1999).

Khalidi-Beyhum (1999, pp 38-9) recounts that the issue of poverty has been especially politicised in Lebanon. Until 1997, official government studies on the problem had been few and far between and it has been difficult to study the phenomenon over time due to the inconsistency of datasets and methodologies (Khalidi-Beyhum, 1999).

The key actors to initiate debate and gather data on the subject have therefore been international development agencies such as the UNDP (see Nehme, 1997b; UNDP, 1998; MSA and UNDP, 2006, 2007; Laithy et al, 2008) and UN-ESCWA (see Haddad, 1996; Khalidi-Beyhum, 1999). Very few Lebanese academics have attempted poverty studies (for an Arabic-language example, see Dah and Hijazi, 1997). The predominant definition of poverty used in all of the studies that have appeared has been money-metric and income-based with the cut-off line ranging between US$200–$300 per month. An early study by the UNDP and MSA (1998) used a broader definition of basic needs and access to services.

The first poverty study to be carried out in Lebanon was in 1960 by the French International Institute for Research and Training for Standardised Development

(IRFED), which estimated that half of the population lived in poverty and close to 9% were extremely poor or 'destitute'. It was estimated that 4% of the population was rich, with claims on 32% of national income. On the eve of the 1975 civil war (in 1974), the percentage of the population living in poverty had decreased to 22% while the middle-income group had expanded from 32% to 57%.

It was not until 1996, with the publishing of a study commissioned by UN-ESCWA (Haddad, 1996), that the phenomenon of poverty was forced upon the public arena as a problem in need of urgent government attention. Although doubt has been cast on the methodological rigour of the study, its value and timeliness are well recognised. Haddad (1996) claimed that 28% of Lebanese households lived below the absolute poverty line and that the situation was especially worse for female-headed households.[3]

In 1997, another poverty study was published (Dah and Hijazi, 1997), in which the authors challenged some of Haddad's (1996) conclusions. They estimated that only 21% of the population was living below the poverty line. Both studies nevertheless reached similar conclusions about the nature of poverty in Lebanon, which they defined as income-based.

In 1998, the UNDP collaborated with the MSA in the first official post-war survey of living conditions in Lebanon, which was based on an alternative conceptualisation of poverty that sought to measure unsatisfied basic needs. This was viewed as a way of getting round the problem of the unavailability of relevant data. Unlike the two previous studies mentioned above, this one was not income-based. Needs were defined according to a relative definition of poverty in Lebanon, resulting in the division of the population along five degrees of needs satisfaction:

- very low: 7.09%;
- low: 25%;
- intermediate: 41.6%;
- high: 21.9%;
- very high: 4.51%.

Khalidi-Beyhum (1999) notes that it took the Lebanese government a full year before it made public the findings of the study (UNDP and MSA, 1998). This epitomised the institutional denial of the existence of socioeconomic deprivation in Lebanon.

The 2007 national poverty survey (mentioned at the beginning of this chapter) built upon a study published jointly by the MSA and UNDP-Lebanon (2006) (in partnership with the Central Administration of Statistics of Lebanon), which compared changes in deprivation levels since the first 1997 study took place. According to the 2007 national poverty survey, 28% of the Lebanese population are poor and 8% are extremely poor (cited in Laithy et al, 2008). Inequalities in consumption are also significant: the bottom 20% of the population accounts for 7% of total consumption levels in contrast to the top 20%, which accounts for over 43% (Laithy et al, 2008). These levels of inequality are similar to the average for the MENA region.

Some general features of poverty that the studies point to are as follows:

- *Regional disparities.* Poverty is worst in rural areas. Two thirds of the extremely poor live in rural areas and they account for more than a quarter of the population in those areas. Disparities also exist between the different regions, with Beirut and Mount Lebanon being the most prosperous. Lebanon's poorest rural area is North Lebanon and the poorest urban areas are the Beirut outskirts (UNDP and MSA, 1998; Laithy et al, 2008). The capital city continues to occupy the favoured position in Lebanon's post-war development, for example it took up the largest share of the *Horizon 2000* budget (34%) (Khalidi–Beyhum, 1999, p 58). Harb El-Kak (2000, p 133) argues that if post-war development is to be balanced regionally, then a top priority is to develop a sense of regional identity and belonging as opposed to sectarian or clientelistic affiliation.

- *Employment.* The studies suggest a strong correlation between unemployment and poverty. Three quarters of families whose primary breadwinner works in agriculture are poor, and 40% of those are extremely poor. Urban poverty tends to be concentrated among families whose main breadwinner is employed in government or industry. Khalidi–Beyhum (1999) adds that what is significant about economic growth in Lebanon since the 1970s and 1980s is its low labour-intensiveness.

- *Household structure and size.* The average national household size is 4.7 members, yet this is superseded by the size of the average poor family in Lebanon. The dependency ratio of poor households is estimated at around 4:1 while that of the national average is 3.3:1. Thus, the young and older people constitute a significant proportion of the poor. The most vulnerable households are those that are female-headed (Latihy et al, 2008). Widowed or single mothers with three or more children constitute the largest category of the poor (Latihy et al, 2008, p 15). This was corroborated by my own research in the four countries.

- *Education.* A connection is also suggested between education and poverty. The poor tend to be illiterate or have very low educational achievements (Laithy et al, 2008). Children of poor families attend public schools and they experience a higher drop-out rate.

- *Healthcare.* Most poor families cannot afford medical care or health insurance. It is estimated that over 50% of the population is without health insurance (UNDP and MSA, 1998).

- *Environment.* Poverty tends to be concentrated in overcrowded urban centres or in small dwellings with a higher ratio of persons per room than the rest of the population.

While these studies make significant assessments about the nature of poverty in Lebanon, they fail to consider the social dynamics that surround the experience of human deprivation. Indeed, they do not account for either the subjective experience of poverty or an actor-oriented perspective to it, both of which can reveal deeper insights about the nature of the phenomenon.

Since the civil war was the most important cause of poverty, which severed the social fabric in Lebanon, it is thus incumbent to consider how the same social and political forces that partook in the war continue to exist in the post-war era and shape human welfare today. Thus, examination of processes of social cohesion and exclusion becomes pertinent to Lebanon.

It is here that we need to acknowledge the critical role played by religious affiliation, which remains a vital axis of social and political organisation in Lebanon today. Many observers still argue that sectarianism is more entrenched today than it was before and poses serious threats to national cohesion. Yet building social cohesion is vital to the process of post-war national reconciliation (Salibi, 1988; Nauphal, 1996; Nehme, 1997b; Destramau, 2000; Harb-El Kak, 2000). Melki (2000) assigns social cohesion an intrinsic role in the formulation of equitable development policy. He gives the examples of post-war Chile and the post-Second World War European nations whose development strategies were founded on a strong sense of national solidarity and nation-building.

Yet Melki (2000) fails to appreciate that unlike the nature and history of the state in today's advanced capitalist democracies where social cohesion and nation-building did indeed provide positive precedents for the welfare state, Lebanon manifests different traits in the make-up of the state. These are described below.

Residualism and "the dream of a welfare state'"

Social policy in Lebanon may be classified as residual in nature (Hong, 2000; Kabeer, 2004) due to the marginal role of the state. Thus, social services are mainly contracted out through the private sector or provided through voluntary organisations. From the 1960s up until the mid-1980s, Arab states accumulated wealth on exogenous revenues such as oil (in the case of Lebanon, tourism and financial services) and it was these rent-based revenues that made possible public investment to create jobs and improve social services (Destramau, 2000). Thus, even though internal taxation and political citizenship have not provided the foundations for the welfare state in the Arab region, there existed within society strong networks of welfare provision.

Apart from impacting on standards of living, what the civil war did was to reinforce inherent deficiencies in the Lebanese state. The lack of internal political cohesiveness that many attribute to Lebanon's strongly sectarian structure led to the virtual collapse of the government in the 1980s. Lebanon is thus a prime example of nations with weak states (Migdal, 1988; Salamé, 1990), which makes the subject matter of this book ever more significant and is key to its underlying rationale.

The retreat of the welfare state in high-income countries due to economic globalisation as well as fiscal and political crises is now widely recognised (Clarke, 2000; Rodger, 2000; Fitzpatrick, 2001). In lower-income countries, the prospects for copying Western models have always been grim, except perhaps for some countries in the Far East, although Hong (2000) argues that even China has a very distinct welfare system from other developed countries. Such bleak prospects are further undermined by international development institutions such as the IMF and the World Bank whose programmes of structural readjustment have made social funds and social safety nets the basic regime of government-based social initiatives in the whole of the Southern hemisphere (Deacon, 1997; Nehme, 1997a).

Lebanon has always followed a laissez-faire system so it has not had to undergo structural adjustment programmes like other Arab countries, although its external debt stands at just over US$40 billion, twice as much as its GDP. It is widely considered that the only era in modern Lebanon's history when there truly was a socially conscious developmental state was in the period 1958–64 under President Fouad Chehab. This was the same government that commissioned the 1960 IRFED poverty study referred to earlier and was the only government to seek to redress the imbalanced regional development in the country by setting up a Ministry of Planning and numerous public works programmes (Corm, 1998; Khalidi-Beyhum, 1999; Harb El-Kak, 2000).

Historically speaking, Thompson (2000, p 72) argues that "the dream of a welfare state evaporated" when Lebanon gained independence from the French mandate in 1943. According to Thompson (2000, p 72), the French authorities of the mandate allied with the local Lebanese elites and encouraged the building of a political system of "liberal paternalism" constituted of "mediated rule and gendered hierarchy of power". This directly undermined the long-term political credibility of the Lebanese state and citizens' capacity to claim their social rights.

The problematic of citizenship in the context of the Lebanon is indeed useful in demonstrating the fundamental features of Lebanese sociopolitical identity today and thus forms a strong basis for the research project at hand. Commentators on social policy in the South consider that citizenship should be the prime vector of political identity (Cornwall and Gaventa, 2000; Kabeer and Cook, 2000) yet there are fundamental obstacles to the ideal of citizenship in lower-income country contexts, which are due to other forms of subnational identity being more important and effective at achieving human welfare. The case of the Lebanon demonstrates this.

Destramau (2000) recounts the dilemmas facing states in the developing world. Although she argues in favour of strengthening state institutions and political citizenship in the Middle East to fight poverty and exclusion, she recognises that the role of government has been irreversibly reduced on the financial front by economic recession and on the political front by international aid agencies. She argues that states in the Middle East must redistribute rights, which she equates with power, to society in order to encourage a new type of social contract based on state and civil society partnership. Yet, as Harb El-Kak (2000, p 132) notes:

> [I]n a country where sectarianism and clientelism structure the political system, to what extent can public actors, private markets, civil society organisations and community groups become partners in the development process?

Harb El-Kak (2000) mentions two distinctly cultural features of sociopolitical life in Lebanon that need to be taken into account if an adequate analysis of social policy in lower-income settings is to be reached: sectarianism and clientelism. Indeed, the state in the Middle East has been "hijacked" by elite groups and has thus furthered the interests of specific corporatist, clan-based or regional forces (Destramau, 2000, p 314). The experience of citizenship in Lebanon has thus been distorted by communitarian and primordial loyalties that have consistently brought state and society into conflict. This is explained as follows.

The first impediment to citizenship has been a highly fragmented experience of nation-statehood in Lebanon. There are several explanations for this. The most important juxtaposes Arab nationalism, a feature primarily of the Muslim communities in Lebanon, with Lebanese particularism, a feature mainly of the Christian communities who believe in a historical Lebanese nation (Shalaq, 1993). Other commentators argue that Lebanon's problem is essentially one of modernisation (Salibi, 1988). The 1975 civil war was, as it were, a war against the privileged modern cities epitomised by Beirut, which was waged by dispossessed rural peasants (Beydoun, 1994b). Both literally and symbolically, national space in Lebanon could thus be considered as having no centre, only communitarian 'islands' that keep each other in check (Beydoun, 1994a). As a result, the state is merely a political actor among many others, which appropriates for itself resources from the public domain (Hannoyer, 1994).

The second impediment to citizenship has been the effective fusion of private and public interests in Lebanon, which contradicts the distinction between personal relations and civic relations in democratic thinking (Beyhum, 1994). The problematic of public space in the Middle East, as in Lebanon, is essentially one of urban space producing fragile democracy, stark social disparities and discord between state and society (Hannoyer, 1994). The discussion of 'space' in the Lebanese context takes on two levels: first, the territorial divisions imposed by inter-communitarian fault lines and urban misery, and second, the overlap between private and public spaces, which has given rise to new associational structures, namely patronage and clientelism (Bonne, 1995).

The final obstacle relates to how citizenship legislation is permeated by religious morality and the identification of the citizen within the collective of a social group. Legislation precariously mixes laws of the land with blood ties. For example, the constitution distinguishes personal status law as falling under the individual's religious background and other laws (Davis, 1997). And although legislation proclaims the political equality of all citizens, access to key public sector posts reflects the confessional distribution of the populace. Thus, for example, only the three main communities (Maronite, Sunni and Shi'a) can acquire the highest governmental posts.

Consequently, the Lebanese define their relationship with the state simultaneously as individual citizens and as members of a group (Destramau, 2000; Thompson, 2000). In spite of Destramau's (2000) plea for the revival of political citizenship, Thompson (2000, p 72) argues that, historically speaking, the expansion of rights in Lebanon simply institutionalised a system of "citizenship hierarchy".

In the absence of strong government and the effective implementation of citizenship rights in the Lebanon, there has been an increased reliance on elitist and religious intermediaries for both political representation and social protection especially for unstable urban populations (Denoeux, 1993; Bonne, 1995; Harb El Kak, 1996; Melki, 2000; Thompson, 2000). Organisationally, these intermediaries behave very much as informal networks and are forged by relations of personal dependence, which operate on the basis of favours as opposed to rights (Denoeux, 1993; Bonne, 1995).

The historical role of informal urban networks in Lebanon has been to adopt dispossessed rural migrants and the newly formed urban elites who were not absorbed into the official power system. Crucial to their success has been the fact that the economically and socially deprived do not perceive of themselves as a class and therefore do not organise as such (Denoeux, 1993). These networks are the principal purveyors of electricity, drinking water, schools, hospitals, pharmacies, housing loans, training colleges, regular family allowances and even the paving of roads for tens of thousands of people (Denoeux, 1993; Harb–El Kak, 1996).

Conclusion: religious welfare in Lebanon and beyond

It is clear from the above discussion that it is impossible to consider the sociopolitical situation in Lebanon without paying some attention to the role of religious identity. Yet even though religious differences add pressure on Lebanon's political tensions, it is well recognised that religious institutions were among the most active emergency relief providers during times of civil emergencies including the civil war (Nehme, 1997b; Harb–El Kak, 2000; Melki, 2000).

> Civil society and non-governmental organizations in particular played a critical role during the years of the conflict, often filling the vacuum left by the absence of formal government.... Many of these groups had a religious or confessional background, serving the needs of target communities. The NGOs provided emergency assistance and relief, health care, education and rehabilitation among other services. Their role in providing social support cannot be underestimated. Today, these groups are continuing to redefine their role, from relief providers to development agents. And are finding their comparative advantage. (Khalidi-Beyhum, 1999, p 56)

> Charity, in the name of civil solidarity, is promoted as a social bond, a moral attitude, but also as a Muslim[4] value and duty; religious alms are encouraged, channelled through state institutions, religious associations and private gifts. (Destramau, 2000, p 311)

What constitutes the 'comparative advantage' of these organisations? This book contends that it is necessary to view these social actors as engaging in vital survival strategies. Religious organisations are a fixture of civil society in Lebanon (Khalidi-Beyhum, 1999) as they are in the rest of MENA (UNDP, 2003). They represent civil society institutions (Esposito, 2000). Yet their role has almost always been documented for its political character and less for its welfare rationale (see, for example, Harb El-Kak, 1996).

The government in Lebanon has actively encouraged religious organisations to offer welfare services. Some expert observers are highly sceptical as to the implications of this for national harmony. Others have argued that the work of such organisations is vital and had it not been for them, regions such as the South of Lebanon would have lost all sense of solidarity with the rest of the nation (personal communication, 2001). Religious morality already permeates the political system in Lebanon, as has been demonstrated above, and it is clear that, whether for good or bad, it will not go away.

Yet development institutions in Lebanon as in the rest of MENA, such as the EU, UNDP, UNICEF and the World Bank, do not collaborate with these organisations. Nor is there any substantial exchange of ideas between them about the social programmes that they are involved in. It is clear that when many of the religious organisations came into being in Lebanon, especially the more prominent ones, one of their primary objectives was to achieve political legitimacy for which the provision of social services was the key stepping stone. The public services provided by the Lebanese militias are well documented in this respect (Harik, 1994). However, as these actors have settled down into their political careers, they have inevitably become less militant and have begun to formulate discourses that have wider developmental content (Hagopian, 1989).

If a strategy for social policy is to start somewhere in Lebanon, as in the rest of the region, then why not with the institution (in this case religion) that both poor and dispossessed groups turn to for social protection and with which the vast majority of the population, regardless of socioeconomic status, identifies most profoundly?

The next chapter begins to explore what religious welfare looks like on the ground in Lebanon.

Notes

[1] All three political figures are addressed as 'president' in Lebanon since they represent the leadership of their respective communities.

[2] It is estimated that internally displaced people account for at least half of the poorest populations in the country (Haddad, 1996).

[3] In a personal communication (16 August 2001), the head of the poverty programme at the UNDP confirmed that 43% of households living in poverty were headed by women. The situation of women is exacerbated by social discrimination, hence they are more likely to take up precarious and badly paid jobs.

[4] It is useful to remember that Islam is not the only religion in Lebanon, even though the author here (Destramau, 2000) specifically refers to Muslim values. The same argument may be made of Christian groups in Lebanon, as is being argued in this book.

FOUR

A philosophy of social service: faith or social insurance?

Introduction

"I don't have social insurance. I just have God's mercy." (Service user, MSA)

"We pray so that God protects us from misfortune. We don't have social insurance." (Service user, Caritas)

"I only found Caritas and Jesus." (Service user, Caritas)

"I only found God and Emdad." (Service user, Emdad)

Religion and social policy; faith and social insurance: it is, perhaps, poor analytical style to argue on the basis of simple dichotomies but throughout the fieldwork carried out for this book, I have been confronted with the extent to which each of these four concepts challenges and indeed substitutes its counterpart. Religion is indeed an axis of spontaneous social and political action in Lebanon but, also, faith in God is as important for the service provider who believes that their work will be blessed by the Almighty as it is for the service user who ultimately depends on God to protect them from misfortune or lead them to a welfare organisation. As all research participants confirmed, religion as a basis of social welfare remained a force to be reckoned with. Yet, as I subsequently argue, this situation was more a matter of supply than demand.[1]

Although the focus of social welfare in this book is religious, what I aim to demonstrate is that religious welfare operates on a continuum where the dividing line between the secular and the religious is not so sharp. Indeed, religion itself is interpreted and used by social actors in different ways. The RWOs that took part in this research bear testimony to this situation as they are themselves a heterogeneous mix. This will raise interesting questions about how problematic religion is as a basis of social welfare. The discussion at this point addresses the second of the main questions outlined in Chapter One:

- How does religious affiliation inform social action and shape the conceptualisation of human well-being in Lebanon and the wider Middle East?

This chapter thus seeks to identify the positions and roles of the social actors involved in this research within the moral contexts and institutional discourses that produce and sustain the phenomenon of social service provision in Lebanon. I shall refer to this task as an exploration of the philosophy of social welfare in Lebanon. Thus, I aim to give further definition to the arguments of this book by answering the following key questions: Who does social welfare? Why do they do it? What meaning do they give to it? This has fundamental importance for understanding the nature of social action in Lebanon and the future value of comprehensive social policy there.

Analytically, the aims of the argument at this point are:

- to understand and describe the moral values and motivations underpinning the initiative for social action, which follows the actor-oriented approach of this qualitative research;
- to produce profiles of the identities of the welfare actors and institutions I researched, which follows the basic formula of ideal types discussed in my research rationale;
- to highlight the intricacies of the power structures and discursive processes that place the disparate social actors involved in this research within a more coherent institutional and relational order.

The argument is thus pitched at the rhetorical level of social policy making in Lebanon since it is concerned with what welfare actors said they were seeking to achieve.

Such a form of enquiry ultimately reflects a political concern to evaluate the extent to which social action in Lebanon responds to what are perhaps the most fundamental issues of social policy: Whose welfare do social interventions ultimately address? How can we be sure that social interventions have achieved an adequate result?

The narrative is structured along two lines of argument:

- The failure of a welfare system based on state social protection in Lebanon leads to and is reinforced by an alternative/competing system of religious welfare based on the emotional/spiritual notion of faith and religious identity. This contrasts with the monetary contribution or rights-based notions of social insurance.
- This value system based on religious welfare is itself negotiated and sustained through power processes that bear significantly on the extent to which faith-based social action in Lebanon promotes progressive social transformation or maintains a status quo of inequality.

The key conclusion I make is that social welfare in Lebanon is an area of public policy that has yet to achieve full legitimacy and gain intrinsic value. Consequently, although religion offers an alternative philosophy of welfare based on the notion of *social service*, there remains a strong emphasis on short-term service provision and need fulfilment in the definition of welfare. This reinforces the line of argument running through this chapter, that welfare is of instrumental value in Lebanon. Key questions will thus be raised about what the real possibilities are for the role of the state in social welfare and the extent to which the non-governmental organisation (RWO) sector has a socially viable agenda. Answers to these policy-oriented questions will be proposed in the course of this book.

It is important to note that since the bulk of the research for this book was conducted (2000–05), there have not been any major changes at the level of the RWOs in terms of their welfare activities. However, it is on a government level where some progress has occurred, with more organised activity taking shape in the form of a Social Action Plan, which expresses an intention to deal with poverty and social justice, led by the initiative of the UNDP (Laithy et al, 2008). These developments have been described in more detail in Chapter Three. The primary research reported in this chapter as well as in Chapters Five and Six has been validated by further fieldwork in 2008 with the same research participants, which confirms that the analysis of religious welfare presented in this book remains robust.

I will explore four key themes in this chapter. First, I consider the motivations inspiring social service from the twin angles of individual value-positions and formal institutional standpoints. Second, I then identify the nature of welfare as a philosophical discourse. This includes how religious welfare is conceptualised and I distinguish between three modes of religious expression: organised religion made up of rules of conduct and practices of worship, sectarianism as political ethnic identity and faith as a personal spiritual experience. All three modes of religious expression, as I shall seek to show, interact with social welfare in varying ways.

Third, the discussion then looks more concretely at the decision–making and policy elaboration processes that translate the philosophical motivations and values into policy objectives. In so doing, the key power processes that control the agenda of social welfare in Lebanon are revealed. Finally, the argument is brought to a close by considering the paramount question in this chapter, which relates to the extent to which social welfare is of intrinsic or instrumental value. The chapter then ends with some concluding thoughts.

Conceiving social welfare: from human solidarity to identity politics

The conception of social action was a key axis of enquiry in this research: How did an employee end up working in a welfare organisation? Why were social welfare institutions established? Why did the small government agency that later became the MSA only gain an official ministerial portfolio in 1994 after falling under the wings of a string of different ministries since the 1960s? The fact that sporadic personal initiatives became formally institutionalised or that the MSA took a long time to be recognised as a valid entity of government are crucial for understanding the nature of social action in Lebanon and its future value as a basis for social policy.

To explore this proposition, I shall consider two themes that emerged from interviews. The first is the personal motivations that inspired social actors to engage in social action. This theme highlights strongly how non-state actors are virtually replacing government in the provision of social services in Lebanon. It raises many issues about the identity and motives of these actors through the discussion of who should take responsibility for social welfare.

From this individualistic consideration of welfare initiatives, I consider a second theme, which takes an institutional perspective of social action. This entails discussion of how the RWOs and the MSA came into being and, subsequently, the roles they perceived themselves as fulfilling in society. This is crucial for contextualising the organisations in their local environments and for mapping out their positions within the sociopolitical hierarchy. It will show how the values that motivated social actors to engage in social action bore upon the extent to which the organisations in question reproduced existing social inequalities. This part of the discussion culminates in the presentation of five typologies of RWOs, which draw on the experiences of religious welfare in Lebanon, Egypt, Iran and Turkey.

The critical argument here is that social service is predicated on a contradictory dichotomy. On the one hand it draws on a deeply humane philosophy of human solidarity and duty to others who are less fortunate. But on the other hand, it does not always escape political co-optation. In the case of Iran, religious welfare is a para-state activity, with undertones of social control (Saeidi, 2002). Often, social service is also a source of social prestige to which social actors become very attached. In Lebanon, social welfare is an expression of identity politics, which can act to further sectarianism.

Personal value-positions and motivations

The impetus for social service in Lebanon, as in Egypt and Turkey where there is an increasingly active civil society, is a dynamic society-based phenomenon. It is located within a refined discourse of religious morality and human solidarity but it can be underpinned by communitarian and regional orientations that are particularly prevalent in Lebanon and can undermine affiliation to the nation-state. Illustrations of this are as follows.

Religious faith

In the case of Lebanon, the empirical research confirms that religious faith remains the prime motivator for social service at both individual and institutional levels. As a general rule, identity defines the parameters of the initiative for social service: family, regional, communitarian and religious identities were the most prominent. Nationhood or citizenship tend to have rhetorical value.

Religious motivation is, however, the most prominent because it possesses the comparative advantage over other forms of welfare in terms of resources, moral authority and practical social skills. A similar situation can be found in Egypt and Turkey. There are many reasons for this, which will be considered later when the notion of religious welfare is addressed. Based on the Lebanese case, suffice to say here that the religious impetus for social welfare is strong because of two main factors.

First, the mere fact that the political system in Lebanon is based on religious identity plays a significant role. Second, on another level, religion continues to hold tightly the moral imagination of Lebanese society and, as such, it is very common for lay people to rely on faith in God, to abide by Islamic principles of *zakat* (obligatory almsgiving) and Christian principles of charity in their everyday lives. In effect, the religious initiative for social welfare in Lebanon rests on these two contradictory pillars: the purely political and the purely humanistic.

> **CAR2**[2]: [T]he sects in Lebanon are an organism which exists, not just in politics....The sectarian organisations are more important than others because they can attract more help since the religious factor is essential in the construction of Lebanese society. Secondly, the sects are not something abstract. They have spiritual and financial power. The *Awkaaf* [religious endowments], Christian and Muslim are an economic power.

> **MSA1**: The sects and religious organisations are among the most powerful of organisations. They have resources and a kind of social authority due to the overwhelming culture ... for decades they have been providing services even before the establishment of the Lebanese government.

> **MSA4**: [T]hese people have a mission....A nun or priest can devote a hundred per cent of their work to social service.... It is normal that the priest or nun's work is better than the rest.

The extent to which religious teachings and heritage act as the driving force behind social action varies among the Lebanese RWOs. Emdad, Caritas, Urfan and the Antonine Nuns are indeed based on formal scripture and religion was something they applied directly to social work. Dar Al Aytam is, to a certain extent, the exception since its religious character is more implicit: basic moral precepts about human conduct, about who needy groups are and about interpersonal relations based on Islam. Its employees tend to speak of "doing good". Thus, as DAR11 argued, religion was more about general manners and correct social conduct.

DAR1: It [religion] continues to be the most essential and biggest influence … through the ideas of *takaaful* (solidarity) and helping others. God will help those who help orphans and if someone does good things they will feel content and on judgement day people will be rewarded … I don't consider that these values are not human values.

DAR4: We shouldn't let religion take over. Otherwise we would have helped only one group of people. Those who follow religion correctly would know that anyone in need should be helped.

Human fellowship through emotional bonding

All interviewees tended to argue that religious values and human values were indeed fundamentally the same. The initiative for social service was thus as much a form of worship and pleasing God as it was about social solidarity (*takaaful*), empathy and a sense of collective identity based on basic human nature (*fitra*), which is naturally inclined to do good. The concepts of *takaaful* and *fitra* are Islamic and their significance will be discussed at a later stage. The Christian communities also use the concept of solidarity. The connection between religious and human values appears to be strongest at Caritas and Emdad.

At Caritas, the initiative for social service is based primarily on a humane instinct to respond to those who are needy and poor. It signifies recognition and love of the other and is built on honesty, as CAR5 explained. It did not discriminate by colour, race or religion. CAR5 also argued that the impetus for social service was not about charity or pity but about preserving the dignity of those who were suffering.

To this extent, the common feeling expressed by members of Caritas was that "all those who are needy are our relatives" (CAR2). CAR2 added that the religious instinct was always a forerunner to humanism but never the other way around. To exercise this human instinct was, according to Caritas employees, the true spirit of Christianity since Jesus came to save the human being and not just the Christians. Nevertheless, all interviewees at Caritas as in all the other RWOs were quick to acknowledge that both Islam and Christianity encouraged good work.

CAR2: The person who has a religious instinct definitely has a human instinct but the person who has a human instinct may not necessarily have a religious instinct … but the spiritual depth came with Christianity and Islam which made of this a duty….

CAR5: Recognition of the other, love of the other, honesty between the two, these are the essential issues of social work…. Our aim is the human being … whatever the person's religion, faction. God who created the world did not say this is Muslim or Christian.

Remarkably similar ideas were expressed at Emdad and Al-Qard Al-Hassan where social action was merely an enactment of human nature, which is instinctively predisposed to do good. In these organisations, employees often expressed the view that human nature was filled with a sense of social and moral responsibility for fellow humans, a characteristic distinguishing humankind fundamentally from the animal state because it was exalted by God.

According to H4 and H13, the ability to *feel* with others, respond to the needs of our neighbours and relatives and give without exchange was a human duty, which was also a legal Islamic one no less incumbent than prayer or fasting. The possibility to feel compassion with others and serve them was the ultimate fulfilment of one's humanity and, therefore, a form of direct worship whereby the beneficiary was not only the one whose material need was satisfied but also the helper who earned God's blessings.

> **H4**: You feel that humanity. It's your *fitra* to help people. Sometimes you meet someone not from your religion and they are victims, you want to help them.

> **Author**: What is *fitra*?

> **H4**: Something internal, created that makes people do good, not evil.

> **H13**: [W]hen the issue is social, it is about humanity ... people whose philosophy in life is secular/materialistic are far away from this world. That is why most of the people who work in the social sphere have a humane or religious character. Whatever their religion, ... they see the human depth of the issue and ... they have an obligation to fulfil towards other human beings.... In all religious texts, Qur'an, Bible, there is an orientation that all human beings are siblings.

The human *heart* was thus the locus of initiatives for social welfare as it was where the feelings of collective identity, solidarity and empathy were felt. This feeling fed directly into *takaaful*, which also included the idea of financial sponsorship. H13 elaborated this idea further by noting that the prerequisite for social service was not just to have the financial capacities but also to feel "close to society" and be part of it. This was expressed as having a deep sense of humanity.

Becoming employed in a welfare organisation

In terms of employees' more personal motivations for entering the social sphere, religious convictions and a shared social or political background with the RWO they worked for tended to play a determining role in the person's professional eligibility. All employees at Emdad and Al-Qard Al-Hassan have an ideological affiliation to Hizbullah. All employees at Urfan have an ideological affiliation to a particular Druze leader. At Dar Al Aytam, the affiliation is usually towards the old ruling families of Beirut and whoever the serving Prime Minister of Lebanon happens to be. In this sense, the Hizbullah RWOs are no different from all the other RWOs in Lebanon.

At the same time, it is not uncommon for employees to enter the field of social service by coincidence or for professional fulfilment. This is especially the case at Dar Al Aytam, which again highlights the more subtle influence that religion plays in social work at this RWO. Nevertheless, this does not preclude the possibility that employees at this organisation have the same political tendencies. I was not able to verify this hypothesis completely but the data point in this direction.

International actors

The role of international actors in instigating social services is crucial although controversial since, according to staff at the RWOs, it tends to be politically motivated.

Emdad was set up in Lebanon by Ayatollah Khomeini and is named after a similar state-owned welfare organisation in Iran, by which it is both ideologically inspired and partly funded. Caritas is part of the well-known international Catholic organisation, Caritas Internationalis, but it was set up in Lebanon by a local priest. Almost all of the programmes offered by Caritas in Lebanon were either set up by a foreign body or funded by one. The Antonine Nuns were a Lebanese order but had a foothold abroad through social centres that they ran in Australia, France and the US.

Dar Al Aytam was the organisation that least favoured international interference in its work. There was general mistrust expressed by its employees of international agencies that engaged in development or social work since they were considered as having political agendas. There was a general perception among the other RWOs however, that Dar Al Aytam received generous donations from Saudi Arabia. Indeed, this RWO has presided over a regional Arabic social welfare forum.

Politicised motivations

The most controversial issue related to the initiative for social welfare in Lebanon, as in the rest of MENA, is its vulnerability to politicisation, a point recognised by all staff at the RWOs including the MSA staff. This process, however, is complex and multidimensional. It highlights the prominence of identity politics and sectarianism in social welfare in Lebanon.

On the one hand, staff articulated the straightforward situation where an aspiring politician or political body offered social services in exchange for political support. I asked interviewees at Emdad, Urfan and to a certain extent Dar Al Aytam to comment on this issue since they had direct links or affiliation to key political figures. While the RWOs downplayed the influence of these connections on their motives to do social work, it was explained implicitly that some service users at these RWOs, particularly Emdad and Urfan, would be politically influenced by them.

> **H4**: [T]here are people who have strategic objectives... They're helping in order to be able to develop an audience and a support base, a faction.... They teach children, open schools.

> **CAR5**:The other factor apart from the religious drive to do social work is money and power, politics through social work to win votes.

On the other hand, the politicisation of social services in Lebanon can stem, according to some RWO staff members, from the fear some sects have for their overall survival in Lebanon. Social services provision reflected a desire to preserve sectarian identity. This was communicated off the record to me by a senior manager at Caritas and was also alluded to at Emdad and Urfan.

Politicisation as patronage appeared to exist most at Urfan where affiliation to an important political figure was considered the only sure means of survival for the RWO. The political figure benefited from the organisation through strengthening his support base and helping his supporters access services. In return, the organisation gained easier access to funds, resources and social standing.

> **URF2**: A political will converged with a religious will and unified around the establishment of an organisation [Urfan] concerned with knowledge, education, morality.

In any case, the vast majority of staff members who were interviewed agreed that all welfare organisations in Lebanon needed political backing in order to be sustainable.

> **H4**: Our organisations are strong because they have backing that defends them. That is known.... No one would listen to you if you didn't have that.

Dar Al Aytam was the most adamant that a true welfare organisation remained "far away from politics", as DAR3 noted.

Politics in the Hizbullah social welfare sphere

A final dimension of the politicisation of welfare in Lebanon was found in the cases of the Emdad and Al-Qard Al-Hassan, two of an array of social services centres affiliated to Hizbullah, where the discourse of human solidarity stood side by side with that of political mission. Here, the motivation to engage in social service was expressed in the distinctly political terms of a resistance movement. Hailed as a mass mobilisation of popular will in the Shi'a sect in the 1970s and 1980s against poverty, oppression and marginalisation from mainstream Lebanese politics, social action reached its ultimate expression in the resistance struggle against Israel.

This located the initiative for social service in an instrumental role within the much wider Islamic/Shi'a discourse of *Al Hala Al Islamiya* or the 'Islamic case'. According to H1, one of the protagonists (although by no means the instigator) of this vein of social initiatives to revive the Shi'a sect was Hizbullah. Indeed, both Emdad and Al-Qard Al-Hassan were created through private initiatives feeding on the wave of political awakening and social transformation that had beset the Shi'a popular masses. Nevertheless, the social movement that has now become a group of welfare organisations working under the patronage of Hizbullah is today characterised by its organised and very clear political vision for resistance against Israel and the social transformation of the Shi'as in Lebanon.

Social service as political resistance is in this context a metaphor for the struggle against all forms of oppression. It represents a natural step towards the formation of a coherent political identity and, therefore, control of one's destiny. However, the fact that this is only one strand of Hizbullah thinking on engaging in social service is reinforced by the general consensus among interviewees at Emdad and Al-Qard Al-Hassan that their organisations would still exist regardless of the existence of Hizbullah. This, they explained, is because these organisations did not cater specifically for the resistance fighters but for their surrounding population, otherwise known as the 'resistance community'.

The situation described above reflects and reinforces the weakness of the Lebanese state in the social sphere. A look at the history behind the establishment of the RWOs in question and the MSA clarifies this argument. To this extent, I propose a typology of the welfare organisations in Lebanon. For broader comparison, this is further supplemented by insights on Islamic welfare in the cases of Egypt, Iran and Turkey.

Establishment of the MSA and the five RWOs

The formalisation of random and personal welfare initiatives through the establishment of an institutional cadre is perceived by junior and senior staff members alike as an important step in achieving more effective and sustained results in social action. It gives welfare actors social and political currency, which inevitably shapes their roles and purposes in society.

Formalisation as official entities: frustration and success

Institutionalisation had different impacts for the MSA and the RWOs. According to civil servants such as MSA5 and MSA7, the 1975 civil war changed, indeed confused, the identity and mandate of the MSA whereby it became no longer responsible just for treating *social cases* and providing social care but was now having to deal with the more complex issue of poverty. It was generally recognised by both civil servants and outside commentators that the golden era of this state body existed only in the period 1956–63 when, according to MSA7, there were more resources and a true social policy led by competent, impartial individuals with "real social thinking".

The main reason given by interviewees at the MSA for setting up the ministry was to respond to social needs immediately after the end of the civil war. MSA15 also mentioned political pressure to create jobs and please certain sides. MSA4 attributed the establishment of the ministry to the need to fulfil the purely administrative function of bypassing bureaucracy to provide faster services to the public.

The unequivocal need demonstrated by the RWOs for formal institutional status as a means by which to deliver more effective service contrasted sharply with the MSA whose status as a legitimate and autonomous entity remained contested for a while. Indeed, whereas the institutionalisation of private welfare initiatives brought about greater effectiveness and coherency, the establishment of the ministry did not make it a more coherent body. To this end MSA7 argued strongly that the MSA merely became more politicised once it became a ministry.

The sense of positive achievement expressed at the RWOs overshadowed the impotence and frustration felt by civil servants at the MSA, although the level of conviction in social service was just as strong in both settings.

A typology of RWOs

In terms of the circumstances that led to the establishment of the RWOs, it is possible to distinguish five 'types' of religious welfare. Some organisations like Emdad and Urfan overlap since they too are led by clerics.

Type 1: The religious order

One type is the organisation set up by clergy such as Caritas and the Antonine Nuns. This welfare organisation is part and parcel of a religious body, such as the Catholic Church or a religious order. It may employ lay individuals but the managerial cadre is reserved for clerics who carry out the social services themselves. This is in line with Christian social activity around the world.

Type 2: The elite family

Another type is directly linked to the elite families of particular communities such as the case of Dar Al Aytam or Urfan. Dar Al Aytam was set up by prominent Beirut families in 1917 as a response to the social hardship caused by the First World War. These families established an Islamic orphanage to care for orphans and widows living in the capital city and its suburbs. Likewise, Urfan was a joint endeavour of the religious and political elites in the Chouf region.

The charitable activities of upper-class families in the Middle East have a long history. Indeed, it was often under the banner of charity that such families engaged in public action across the Arab world and Middle East. In Egypt, in 1882, the first feminist movement mobilised in this way under the name of the Women's Educational Society. The 1940s and 1950s witnessed waves of anti-colonial movements in the region, and these were often led by aristocratic families. In Turkey today, it is very common for prominent families to follow a long tradition in Turkish history, which is to set up charitable public institutions such as schools, and universities, otherwise translated from the Islamic concept of *waqf* (religious endowment) into English as 'social foundations'. Undoubtedly, the role of wealthy and powerful families remains central to the political make-up of the Middle East, particularly the Arab world where patriarchal and feudal structures have persisted.

Type 3: The popular political movement

The third type is perhaps the most revolutionary and indeed the most politicised. It is the one under which Emdad and Al-Qard Al-Hassan fall. This type of RWO can also be found in Egypt, Morocco and the Palestinian Territories in the example of movements with a clear Islamic ideology, such as the Muslim Brotherhood, Justice And Charity Movement and Hamas. It is important to pause here and consider the literature on Islamic social movements. Sutton and Vertigans (2005) and Makris (2007) make a distinction between radical Islamic movements such as Al Qaida, and mass organisations such as Hamas, the Muslim Brotherhood and Hizbullah. This book shows how important a social welfare perspective is for understanding the character of Islamic groups, particularly those falling under the category of mass organisations.

I prefer to use the term 'popular political movement' to denote these mass organisations since a key facet of their identity is their populist character expressed through their discourses on anti-imperialism (usually American), social justice and their active involvement in social welfare provision. Salamey and Pearson (2007), in analysing the particular case of Hizbullah, speak of a populist proletarian movement, which is part of an anti-imperialist international alliance. This, they argue, takes better account of the particular political discourse adopted by Hizbullah.[3] Here, the populist pro-poor discourse feeds into one of resistance not just against neo-colonial dominance but also against poverty and ignorance.

In the Western social policy literature, populism is viewed with disdain due its connection to conservatism and traditionalism (Hall and Midgley, 2004). However, populism can help explain the dynamics of social policy in the Middle East, not just during and after the colonial era but also with respect to the current involvement of Islamic social movements in social welfare in the region. Hall and Midgley (2004) credit populist approaches to social change with a long history of substantial achievements in the developing countries of the South. The success of Hugo Chavez in Venezuela is one such recent example (Salamey and Pearson, 2007). The awareness raising of Paolo Freire in Brazil, the social movements of India and Latin America and the expansion of social services in Argentina under President Juan Peron in the1960s were all inspired by forms of populism, which had the strength to attract the "people" around a sense of common identity (Hall and Midgley, 2004). Indeed, Walker and Wong (2005) attribute the success of social policy in the 'tiger' economies of East Asia to the influence of Confucianism and the prime political objectives of nation-building and regime legitimisation.

As I have argued elsewhere (Jawad, 2008), the support of populism here is not based on nostalgia or on romanticism. Rather, it draws attention to the value of positive local grassroots action, which is not something we hear of every day in the region of MENA. In this respect, there is a strong sense in which the Hizbullah welfare organisations started from scratch, as popular local initiatives that grew gradually into a sophisticated and organised institutional cadre able to command a high level of resources and moral authority. In the case of Lebanon, at the heart of the establishment of Emdad and Al-Qard Al-Hassan was the awareness of a need for direct action in the face of prolonged human deprivation or, in more political terms, in the face of a long-term political project of resistance and social transformation. Here, the reference is to the Shi'a Muslims of Lebanon and the renaissance, which was inspired by the charismatic Iranian cleric, Imam Musa Sadr.

> **H1**: [T]he social work and social services of Hizbullah ... started with the establishment of Hizbullah because Hizbullah began from among the people and with the people ... our religious scholars and brothers and relatives and leaders ... incite us not to stay silent in difficult circumstances.... Since the beginning we were clear with ourselves and our people.... It is not just an issue of a group of religious young men or scholars who decided to face the enemy with one or two isolated operations. We knew that we were setting up a project from the very beginning.... Resistance is not located among the elected and the diplomats.... Those who do resistance work are the popular forces and the disempowered who are patient and resilient.... In just a few years we were able to establish a group of organisations which have become the cosmos of the resistance movement.

Yet H1 is very clear that Hizbullah is not "trading in people", as he puts it:

> **H1:** We don't have such a thing where a service is given in exchange for another.... The human standard is when people serve each other because there is a need. We serve other people because they are human … if we don't we would be lacking in emotions … and our sense of the existence of others. When this is the prevailing philosophy, society will be sound.

Type 4: The international humanitarian relief organisation

We also cannot neglect the cross-national influences that feed into Islamic welfare, as indeed Christian welfare. Emdad in Lebanon was directly inspired by Emdad in Iran, which is otherwise known as the Imam Khomeini Relief Foundation. Today, Emdad-Iran has an almost untouchable status as it falls under the control of the supreme council. Underpinning both organisations is a Shi'a identity. The same may be said of Sunni-based RWOs where the staff members of different RWOs in different countries are ideologically affiliated to the Muslim Brotherhood for example. These cases denote a fourth type of RWO, mentioned above, which is especially evident in the cases of Iran and Turkey.

Insani Yardim Vakfi and Deniz Feneri Denergi in Turkey have risen to prominence in the last decade for their extensive international relief efforts to emergency situations around the world. Their attention also turns to the domestic front and they distribute aid within Turkey. They are very similar to the British Islamic humanitarian organisations such as Islamic Relief and Muslim Aid. Emdad-Iran is also beginning to cross international borders although it primarily denotes a fifth type of Islamic welfare organisation, particular to a theocratic state.

Type 5: The para-state organisation

This fifth type has already been described at length by Saeidi (2002, 2004) as a para-state organisation, otherwise called in Persian *Boniyad*. The general public perception in Iran is that Emdad *is* the welfare arm of the state. This view differs from that of staff members who argue that it is a 'holy organisation' set up by Imam Khomeini to serve the people. Indeed, the populist association emerges again here, with staff members arguing that the local population is more likely to donate to and support an NGO that it trusts.

As Saeidi (2002, 2004) argues, Emdad is part of a large constellation of social welfare institutions in Iran that offer a variety of services, sometimes to the extent that they duplicate services. Since 1979, social policy in Iran has increasingly been used as a tool of social control and political legitimisation. In this sense, the formal apparatus of government in Iran is an administrative structure since welfare organisations such as Emdad respond directly to the supreme leaders. According to Saeidi (2004), the *boniyads* reinforce the "financial authority of the religious leaders without accountability".

The nature of welfare: social service and religious faith

This section defines the nature of welfare that the MSA and the RWOs in Lebanon articulated and, departing from this, their definition and judgement of religious welfare. It is important to note the distinction made here between the definition of social welfare generally and that of religious welfare. This is in order to account for the interaction between religion and social service; indeed, as part of the discussion of the instrumental role of welfare in this chapter, I review the extent to which religion and social welfare have an arbitrary or intrinsic relationship.

The aim here is to explore the conceptualisation of social welfare among research participants and highlights two key propositions:

- Social welfare is dominated by a service-oriented and needs fulfilment approach to human welfare. Yet, the nature of welfare was also understood by the research participants in terms of a human *service* or "doing good". Social service thus has two connotations: on the one hand, there is the literal meaning of a direct short-term service and, on the other, there is the more profound meaning of feeling with another person's suffering and giving of one's self altruistically for the common good.
- Faith acted as a critical counterpart to social insurance (understood as rights-based or contribution-based social protection in the traditional Western European sense) in conceptualising the nature of welfare and the means of accessing it.

The extent to which we may speak of a philosophy of welfare among the organisations is important for determining the extent to which welfare played an instrumental role. The family (nuclear then extended) emerges as the basis of the good society.

A philosophy of social service

The concept of social welfare is effectively denoted in the Arabic context of the organisations by the term 'social service', understood broadly as an altruistic act of human solidarity. The notion of service is very significant in the literature on the role of religion in development, particularly to Kumar (2003) who focuses on the *gram seva* or village service that was promoted by Gandhi to foster rural development in India. To the extent that the RWOs and the MSA had a philosophy of welfare, they argued that they were acting out of humanity for the sake of humanity.

The main argument to be made here is the following: as a social exchange, social service in Lebanon has slowly gained in legitimacy over the years and begun to take on board the new development thinking, especially since the civil war. The conceptualisation of social service by service providers and users encompasses both material and moral dimensions but it remains largely driven by a service provision approach to human need even though some RWOs do run programmes that allow beneficiaries to achieve structural changes in their lives.

Evolution in social thinking

According to DAR2, DAR4 and MSA9, social service evolved over the years to gain in status as a science and specialism in its own right. It started as a voluntary activity based on a sense of personal mission or charity. This explained why social service in Lebanon and the Arab world generally had tended to be viewed as a second-class activity. However, according to interviewees, social work was only just starting to shed its rudimentary definition as relief assistance. In the particular case of Lebanon, the civil war had disrupted and delayed the evolution of the concept beyond urgent relief.

> **DAR2**: It is an error of our societies to view social work as consisting of a bunch of miserable children to whom we give whatever we don't need at home and some money. They live as if on the margin or by accident.... Since I entered this field, the view of social work has evolved a lot though there are circumstances which give a bad impression ... that social work is the monopoly of the wives of presidents and ministers ... as if it is just women's work.

> **MSA9**: It is not a money-making field and social work in Lebanon started as voluntary.... But it is no longer a question of mission, it's become a science. You study it and gain a qualification.... We are able to change society....

The sense of evolution was expressed across all the RWOs, which noted how when they had started working, their idea was merely to satisfy needs and provide social assistance randomly. However, they eventually opened health and education centres since they found the need for such services in society to be great. This idea was especially expressed at Emdad and Urfan.

The most extreme transformation in the understanding of social service among the organisations was at Caritas. The most important reason for this was the need to adapt to the circumstances of the post-war era and engage in development work.

> **CAR1**: There is a whole conception of social work which must now change. We no longer work for people but we work with them.

> **CAR3**: We are moving from direct services to giving people the capacity to work and provide their own services ... education is a direct service, micro-credit is not a direct service. You are giving the

person the means by which to serve themselves as they wish when they want, not when you want.

Material and moral support

Social service was also understood as a combination of both material and moral support. On the one hand, it consisted of the effective identification and satisfaction of material needs, and on the other, it was about humane treatment of the needy or disempowered whereby they were given a sense of hope and worth. An important dimension of this was the possibility of helping beneficiaries gain self-sufficiency. As H13 noted, social service had to prevent beneficiaries from becoming "captives to assistance".

> **CAR5:** You see someone who is in need, you want to do something but it is not charity or pity. You want to preserve the person's dignity and help them in a direct way without insulting them. That is social work.

> **Author:** Not that you are better than them and they depend on you?

> **CAR5**: No, when the ladies come to collect money from me, I don't sit behind my desk. I am like them.

> **H1:** We should take the hand of the person we are serving and tell them you are a normal human being … don't just think about how to secure food and health for you and your family, you have an opportunity to develop.

> **H13:** The idea is not for us to go down to their level but for them to come up to ours.

Definitions of social service: MSA, RWOs and service users

At the MSA and RWOs, the definition of social service was stretched across a wide spectrum. At the heart of the definition of social service lay the issue of whether social service was restricted to mere service provision or was in fact providing something more than that. It should be noted that the definitions of social service became more homogeneous at the level of the RWOs; indeed, their emphasis changed quite significantly towards satisfying social needs, as will be discussed subsequently. Below are the views voiced at the MSA, which illustrate narrow to broad definitions of social service:

> **MSA4**: Social service is about the mother and child. We could go into it through family medicine, a paediatrician, gynaecologist. We must specialise.

> **MSA3**: [It is] intervention in social affairs to correct the individual and family's situation and from there the local community/society. There are many reasons which cause the individual to go out of society.

> **MSA15**: It is a very baggy and big concept: schooling, employment, unemployment, poverty, the mother, the child, development, rural areas, national spirit, the economic situation, sanctions, politics, Israel, displacement, all constitute social pressure. The MSA must take care of all these issues.

These definitions highlight the four major dimensions of welfare that emerged from the research. First, the baseline idea of service provision: this was present in all of the RWOs and was most borne out at the MSA where emphasis was paid to delivering fast and easy social services since the aim behind establishing the MSA was to bypass government bureaucracy. MSA4, MSA5 and MSA7 noted that the MSA did not offer money, only services, and operated an active referral system. Even the relationship between the MSA and the RWO sector was based on service provision.

> **MSA5**: They [RWOs] are educating children. It is service-oriented. Private organisations are offering multiple times more services than the government.

> **MSA9**: We have a coordination committee in the … area which includes all local community organisations. We exchange services. We direct people to other organisations where the service is available.

However, staff members at the RWOs and beneficiaries were very aware that there was a dire need by the public for health, education and social care services. Moreover, all of the RWOs including the MSA noted that no sector could bear the brunt of delivering comprehensive services alone. Only at the Hizbullah RWOs was the view expressed that government had to take full responsibility for providing services.

Social actors also considered that the follow-up of services made a difference to their impact. This was particularly the case where there was educational follow-up of the families that were being assisted.

> **MSA12**: Some organisations provide services, no effective follow-up and that is not sustainable.

The second main dimension of social services was the idea that they work towards or directly feed into development. At the MSA local development services centres and Caritas, social services directly fed into community development. All the other RWOs saw themselves as doing development mainly through the educational and vocational services they provided. The concept of development is explored in the next chapter.

The third dimension equated social service provision to a political project of resistance. This was mainly the case in the Hizbullah organisations where social service gained the same status of struggle against oppression as the more conventional meaning of political resistance against an invading enemy. Fourth was the idea already touched on, which is that of social service as a humane exchange and an expression of human solidarity: recognition, respect, indeed love of other fellow humans.

From the beneficiaries' points of view, social service was very much about social care and educational services as it was about the humane treatment they received from the RWOs. The human contact was also emphasised by beneficiaries who later volunteered for the RWOs that had helped them.

> **H10 (B1):** They have a conscience and manners. They talk in a nice way to beneficiaries. They never turn a family away empty-handed.

> **CAR7**: Support to the mother. Schooling. They gave me a job. They take the kids to summer camps and they don't make the child feel like a victim or feel financial pressure. We have no car. Social service is in everything, clinics, dental care. I pay everything in instalments. I knew how to take care of my children too because I'm a teacher, I knew how to act.

Thus, some beneficiaries made a point of showing that they were not totally dependent on the RWO that helped them. This same feeling of dependency caused some widows, such as DAR7 and DAR8, to feel embarrassed about receiving social assistance.

Needs fulfilment

Responding to human need and fulfilling human need was the common denominator of social services for all interviewees. This primarily denoted basic needs such as food, clothing, education and health services. For organisations that believed in creating autonomy for the family (Emdad, Caritas, Al-Qard Al-Hassan and to a lesser degree Dar Al Aytam), income-generating projects or income allowances were provided as the means by which such needs could be fulfilled.

Other key concepts about the nature of welfare included happiness and an equally common one was preventing deviance (or moral rectitude). Moral education and awareness-raising thus became important determinants of welfare.

All of the organisations considered that religious education was as fundamental as academic education. Hence, the spiritual dimension was an important facet of human needs and all the RWOs advocated a holistic philosophy of social welfare.

> **Author**: Where does religion start and end for you?

> **DAR11**: From need, when someone comes to you and is in need.

> **H6**: It is a blessing from God upon you when you can satisfy people's needs.

Security, broadly understood as safety from harm or uncertainty as well as access to basic needs, was mentioned mostly at the Hizbullah RWOs, with one official noting that securing housing for beneficiaries was important. Also, resistance against oppression was a critical dimension of the nature of social welfare according to these Islamic organisations.

According to Emdad interviewees, from an Islamic point of view, the inability to fulfil essential needs was at the core of the definition of poverty in Islamic Shari'a law. The latter added a temporal dimension in order to convey a sense of degrees of poverty. The poor person was thus someone who did not have their essential needs for a day, month or year. Food was the key need here.

Altruism and duty

To engage in social service demanded that the person had a desire to give altruistically. The focus on human need was the principal means by which to ensure this.

> **DAR2**: Ideal social work must consist of no distinctions, no factionalism, no politics, no fanaticism. The worker must have the spirit of volunteerism, transparent work and good reputation."

> **ANT1**: When I serve for free there is a spirit of humanity and spirituality but when I want to make a profit I no longer look at the person.

> **H1**: The human standard is to serve others because there is a need. We serve others because they are human … if we don't we would be lacking in emotions and feelings, a heart and our sense of the existence of others.…

The emphasis on altruism was made by some RWOs such as Dar Al Aytam where it was argued that a truly charitable RWO should not even depend on government for funding otherwise it would be susceptible to political interference from the state. Only Dar Al Aytam and the critics of religious welfare at the MSA such as MSA1 and MSA7 spoke with fervour about enforcing human rights conventions in social welfare.

> **H2**: A feeling we always have is that offering assistance is not a favour: it is a duty and a great human service....

Yet, this view was contrasted by an orientation towards charity in social service.

Charity and paternalism

As social interaction, social welfare was firmly located in the domains of charity and altruism. However, the organisations that offered income-generating and micro-credit projects were the ones most able to go beyond the idea of charity, namely Caritas, Al-Qard Al-Hassan and the self-sufficiency programme at Emdad.

> **H2**: We even prefer that the family does not benefit from Emdad. That it depends on itself. Since there might be Emdad today but not tomorrow.... We find a job opportunity for the family or we teach the family a vocation....

Only at Caritas was there the idea of treating its beneficiaries as partners and an important reason for this was the change in Caritas's donor funding policy, which was obliging the RWO to become autonomous.

> **CAR3**: In my department, the vision is economic independence ... you have to depart from the capabilities of the person you want to fortify. I can't improve their social situation for them, they have to do it themselves ... I want to help them see what they want to do.

The other RWOs tended to have a rather paternalistic attitude towards their beneficiaries not least because they considered that the essential problem of many of them was ignorance and backwardness.

The family: basis of the good society

At the heart of the sense of duty towards fellow humans lay a deeper affiliation to one's family. Given the emphasis on religion and ascribed identity, it was not surprising that the cohesive family (nuclear and extended) should indeed be the social unit that the RWOs and the MSA believed to be the basis of the good society.

> **MSA6**: If development has as its final goal the human being, then the human being, the family and society are the objective ... development is no longer about self-interest but the common good, embodied in the family.

In practice, it emerged during fieldwork that the focus on family welfare was undermined by the fact that all of the organisations, by nature of their work being social care, concentrated their attention on vulnerable social groups: children, orphans, single mothers or female-headed households, older people and disabled people. Men, interviewees unanimously argued, could always find jobs and survive alone.

All the RWOs including the MSA were ideologically against excessive dependence on institutional care. Through my observational work, however, I would argue that attachment to religious identity was more likely to be an attribute of organisations that strongly opposed institutional care. The debate about the quality of social care will be discussed in the next chapter but it is useful to point out here that this was framed by MSA1 as essentially a problematic of modernisation versus tradition and the classic dichotomy of quality versus quantity.

Fee-paying services

One of the most noteworthy elements was the fee-paying component of welfare and this was where the philosophy of altruism became rather blurry. On the one hand, the RWOs that had their own schools (Emdad, Urfan, the Antonine Nuns) ran them as private establishments and this formed an important source of revenue.

Moreover, all the RWOs were very clear that they could not provide their beneficiaries with all their needs and Caritas specifically asked parents to pay for certain services in order to ensure that the family maintained a sense of responsibility for its own affairs. Likewise, in the case of the nursing homes for older people run by Dar Al Aytam and the Antonine Nuns, full-time residents paid for their stay in the home although this tended to be proportionate to their incomes.

In the case of Dar Al Aytam, the very philosophy of welfare that the organisation had (developing people's capabilities) meant that it could offer recreational and activity-oriented services to older people, which they could pay for. In the case of Al-Qard Al-Hassan, members of the organisation did stress that the latter was not a bank, although the micro-credit centre I visited could be passed off as one. Even the MSA local development centres charged a minor fee for medical consultations.

We cannot, however, underestimate the lack of resources and financial constraints that interviewees consistently noted impeded the flourishing of a fully fledged vision of social welfare. All the RWOs pointed out that providing fee-paying services constituted a substantial source of their revenues.

The role of the state

The contribution of the state towards the making of the good society remained marginal according to staff members. All the RWOs, including the MSA, believed that the government's role should remain legislative and financially supportive towards the RWO sector. Paradoxically, however, Emdad, Al-Qard Al-Hassan and to a certain extent Urfan believed that social services should be the full responsibility of the state. Indeed, interviewees in these organisations argued that the religious mission they felt gave them justification to engage in social work even though this type of welfare was more personalised and focused on specific religious communities. This situation emphasised the predominance society enjoyed in the social sphere over the state in the Lebanon.

> **MSA6**: We are still a society based on primordial, ascribed and tribal ties. We still haven't become a civil society where we are under the rule of law and associations, recognising others, depending on dialogue.... Relatives, villages, regionalism, women's association, that is how help is sought.

Religious welfare: faith versus social insurance

There was overwhelming emphasis among service providers that religious welfare possessed the comparative advantage over other types of welfare in resources, moral authority and practical skills. Indeed, religion brought to social welfare a holistic approach to human need and a wide-ranging repertoire of concepts and social programmes.

> **CAR1**: We are with the human being, for every human being and for the whole of the human being.

I have already argued at the beginning of this chapter that RWOs have a long history in Lebanon and are much more powerful than government in the social sector. As CAR1 and CAR2 argued during fieldwork, religious organisations were able to appeal to local society in ways that no other social institution could, including government.

Historically speaking, the civil war was a major factor triggering the mushrooming of social welfare RWOs and new sectarian welfare organisations continue to enter the social arena such as the Ahbash, which is a branch of Sunni Islam. The oldest and perhaps richer organisations are Christian and Sunni since they have had the closest contact with government in the past as well as international financial support from both the West and the Middle East. The Shi'a welfare organisations have been the latecomers but have flourished nonetheless, in a very short space of time.

In exploring the nature of religious welfare in Lebanon, I distinguish between three modes of religious expression that were manifested by the various organisations and social actors during fieldwork:

• religion as an institutional entity entailing rules of ethical conduct;
• faith as a personal spiritual experience, which is not necessarily manifested in ritualised practices;
• religion as pure political ethnicity expressed as sectarianism.

There are two lines of argument that I will engage with here about the nature of religious welfare. The first deals with the importance of factoring into the conceptualisation of social welfare the emotional and spiritual roles of faith in God for both the service user and service provider. This is one of the most challenging ways in which religion reshaped the understanding of well-being and social action during the fieldwork.

The citations referred to in the introduction to this chapter bear testimony to the importance of religious faith. The nature of the juxtaposition between social insurance and faith lies in how service users who turned to RWOs often did so because they had no access to employment-based or statutory social protection. Thus, religious faith was an alternative form of human welfare not only because of strong adherence to a particular religious tradition but also because of the mere lack of social protection measures.

The second line of argument entails questioning the extent to which religion had an intrinsic or arbitrary value for welfare actors in this research. This will entail exploration of the assessments that service providers and service users made of the influence of religion on welfare services.

Degrees of religiosity among the RWOs

The organisations that participated in this research fell on a spectrum of religiosity, with Dar Al Aytam being or at least claiming to be the least religious. Thus, we may speak of basic religious morality that underpinned all of the RWOs but speak of a clear clerical character in four of them, excluding Dar Al Aytam.

In all the RWOs, dependence on religious faith and God's blessings was considered intrinsic to social service. This was evident even among beneficiaries, who tended to express faith in God and affiliation to the welfare organisation that had helped them. Social service was also for service providers a direct interpretation of their religious faith. Faith in God was crucial for the flourishing of social work.

> **DAR2**: The new generation says "do a good study and you will do a good job", not "let's depend on God and He'll help us" … yet I feel

that in social work, one should always give it importance: the emotional ... if you don't have that spirit of faith; one plus one does not equal two in social work ... of course you need logic but ... sometimes, you want something and God puts you in the right circumstances so that He sends it to you.

Yet there were noteworthy distinctions among the RWOs' degrees of religiosity, for example language use varied between the Muslim organisations Emdad and Dar Al Aytam: whereas Dar Al Aytam spoke of donations and religion as a civilising force, Emdad used the religious terminology of *saddaqah* (almsgiving) and religion as worship. Whereas Emdad actively installed collection boxes in the streets bearing Islamic sayings, Dar Al Aytam considered this an improper and unorganised way of collecting funds, preferring that donations be made in person to the RWO.

What was even more striking was how the MSA's local development centres took on the character of the local communities they were serving and themselves were religiously homogenous. Indeed, employees at the RWOs considered that even the MSA was influenced by sectarianism. I shall focus briefly here on the incorporation of religion into the work of the organisations.

RWOs' definitions and judgement of religious welfare

So how did the RWOs define religious welfare and incorporate it into their programmes and services? Here, I review the three largest organisations: Caritas, Emdad/Al-Qard Al-Hassan and Dar Al Aytam. All the RWOs except Dar Al Aytam considered religious and spiritual education an intrinsic part of their work although what Dar Al Aytam called basic moral education often amounted to religious education. All the RWOs considered it crucial to preserve the morality of their beneficiaries since, they argued, need and poverty led to deviance and sin.

The logic of preventing deviance was evident in many different ways and will be discussed more fully in Chapter Five. Suffice to say here that from the point of view of the RWOs, helping people know their religion was another way of helping them fulfil their humanity. Caritas and the Antonine Nuns did regular spiritual exercises with their employees, and the other RWOs tended to hold religiously oriented social and educational seminars for adults and children.

Caritas

Employees were very clear that their work was socio-pastoral.

> **CAR1:** A person shouldn't be a big man in his intellect and a dwarf in his spirituality.

Caritas intended to start doing spiritual exercises with beneficiaries too although it argued that no one would be coerced into this. The logic behind introducing spiritual exercises was, according to CAR1, necessary for developing a more effective strategy. In the micro-credit and social care programmes, the religious component was applied indirectly, according to members of staff. There were no religion classes as such and one senior manager argued that awareness raising was pointless since people were tired of moralising and they learnt better through action. In this sense, CAR3 saw the spontaneous sense of solidarity or co-existence that resulted from participation in the women's village banks as an indirect but intended result of Caritas's sociopastoral work. The managers of both social care and micro-credit programmes saw themselves as spreading Christianity by example, through their treatment of beneficiaries.

As the welfare body of the Catholic Church, Caritas was actively seeking to reactivate awareness of the social role of the church. In the new social vision Caritas was setting for itself, there was a new emphasis on local parishes becoming more involved in social work and unifying their vision of it according to the Bible as well as encouraging more volunteer involvement. This was part of Caritas's decentralisation plan and its objective of building solidarity at the community level.

There was general consensus at Caritas that all religious organisations in Lebanon have "a message to transmit", including Caritas. It was even felt that the government was influenced by sectarian politics and in particular Muslim interests. Conversely, it was argued that this did not mean that Caritas was discriminatory or sectarian; indeed, all interviewees argued that it was political interference and sectarianism that ruined religion. Religion was thus distinct from sectarianism.

Caritas employees and beneficiaries were quick to name Muslim areas that the organisation worked in. CAR1, CAR2 and CAR3 added that the RWO was often accused of helping too many Muslims and non-Lebanese. Moreover, CAR2 pointed out that there was nothing like poverty and need to solve the issue of sectarianism. Nevertheless, at least one senior staff member argued, albeit off the record, that the organisation was not as non-sectarian as it claimed: Caritas employees were members of Lebanese society after all and sought to further their own interests at Caritas.

Indeed, the same manager added that during the civil war, emergency relief work could not overcome the sectarian influence and Christian welfare organisations did fear for the sustainability of the Christian sects in Lebanon. While nothing was explicitly mentioned in Caritas's policy about helping only the Christian community, CAR3 admitted that it was not always possible to control employees' behaviour. There were senior programme managers at Caritas who did not consider it wrong to direct Muslim applicants who came to Caritas to Muslim organisations. In the end, it was difficult to overcome the religious hatred of the civil war.

Out of all the RWOs, only Caritas expressed interest in engaging more directly with international development institutions such as the World Bank. CAR1 saw this as a necessary step for asserting the ethical role of the church in the face of globalisation.

Emdad and Al-Qard Al-Hassan

Here, religion (all religions and not just Islam) was considered a very important basis of social work and the social order.

> **H7**: Social work is religion.

> **H2**: The world without religion is a jungle.... There would be no humane rules, no morality. Who would be able to claim their rights?

Islam in particular was described by Emdad employees as being full of ideas of social feeling. The closer the person was to their *fitra* (human nature), the more likely they were to follow religion correctly and help others. The qualities of kindness, mercy and the ability to give were described as godly qualities on the basis of which humankind acted as God's vice-gerent on earth. Thus, it was a human responsibility to build the exemplary society as intended by God.

Interviewees recited verses from the Qur'an and many holy sayings (*hadiths*) of the prophet Mohamed, noting that there was a whole culture of social work and resistance to suffering in Islam enacted by the long heritage of (Shi'a) Imams who devoted their lives to the poor. The *hadiths* were a very important means by which to move people to donate money and help others. Many such sayings referred to the importance of helping orphans and the needy and how God blessed those who helped others.

A very common place where the *hadiths* could be seen was on the collection boxes that were located all over Muslim areas in Lebanon. The yellow and blue Emdad boxes always bear sayings about the benefits of charity to the person who donates, such as protection from misfortune and sickness or that by sponsoring an orphan they would go to heaven. Such religious beliefs are a direct illustration of the way in which religious faith defines the meaning of social service and human well-being. God's blessing in the afterlife is a different kind of social insurance.

The understanding of religious welfare at Emdad and Al-Qard Al-Hassan culminated in the idea of social work as a legal Islamic duty like prayer or fasting. Interviewees cited the many obligatory financial contributions Muslims should make on different Islamic occasions called *huquq shari`ya* (legal rights, which fall under the principle of *takleef shar'i*). Thus, the money that an organisation such as Emdad distributed to service users was "God's money" and the families it helped were "God's families".

In the context of the Shi'as, religious welfare formed an important part of their revival and uprising as a community. The pre-eminent role played in the development of this sect by personalities such as Imam Musa Sadr[4] and Ayatollah

Khomeini has already been mentioned and serves to reinforce the way in which Islamic scripture has formed the basis of social transformation among the Shi'a communities.

Dar Al Aytam

The role of religion in Dar Al Aytam's presentation of itself was extremely fascinating in my view because it was ambiguous. The organisation appeared to want to balance the role of religion in its work with its desire to be inclusive and modern. Only two senior members of staff answered frankly that the organisation was Sunni by virtue of its affiliation to Beirut families.

A poignant illustration of the organisation's religious and dynamic character was its name. There were two names under which it operated: the older *Dar Al Aytam*, meaning 'The Islamic Orphanage' and the newer *Muassassaat Al Ri'aaya Al Ijtimai'ya*, meaning 'The Social Care Organisations' (at the time of the research, the RWO had 36 different centres nationwide, with a view to further expansion). Both names were used interchangeably although members of staff who downplayed the organisation's religious leaning tended towards the new name. Interviewees correlated religion with fanaticism in that as soon as they were asked about the role of religion in their work they immediately sought to distinguish themselves from organisations that they considered fanatical.

> **DAR1**: Fanaticism doesn't breed social organisations. It may breed militias and mafias. But not open work like this.…Yes, we are a religious organisation which is not fanatical.

Three senior members of staff did not consider that the Dar Al Aytam was religious at all since it accepted applicants from all sects.

> **DAR2**: What is particular is that we are with everyone.… We serve religion, we don't abuse it.

Both DAR1 and DAR2 called Dar Al Aytam "The largest Shi'a organisation in Lebanon". This point was slightly confused when members of staff proceeded to state what the proportions of beneficiaries and employees by sect were, as I note in Table 4.1. Indeed, it was contradicted when senior staff members accepted that the organisation did fall under the patronage of Beirut's Sunni community.

DAR2 argued that the real tests of whether an organisation was religious or not were (a) whether it only employed people from its own sect and (b) whether it had its own schools where it taught children allegiance to it. Dar Al Aytam, DAR2 argued, did neither of these; indeed, many senior posts were held by people from non-Sunni sects.

Table 4.1 Selective indicators on sectarianism: numerical data provided by organisations; other data produced through observation and interviews (data collected in 2002 – verified again in 2008)

Organisation	Employees	Donors	Beneficiaries		
			Elderly	Children	Total
MSA Centre – GH (Muslim Area)	Muslim (Mainly Shi'a)	Government	–	–	Majority Shi'a
MSA Centre – BH (Christian Area)	Christian (Mixed)	Government	–	–	Muslim: 11 Christian: 81 (successful applications for the year 2002)
DAR AL AYTAM (Sunni)	Sunni: 60% Shi'a: 40% (also employed in managerial posts) Board of Governors: Sunni	Sunni: 7000 Shi'a: less than 20	(Elderly Club) Sunni: 263 Shi'a: 25 Druze: 3 Christian: 2	–	Shi'a: 40% / 45% / 60% / 90% Sunni: 30% / 45% / 60% Druze: 5% Christian: 1%–2% (several figures quoted)
EMDAD (Shi'a)	Muslim Shi'a (Hizbullah Affiliation)	Shi'a	–	–	Shi'a: 90%
AL-QARD AL-HASSAN (Shi'a)	Muslim Shi'a (Hizbullah Affiliation)	Shi'a	–	–	Majority Shi'a
CARITAS (Catholic)	Christian Catholic and Maronite	Caritas Internationalis	–	–	Majority Christian
URFAN (Druze)	Druze	Druze (some non-Druze grants)	–	–	Druze: 80% (?)
ANTONINE NUNS (Maronite)	(Elderly Home) Maronite: majority Muslim: Number not given *(Social Care)* All Maronite Orthodox: 5 Muslim: 1 (gardener)	Religious order	(Elderly Home) Maronite: 234 Other Christian: 167 Druze: 8, Shi'a: 7 Sunni: 7	(Social Care) Maronite: 105 Orthodox: 13 Catholic: 9 Sunni: 11	–

Table 4.1: .../ continued

Organisation	Beneficiaries whom I came into contact with	Employees whom I came into contact with	Presence of clergy amog employees	Spiritual exercises or religious seminars	Beneficiaries in receipt of service become more religious	Designated prayer area on premises
MSA Centre – GH (Muslim Area)	All Shi'a	All Shi'a, only one Sunni	No	Upon request	n/a	No
MSA Centre – BH (Christian Area)	All Christian	All Christian	No	Upon request	n/a	No but premises rented from Archbishopric
DAR AL AYTAM	All Sunni (during the observation sessions of applications for social care, out of 17 applications, 3 were by Shi'as)	All Sunni	No	Religious education for children, seminars for mothers upon request	Yes	In some centres
EMDAD	All Shi'a	All Shi'a	Yes	Yes	90%	Yes
AL-QARD AL-HASSAN	All Shi'a	All Shi'a	No	No	n/a	No
CARITAS	All Christian	All Christian	Yes	Yes (employees now, service-users later)	Yes	No but all staff meetings begin with mass
URFAN	All Druze	All Druze	Yes (70%)	Religious education for children	Yes (hospital = n/a)	No
ANTONINE NUNS	All Christian	All Maronite	Yes (except administrative and medical staff)	Yes (beneficiaries)	Yes	Yes

Note: It is important to note that in 2003, the MSA had 168 contracts with social care organisations; 88% of these contracts were with Christian orders or Islamic organisations.

I was not able to verify this but, as Table 4.1 suggests, Dar Al Aytam's claim to non-sectarianism should be taken with some reservation. The RWO argued that it was more interested in employing competent professionals above all else, and in a casual conversation I had with one member of the staff, the same point was voiced voluntarily.

Dar Al Aytam sought to promote positive Islamic values such as tolerance and free choice. Religion was thus portrayed as a civilising force and open to modernisation. More junior members of staff did stress that the RWO had a religious character and they felt that religion or perhaps what was better expressed as faith in God made them give more to the people they helped. This is a further illustration of how faith guided social service provision in a very intrinsic way.

Thus, what I would conclude was that Dar Al Aytam worked on the principle of religious morality and faith but it did not inflate the role of religion in its work nor did it consider teaching religion a vital part of its mission. It did not employ clerics. But it was, effectively, a practising Sunni organisation.

> **DAR10**: We do not wear religion like a badge but the Qur'an is our banner. It is the constitution that organises society. We work with it but we're not here to teach people morality and religion.

The political locus of religious welfare: elitism and the popular masses

An important distinction arising among the organisations was where they located religious welfare and to what extent it was an activity of the elite clerical establishment or a popularised social initiative.

The Hizbullah organisations placed most emphasis on religious welfare as an initiative arising from among the people and remaining with the people. Very clear criticism was made of the elites and it was on this basis that they criticised secular cultures for depending too much on government to provide social services since they saw this as necessarily undermining fellow feeling and solidarity among ordinary people. The key feature of Hizbullah RWOs, and that which underlies the very essence of Hizbullah's identity, is that they are grassroots organisations that started as popular and unorganised social initiatives aimed at improving the situation of the Shi'as.

This idea resonates as a defence of the rationale behind the importance of supporting the "resistance community" which, H1 states, can only ever be poor since the "elites do not defend resistance movements ... we are all a society of poor people".

In the Hizbullah welfare universe, the political and the social were one entity in the same mission to assert a fundamentally religious identity. Both Emdad and Al-Qard Al-Hassan followed the leadership of Hizbullah but, crucially, both affirmed that they existed independently of Hizbullah as a political party. This was because, ultimately, they were filling a social role and responding to society's needs. However, they admitted that without Hizbullah they would not enjoy the same prominence or command of resources. Thus, employees at both organisations noted that all welfare organisations need to have political backing otherwise they could not survive in Lebanon.

With the other RWOs, religious welfare remained a discourse primarily located among religious leaders (Caritas, Urfan and the Antonine Nuns) or social elites (Dar Al Aytam). Caritas and the Antonine Nuns followed the leadership of their respective churches with all senior decision-making and policy-related posts occupied by senior clerics. Caritas's increased emphasis on decentralisation and stimulating the participation of local community parishes in the work of the organisation was nevertheless presented as step towards a more popular expression of the organisation's religious welfare activities. At Urfan and Dar Al Aytam, there was a clear alliance between the ruling classes and powerful local families of those particular sects with the managerial establishment of both welfare organisations. The ideas will be expanded on in the course of this chapter.

Differences in Muslim/Christian welfare

Another important dimension of religious welfare was how accurate or detailed the different organisations' knowledge was about each other; indeed, was there a concrete distinction between and within Muslim and Christian welfare?

Knowledge of inter-religious welfare practices and orientations was generally scant, with senior members in the Christian RWOs having no knowledge at all of Islamic organisations except for ANT1, who noted that the Muslim communities tended to have a stronger idea of solidarity because of the notion of *zakat*. CAR6 thought that Muslim organisations focused more on orphans.

The predominant impression among Muslim organisations was that Christian organisations had more resources but less demand on their services, certainly less children in their care. Indeed, the point was made that Christian organisations indirectly reduced the burden of poverty on their communities because they were focused on offering free education.

If there was any substantial difference that I could draw between Islamic and Christian welfare, it was that Islamic welfare was more likely to emphasise local funding as opposed to Christian organisations, which had more contacts internationally. Christian organisations were more likely to be in tune with international trends in development and social welfare because of their more spontaneous contact with the West. The Druze sect was an exception in terms of the Muslim organisations in this regard since it felt fairly cut off in the Middle East as it is a minority religion. Muslim organisations were most likely to collaborate with regional actors especially those of the wealthy Arab Gulf: Kuwait and Iran in the case of Shi'a organisations, and Saudi Arabia in the case of Sunni organisations.

Also, there were more Muslim service users at Christian welfare organisations than there were Christians benefiting from Muslim organisations. This was mainly in the area of education where it was very common for Muslim children to attend nuns' schools. Also, Christian welfare organisations were much older than Muslim ones and, as such, Muslim service users tended to go to them more.

Thus, a major difference between Muslim and Christian welfare organisations lay in the volume of cases Muslim organisations received. Service users were more numerous among the Muslims but when probed on this subject further, interviewees in Christian organisations did not think that poverty was more of a phenomenon among Islamic communities, a point contradicted by the Muslim organisations where a key issue relating to the higher numbers of poor families was reported as being the problem of large families. Family planning was less popular among the Muslim families, it was argued by social actors in the Muslim organisations.

All employees in the Muslim RWOs were paid a salary, even if they were clerics, while in the Christian RWOs there was a communal fund where the cleric owned nothing. This, however, did not reduce the degree to which the employee felt ideologically affiliated to the organisation they worked in.

Finally, even though Islamic welfare organisations were relatively younger than the Christian ones, they had in some areas developed a more sophisticated set of mechanisms in welfare provision. *Zakat* and *takaaful* were two such examples where the Muslim felt the obligation to make a financial contribution to those less fortunate. This may have been another reason why Muslim organisations depended more on local contributions than Christian RWOs.

Sectarianism: welfare as identity politics

Perhaps the most important point of contention during the interviews was the extent to which the RWOs were influenced by sectarianism. This was the hardest subject to research although several interviewees were fairly honest about the sectarian biases in their work. The picture was finetuned through observation.

All interviewees distinguished religion, which they saw as a positive force promoting universal human values, from sectarianism, which they saw as a negative force promoting discrimination and political abuse of religion. Yet, all (except Dar Al Aytam) noted that each sect in Lebanon naturally had to take care of its own members since this was how the country was structured, as long as the welfare organisation did not breed fanaticism. Nevertheless, as Table 4.1 shows, the majority of interviewees were of the same sect as the organisation they worked for or benefited from.

The discourse of serving human needs paled into insignificance in the face of such affirmations, as Table 4.1 highlights. Dar Al Aytam and Caritas argued strongly that that they did not prioritise their own sects but no conclusive evidence was given to me by either organisation. In a personal communication with my key informant at the MSA on 25 October 2003, MSA2 said that Dar Al Aytam had undergone a change of policy and was decidedly much more open now to all sects. In any case, Table 4.1 illustrates more clearly the prevalence of sectarianism among the RWOs.

Crucially, the RWOs argued that geographical location played a determining role in their religious homogeneity. This was a consequence of the civil war and they did not specifically set out to help only members of their own sects. Indeed, they argued that they did have branches in areas where the majority population was of a different sect. Yet, it should be noted that such cases were in the minority. Certainly, all the headquarters of the RWOs, and also for some of them most of their branches, were located in areas whose majority population was of the same sect as that of the organisation.

Service users' perceptions of religious welfare

According to service users, the RWOs they benefited from had a defined religious character but this was not discriminatory and the beneficiaries felt comfortable with their RWO's religious identity. Yet, service users at Urfan, Emdad and Caritas claimed that had they applied to an organisation of a different sect, they would not have been accepted. Service users also noted that education and health services were the most important services they needed that religious organisations offered.

A very prominent characteristic of service users is that they wanted a palpable social service: in-cash or in-kind social assistance to alleviate their problem. As such, they were willing to comply with the demands the RWO made on them in terms of religious practice. In this sense, the religious component of social services was more a matter of supply than demand. As mentioned above, this contradicts rational choice theories of religion, which emphasise the importance of demand-side factors in the rise of religious activity (Iannaccone et al, 1997).

> **URF3**: It [Urfan] has religious character but we do not feel that there is religious fanaticism.... There is religious awareness raising. At the same time it is located in an area where there is a well-known majority sect.... If I were to go to another organisation of another religion, it may not accept me because I am of a particular religion.

> **CAR4**: A Muslim organisation would not come here and, even us, if we tried to go to a Muslim organisation they would reject our application ... but we are different, I go into a Muslim area, we were in ★★★ and ★★★ and ★★★. I have a group in ★★★. They are Muslim women.

> **H10 (B6)**: These organisations, whatever happens in the end, they want to attract people to their religion. So they go into social care.

> **Author:** Do you feel Emdad does that too?

H10 (B6): Of course, it is an Islamic organisation with its own rules. If the family isn't practising or it does not pray and fast, it is not necessary that it attends religious seminars but it is placed under the condition that it should follow religion.

Author: But the family does not need to be politically affiliated?

H10 (B1): No. It should just be religious.

DAR8: There is a big role for religion. There are special religion classes.... When the teacher gave us religion classes it benefited us. They make us really feel the Islamic holiday and Ramadan. We are invited to events.

Religion and social welfare: intrinsic or arbitrary relationship?

Perhaps the most important issue to emerge from research in Lebanon regarding religious welfare concerns the extent to which the relationship between religion and social welfare is intrinsic, arbitrary or, more problematically, instrumental. Indeed, to what extent do service providers and users consider that religion impacts negatively on social welfare?

Most service providers in the Lebanese research agreed that there was an intrinsic relationship between social welfare and religion since social work had to depend on faith in God if it was to maintain its altruistic character. DAR2's words cited on page 108 illustrate this. Only three employees at the MSA, two of whom were fairly senior, thought that religion and social welfare should be separate.

MSA7: Religious organisations, I think it is excellent that they should care for the sect and educate it. People react when the sheikh says we should pay *zakat* or the priest says we should help organisations.... But all of them, their background is not social. It's government that should do the work.... Let the religious organisations go back to the mosques and churches and care for the people religiously.... Social care has its appropriate professionals.

ANT1, a senior nun at the Antonine Nuns, did not think that the relationship between social welfare and religion was intrinsic but that religion gave spirit or spirituality to social care, which allowed beneficiaries to know their humanity better. Fulfilling human nature is indeed a recurring theme in the literature on religion within development studies (see, for example, Kumar, 2003; Tyndale, 2003). Again, this is a theme that will be developed more fully in the course of the remainder of this book, certainly in Chapter Five, where the welfare outcomes of religious social services are considered.

The overarching view in terms of the relationship between religion and social welfare that was presented during the fieldwork was that religion was not a negative influence as long as social services were not politicised or influenced by sectarianism.

> **MSA12**: If it is not politicised you can build many things on religion ... sadly religion is politicised.

> **DAR11**: Religion is openness, progress, civilisation, justice, power, forgiveness, all positive principles.

So how were these religious teachings elaborated at policy level and translated into working objectives? The discussion now turns to a more formal introduction of the organisations and MSA as professional welfare actors situated in particular policy contexts within which they articulated their objectives.

Identities, policy contexts and objectives

The aim here is to add texture to the profiles of the RWOs outlined so far by conveying them as dynamic social actors engaged in decision-making processes. The mechanisms through which religious welfare values were articulated as policy are highlighted through three issues:

- the perceived roles of the organisations within society;
- the power processes that determined the definition of policy formulation and objectives;
- the extent to which the objectives acted as palliative measures or pursued far-reaching change.

The research findings confirmed existing knowledge about the weak role of the state in the social sphere in Lebanon and I shall therefore refer to the role of the MSA in social policy and its objectives very briefly.

The key argument that will be made here regards the rudimentary character of state social policy, which stands in stark contrast to the autonomous and dynamic RWO sector. Yet, both ends of the service provision process suffered from a lack agency and choice in determining the type of social services that were offered. There were two overarching issues that I would like to highlight:

- the lack of an adequate definition of the problems and issues the MSA proposed to address, notably poverty, social care and the *social case* and, therefore, ineffective treatment of the causes of these social problems;
- the lack of planning in the MSA's approach to social service due to the destructive effects of the civil war and the lack of political will to assign social policy a more constructive role.

Ministry of Social Affairs: searching for a social policy mandate

The general situation of social policy as expressed by both the RWO sector and the MSA was thus: that there was no social policy in Lebanon in the sense of a comprehensive plan that treated social problems adequately or promoted a viable vision of the good society. According to the majority of interviewees, this was more fundamentally linked to the weakness of the state generally in Lebanon and the side-effects of the war that had kept the MSA catering for immediate needs satisfaction and the solving of social problems ad hoc. To a certain, the Lebanese state suffers from this deficiency more than its counterparts in Egypt, Iran and Turkey, although in all these other countries, social welfare is provided across disparate institutions with very little coordination among them.

> **MSA7**: There used to be a social policy. And it was a very good one.... The war messed up everything in the social field. It became urgent relief. Now we are continuing like that and it is increasing.

In Lebanon, what exists as a result is a ministry totally dependent on the RWO sector for the provision of social services based on contractual agreements through which it partly funds beneficiaries. To this extent, the role of the state in social policy becomes instrumental and confined primarily to administrative and regulatory purposes. As such, the MSA only provides services in kind, not cash.

The MSA's policy revolves around social care and needs satisfaction as opposed to more fundamental work relating to social development, social justice or social cohesion. For 2004, the MSA's total budget amounted to around US$6.7 million, 56% of which was devoted to contracts with social care institutions. This share of the budget is constant.

In 2003, the total number of beneficiaries partly funded by the MSA through its contracts with the RWO sector amounted to 33,039 individuals, a drop of about 50 from 2002. Ninety-eight per cent of these beneficiaries were children between the ages of 0 and 23 who were either in institutional care or day pupils in vocational training. According to various employees at the ministry, the MSA receives between 8,000 and 15,000 applications for social care annually. There is no actual database. In 2004, the MSA was partly funding 2,491 children in institutional care in Dar Al Aytam, 525 children in Urfan and 192 children in the school run by the Antonine Nuns.

Rural development is also one of the objectives of the ministry although this is very much development with a small 'd'. It is confined to small projects that are not funded by the ministry and is geared towards encouraging volunteering and small environmental enhancement projects in rural areas.

There have also been complaints about political interference and sectarianism from both the RWO sector and the MSA.

> **DAR2**: There is no social policy because everyone wants to preserve their own social work.

This situation is marked by a sense of frustration and lack of both choice and agency at all levels of the ministry. It is possible to argue that there were competent and committed people at the MSA but with little power to change things, with blame generally being put on the excessive powers of the ruling political factions, the religious leaders and welfare RWOs. Indeed, junior-level employees at the ministry also expressed frustration at the ineffectiveness of their work and appeared to depict a dynamics of 'them' and 'us' whereby the policy-making body at the MSA was considered to hold a very different view of the effectiveness of the ministry's work.

> **Author**: So your work is more administrative?

> **MSA2:** Yes, that's what I feel.... If you try to enter anything particular … they don't like it … I am trying certain things. They talk a lot that the MSA must improve the social situation of the people but you don't feel anything is being applied on the ground. You feel that the thing most applied is the issue of disabled people. The laws that were issued…

However, the MSA's local centres are noteworthy for the local development work they do. Unfortunately, I am not able to explore these centres further here due to lack of space but I would like to mention a key issue: the centres are very active and represent an important initiative on the part of the government to have a presence in the local communities. Yet, because of the weakness of the state in public life in Lebanon, the centres emphasise how, at the local community level, the state is merely one of many actors in the social welfare sphere.

> **MSA12**: When I enter a particular neighbourhood which is dominated by a particular faction … I only enter with their permission.

Dependence on the RWO sector

The ultimate dependence of the MSA on the RWO sector for the provision of social services is seen as a matter-of-fact situation in Lebanon, with general consensus leaning towards the idea that the RWO sector holds the comparative advantage in terms of resources, effectiveness and the voluntary will to provide social services.

The MSA's dependence on the RWO sector for the provision of social care services is, however, tinged with resentment. On the one hand, there are employees at the MSA who fully support this dependence since they believe that the public sector is too influenced by political and bureaucratic considerations and bereft of resources to provide good-quality services. The contractual relationship between the MSA and the RWO sector was often depicted during fieldwork as a partnership whereby the MSA's role was to provide funding and a suitable legislative environment.

Likewise, some interviewees were quick to draw attention to the dynamism of local society in Lebanon, although the extent to which the term 'civil society' could actually describe the society-based associations that existed on the ground was questionable. Employees of the MSA were very aware of the power of the RWO sector in setting the agenda for social care and defining eligibility criteria. Indeed, it was mentioned that the MSA was actually denied access to some of the more powerful RWOs when it sought to undertake standard inspections of social care organisations.

> **MSA0:** There is an NGO lobby. They gang up against the government and they once filed a lawsuit against the MSA.

> **MSA2:** Of course, I talk to the institutions. I don't really like the idea of large dormitories … some respond. Some organisations see this as the red line … I give my opinion and that's it for them.

All the RWOs advocated that the sector remain autonomous except the Hizbullah organisations, which argued vehemently that the state must take a central role in social services provision. Ironically, Hizbullah is one of the organisations from whom permission was sought by the MSA development services centres when these wanted to work in a particular neighbourhood dominated by the political faction.

The poverty dilemma

The dilemma that has beset the objectives of the ministry with heated debate about its mandate and identity is whether or not to deal with the issue of poverty. Apart from the very real need to review the quality of social care, there is the more fundamental question of whether or not the ministry should add to its mandate the issue of economic and financial hardship and accept this as a valid reason for literally breaking up a 'normal' family (the opposite to its mandate) and putting a child into institutional care.

The problem is that this is already happening to the extent that, according to MSA1, only 15% of children going into care are actually orphans and need to go into an institution. This has been corroborated by other MSA personnel who noted that "three quarters" of children going into care were poor children. The applications officer in charge of cases of orphan children at the MSA noted on 23 October 2003 in a personal communication that applications for orphans had decreased substantially and that all applications had put down financial hardship as a major factor. The case of one of the MSA local development centres also illustrates the ambiguous place of poverty in policy: for the year 2001, up until the month of August, 68% of applications for social care submitted to the centre were due to economic hardship.

Suffice to say here that one camp at the MSA is pulling towards modernisation of the ministry's objectives while another is calling for a return to the ministry's essential aim before the civil war, which was to provide social care to children with no home or family. Both camps, however, agree that the growth in institutional care is unwarranted and advocate measures to encourage family care. In 2008, UNICEF and the MSA announced that they would be launching a major report on the state of children in care in Lebanon. The report has not yet appeared at the time of writing this book.

Rhetoric and reality

There is, in conclusion to this subsection, a strong sense of a gap between what the ministry is meant to be doing and what it actually does. MSA2 and MSA6 were brave enough to call this rhetoric. Almost all agreed that the ministry was not always able to fulfil its objectives and, therefore, solve the real causes of people's problems. A major reason for this was immense pressure from a population with increasingly complex social problems and no clear government plan to deal with this. This, in the opinion of civil servants, called for a redefinition of the dynamics of poverty and the social case.

One clear dividing line in the objectives expressed among the different tiers at the ministry was that between the decision-making body at the ministry and the local development services centres. Staff in the latter centres felt very strongly that their work was about community development and that institutional care was only one aspect of this. Thus, they saw poverty as a very legitimate reason for putting a child into social care since they did not differentiate between poverty and the social case.

In stark contrast to the context within which government policy is taking place, stands the RWO sector to which the discussion now turns.

Five RWOs: identity and social roles

Each RWO has its distinguishing features and I shall illustrate this heterogeneity subsequently. I would add at this point that the Hizbullah organisations and Dar Al Aytam stand at the extreme ends of the list of organisations in terms of their degrees of religiosity and politicisation. They are also two of the three largest RWOs in the study, Caritas being the third.

The main claim to be illustrated here regarding the role of the Lebanese RWOs is as follows: local and international forces tug and pull on an RWO sector that is brimming with a sense of purpose and achievement. This has both a constructive and destructive impact on the extent to which the RWOs are truly applying their rhetoric of human solidarity. Their religious and sectarian fervour exercises a direct influencing factor in this regard. Below are brief portraits of each RWO based on what I propose were their most distinguishing features.

Leadership, growth, power: Dar Al Aytam

Each RWO boasts of its success and of being a leader in the social services sector. Each one attributes to its success the trust, love and credibility it enjoys from its constituents. This is also apparent in similar organisations in Egypt, Iran and Turkey. To this extent, each organisation sees itself as representing the public interest without discrimination by sect or politics or religion.

Only three of the organisations (Caritas, Dar Al Aytam, Emdad) (claim to) have full nationwide coverage and they are the most vociferous about how their growth signals their success and inclusiveness. All the RWOs thus regard themselves as social symbols of their different communities.

Dar Al Aytam is especially noteworthy in this regard, with the head of the RWO dubbed the 'the father of social work'. This is an organisation brimming with the power and confidence of success and growth. Power was understood by service providers as self-sufficiency and size, which are based on an ability to command resources and change the surrounding circumstances.

DAR1: This is the age of power, not weakness.

Resistance and political transformation: Al-Qard Al-Hassan and Emdad

All the organisations appear to be at ease with their sectarian or political identity except Dar Al Aytam. The latter considers that this issue limits the growth of the organisation but there was evidence during fieldwork to disprove this since two of the other large organisations – Caritas and Emdad – have nationwide coverage and as large a budget as Dar al Aytam but they also have distinctly religious identities. I shall provide a brief discussion here based on the Hizbullah welfare organisations.

At the furthest extreme of the political spectrum lie the Hizbullah organisations whose politico-religious mission has already been commented on. Figure 4.1 illustrates the way in which Al-Qard Al-Hassan and Emdad connect with the wider movement of Islamic resistance, which they call *Al Hala Al Islamiya*.[5]

These RWOs are aware that their existence supports "the horizon of the resistance", the business and lay communities that embrace the mission of resistance and lend their services, funding and resources to Hizbullah. After all, the latter is, according to staff members, not only a resistance movement, but a whole society. H6 noted that while Hizbullah is not a fully fledged state, in a manner of speaking, it certainly acts as one. Thus, employees are not just mere staff members who go home when the day is done. But the political dimension

Figure 4.1: Network of supporting links between the *Al Hala Al Islamiya*, Hizbullah welfare organisations and the resistance community

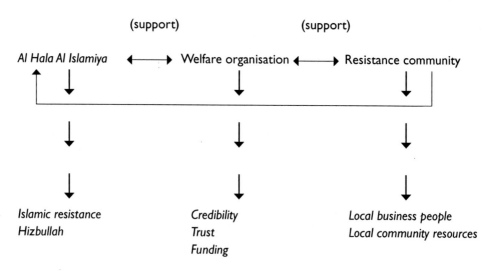

of their affiliation works in synchronicity with the social dimension and not as a form of political exploitation.

> **H1**: They are one entity.... Politics for us is for the people and for society ... I don't serve people so that they support me politically.... The background is much larger than the political and social: it is religion ... for example, one of our brothers may be working in politics and he may have found success ... but we may need him for social work. Without hesitation he will drop political work and make time for social work.

Thus, employees at both Al-Qard Al-Hassan and Emdad did not see that the political affiliation of their organisations interfered with their social work; indeed, at the social level, they believed that their organisations were totally humane and non-discriminatory. To this extent, they reaffirmed that their social work had started well before Hizbullah came into being as an official political party (1985).

> **H2**: Social work started with the prophet Mohamed.

The influence of the international arena: Caritas

The extent to which the RWOs have contact with international actors and the international development scene is also a striking and determining factor of their identity. Only three organisations – Al-Qard Al-Hassan, Caritas and Emdad – are ideologically inspired by international religious movements.

Yet, there is a clear Muslim/Christian divide whereby the Muslim organisations mistrust international (read Western) donors although not all are averse to collaborating with them. Only Dar Al Aytam is categorically against any collaboration with international organisations, which it sees as politically motivated. The Christian RWOs either depend totally on foreign funding (Caritas) or are active in religious missions and social work among Lebanese emigrants abroad (the Antonine Nuns).

Ninety per cent of Caritas's funding, according to CAR1, comes from its sister organisations as well as donor countries such as France and Italy and international organisations such as the EU. While the heavy dependence on foreign actors was seen as a positive element by members of staff since Caritas Lebanon had access to a rich array of resources, it had nevertheless bred dependency on Caritas's international partners although staff members argued that Caritas Lebanon was autonomous in its work.

> **CAR2**: We are part of Caritas Internationalis. That's a point of strength for us because we are exchanging experiences with people.

Loyalty to the local context: Dar Al Aytam

Attachment to the local context is a recurrent theme among all of the RWOs and is considered a key facet of the success of the organisations. But Dar Al Aytam, the RWO most averse to foreign funding, is the one to emphasise most the importance of being rooted in the local context.

What is striking about this RWO is that its understanding of local society does not primarily mean the grassroots of the poor or disempowered but simply members of the local community who embrace the cause of the organisation and donate resources. This, according to DAR2, was the key to sustainability and growth. It was also what defined the organisation's charitable character and explained its openness with its donors and society at large.

Thus, the strong link to the local community relates to the sources of wealth in Lebanon. Dar Al Aytam retains its primary affiliation to the prominent families of Beirut. This special association is fundamental to the very identity and survival of Dar Al Aytam and led DAR2 and DAR10 to question how far Dar Al Aytam has sunk its roots in the other regions where it has welfare centres.

RWOs' policy contexts and decision-making processes

A consideration of how the RWOs conduct policy draws attention to features that are leitmotifs of this book. First, there is the immense heterogeneity and autonomy that the RWOs enjoy in devising their policies in relation to the Lebanese state. In the case of Caritas, it is international donors who hold more sway on changes in policy.

> **CAR1:** We literally found ourselves with our backs against the wall.

Likewise, at Emdad there is an issue about the influence of Iran on the organisation, for example with regard to the smoking policy at Emdad, which is discussed below. A second issue about the policy context in which the RWOs operate is that they consider social planning to be more a feature of the RWO sector. It is quite typical for the RWOs to have five- or 10-year plans, something that is missing at the MSA.

> **DAR11:** Social planning exists more at the level of the RWOs than the ministry.

The Hizbullah organisations are the main exception in this regard. The question of whether or not there is a comprehensive social strategy at the Hizbullah organisations was met with differing responses from interviewees. H1 stated that any comprehensive strategy for social service could only be the job of the state and, as such, all that Hizbullah social services could do was provide a basic standard, merely to keep the local community, and in particular the resistance community, afloat.

> **H1:** [W]e cannot say that we have a social strategy. The reason is we are not a state. One should know their role and size. We have a social strategy that is in tune with our role and resources.... We are not a substitute, we can't be.

Such a view was shared by H13 at Al-Qard Al-Hassan, who noted that this RWO could not solve all of society's problems:

> **H13:** [I]t merely lights a candle in the right direction.

At Emdad, however, the view was slightly different since managers did believe that the organisation had long-term plans that were aimed at the eradication of poverty and deprivation. But the overall consensus was that government should bear responsibility.

The final point about the policy context of the RWOs relates to the process itself of policy elaboration and who the actors involved are. Overall, policy elaboration is a centralised and hierarchical process, as can be found in the other countries that are discussed in this book. The RWOs may be humane in their treatment of service users and they may consult with junior staff members as well as beneficiaries. However, this humaneness comes through as a form of paternalism whereby the RWO 'knows best' and the beneficiaries are happy just to receive help without disputing its quality and terms of benefit. Supply is definitely more powerful than demand in the religious welfare sphere.

One illustration of this centralised and paternalistic approach to policy making is the smoking policy that Emdad introduced at the time of my research in Lebanon, which entailed substituting cash handouts with vouchers as a way of prohibiting smoker beneficiaries from spending their monthly allowances on cigarettes. Although H2 explained that Emdad took time to review such a policy before it introduced it, beneficiaries such as H10 (B3) expressed a kind of resignation to the RWO. One volunteer went as far as saying that the policy was imposed on Emdad by the mother organisation in Iran.

The case varies slightly at Dar Al Aytam, where executive management appears to be more decentralised although DAR10 suggested clearly that the different programme managers at Dar Al Aytam were not given enough autonomy to decide their budgets and run their programmes. The extent to which Dar Al Aytam consulted with local society was expressed as follows:

> **DAR2:** We have, of course, meetings with the families that benefit in order to find out the extent of their acceptance or what they want from us. We always propose that, be it with the elderly who can express themselves, the parents of the children in our nurseries ... whatever the mother does, she will always have more of an opinion.

Through observations I conducted of the exchanges between members of staff and beneficiaries or applicants for services, I found that the relationship was rather paternalistic, with the organisation taking the upper hand in deciding the needs of the beneficiaries and how best to treat them. DAR4, in her account of the relationship between the widows and social workers in the AMAN programme, explained that if mothers did not comply with the terms of the programme, it was halted.

The most participatory approach to policy elaboration was expressed at Caritas, where beneficiaries were described as partners who should solve their own problems. This was not just a matter of principle but also of practical necessity for sustainability since development projects were built on the notion of being self-funded. This was especially the case in the women's village banks programme.

> **CAR3:** We don't use the word 'beneficiaries'. The move from emergency relief to development also means from spontaneous work to planned work. From beneficiaries to participants.

The RWOs' objectives

While the social sector in Lebanon is marked by heterogeneous and sometimes inappropriate objectives, it is united by concerns for human solidarity and moral responsibility, which cut across the ideological dividing lines. Based on this, I would argue that the possibilities for transformational action would surely be enhanced if more concerted efforts were invested into unifying the objectives of the sector – not least through strengthening the role of the state.

General overview: heterogeneity and ambition

The general claim I will make is as follows: whereas the policy objectives of the MSA whittle down to those of the programmes it offers, the RWOs present a more confident agenda backed up by a very clear social and at times political vision. The domain of social welfare is theirs to determine even though they look to the government for financial and legislative support.

The most striking issue is how heterogeneous the objectives are and how autonomous the RWOs are in setting them. Nevertheless, the RWOs and the MSA are united by more fundamental objectives than they are divided, even though they differ greatly in terms of the strategies they employ. They share common goals in terms of social care, child and family welfare, satisfying human needs, educating society, helping beneficiaries attain self-sufficiency and moral responsibility. Indeed, the issue of poverty remains a chimera for most of them and is putting all their objectives to the test. Finally, all the organisations distanced their work from political objectives and were thus united by a strongly moral discourse, which prioritises the prevention of deviant behaviour as opposed to encouraging social cohesion.

What divides the RWOs are the following issues:

- how far they have incorporated development discourse into their objectives;
- where they stand in terms of the issue of institutional care and how best to deliver social care;
- to what extent they see their work as political or religious;
- what role they believe the MSA should have in the social sector;
- how much influence international actors have on the agenda of each RWO.

The main argument that summarises the objectives of the organisations draws attention to the mixed blessing of their very heterogeneity, which breeds lack of coordination. Even though all the RWOs speak in the name of humanity, the fact that they occupy different moral platforms contradicts their claims to universalism.

The Hizbullah welfare organisations in focus

It is instructive to focus here on the Hizbullah organisations whose objectives are the most complex. Table 4.2 outlines the objectives and target groups of all the RWOs. In the case of Al-Qard Al-Hassan and Emdad, resisting oppression in all its forms encompasses the broad objectives. These thus reflect a distinct sociopolitical agenda, constituting ultimate/underlying and immediate/obvious goals.

Both organisations affirm their objectives as purely social and these we may call the immediate or obvious objectives since there are clearly a lot of people living in dire need. However, both RWOs also recognise that there are consequences (both intended and not) resulting from their affiliation to the resistance community. Under this heading lie what we may call the ultimate/underlying objectives, which link back to the overall ideological vision.

The ultimate objectives entail ensuring the steadfastness of the resistance community, which refers to the support base (both potential and actual) of Hizbullah. To this extent, social services are provided out of duty to the resistance community and they constitute only the bare minimum, enough for the community not to perish.

The more immediate and obvious objectives are two-pronged. With regard to the first objective, there is a humane discourse of needs satisfaction and helping the individual regain self-sufficiency, hope and dignity. This is seen as the redressing of injustice but also, in more pragmatic terms, as a means by which the person is not a burden on society. "Relieving a burden off society" was an often-used phrase to describe these RWOs' work.

The other main objective is seen as complementary to the first and also acts as a strategy: it is a highly moral discourse of protecting the individual within society from deviance. Unsatisfied needs and poverty are considered to lead directly to deviance, criminal and dishonest behaviour, and sin. Whereas the resistance movement has a political vision, the RWOs articulate a genuine social vision, which rests fundamentally, in the words of H2, on the notion of "building the human being": one who is exalted, dignified and strong.

While this vision of society is inevitably normative since it is wholly based on the Shi'a interpretation of Islam, it is depicted in universal terms. It is about returning the human being to their essential human nature, their *fitra*, which, according to H13, is peaceful, good and beautiful. Only by returning to this essential humanness can there be true solidarity among humans. *Takaaful* (financial sponsorship/social solidarity) thus becomes both an objective and a strategy in this social vision, which we may call, in the words of H13, "the humanisation of society".

Table 4.2 The RWOs and their objectives

RWO	URFAN	DAR AL AYTAM	ANTONINE NUNS	CARITAS	AL-QARD AL-HASSAN	EMDAD
OBJECTIVES	• Religious and academic education • Hospital care	• Developing capabilities, human development • Social care	• Social welfare • Education • Health clinics and health care	• Social justice sustainable human development: protection of human dignity	• Micro-credit • Building social solidarity • Satisfying urgent needs	• Responding to needs: social, health, educational, spiritual for human autonomy and dignity
PRIORITIES	• Responding to needs of the Druze community • Preserving identity and morality of Druze community	• Responding to local needs	• Preserving identity and sustainability of Maronite community at home and abroad	• Developing social role of Catholic Church • Responding human needs • Moving from emergency relief work to development	• Political project: serving the resistance community	• Preservation of moral fabric of society and preventing deviance • Teaching service-users correct religion • Political project: serving resistance community
TARGET GROUPS	• Priority target group: Druze	• Children • Elderly • Orphans • Widows • People with disabilities (physical and mental) • *social cases* (children from broken homes)	• Children • Elderly • Handicapped • Homeless	• Women • Female-headed households • Orphans • Elderly • Immigrants • AIDS victims • Drug addicts	• Service-users not poorest of the poor since should be able to pay back loan	• Orphans in nuclear and extended families • Single mothers female-headed households • Families without main male breadwinner

Social welfare: instrumental or intrinsic value?

To synthesise this chapter, I shall now review the key issue of how far the RWOs and MSA can be considered as providing something more than needs satisfaction. Indeed, how far do their endeavours mean that social welfare in Lebanon stands as a legitimate entity in its own right, a comprehensive and feasible vision of the nature of the good society?

Although all interviewees in my research emphasised the human alliance as being at the heart of social service, the rhetoric of solidarity fell short of providing a coherent appraisal of social welfare due to several impediments. This means that instead of a vision of the good society as the end of social action, there is an instrumental use of social services.

On the one hand, the RWOs very clearly advocate the importance of equipping their beneficiaries with the tools of self-sufficiency, be it through an income-generating project, vocational training or the decent upbringing of children. The adage of teaching people to fish instead of giving them fish is often repeated among RWOs in Lebanon and indeed the rest of the developing world. The micro-credit programmes at Caritas, at Emdad and to a lesser degree at Al-Qard Al-Hassan are immediate examples of this philosophy.

I would also argue that providing academic and vocational education should also bear its fruits provided that children are not too damaged by institutional care and the marketplace can absorb them when they start to look for jobs.

Nevertheless, interviewees argued, as I have in this chapter based on my own observations, that institutional care, as articulated in the discourses of welfare actors, is too focused on the fulfilment of physiological needs. It thereby falls short of ensuring the emotional needs and psychological stability of children. These issues will be alluded to in the next chapter. In the case of Emdad, this RWO gives out much financial and social assistance and advises families to become more religious but staff members agree that Emdad has created dependency and is not helping the vast majority of its beneficiaries who are single mothers or members of female-headed households to become professionally active.

Sectarianism is also a key way in which welfare is used instrumentally. At Urfan, there is a purposive focus on providing educational and health services to the Druze community just as the Antonine Nuns are primarily concerned with the well-being of the Maronites in Lebanon and abroad. Al-Qard Al-Hassan and Emdad staff are also proud that there are finally in Lebanon effective Shi'a welfare organisations.

Another way in which welfare is instrumentalised relates to how far RWOs are able to build links with the local communities where they operate. Dar Al Aytam is actively constructing large social institutions in different regions but it remains a fundamentally Beirut-based organisation. Caritas is elaborating a sophisticated vision of social justice and human development but were it not for its donors changing funding priorities, Caritas would still be giving cash handouts and doing mainly social assistance work.

A final point is the extent to which the RWOs consider themselves symbols of their respective communities and enjoy the social prestige that accompanies their line of work. Thus, social work is a means by which to assert their social standing in society. Yet, a senior staff member at Caritas stressed the importance of not mixing prestige with social work in order to retain the spirit of the Bible.

Dar Al Aytam is the most noteworthy in this regard as illustrated by the street decorations that the organisation puts up every year during the month of Ramadan (although Dar Al Aytam is not the only organisation to decorate during Ramadan). The funding for the decorations is provided specifically for this purpose by Beirut families. The decorations are specifically for Beirut. Such acts add a very different dimension to the nature and role of welfare in society. I would argue that they tinge welfare with social and political connotations, which emphasise the immense sway on public opinion that RWOs in Lebanon enjoy.

All the factors mentioned above constitute, I would argue, limitations to a more coherent vision of the good society in Lebanon. These issues will be explored more fully in subsequent chapters, specifically Chapter Seven. What I shall argue at this point is that social welfare as a viable end of public policy in Lebanon is questionable since concern with social welfare invariably acts as a tag-along to economic growth in the official government discourse, a prop for political interests or a badge for social status, as I have sought to show in the case of the RWOs.

Only one very senior member of Hizbullah during the research articulated an ideological rejection of capitalism and advocated more government intervention. But even here, it was argued that social services were secondary to the objective of military resistance.

Conclusion: social service as religious faith and instrumental welfare

This chapter has unpacked the values that underpin religious welfare by asking who defines the parameters within which social welfare exists as a value system in Lebanon. Religious welfare has thus been situated within the moral contexts and institutional discourses that give it meaning. Such an analytical approach is important if we are to look forward to the future development of social policy in Lebanon.

This chapter has fulfilled two tasks. The first has been to set out key parameters for this book by (a) identifying the key actors involved in defining social welfare in Lebanon and (b) unpacking the underlying values and motivations behind social action and religious welfare in Lebanon. Thus, I have argued that while religious identity and welfare are expressed heterogeneously among the organisations taking part in this research, the common denominator of spiritual faith unites them in their conceptualisation of welfare and their articulation of it into policy goals. The first conclusion I have thus drawn is that religious welfare is based on a fundamentally different value system to that of mainstream social policy thinking, barring perhaps corporatist states where Catholicism has played an influential role in social policy (Van Kersbergen, 1995).

I have framed this as a juxtaposition between the emotional and spiritual logic of faith, which ties welfare to protection and blessing from God for both service user and service provider and the more standard thinking of social insurance (social protection based on income benefits and allowances against risk or vulnerability), which is a right of citizenship or occupational contribution. This juxtaposition also pins down the nature of welfare philosophically to the principles of service and altruism, which resonate in the literature on the role of religion in development. The nature of the juxtaposition between faith and social insurance is that service users turn to religious welfare not only because of their religious orientation but also out of the inability to access employment-based or private social protection schemes. But social service also means short-term needs fulfilment.

Indeed, in the absence of a viable system of state social insurance in Lebanon, I have proposed three types of welfare that offer measures of 'social protection': (1) the elite family, (2) the religious order and (3) the popular political movement. These were supplemented by two other types drawn from the cases of Iran and Egypt: (4) the international humanitarian relief organisation and (5) the para-state organisation. All of these work on the basic precept of religious faith, which the service provider acts on to help those in need, and the service user finds themselves obliged to seek recourse to because of the lack of material services of social assistance either from the government or from an employer.

I have illustrated three modes of religious expression in order to explore how they bear upon social welfare. I have suggested that there are qualitative differences among:

- religion as an organised social institution based on rules and practices, which may or may not intermingle with politics;
- faith as a personal spiritual experience, which may be separate from organised religious practice;
- sectarianism, which is the purely political face of religion and is expressed as ethnic identity.

All three modes of religious expression have been explored in this chapter in terms of their varying influences on the conceptualisation and elaboration of social action.

The second task fulfilled in this chapter has entailed framing the descriptive dimension through a more analytical and politically sensitive perspective. This has entailed looking at religious welfare values in terms of policy rhetoric. For this purpose, I have outlined the objectives of the organisations and also the power dynamics and decision-making processes within which such objectives are determined. This has served to raise questions about the final agenda of social welfare in Lebanon. Certainly, I have suggested that the religious content of social welfare in Lebanon may be more a matter of supply than demand, with service users concerned primarily to satisfy their basic needs.

I have framed this dimension of the discussion within the competing usages of welfare instrumentally, for political or personal goals, and intrinsically as a viable end of public policy, which seeks some notion of the good society. I have suggested that social welfare in Lebanon is annexed to political ambition or social status. Social welfare thus needs to find its place as a legitimate and coherent entity of public action.

The RWO sector, I have argued, is a dynamic and progressive channel through which social welfare can gain legitimacy although the sector's monopoly of the social sphere contrasts alarmingly with the rudimentary character of state social policy. While the dynamism of society-based associations has a positive impact on political and social development, I have also argued that the RWOs are rooted in sociopolitical networks that promote hierarchical power structures through family alliances, regional alliances, patronage alliances and sectarian alliances. Welfare is thus expressed as charity and paternalism first and foremost although this is articulated in the language of human obligation. Human solidarity is, as a result, the weakest social bond.

From this platform of welfare philosophy and policy rhetoric, I now progress to a consideration of the mechanics and dynamics of service delivery, consumption and evaluation: in other words, the 'reality' of service delivery on the ground.

Notes

[1] Rational choice theorists of religious change (most notably Iannacone et al, 1997) emphasise the demand side of religious affiliation, arguing that consumer choice in the late modern era has led people to pick and choose religious traditions according to what suits them. This is a demand-led perspective of the religious market. Religious groups thus compete with each other to respond to the needs of the demanders. Based on the data in the countries I have studied, the demand-side argument does not explain religious welfare. Service users of religious welfare in the Middle East are very often desperate, poorly educated families who respond to the requirements and instructions of the organisations that help them.

[2] Interviewees are denoted by an abbreviation indicating the organisation they were connected with – ANT: the Antonine Nuns; CAR: Caritas; DAR: Dar Al Aytam; H: RWOs affiliated to Hizbullah (Emdad and Al-Qard Al-Hassan); URF: Al Urfan Al Tawhidiya; MSA: Ministry of Social Affairs – followed by a number.

[3] Imam Musa Sadr, the spiritual father of the Shi'a factions Amal and Hizbullah in Lebanon, began a pro-poor movement bearing just that name 'Harakat Al Mahruumin', translated from the Arabic as 'movement of the oppressed'.

[4] Imam Musa Sadr was an Iranian cleric who became politically active in Lebanon in the 1960s and 1970s and is single-handedly attributed with instigating the Shi'a revival

there. He disappeared mysteriously while on a visit to Libya in 1978, which has earned him near-iconic status in Lebanon.

[5] Harb (2008) calls this the Islamic sphere.

FIVE

Systems of provision and welfare outcomes: defining and treating the causes of poverty

Introduction

The discussion now focuses on the actual mechanics and dynamics of service provision, consumption and evaluation. It builds on the claims made in the previous chapter about the extent to which welfare in Lebanon has the scope to act beyond short-term or instrumental goals. This chapter is thus concerned with one key question: to what extent do policies and programmes offered by the MSA and RWOs in Lebanon adequately define the object(s) of their interventions and, thus, respond to the causes of human impoverishment as opposed to its symptoms? Hence, this chapter addresses the third and fourth central questions mentioned in Chapter One:

- How is the conceptualisation of social welfare packaged, implemented, delivered and evaluated in practice through social actors, welfare institutions and policy tools?
- What are the key issues raised about the configuration of social policy in Lebanon and the rest of the region?

The chapter will draw on empirical illustrations from the two types of social care and micro-credit programmes that I researched in Lebanon as well as add insights from Egypt, Iran and Turkey, although reference to these will not be as detailed. The social care programmes in Lebanon are listed below, according to the RWOs that provide them. None of the programmes under social care contains a monthly allowance component except programme numbers (1), (3) and (5), which were all based on family care. The elderly component aided the research to the extent that it highlighted issues of social care but I did not focus on older people in the research.

Social care programmes

(1) 'Social Care' (families/orphans): Emdad
(2) 'Alternative Care' Programme: Dar Al Aytam
(3) 'AMAN' (widows and orphans) Programme: Dar Al Aytam

(4) 'Al Umr Al Madeed' Elderly Nursing Home: Dar Al Aytam
(5) 'SALVE' Widows and Orphans Programme: Caritas
(6) 'Social Care': Urfan
(7) 'Social Care': Antonine Nuns
(8) 'Dar Al Rahma' Elderly Nursing Home: Antonine Nuns.

Micro-credit programmes

(1) 'Self-Sufficiency' Programme: Emdad
(2) Small Loans and 'Ishtirakat' Programme: Al-Qard Al-Hassan
(3) 'Women's Village Banks': Caritas.

The main aim of this chapter is to consider more closely the effective experience of service provision and use on the ground beyond the rhetoric of policy, which I highlighted in the previous chapter. The result of this present enquiry will be to understand how services target, respond to and are received by service users. Hence, this chapter explores the key points of contention in the very definition of the objects of social interventions and the formulation of policy by the organisations.

The review of the definitions of the key concepts guiding the policy-making process will also allow exploration of the fourth research question of this book. This chapter will provide the beginning of an answer to the key issues surrounding the configuration of social policy in Lebanon. The present discussion will also include the definition of development among the organisations researched. Development cannot be ignored in lower-income contexts since it is at the heart of public policy and is, therefore, of critical importance for understanding human well-being. Indeed, I have already shown in the previous chapter the importance of development in the policy discourses of the organisations.

The chapter deals with three broad themes. The first entails identification of the object of social policies and programmes by exploring the key points of contention in policy making. The key debates are framed in terms of dilemmas in defining the social problems that policy makers sought to solve. The discussion then moves on to mapping out the mechanics and dynamics of service delivery and consumption. This considers core issues of system operation and service provision and entails a process analysis of how and why service users and providers come together at the intersection of service delivery. This point of the discussion will provide interesting insights into the actual role and perspectives of service users in social welfare in Lebanon. Finally, the argument is brought to a close by looking at how welfare is measured as an outcome, indeed who 's involved in service evaluation. The latter will be based on the welfare organisation's own subjective perceptions of welfare outcomes. I do, however, supplement the views of interviewees with my own observations.

This chapter reinforces key issues that were raised in the previous chapter concerning who ultimately controls the agenda of social policy in Lebanon and how far social action effectively deals with the causes of human impoverishment.

Definitions and key policy dilemmas

Five key terms emerge as central to the policy-making process in Lebanon (and to a certain degree they are corroborated in the regional context). These are:

- human need;
- poverty;
- the 'social case' (closely linked with poverty);
- social care;
- development.

These definitions are framed as the core dilemmas of policy making. I shall also incorporate into the analysis new terms that had resonance for research participants, the most striking of which is the notion of *istid`aaf* (oppression, disempowerment). The aim here, then, is to set the scene for this chapter by asking to what extent the system of service provision in Lebanon adequately defines the object of its interventions and, thus, responds to the causes of human impoverishment (as opposed to its symptoms)?

The entry point into this discussion will be a consideration of the pivotal concept of human need. I will argue that challenges in defining human need adequately were the source of inconsistency in the elaboration of policy at the MSA and RWOs.

Issues in fulfilling human need

Chapter Four referred briefly to the importance of needs fulfilment in the conceptualisation of welfare by the social actors. Here, I will consider the following facets of needs interpretation:

- how needs are defined by service providers and users and, as such, how far they aid the elaboration of policy;
- the extent to which needs fulfilment acts as a merely short-term curative treatment of poverty.

The main claims I make here are the following. In terms of the understanding of human needs, human needs are classified by service providers in two ways: (a) individual short-term deficits such as insufficient money for food or for paying school or hospital bills; (b) structural and qualitative deficits such as emotional, spiritual and psychological needs. This leads to a focus on needs as outcomes on an individual basis as opposed to relational processes. It is a rudimentary treatment of human need, which is nevertheless counteracted by an awareness of the multidimensionality of human deprivation, in particular the spiritual and emotional kinds.

Yet the primacy of the needs discourse as the most critical warrant for receipt of social services is nevertheless undermined by political and sectarian interference as well as the internal constraints within social and micro-credit programmes themselves. This leads to potential questions about the extent to which services can be considered as responding accurately to the needs that are defined, in particular children's needs.

Material and moral

There is a multidimensional conceptualisation of human need spreading across a material/moral continuum: social, economic, cultural, intellectual and spiritual. The work of the RWOs and the focus of the MSA show a concern with both material and moral types of need, although material needs take precedence.

The material, or narrow, understanding of human need entails the physiological and very basic components of daily living. Urgent physical/material needs for children are the first priority: feeding, clothing, education and health. This is particularly well demonstrated in institutional care where the sheer numbers of children make it practically impossible to give truly personalised attention to them.

> **MSA1**: People are still favouring quantity over quality. They may as well keep the child off the streets and they will observe the child in a school. The main thing is that the child is eating and drinking.

MSA2 added that the kinds of services which the MSA considered as adequate for the needs of children in these cases were good nutrition, healthcare, security, space and the number of personnel working. Nevertheless, such needs were understood as essential rights of children, which are usually covered by the family. All civil servants recognised that children also need affection and family warmth in a way that they would not receive from institutional care. This issue has been the source of heated debate in Lebanon, with many service providers calling for a redefinition of children's needs.

> **ANT1**: But the child does not want to just eat and drink. He needs love and affection and care from the parents.

The broadening of the definition of need should incorporate any deficiency in the essential components that make up decent human life:

> **ANT3**: The needy have no one. Sometimes the family is totally destitute. A family with children. The father who has stopped working

like nowadays. The grandmother is at home and needs medication but he can't even get food for his children.

All RWOs noted the importance of meeting people's spiritual needs and at Caritas these ideas were aptly summarised as follows, showing a sense of the hierarchy of human needs:

> **CAR1**: You take the human being in all their dimensions. Sometimes you work more on urgent needs. If someone is hungry or without clothes or sick you can't talk to them about God first. You need to respond to their most urgent needs and then perhaps without even talking about that, just from the way you deal with them, they will start to talk to you about that [religion].

The discourse of need in Lebanon is thus heavily underscored by moral concerns.

Needy groups were felt to include older people, disabled people, drug addicts, 'social cases' (see below), orphans, people with AIDS, deviant girls, socially marginalised groups and the poor.

From the point of view of service users, the needs they were most concerned with were immediate material needs such as feeding and educating their children or, where possible, receiving financial assistance. They also valued the moral support that RWOs gave them. The spiritual and moral dimensions of human needs were introduced by the RWOs as a result of their basic religious philosophy although sometimes service users requested religious guidance classes. This is another illustration of the importance of the supply side, in contrast to rational choice theory.

Need or poverty?

An association is constantly made between lack of income and unsatisfied needs. The concept of need thus exists in the same lexical constellation as poverty and disempowerment.

> **CAR8**: The father who has lost his job. I don't like the word poor ... we never us that word, we just say needy or deprived.

Paradoxically, at Dar Al Aytam, a focus on need means that the beneficiaries of this organisation do not always have to be among the poorest since some categories of people may have a need stemming from a physical or social disability but they may be financially well off, for example disabled people, widows and especially older people. Indeed, even Emdad, Urfan and the Antonine Nuns run schools that are fee-paying. And ANT5 from the Antonine Nuns noted that their social services also catered for the middle classes.

> **DAR2**: We help the needy and the poor so that they become more able, gain capabilities. We always say the most needy and the poorest because sometimes people need your service but they may not be very, very poor, for example the handicapped or school drop-outs, although the majority are poor.

Displacing need: political interference

Political interference and personal favours (*wasta*) as well as sectarian discrimination were recognised by service providers as key impediments to the needs discourse across all of the organisations but no interviewee admitted that their organisation was at fault. Indeed, at Urfan and Emdad, interviewees qualified their discourse of human need by saying that both the Druze and Shi'a communities were among the most needy in the country.

> **URF1**: Even if the organisations are oriented towards their sects, that is humane work because the person from the sect ... is also a human being in need of social care.

At the MSA, however, it was made very clear – for example by MSA4, MSA5 and MSA15 – that political interference does influence the decision-making processes in social care applications and contracts.

> **MSA15**: There may have been whimsical distinctions made in offering services to people who were affiliated to particular political factions or religions. That is natural due to the absence of government in reaching all society. But that doesn't mean that those social, voluntary and charitable services do not impact positively....

> **MSA0**: People who really need don't receive [help].

Need fulfilment or social development?

In accordance with the definition of needs presented above, the understanding of needs fulfilment involves the straightforward satisfaction of the essential material needs of daily living. However, the reality is that a vast segment of the public is still unable to secure the basic requirements of life such as healthcare, education, and housing.

> **MSA10**: The main strategy is satisfying people's needs.... Our programmes change during the year according to what needs there are and if we feel they are truly satisfying needs.

> **DAR3**: The first thing is to respond to the needs of the local community ... we may get involved in housing issues since this is a need. This is social work: responding to the needs of society.

> **H7**: We are helping the family with its daily living needs: health and education.

Some claims were made about the developmental potential of needs satisfaction. Here, satisfying human needs underscores a complex human exchange based on compassion, solidarity and the preservation of the dignity of needy people. It thus liberates the individual from constraints that could to lead to incorrect behaviour. As such, there are moral undertones inherent in preserving the religion of the needy.

A key idea that was voiced mainly at the MSA and Dar Al Aytam is that needs satisfaction is more effective than merely giving the family money. Parents at Urfan who had children in institutional care said a similar thing.

> **MSA7**: If I give money I don't know how the person will spend it....

A lack of resources and sufficient budgets in the RWO sector and the MSA local development services centres was felt to impede the capacity for comprehensive coverage.

> **MSA15**: It is normal that services being offered by the RWOs are not covering all needs, due to a lack in finances and resources.

Similarly, for some organisations, notably Hizbullah and Urfan, it was argued that all that these RWOs could do was to satisfy needs since anything more than that would be development and they did not have the resources to do development work.

> **H1**: We don't have a strategy to develop this society in the sense of helping it reach its aims and needs ... we can't provide more than the basic minimum standard ... the population stands on its feet and retains its sense of dignity.

Yet, in contrast, Caritas and Dar Al Aytam link the satisfaction of needs directly to more developmental work. Caritas is the only organisation to draw a clear line between needs satisfaction through social assistance and needs satisfaction through development projects.

> **CAR3**: We are doing local development now based on local needs and capacities.

CAR3: The war grew and so does Caritas, since it is following where there is need. But it is all emergency relief. We had a social body which covered the emergency relief needs and there is also another body called 'Pre-planning and Projects' so that at the same time … you can see how fully aware the founders of Caritas were then … you can't just do emergency relief work. So they had a vision at the time, which is social justice and human development that is sustainable and holistic.

The different names for poverty

Poverty is for service providers a multidimensional concept with a particular emphasis on ignorance (or poverty of the mind) and lack of income. The Islamic concept of *istid`aaf* (oppression, disempowerment) emerged as a key signifier of poverty but added to it political connotations which, in some respects, recall the Western concept of social exclusion.

Nevertheless, I would argue that the operationalisation of the concept of poverty by RWOs and the MSA to inform policy and programmes has yet to be fully implemented since not only is the MSA in a dilemma as to whether or not to fully take on board the problem of poverty but the RWOs themselves do not always deal directly with the issue of poverty or reach the poorest of the poor.

Focus on social care and needs produces preventative measures in the treatment of poverty and sometimes even shifts the focus altogether from low-income groups to social groups that are traditionally deemed as vulnerable or weak: orphans, children, widows, older people, disabled people and sick people. These claims are illustrated below.

Recognising and integrating poverty into policy

I have already discussed briefly in Chapters Three and Four the problematic of poverty in the MSA's social mandate. I shall thus focus here on the RWOs.

There is consensus across the organisations that there has been an increase in impoverishment and socioeconomic polarisation in Lebanon since the end of the civil war period (beginning of the 1990s). Yet, in their policy discourse at the time of the research, the concept of poverty appeared not to have quite achieved the legitimate status of a social problem that has to be addressed directly. Indeed, although the use of the concept was prevalent in the language used by interviewees, as the many citations already quoted illustrate, its place in policy was undermined by other considerations, notably social care, the social case and, most importantly, need. The concept of poverty was also sometimes replaced altogether by others that were felt to be kinder such as "needy" or more comprehensive such as *istid`aaf*.

This issue may be roughly split between RWOs that provide social care services and those that provide micro-credit services. It translates into a rather contradictory situation where social care deals indirectly with poverty but does reach the poor whereas micro-credit services deal directly with the issue of poverty but do not always reach the poorest of the poor, indeed do not always treat the root causes of poverty. These ideas will be explored more fully in the course of this chapter.

Causes of poverty

The causes of poverty according to service providers are fourfold. First is unemployment or insufficient income to meet daily essential needs. Much emphasis was placed on earning a regular or stable income. At Urfan, URF1 noted that 75% of the problem of poverty is income-based. Poverty starts, therefore, as a problem of unemployed male providers or indeed of the loss of the male breadwinner through death or sickness or abandonment of their family.

Second, bad economic policy and bad government are blamed for the problem of unemployment and low incomes; indeed, all interviewees felt that only the government could solve the economic crisis comprehensively.

The third important cause of poverty is ignorance and bad income management. Ignorance does not just mean low educational attainment but also lack of awareness in managing one's affairs. A famous *hadith* of the prophet Mohamed was often cited at Emdad: "I do not fear for my nation from poverty but from the lack of good management". In this sense, service providers spoke of "poverty of the mind" or "social poverty" whereby irresponsible behaviour leads to economic hardship. Having too many children was often mentioned as an example of such irresponsibility and as a main factor in increasing economic hardship.

The final main cause of poverty cited was of course the civil war and the large displacements that forced many families to uproot and never retrieve the standard of living they had enjoyed before the war. Indeed, many of the service users I met were either displaced families or families where the father/husband had died during the war. All of the RWOs who took part in this research, with the exception of Dar Al Aytam, came into existence in the few years preceding or during the civil war.

The importance of income

While all interviewees clearly defined poverty as primarily income-based, the importance given to income in their programmes varied, which is a contradictory point. Emdad was most explicit about its criteria on benefits based on level of income. The other RWOs that had programmes with cash-handout components – that is, the orphans programme at Caritas and the AMAN Programme for widows and their children at Dar Al Aytam – also had income supplements. These social care programmes, which have a monthly family allowance component, terminate payments once the family begins earning for itself but the family still continues to benefit from health and educational subsidies. This is also the case at Emdad. Likewise, the micro-credit programmes are less concerned about the person's level of income as their ability to pay back the loan. Thus, income is a criterion only in as far as it provides the basis on which loan repayments would be made.

At the time of the research, the RWOs noted that the minimum wage set by government was US$200 per month although one interviewee thought that it was US$300 per month. In any case, all agreed that it was too little and that a family of five needs at least something between US$450 and US$1,000 per month to cover its most essential needs. All of the service users I came into contact with were earning between US$200 and US$300 and they all had children to fend for.

Income meant something to the RWOs in the extent to which it indicated how far the family is fulfilling vital needs. But conscious of the limited resources they worked with and the fact that a family would not always use a loan or cash assistance wisely, also that the vast majority of service users were women with very low standards of education, if any, the RWOs preferred to offer social care services. Indeed, as one senior nun in the Antonine order noted, by offering social care services, an organisation is able to cover a larger number of beneficiaries than if it were offering cash handouts to families in their homes.

As a result, by far the most important indicator of poverty and indeed the one that receives most attention from social services is the inability of parents to pay for their children's education. Also, access to health services and nutrition are key indicators.

Other dimensions of poverty

The understanding of poverty was cast over a much wider array of variables than those just described. All social actors emphasised the social, spiritual and mental dimensions of poverty. Interestingly, social workers at the MSA were the only interviewees to totally separate poverty from the social domain, which they saw as a matter purely related to family breakdown and the incapacity to meet a child's vital needs.

Poverty also tended to be described as particularly serious in rural areas and more an attribute of Muslims, especially Shi'a communities, who tended to be less educated and have larger families.

For RWOs, part of the urgency to deal with the problem of poverty was because it made people vulnerable to deviance and sin. This highlights the deeply moral connotations of social life in Lebanon and the emphasis on behaviour correction, which is the result of a deeply religious approach to social problems. It also explains the immense importance that the RWOs give to guidance, education and awareness raising for service users, epitomised by the concept of social care.

Only one interviewee, CAR3, equated poverty outright with social exclusion (discussed in the next chapter) defined in all its forms: economic and cultural. Yet all interviewees referred to the poor as being a socially cut-off family or individual who had no one to turn to or provide for them. Thus, the poor needed to be strengthened. The rich had to raise the poor to their level as opposed to them going down to the level of the poor.

This view of the poor as having no one to turn to emphasises the role of charity or direct social assistance where service users become dependent on the RWO. This was especially emphasised at Emdad. Yet, at Caritas, the view presented was totally the opposite. Poverty is specifically about dependency, therefore poverty reduction would only occur through economic autonomy, which in turn is best served by programmes aimed at development. Only Caritas saw itself directly engaging in development work to combat poverty.

Poverty as oppression and disempowerment: istid`aaf

An interesting concept used in the place of poverty, which also broadens the understanding of the concept, giving it religious depth and political connotations, is *istid`aaf*. The concept is used at Emdad and Al-Qard Al-Hassan, which explains its political appeal, but DAR4 at Dar Al Aytam also referred to it.

Of Islamic etymology, *istid`aaf* is a baggy concept, sometimes defined in a rather muffled way by RWOs, which nevertheless encompasses poverty. *Istid`aaf* is considered a kinder and more comprehensive alternative signifier to poverty. I should mention here that I was not able to verify the use of the concept of *istid`aaf* beyond the definitions attributed to it by social actors. These were as follows:

- It is a religious concept with powerful political connotations, used frequently by interviewees to refer to the poor but actually surpasses a narrow income-based definition of poverty. *Istid`aaf* means variously deeming someone weak, forced impoverishment, victimisation, disempowerment, oppression and usurpation of rights. It affects both rich and poor but is more a quality of the poor. The main usurper of rights in the world today is, according to interviewees, the US and, as such, all poor countries, certainly all Arab countries including their leaders, fit into this category of disempowerment. Indeed, *istid`aaf* includes non-Muslims. Yet, the disempowered should stay silent but must fight for their rights. Ayatollah Khomeini's revolutionary call is often cited at Emdad: *oh oppressed of the world, rise up!* The Qur'anic conceptualisation has begun to bear much resemblance to its biblical cousin: *the meek shall inherit the earth. Istid`aaf* therefore has connotations of social injustice and pity for the poor and thus is a call for a kind of revolution. Thus, the term has become a category of human deprivation worse than poverty or, at least, it is the most severe form of poverty.
- The concept is ambiguous and slightly overstretched in the usage made of it at Emdad. Interviewees sometimes contradicted themselves by noting that everyone is *mustad`af* (adjective of *istid`aaf*), although not everyone is poor. *Istid`aaf* is thus used at Emdad as a generic label into which are awkwardly packed categories of service users who do not fit into the standard eligibility criteria of the RWO but who are nevertheless worthy of social assistance, for

example drug addicts (who are ashamed to be called as such), fathers who work but are unable to fend for their families, older women who have never married, elderly parents who have young children but cannot fend for them. Thus, the whole of the Lebanese population could be considered *mustad`af*, yet the concept is effectively translated to mean poverty because an orphan may not necessarily be a *mustad`af*.

The social case (Al Hala Al Ijtima`iya)

The discussion now turns to one of the most contentious issues of social policy in Lebanon, which also appears to occur in Egypt, a resounding issue that has shaken up the core of the social care approach adopted by the MSA and which allows us to come closer to answering the question of how well social policy in Lebanon understands the object of its interventions – the relationship (or lack of) between poverty and the social case. Before engaging in this discussion, I shall briefly outline here what the social case means. (According to MSA1, one of the key reforms under way in the World Bank–steered reform of the MSA is to revise how the MSA defines poverty and the social case.)

As the key unit of analysis that the MSA's social care policy seeks to correct, the social case underwent a change in definition mainly during and after the civil war due to the urgency of dealing with the problem of poverty and financial hardship. As MSA2 explained, the objective of the MSA when it was first set up was to provide *iwaa* or shelter for orphans and children who had very difficult social cases, those who had no chance at all of living within a family.

> **MSA2**: ... a child who is unable to stay with their family due to a specific problem in the family such as addiction, divorce and there's no one to take care of the child ... a very sick father or mother ... imprisonment of one of the parents....

The social case arose fundamentally from the incidence of family breakdown due to the reasons mentioned above, although equal emphasis was placed by interviewees on the immoral behaviour of parents. For example, parents who gambled, committed incest or were 'sexually deviant' also fell into the category of the social case.

The crux of the concept is that a child is in danger if they stay with their parents once the latter are deemed unfit to bring up the child. It might be that the child's needs are not being met or that they too are at risk of becoming deviant. Thus, the child has to be removed from their family and put into institutional care. But the critical issue is that the child's parents are alive and they have to retain responsibility for the child. Indeed, the child has to return to the family home once the family problem has been solved. Key characteristics of the understanding of the social case are that it is not related to income since it is specifically related to moral behaviour and family cohesion.

But this does not mean that the concept has automatic currency among the RWOs. The relevance of the concept is disputed particularly by Emdad and Caritas, which do not support institutional care. Interestingly, they are the only two RWOs that have income-generating projects for the families they support.

Poverty and the social case

Strong opinions were voiced by service providers for and against the conflation between poverty and the social case, with all nevertheless agreeing that poverty is the principal cause of the social case. What is evident is that low income and financial hardship were cited as key components of most of the applications for social care. Thus, conflating the issues of poverty and the social case has important consequences for the appropriateness of the measures adopted to deal with the needs of society.

Convergence

Strong views were expressed that the social case should and does take precedence over the problem of poverty strictly defined as lack of income. Thus, poverty is itself a social case, or at least is separate from the social case but nevertheless an integral component of it and almost always connected to it. Poverty per se is not the problem, according to interviewees, but the consequences of poverty such as unsatisfied needs and family breakdown are, which is why poverty is considered a social case and therefore an issue that could be dealt with through institutional care.

This view was held by a couple of senior managers at the MSA, and staff members at the development services centres and all employees at Dar Al Aytam and Urfan. At the Antonine Nuns and Caritas, this view was less widely shared.

> **DAR4:** We can't differentiate between poverty and these cases because poverty is one of the reasons for divorce, drug addiction, they are all linked together … when there is a lot of poverty it is better to keep the child off the street. Take him in, educate him.…

> **URF3:** If my income is 600,000LL or 700,000LL, a stable income, I would keep my child with me. So that is a major reason why a child should be removed from their home.

Moreover, DAR2 argued that poverty is much easier to solve than the social case. Indeed, she argued that Dar Al Aytam's work is focused on the social case and not poverty, unlike the other social institutions in Lebanon.

> **DAR1:** Poverty is easy, its solution is material/financial. You can feed them and take care of them.… If you go to any other organisation on

a Saturday, you won't see any children because for them it is a problem of poverty, not social cases ... not here....

Divergence

The point of contention regarding the mixing of the issues of poverty and social cases is that parents who are alive, in stable marriages and whose only real problem is low income or an inability to pay for their children's most basic needs, most notably their education, are removing their children from the family environment to put them into institutional care.

Social workers and junior managers at the MSA and Caritas thought that the social case and poverty were two separate entities: poverty could be dealt with more effectively by helping the family directly with cash and keeping the child at home.

> **MSA2**: The social case does not mean poverty. It is a big illness, imprisonment, addiction, those things ... a child who goes into an institution on account of the MSA may not have any real problem at home but it is just that their parents can't pay for their education.

> **CAR6**: Some children are going into boarding when they should not, for example both parents are alive and work but they may have financial difficulties. So the child goes into boarding so that the parents can save money.

Same cases, different approaches: Dar Al Aytam and Emdad

Such comments are supported by the distribution of cases in the organisations that do take children into institutional care. The case of Dar Al Aytam is particularly noteworthy since it is the largest social care institution with around 7,500 children in care. It is true that Dar Al Aytam is known in Lebanon for taking the most difficult of social cases: illegitimate or abandoned children whose parents are unknown.

The extent to which children whose parents are alive but have low incomes are accepted into care was qualified by employees at Dar Al Aytam in different ways such that they reinforced the argument that families whose only problem was financial hardship were not easily accepted, although DAR4 confirmed that "the social cases ... all have families and parents".

DAR3 and DAR11 pointed out that when income was an issue in the application, it was in particular cases where the family was very large (15 children) and could not take proper care of all the children. DAR4 added to this extreme circumstances of ignorance and backwardness: parents who were too simple or too irresponsible were deemed unfit to take care of their children. Families living in rural areas were the typical case.

Yet for the year 2002, only 8% of children at Dar Al Aytam returned to their families after the improvement of their families' circumstances. Furthermore, 85% of children at Dar Al Aytam went home for holidays or weekends, which meant that their families were in good enough circumstances to receive them.

The conclusion to be drawn is that the arguments made by organisations defending the consideration of poverty as a valid reason for entry into institutional care do cause some doubt. One way of highlighting the weakness of such arguments is by comparing the circumstances of the families benefiting from Dar Al Aytam and those benefiting from other RWOs such as Emdad. If we put aside the cases of foundlings and abandoned children who cannot even be taken in by their extended families, we find that Emdad is indeed catering for the same kinds of cases as Dar Al Aytam, yet Emdad has adopted a policy of family care and income maintenance whereas Dar Al Aytam only adopts such a policy in the very strict case of families where the male breadwinner has passed away.

Social care: institutional care versus family care

The problematic of social care rests primarily on the tension between institutional care and family care, both of which are valid although imperfectly applied options of social care. As things stand, there is excessive and unwarranted dependence on institutional care because this is the cheaper and easier option for both RWOs and parents alike. Recent contact with the RWOs suggests that the overdependence on institutional care is being reviewed and that changes in policy are due. Nevertheless, the over-reliance on institutional care calls into question how adequate the quality of care is to children who enter institutions and how accurate the assessment of the needs of the population is. The extent to which social care is aimed at more long-term objectives than needs satisfaction is upheld by the access to education that social care institutions provide. But whereas such institutions work on the child, they work less on the child's social context, casting a shadow on the impact of their work.

Defining social care

The concept of social care is used in two ways by the RWOs, the first being the more dominant meaning: (a) as a social programme aimed at providing an alternative home for traditionally dependent social groups such as children, among whom orphans figure very strongly, older people and widows; (b) as a general approach to social service, which is based on needs satisfaction and implies a rather paternalistic relationship between providers and users of welfare. This contrasts with notions of development, which will be discussed later in the chapter.

Social care figures most in the discourse of the organisations that provide institutional care: Dar Al Aytam, Urfan and the Antonine Nuns and, of course, the MSA. At Caritas and Emdad, the concept also exists but in a much more diluted form since it is taken for granted that social care must occur within the family.

This changes the role and identity of the organisation, as it does the meaning and role of social care in their work. Caritas and Emdad tend to view themselves less as social care organisations and more as a development organisation in the case of Caritas, and a cooperative, social organisation in the case of Emdad. As such, they are the only two RWOs not to have contracts with the MSA for institutional care.

The evolution of the understanding of social care started in the very basic form of orphanages and direct social assistance for children among RWOs. Thus, as a service, social care was originally designed to cater for orphans, foundlings and children from broken-up families and to a large extent, this rudimentary understanding of social welfare continues among RWOs.

> **MSA1**: [R]eligious organisations continue to be distinguished by their work in providing social assistance in a specific way and ... social care type of work.

To this extent, a central tenet of this type of work is to provide *iwaa* (shelter); indeed, according to MSA2, the MSA currently only focuses on basic infrastructural conditions (buildings in good condition, with space and sunlight) and fulfilment of physical needs of children when it conducts inspections of the social care institutions. The MSA funds 30% of the cost of 40,000 children who are in institutional care or are doing vocational training at RWOs that have contracts with the MSA. This amounts to just under US$3 per child per day and US$2 per day for day pupils.

While some of the RWOs continue to concentrate their social care services on providing an alternative home for children, the concept has evolved, according to DAR2, to take on a much more holistic approach to human need.

> **DAR2**: Comprehensive social care.... It is not eating and drinking. It is upbringing and health and preventative care and work with the family.... Development is part of social care.... We don't have social care as it is used in the traditional Arabic meaning of *iwaa* [shelter].

> **MSA4**: Social care has a vast meaning: you start with the poor who cannot educate their children, you remove the child.

> **CAR3**: The mother gives social care to her children ... so that they become autonomous and independent. The organisation is the same. It should stand by the poor person until he becomes better.

The problem of education

Education occupies a central position in the rationale behind social care. This issue will be explored more fully when the problematic of institutional care is explored subsequently below. What is important to mention at this point is that parents' need to educate their children in good schools becomes conflated with an overall need for social care services simply because the only access low-income parents have to good private schools is through institutionalised childcare.

Thus, some of the RWOs described in this book view themselves primarily as schools, which later open social care centres. A typical case is Urfan. At the other extreme is Dar Al Aytam, which views itself as a social care organisation par excellence and sends its children to public schools.

The desire that some RWOs have to maintain their role as academic institutions puts them at odds with the MSA, whose main policy for social care is that children should be admitted into an institution and attend a public school. But it also creates the rather contradictory situation of social care institutions often amounting to no more than boarding schools with children going home on weekends and during the holidays.

The example of how the problem of education creates contradictions in the meaning and role of social care is also reinforced by the existence of fee-paying social care services. This is especially the case in services provided to older people particularly by the Antonine Nuns and Dar Al Aytam.

Other contradictions will be borne out subsequently when the rationale for institutional care is explored below but the main conclusion to be drawn about the concept of social care is that there is a need to review the system and policy being followed by the MSA by reassessing the needs and situation of the target population and the impact of the different forms of delivery of social care on children.

Institutional care: a harsh reality

The option of institutional care is presented as a necessary although difficult choice. It applies to social groups, particularly children, who have no one to take care of them, who are in danger of not having their most essential needs satisfied or who are at personal risk if they stay at home. For proponents of institutional care, the organisation could and does substitute the natural family.

Institutional care is not, however, bereft of contradictions or indeed of criticisms about the quality and impact of care provided to children. The key sticking points are as follows:

- the ability of the organisation to provide the child with enough affection and personal attention;
- the size of the organisation;
- the length of time the child stays in the organisation;

- how valid the need is for the child to enter institutional care in the first place;
- the responsibilities of family members towards the child going into care.

I shall review the first and most important shortcoming, which is the ability of the RWO to satisfy the needs of the child through institutional care.

All service providers admitted that no one could replace the love and personalised care of the mother and father towards the child. They also admitted that there were shortcomings in the extent to which a child could be given enough affection in a social care institution; indeed, some felt that the child hardly received any affection.

> **ANT1**: It is about taking care of the child but if that is all you do and you don't give affection, you have not done anything … what matters to me is that the child has a future, a normal life, even if they are deprived of their parents.

At Dar Al Aytam, proponents of institutional care nevertheless pointed out that the organisation seeks to maintain contact with the child's parents and that the child is kept busy with many educational and recreational activities in order to compensate for the lack of affection. However, more junior staff members noted that children are unhappy and DAR5 noted that the relationship between the carer and the children is not always very close since they are after all strangers to each other.

At Urfan, the other RWO providing institutional care, interviewees were clear that children in care are only receiving their basic needs and are not always happy.

> **URF1**: In boarding, what is being provided for the child? Their food, education, some of their personal needs … not much more than that.

What this situation highlights is the ultimate contradiction that has already been referred to above, that social care institutions are merely turning into boarding schools. Indeed, proponents of institutional care as well as many parents point out that children live much better in social care institutions than they do at home. In the case of older people, it also highlights the way in which social care simply turns into a private nursing home for older people whose children are not available to take care of them or who are well-off and independent enough to want to live in a nursing home.

The most striking issue is that some social care institutions, notably Urfan, feel they can do very little to change MSA policy. This creates an alarming situation whereby only 5% of children in boarding at Urfan actually need to be there.

> **URF1**: There is a system which MSA forces the parents and organisations to accept....

Institutional care is a cheap way of giving a service to large numbers. Moreover, it is lucrative. At Dar Al Aytam, salaries are adjusted according to the number of children in care: the more children there are, the higher the salaries.

Family care: expensive rhetoric?

Among the key proponents of family care at Caritas and Emdad, there was a strong feeling against institutional care for both older people and children. But there was evidence to suggest that family care was an ideal that was difficult to apply.

First of all, for both RWOs the rationale for family care was clear: it was a matter of ideological conviction – to maintain the family unit – and also a matter of what would ensure the best outcome measures for children. However, at the MSA, family care is considered too expensive and complicated. There is a family affairs division at the MSA, which has even set up income-generating programmes for families but its budget remains small since institutional care is more important.

At Caritas and Emdad, social care categorically means family care, even if it means finding extended family, or helping the family find a house or supporting the mother through helping her to remarry or find a job. Staff in these RWOs argue that both scientific studies and their own experiences in social care provided ample evidence that family care has a better impact on the child. Children growing up in institutions would become hostile and not integrate well in society. Thus, they criticise the MSA for not supporting family programmes enough.

Likewise, there is concern over the case of older people and the justification for putting them into nursing homes. To this extent, social care becomes intrinsically a problem of family cohesion. MSA3 emphasised how social care is fundamentally concerned with the child's integration into their family and it is when such integration is not possible that the child has to be removed. At Emdad, H2 argued that removing family members to put them into institutional care is firmly against the spirit of the Qur'an, which calls for love and solidarity within families.

But according to DAR3 and DAR10, a family care programme would not be successful since parents could not be trusted to spend their family allowances correctly on their children – many parents are simply too ignorant and lack discipline. These ideas were also expressed by managers and parents at Urfan.

Restricting family care programmes to families looking after orphan children is thus a very striking practice and is one way in which family care may be considered as being overcome by a certain amount of rhetoric.

Emdad is a case in point. Out of 5,000 families receiving aid, 70% are looking after orphans. Indeed, some families that Emdad support have put some of their children in institutional care that is run by another important Shi'a welfare organisation in Lebanon. H4 pointed out that families are free to put their children into institutional care if they want. Many mothers who need to work or who are single are burdened financially and psychologically by their children. H2 argued that parental irresponsibility and ignorance is also another factor contributing to this phenomenon. H2's defence of family care highlights the arbitrariness of the choice between institutional and family care.

> **H2:**There are two scenarios. Each has its advantages and disadvantages.... What we do is say what the rule is. We need an ideal example to copy in society. We do that by not opening orphanages or elderly homes or other services which harm society.... There will always be people who do wrong.... This [family care] is an ideal which we cannot abandon in order to follow what is not ideal simply because the ideal won't work....

Among the mothers with whom I came into contact who were benefiting in some form or another from Emdad, there were varying responses as to why they chose to keep their children with them or not. All currently had, previously had or were looking to put their children in institutional care organisations. Their circumstances were similar in terms of lack of income and their responsibility for their households, yet there were varying responses:

> **H9 (B1):** I can't read or write ... so it would be better to put the child in boarding school.... My kids are young, I can't run after them ... I have to be a bit strong and put them in boarding....

> **H9 (B2):** I preferred to keep them with me. I have four kids. [This mother could not work due to poor health. Her child had been in social care institutions and had studied well but she missed him so she brought him home.]

I would argue that both the MSA and social care institutions complain a lot about families not taking responsibility for their children but are in actual fact doing little to improve parenting, as to do so would surely mean intervening directly in issues of marriage guidance, family planning and reproductive health.

What is needed is a reassessment of the eligibility criteria that allow children to be put into institutional care. Also, the subject of education needs to be dealt with. Parents do not want their children to attend public schools but on the other hand, financial burdens make institutional care or boarding schools an appealing choice. It is incumbent that the impact of such care on the child be reviewed.

Development

Although concern with development policy per se is not a determining dimension of this book, it is safe to argue that the dividing line between social policy and social development in lower-income country contexts is not always very clearly marked (Kabeer, 2000). The RWOs described in this book have both direct and indirect links to international development organisations as well as mainstream development thinking, although their views of international actors varied. It is thus necessary to consider the role of development in the work of the organisations. Although development was found to be an endeavour in its infancy, discussion about development had the positive impact of fine tuning the issues relating to the elaboration of social policy among the organisations.

The main argument that I shall make here is that development emerges as the single biggest challenge of policy making in post-war Lebanon. Acting as the new organising axis for progressive social change, it poses serious questions about the traditional monopoly of social care over welfare services provision in the country.

As the argument will subsequently illustrate, development is understood, broadly speaking, to mean a progressive social vision based on building productive and self-sufficient individuals living in a society that promotes social justice and equality. Development in this sense inherently depends on long-term planning for positive social transformation. But the reality of development work at the RWOs raises three points of contention with regard to the way social actors define where their organisation is located in terms of achieving the goals of development:

- developing capabilities or socioeconomic investment;
- individual or social development;
- means versus ends of development.

These are explained below.

Semi-marginal status

There is a semi-marginalisation of development discourse among the RWOs and MSA, which may partly explain why service users are not very familiar with the concept of development. Even some junior members of staff at the RWOs and the MSA were not very clear about the role of development in their work, which is more concerned with social care. Development is almost always associated by service users and many members of staff with education and vocational training. Only service users in the micro-credit projects understood development in terms of income-generation and job creation, and most specifically the idea of growth and flourishing.

Social care versus social investment

Among the RWOs and MSA, concern with development was overshadowed by the more central axis of social care. And the synergy between development and social care was not always agreed on by service providers.

MSA1, for example, was very clear that development and social care were two different things but he acknowledged that there was no "wall of China" dividing RWOs that undertook social care work and those that undertook development. Indeed, at the MSA, although there is a social development department, its budget is considerably smaller than that for social care. It is at the MSA local service centres, also called 'local development centres', where community development has greater resonance.

MSA9, who is a branch manager at one of the centres, considered that the work of the centre had more to do with local community development than social care since the centre was more actively involved in coordinating services in the local area and acting as a platform for knowledge sharing where local community residents came to share ideas and experiences and solve their problems.

In contrast, MSA12, a branch manager of another MSA centre, thought that the work of the centre was "lightweight" development. Educational services and awareness raising, she argued, were only one dimension of development and they did not prevent the same problem from occurring again.

At the RWOs, social care overshadowed development. The annexing of development to social care was most pronounced at Dar Al Aytam.

> **DAR2**: Development is part of comprehensive social care. We do not
> have social care as it is used generally in Arabic society to mean 'shelter'
> [*iwaa*].... Comprehensive care is for us the main heading.

In this sense, service providers expressed an understanding of development that complemented social care, indeed which draws from mainstream development thinking ideas about self-sufficiency that gave social care more depth and wider impact.

> **CAR2**: [Development is] about work with the human being in all
> their dimensions so that they become autonomous.

The appeal of the concept of development for service providers lay precisely in its intrinsic correlation to human autonomy. This stood in contrast to the dependency culture that has grown around emergency relief assistance. CAR3 argued that a focus on development necessarily meant a move away from charity and dependency to the cultivation of notions of rights and obligations among service users.

Thus, although development was considered to achieve results that are more sophisticated or structurally transformational than social care, the final objective is still social care for the organisations. RWOs called the synergy between development and social care *developing capabilities*.

> **DAR2**: If we don't develop their knowledge capabilities, we would not
> have done anything. It is not just about eating and drinking in the end

> ... our concern is more than just their natural rights. It is so that they
> too become agents of development in there area or community.

Developing the capabilities of children through education and vocational training, of older people through social activities, of disabled people through rehabilitation, of widows through guidance and training seminars on parenting were all ways in which the RWOs considered themselves to be actively involved in development work through social care. This meant that for most of the organisations, except Caritas and Emdad, the key targets of their services were women, children, older people and disabled people.

> **DAR4**: They [women and children] are disempowered.... Are you
> going to work with men who can work and help themselves?

To this extent, the focus on developing capabilities may be considered *more the means than the ends of development.* The discourse of developing capabilities among RWOs contrasted with the other main definition of development, which was recognised by the RWOs but which most noted was outside of their remit. This is development conceptualised as *socioeconomic investment* based fundamentally on employment creation, infrastructure and economic development. Here development was understood ultimately as a process intrinsically dependent on long-term planning, a dimension of policy making that was considered to be lacking at government level in Lebanon. At the heart of this understanding of development was that it treats the root causes of social problems.

> **CAR2**: We don't give help that solves the symptoms. The concern is
> much more far-sighted – to solve the big problem.

RWOs often argue that real development work is a government responsibility, which leaves the RWOs most comfortable with the jargon of community development, which matches their resources and capabilities better. However, Emdad, Caritas and Al–Qard Al–Hassan are more directly involved in income-generating and job-creating projects through their micro-credit and self-sufficiency programmes. These programmes have a more socioeconomic dimension, as discussed below.

Income maintenance or generation?

Emdad and Caritas are the only two RWOs actively involved in providing direct financial assistance to beneficiaries. Yet both RWOs have a different approach to cash handouts, with Caritas making a clear decision to break away from such a short-term view of social service.

According to CAR 1, cash handouts typify the emergency relief mentality of the war era, but post-war, it is now necessary to "educate people about other things". The need to move beyond cash handouts is the result of both a decline in funding and a change of policy direction towards development. This does not mean that local people understand or accept the change in direction – CAR1 lamented that Caritas has lost popularity in Lebanon as a consequence. But CAR3 fortified this idea by adding that the organisation now has to "direct people and teach them their obligations and responsibilities, teach them to demand their rights".

For Emdad, although financial assistance offers only superficial treatment for social problems, it fulfils the very important role of satisfying urgent needs such as paying hospital bills or buying medication. Emdad employees emphasise the need to follow up the families to make sure that the money given to them is spent correctly. Likewise, H8 noted that the number of families with economic difficulties is so large that it is not possible to offer them enough guidance. The issue of dependency also exists, albeit it is sometimes unavoidable:

> **H4**: When the family has four or five children, all of them under-age at school, the mother is barely able to bring them up. She is bound to depend on us.

> **H6**: The problem in our society is that many people like to benefit and that's it ... they get monthly allowances ... without working and getting tired.

The point is that regardless of the normative appeal of moving towards a more long-term approach to financial assistance, the situation at Emdad suggests that service users are still in desperate need of cash. Over 29,500 families benefited from one-off cash handouts from Emdad between 1987 and 1998. Based on figures provided by Emdad for the same period, just over 50% of the social services offered were for the satisfaction of urgent social needs such as medication, household items and maintenance, and marriage. I would argue that the extent to which it is feasible to move away from this emergency assistance thus needs further investigation.

Social care does include income-related services in two particular cases: (1) families of widows and young orphans at Caritas and Dar Al Aytam; and (2) families who have lost their male breadwinner, regardless of the reason. Such social care involves family care-based services. A key component of the Caritas and Dar Al Aytam programme is vocational training for mothers. Both RWOs also try to find employment for widows or their children where this is possible.

Emdad is the only RWO to offer actual income generation loans for such families, in which case it trains any non-disabled member of the family to start their own business, such as a small kiosk, a chicken farm or a bakery. In the rural programmes it supports in South Lebanon, the programme even includes the rehabilitation and retraining of male breadwinners who have lost their livelihoods due to accidents or illness. While Caritas does offer loans to families to start their own businesses, Emdad is the only RWO to do this as a set programme.

Crucially, men were hardly ever beneficiaries of such programmes (with the exception of some Emdad cases) since all the RWOs hold the idea that men could easily find work and it is their dependants who need to be supported.

As a component of social care services, income maintenance remains by and large a symbolic gesture confined to programmes supporting family care only. This includes the AMAN Programme at Dar Al Aytam, the SALVE Programme at Caritas and the Social Care Programme at Emdad. Only the latter programme includes a wide variety of beneficiaries such as older people or sick fathers. Recent correspondence (in April 2008) with the manager of the AMAN Programme at Dar Al Aytam indicated that this particular family welfare programme would be introducing a micro-credit component.

> **DAR4**: Our objective is not the money. Don't focus on that.

As such, the value of monthly family allowances remains quite low. At the time of the research, the highest value did not exceed US$50 per child at Caritas while Emdad offered as a general rule US$20 per person per month and increased this by six or seven dollars per extra person. Family allowances are adjusted according to the number and ages of people living in the family. The minimum income the family had to be receiving was US$200 or, according to Emdad, US$30 per person. As such, the idea is that the family allowance will cover 10% of minimum income. Dar Al Aytam refused to give any idea of the value of the family allowances it offers but DAR3 did mention that they aim to cover 10% to 15% of the minimum income of US$200 according to the needs of the individual, suggesting that the family allowance at Dar Al Aytam is roughly the same as that offered at Emdad. The maximum allowance Caritas gave the family was US$200.

The rationale behind income maintenance varied. At Dar Al Aytam and Caritas emphasis was placed on the family allowance as justifying the intrusion of the RWO into the life of a family.

> **CAR5**: Through the financial aspect you can really go into the family
> ... it is a kind of tactic ... you are visiting to pay them something and
> that helps you get closer: it is a monthly relationship.

> **DAR4**: Financial help is an entry point to work with the family.

When probed as to whether or not the RWO thought that the family would refuse to work with them if they did not offer financial help, vague answers were given.

Conversely, at Emdad, income maintenance was understood as an important source of sustenance and even autonomy for the family, although this was mainly in the cases where bank accounts were opened for families with orphans.

> **H1**: After a while the mothers began to feel that they were the ones spending ... they began to feel responsible.

But for all the other families receiving allowances, it was recognised that the income provided would not go very far.

> **H5**: We are just giving the family the cost of bread each month. The really essential part is the other assistance: education, health....

To a certain extent, Emdad's work does appear to be overshadowed by the mere provision of cash handouts and direct health/educational assistance. This is reinforced by the sheer numbers of families that Emdad helps, which is a key impediment to regular follow-ups and family visits. Indeed, many families collect their allowances in person. This relief assistance mentality with no follow-up was also found to be the case with service users of RWOs in Turkey, suggesting that there are wider questions about policy coherence. Visits to local families in Istanbul benefiting from Deniz Feneri Denergi suggested a rather ad hoc pattern whereby a family may receive one-off assistance but then lose contact with the organisation even though its needs have not been resolved. In some extreme cases, this leads to illiteracy among children who are obliged to work in order to provide an income for their families. Like Lebanon, these families are female-headed households.

In Lebanon, personal contact with the families is maintained in some RWOs, for example at Emdad through the reps and social workers who visit the families bimonthly to pay them their allowances (the visits are bimonthly in order to cut costs). Most emphasis appears to be placed on the religious and moral education of the families who are not able to engage in income-generation projects. There is also help with household income management.

Conversely, Caritas and Dar Al Aytam give more emphasis to the follow-up services given to the family apart from the financial allowance, namely vocational training, support with household income management and family counselling. At the AMAN Programme at Dar Al Aytam, the widows even have monthly meetings where they share experiences about various issues relating to childrearing. Dar Al Aytam's philosophy is to form a support network for widows who, by and large, have no extended family support to rely on.

It is nevertheless clear that for all three RWOs, what is more important than the allowances are the other services that are offered to the family. Where no family member is working, the RWOs cover the full cost of services but once the widow or her children start earning an income, it is expected that they contribute. Indeed, there are many cases of families no longer receiving the monthly allowance but still benefiting from health and educational services. At Emdad, the children of the families it supports attend its own schools and receive medical care from doctors who are on contract with Emdad.

The emphasis that Caritas and Dar Al Aytam give to training mothers and helping them integrate into the marketplace is not evident with the families that Emdad helps, except those who enter the Self-Sufficiency Programme.

Mechanics and dynamics of service delivery, consumption and evaluation

The discussion now moves to a consideration of the processes through which services are delivered and consumed. It focuses on the point of service delivery at the intersection of the service provider–end user relationship. I examine service delivery and use along the following axes:

- terms of benefit: eligibility criteria and needs assessment;
- service users' choice of welfare provider;
- knowledge and use of government services;
- access and coverage;
- sources of funding.

The main conclusions I shall draw are the following:

- the total control the RWOs have in deciding the needs of applicants;
- the passivity of service users and their desperation for assistance;
- the pivotal role of local social/political ties not just in providing funding to RWOs but also in helping users access services (leading in some cases to the distortion of access by *wasta*);
- the limitations of the distributive effects of social care services;
- the importance of geographical location in the sectarian homogeneity of the service delivery dynamics and mechanics;
- the fact that the religious component of services is more a matter of supply than demand although religion is a critical channel through which services are accessed.

Terms of benefit

Here, I look at the dynamics of the application process, who the key decision makers are and how applicants effectively become accepted by the RWO. Of key concern is the issue of how the needs of applicants are assessed by service providers, which will eventually inform my enquiry into how well services respond to the needs of services users. This also demonstrates how some of the key political processes outlined in Chapter Three influence terms of benefit.

Where social care is concerned, the role of the MSA in the application process is intermediary and administrative. Thus, it is at the RWOs where the real assessment of applicants' needs and investigation into their eligibility occurs.

> **MSA12**: If the RWO rejects an application, there is no point in the MSA accepting the child.

Eligibility criteria and needs assessment

All the RWOs and the MSA adhere to their own eligibility criteria on the basis of which they make value judgements on needs assessment. To this extent, they act as the experts. As such, the needs assessment phase of the application process occurs in a rather clinical way, with the RWOs defining what the problem is and how best to treat it.

> **DAR3**: Here is where we put our finger on the wound and we know what the problem is … we do the social study, we transfer the child to the programme in question.

> **H3**: Our decision is more appropriate.

The key issue here is the way in which problem diagnosis is a one-sided approach whereby the RWO has the remedy and if the service user does not comply, it is they who are at fault, according to staff members. The reason given for this by service providers is that the social programmes they offer are properly designed. When I asked DAR4 what she meant when she said that mothers collaborated well with her in her programme, she replied:

> **DAR4**: The mother applies what the programme is asking of her … if the mother is not responding it means she does not care and we cannot accept that … our work cannot go to waste … but the cases where there is no collaboration are rare.

To a certain extent, the RWOs cannot be blamed for their paternalistic approach to needs assessment. They argue that service users are simple-minded, often poorly educated or illiterate. I would also argue, through the observations I made, that the very fact that service users tend to be the dependants of male breadwinners – like widows, children, older people or disabled people – means that they are less likely to be able to make a sound judgement of their needs. This may also explain the passivity of service users even if, in certain cases, they disagree with the RWOs they are benefiting from. A case in point is the decision by Emdad to stop distributing cash handouts to beneficiaries who are smokers and to give them vouchers instead (discussed in Chapter Four).

> **H9 (B3)**: He told me he wanted to give me a voucher for the supermarket. I had to try to stop smoking. I said, God willing. I know smoking is dangerous but everyone has something.…

The only RWO to show a fair amount of reflexivity is Caritas. In part, this is due to the change in direction that the organisation is undergoing, which entails decentralisation and therefore encouraging service users to solve their own problems and find their own resources. This echoes the developmental approach that Caritas is following, in some of its programmes anyway. Thus, the idea of service users as partners and decision makers in their own right is pushed forth with force.

> **CAR1**: Needs assessment is the hardest thing we need to do now ... we don't do things for them but with them ... the execution, the choice of project...

In this regard, CAR3 focused a lot on the importance of probing deeply into service users' needs and to find out their root needs in order to solve the causes of their problems. CAR3 spoke of "undeclared needs" yet even this highly participatory approach to needs assessment does not escape the view of the RWO as the expert who defined needs.

> **CAR3**: You need experts and social scientists who can distinguish.

Caritas's reflexive approach to needs assessment is backed up by the voluntary admission of staff members that their approach to social service has to change in order to adapt to post-war circumstances and that the organisations have made mistakes in the past by getting involved in too many projects and misinterpreting the needs of service users. But the change in approach to the needs of the Lebanese public that is occurring at Caritas is ultimately a reflection of the change in donor policy.

Where eligibility criteria are concerned, it is also important to note the extent to which they are truly applied. The way in which the issue of poverty has forced itself onto the agenda since the 1990s is a case in point. This leads us to note that although the social situation of the applicants to the RWOs has changed, bringing with it new needs, the eligibility criteria have continued to address the problem of social care. The situation existing today, therefore, is that the social case still overshadows poverty.

Likewise, there is an implicit pre-selection process that occurs the moment the applicant reaches the welfare organisation. This is dictated by the geographical specificity of the RWOs, which means that applicants tend to be religiously homogenous.

Service users' social acquaintances also play an important role in accessing services. This will be made clearer when we consider in a later subsection the reasons why service users choose to go to particular organisations. Both of these cases are illustrated in the family care programme at Caritas where it is specified from the start that the families will be chosen from the Beirut and Mount Lebanon areas. Indeed, selection processes often occur through local places of worship that know of families with orphans. Thus, the patterns of entitlement that service users are subject to are also heavily dictated by geographical and sectarian factors.

Benefiting from more than one organisation

A very striking feature of the terms of benefit is that service users can call on several welfare organisations at any one time, with the knowledge and acceptance of service providers. The most obvious example of this is at Emdad, where typically a family that is benefiting from Emdad would have one or several of its children in institutional care at another well-known Shi'a organisation. H7 explained that the major reason for this is that Emdad's eligibility criteria are concerned with helping families who cannot earn a stable income. No other Islamic welfare organisation in Lebanon gives beneficiaries monthly family allowances. As such, if a family benefiting from Emdad receives a one-off donation from another RWO, this is not to be held against it.

> **H4**: The more organisations there are, the better. We cannot claim to be providing for all the needs of the families.

> **H5**: The family is free but we do not accept that the family benefits from an organisation which is against us.

For some service users this situation becomes a living for them:

> **DAR7**: I get a bit from here, a bit from there, we get by.

Indeed, in discussions with beneficiaries at Dar Al Aytam, all of them stated that they had benefited or were still benefiting from another RWO, even though Dar Al Aytam was the main organisation that was helping them. Conversely, this is against the eligibility policy at Caritas. Thus, the SALVE Programme coordinates closely with seven other RWOs in its local area so as to ensure that service users do not benefit twice.

> **CAR5**: We coordinate in the same area so that we don't take the same families.

Not all Caritas employees were as strict, however. Furthermore, some service users were very satisfied with Caritas and did not think of approaching another RWO.

Service users' choice of welfare provider

There are three main ways in which service users end up benefiting from a particular RWO. This provides very important insights into how institutionalised or indeed universal social welfare is in Lebanon. Further research I conducted in the region suggests that Lebanon is not unique in the extent to which the use of social welfare services occurs in an informal and perchance way. This is explained below.

First, service users come to the RWOs themselves. Several factors influence this process. The most common reason service users mentioned was that their neighbour, friend, relative or local priest had advised them to apply to the RWO. Quite frequently, that person had also benefited from the services of the organisation or knew members of staff there. This was especially the case when priests referred applications to the RWOs or when volunteers at the RWOs knew people in their village or neighbourhood whom they advised to approach the organisation. The geographical and sectarian delimitation of this process is very evident. Indeed, both service providers and users were clear that applicants tended towards organisations from their own sects.

> **DAR11**: Christians go to Christian organisations and Muslims to Muslim organisations.... That is how society is made up.

> **H4**: In the past, before Emdad, these people [service users] turned to Christian and Sunni organisations, but now ... there are Shi'a organisations and they turn to them.

In contrast to the above comments, DAR2 pointed out that it is the politically and religiously neutral character of Dar Al Aytam that attracts its service users.

> **DAR2**: Those who are not in factions put their children with us.

The service itself also plays a role in the choice of organisation although to a lesser extent. Education is a very important reason for applicants. At Urfan, one parent was adamant on placing their child there, in a boarding school environment, even though there was a state school "10 metres from my house". To this extent, there were Muslim parents who applied to schools run by nuns since the standard of education was generally higher there. In the case of the micro-credit programmes at Caritas and Al-Qard Al-Hassan, service users thought that the eligibility conditions were much easier than those of a normal bank.

Generally, what can be argued is that service users are not very fussy about the organisation that they finally benefit from. Indeed, many had no idea that such organisations existed or no initiative to approach them. Thus, it is also common, although less so, for the RWO itself to approach service users. The local reps at Emdad play a critical role in finding out about deprived families in their neighbourhoods. Likewise, local parishes and churches play a crucial role in referring Christian organisations to needy families. In the case of Dar Al Aytam, when a new programme starts, the RWO contacts local doctors and uses its social workers to access potential service users. Other RWOs such as Al-Qard Al-Hassan advertise in the local press.

A third method, whereby RWOs refer applicants to each other, also exists. This emphasises how coordination can occur among RWOs of the same sect as well as how inter-sect contact maintains the sectarian homogeneity of service users.

Knowledge and use of government services

It follows that knowledge of government services is scant and where service users have experience of government services, they do not have very good memories of it. Nevertheless, the MSA local development centres do have a strong user base in their vocational training courses, literacy courses and reproductive health services. For some service users, the religious neutrality of the MSA centres is a significant dividend although the centres also comply with the religious orientation of the community they are located in. The negative view of government social services is most expressed at Emdad.

> **H7**: People don't know what the MSA is.

> **H10 (B5)**: When you go to get medication from the Ministry of Health, they make you despair. They keep sending you to get papers and do things....

However, one volunteer sister noted that some of the widows whom Emdad was helping had taken part in one of the literacy programmes offered by the local MSA centre.

Likewise, at Caritas, some service users had a more positive experience with the local development centres. CAR7 (B2) was given one-off assistance from such a centre and CAR4 (a social worker) pointed out that she had collaborated with her local MSA centre on a session for income generation with women but that the centre is limited in the services it provides.

Other service users thought that for them to benefit from the MSA, they needed political contacts (*wasta*). In any case, the overall situation was that service users were not interested in approaching government services; indeed, those who had an opinion about them did not expect much from the services the MSA provides.

The research for this book also included contact with service users at the MSA local development centres. On one occasion, this was in the context of vocational training courses (hairdressing and make-up) and adult and children literacy classes for which the MSA is well known. Beneficiaries wanted to attend such courses but could not afford to attend those offered at private colleges. The courses offered at the MSA were much cheaper. Frequently, service users hear about these vocational courses by word of mouth. Geographical proximity is also a key issue in their choice of course.

Access and coverage

Access to services is determined by several factors:

- eligible need;
- *wasta*, or political interference;
- the applicant's sect;
- geographical proximity;
- the make-up of the programme;
- having knowledge that a service exists.

What all interviewees confirmed is that there are members of the public who are in need but do not always access services.

> **MSA4**: It is possible that a part of them, their place should have been taken by those destitute ones outside.

All the RWOs argued that need is always the principal factor they consider in an application although they acknowledged that sectarian and political interference is a reality, albeit one that they tried to avoid.

The primacy of place given to need as the main criteria for users' access to services was also impeded by the issue of quotas in social care. The number of children partly funded by the MSA that each social care organisation can accept is set by the MSA in its contractual agreements with the RWOs. In the case of Urfan, the need to fill places at the expense of children truly warranting removal from their family environments was made clear by URF1. This results from the fact that there is a high demand for Urfan's educational services, which leads parents who simply want to educate their children but cannot afford good private schools like Urfan's putting them into institutional care so that they can be subsidised by the MSA.

All the RWOS have nationwide coverage except Urfan and the Antonine Nuns. Urfan is very clearly located in Druze-populated areas and the Antonine Nuns are primarily focused on Christian areas. As such, from the start, the geographical location of programmes limits coverage.

Nevertheless, several key points of debate arose about the scope and content of coverage. Dar Al Aytam is confident that it covers all Lebanon and all sects although there is a clear Beirut bias in both the location of programmes and the regional origin of the beneficiaries. This was illustrated in Table 4.1. Yet, Dar Al Aytam does offer its services to non-Lebanese nationals.

Emdad too portends to have nationwide coverage although the centres covering the Christian parts of Lebanon are Muslim-dominated localities. Yet members of staff at Emdad are very clear that their services cannot cover all the needs of service users nor do they cover all kinds of social problems. Moreover, Emdad is very clear about which category of the poor it targets. It specifically excludes unemployed males, otherwise, the general argument goes, it would have to help most of the Lebanese population.

> **H4**: Three quarters of Lebanese society is poor. But we are helping the segment which is below poverty ... meaning the one that cannot satisfy its most basic daily needs.

> **H3**: If we were to go into the subject of those who cannot work then we have entered the subject of unemployment and that is a large segment of society.

Recognition of the inability of programmes to reach the poorest of the poor and the truly destitute was also shown by CAR3 at Caritas, although in a different way. In support of Caritas's move towards decentralisation and increased prioritisation of local needs, CAR3 noted:

> **CAR3**: In a standardised programme the masses will pass through but not those at the fringes. You need to partition the programme to channel it so that it reaches specific categories of people.

As such, CAR3 gave examples of programmes whose very eligibility criteria impeded needy groups from benefiting. With reference to a fishery programme in the south of Lebanon, CAR3 noted:

> **CAR3**: I put them in a programme just for them which will reach the poorest of the poor because we were able to understand their true needs.

Apart from the issue of reaching the poorest of the poor, RWOs implicitly reserve their services for their own sects, a point that has already been discussed. Some RWOs have explicit criteria regarding the religious practice of service users while others do not.

Sources of funding

The RWOs enjoy a wide-ranging array of sources of funding, most of which are private and society based. Those who do receive government support are the RWOs that have contracts with the MSA for social care or vocational training. Table 5.1 illustrates the various sources of funding the organisations have, as well as the reasons why donors give to them. The organisation that depends most on fee-paying services and private investments is the Antonine Nuns. The organisations that depend most on charity are Dar Al Aytam and Emdad.

Two key issues arose during discussion of this theme: first, the sustainability of charity as the organisations' key source of income. At Dar Al Aytam, staff members confidently replied that their organisation is well established and that their funding source is too. The fact that prominent Beirut families uphold Dar Al Aytam is the key reason for this. Second, the focus on local society at Dar Al Aytam is considered the most important element in ensuring its autonomy and sustainability.

> **DAR3**: Local good work is most guaranteed.

> **DAR2**: Those who donate abroad don't just pay for nothing.

In contrast, Christian RWOs are the least likely to depend on local donations; indeed, it was felt by all employees that local society needs to be educated about the importance of donating money. The dependence of such organisations on foreign funding or fee-paying services does not, however, affect local society's sense of affiliation to them.

The importance of this issue relates to the extent to which local society in Lebanon could appreciate the importance of social welfare and the way in which human deprivation is a structural issue that demands social responsibility. Among the Christian organisations, this is especially evident.

> **CAR1**: At the level of the wealthy classes in Lebanon we've a lot to
> do in terms of solidarity. Very rarely do they show interest.

To this extent, funding is understood as an act of solidarity and this is an idea that is worked on strongly at Al-Qard Al-Hassan, which sought to raise funds for the loans it gave out through solidarity funds or financial sponsorship programmes. To this end, Al-Qard Al-Hassan had set up the *Ishtirakat* Programme, which was listed at the start of this chapter. Thus, ANT1 noted:

> **ANT1**: Muslims have more spirit of collaboration than our
> organisations because in their religion help is obligatory ... in ours
> it is not.

The situation of Urfan is similar to the Christian RWOs. The concept of *zakat* is not very well cultivated among local people and it is left up to wealthy individuals in society to make substantial donations. The role of political contacts is thus greatly emphasised:

> **URF1**: Social organisations are obliged to make relations with specific
> personalities in order to ensure for themselves funding.

Table 5.1: RWOs' bases of funding and reasons why contributors donate money (date from 2002, verified in 2008)

RWO	MSA or Ministry of Health contracts	Fee-paying services in Lebanon	International	Private/local donations (includes religious) in Lebanon	Contributors' reasons for donating money
DAR AL AYTAM	28%–30%	Elderly Club and Home are totally self-funded	None (one-off donations from Saudi Arabia)	80% of funding = Beirut families	'Doing good'/Islamic charity, family tradition, social prestige, trusted RWO, preventing crime, Ramadan charity, decorating Beirut
EMDAD	None (vocational training pending)	Schools = 30% (author's estimate)	Iran = 10% (administrative costs) – further research in Iran suggests this percentage is significantly higher	60%–70% = (collection boxes) and Islamic charity	*Khumus*, Islamic religious events, Islamic charity, earning God's protection/ blessing, preventing crime, supporting the Resistance Movement
AL-QARD AL-HASSAN	None	Administrative fee/loan = 20% (author's estimate)	None	*Ishtirakat* Programme = 40% Islamic donations= 40% (author's estimates)	Same as EMDAD, plus saving money
URFAN	35%	35%	20% (Druze immigrants)	10% (employees donate *zakat*)	Supporting an important Druze social/political institution – 70% of funding via Walid Jumblatt
CARITAS	None	Village banks charge interest (USAID funding)	Caritas Internationalis and other countries, e.g France, Italy = 90%	Rent from real estate	(Not enough reasons to encourage local donations) charity, family tradition, fasting month
ANTONINE NUNS	30%	All schools, homes and clinics except orphanage	Fee-paying services in France, the US, Australia, Canada	*Awkaaf* (endowments) and Religious Order Fund	Charity and donations in kind

Donation as an act of religious worship is expressed vividly at Emdad whereby many holy sayings of the prophet Mohamed are recited to show how donations or *saddaqah* earn the contributor God's blessings and protection. These sayings are often printed on the 33,000 collection boxes that Emdad has put up all over Muslim areas in Lebanon.

The final point to mention is that funding is dwindling for the organisations, particularly the Antonine Nuns, Caritas and Urfan, which mention cutbacks in employees' wages and personnel in order to make ends meet. In the case of Caritas, the cutback in funding has been largely due to the withdrawal of international donors and the increasing emphasis on making projects fund themselves locally. Likewise, contributions from local people have dwindled due to poor economic circumstances.

Social welfare as measure of outcomes

Social welfare as an outcome of social policy is denoted by a variety of measurements that generally conform to a notion of human well-being broadly defined as a state of psychological ease and the satisfaction of essential material and emotional needs. The aim here is to consider two main issues: first, who is involved in evaluating social programmes at the RWOs and, thus, to whom these organisations are accountable; and second, the actual measures of welfare that are used by the RWOs. I also consider the actual assessments of social services that service users made and what expectations they had of such services and the actors who provided them.

The main claim to be substantiated in this regard is that service providers adopt a paternalistic and 'expert-oriented' approach to service evaluation. Often, they show a fair amount of reflexivity and consultation with junior staff members and service users; indeed, all the RWOs argue very strongly that the secret of their success is their transparency and credibility.

But programme and policy evaluation remains a highly centralised and hierarchical exercise, with accountability, particularly to the founders and donors of the RWOs, staying at top management level. To a very large extent, the poor level of education among service users is cited as the main reason why the RWOs are the key decision makers. I was able to verify that service users were indeed poorly educated but I would argue that poor educational attainment does not annul a person's ability for sound judgement. Nevertheless, the outcome measures the RWOs refer to confirm their holistic understanding of human well-being, albeit the actual rates of success do not always conform to their stated vision.

Accountability and evaluation

Policy evaluation is the weakest point in the social welfare sector in the Middle East. Here, I consider the structure of channels of accountability and how services were eventually evaluated by social actors.

Accountability

Four actors were involved in the discussion regarding who is held accountable for social welfare in Lebanon: the MSA, the RWOs, the donors and the service users. This made clear that accountability is an activity reserved for top management. Where the lower echelons in the hierarchy are concerned, it is very common to substitute the concept of accountability with "giving an opinion" or to annul its need altogether by emphasising that the RWO in question is very transparent in its work. In yet another case, trust is a factor that replaces accountability altogether.

Where the MSA is concerned, while it could not be said that there are strict channels of accountability between the MSA and the RWOs, the two do keep each other in check, as it were, to a certain extent. The MSA does have certain regulations about the standard of social care and criteria for which organisations it establishes contracts with. As such, each social care institution has to undergo regular inspections by MSA social workers in order to ensure that they are not mistreating children. But although contracts are hardly ever broken and social workers such as MSA7 complain that it is very hard to inspect some social care institutions let alone gain access into them, there is the possibility for mutual accountability at the National Council for Social Welfare, which is presided by Dar Al Aytam.

> **MSA3**: The organisations observe us and criticise our mistakes and we criticise theirs in order to maintain good services.

But DAR2 had a different view of the role of the national coordinating body, which clearly places the MSA in a position of accountability to the RWOs.

> **DAR2**: We coordinate that way to monitor the MSA's policies so it doesn't do anything wrong.

The sense of the RWOs having become too powerful vis-à-vis the MSA was expressed by several civil servants even at the highest levels, to the extent that doubt was cast as to how effectively funding is reaching the children it is meant to go to. I have already alluded to these power struggles in Chapter Four.

Yet the RWOs all see themselves as a better channel for social service delivery because they escape the political interference that influences the MSA. When queried about whom their accountability was to, the most common responses were (a) the RWO is very transparent and all its accounts were clear, and (b) it does consult with parents and junior staff and ask for their opinions. Indeed, local donors are given tours of the projects their money funds and in specific cases they are shown the actual accounts.

H2: There is transparency. Nothing is hidden.... If you are the financial sponsor for an orphan, we can tell you exactly what has been spent on them and how much money you gave them.

However, accountability remains a matter for top management and executives who are the experts. I argue here that there is a need to be less centralised in the taking of major decisions and policies.

URF2: There may be consultation and we do ask opinions ... you can only consult with people who really know about the subject....The parent may see something from the point of view of their child and only their child would benefit. Consultation is with experts.

Such a view appears to stand in contrast with the RWOs' stated vision of representing society and being close to the local people. URF4 offers a different view:

URF4: We are not a private organisation ... we have our region and community who are going to ask us.

In the Caritas women's village bank projects, borrowers do not have to be accountable either to Caritas or to group members over how money is spent due to the strong community ties and trust among them.

CAR4 (B1): Everyone is free. Everyone in the village knows each other.

In conclusion, the RWO sector is too powerful and autonomous to be held accountable by a government that it considers weak and overwhelmed by political interference. On the other hand, the RWOs have a compassionate paternal authority over their service users whose best interests they pursue. The latter often tend to appear resigned to the decisions made by the RWOs since what matters to them most is financial relief.Thus, service users do not expect to hold RWOs accountable and donors work on the basis of trust with the RWOs since they are often personally linked to the founders of the RWOs through family, political or community ties.

This leads to the final issue of how far the RWOs themselves are protected from accountability by their political connections. All the RWOs enjoy some form of patronage or political protection by powerful figures, otherwise known as *mahsuubiya* in Arabic.The extent to which *mahsuubiya* gives the RWOs automatic immunity from *muhaasab*, the Arabic term for accountability, thus leaves much room for thought.

Evaluation

From the preceding discussion of the issue of accountability, it thus follows that the evaluation of services is concentrated at the RWOs too. This is not to say that the RWOs do not recognise their mistakes and are not critical of their achievements. Emdad, for example, admits that only 20%–30% of income-generation projects for families succeed, partly due to the unfavourable economic conjecture but also due to the poor preparation and training of the families that Emdad has undertaken.

All the RWOs stress the importance of the detailed studies they do before starting any new projects. Indeed, much emphasis is placed on following up families and regularly reviewing the eligibility of cases benefiting from the organisation. Project and programme managers at the RWOs are generally quite reflexive although at times they appear resigned to the status quo, such as at Urfan, where the MSA policy of institutional care is accepted even though only 5% of the children actually going into care at Urfan truly need to. In other cases, this RWO reserves final control of decision making to itself.

> **CAR5**: We have bad points: we did projects which were not for us. We are doing too many things, we should specialise.

> **H5**: We do evaluation without marginalising people's opinions … but the main thing is that that does not contradict our aim, politics, principles or mission.

> **ANT1**: I ask myself if we are helping or harming.

Among the RWOs, Caritas is perhaps the most reflexive since it is undergoing substantial restructuring of its whole policies. But it is at the MSA where loud calls for the revision of social care policy are being made. Critics within the MSA emphasise the quality and delivery of a system of social care, which favours quantity and is confusing the problem of poverty. Indeed, there is disdain at the fact that serious evaluation of the MSA's work is not being undertaken:

> **MSA1**: Today, no one is really going to evaluate the quality of service that is being offered to the child.

I now examine the actual outcome measure of the social care services reviewed and will end this chapter by looking at how far the RWOs' assessment and response to the social needs they define address the reality of needs among service users. I begin first with a brief look at service users' own assessments and expectations of welfare services.

Beneficiaries' assessments and expectations of welfare services

There are two overwhelming conclusions that arise regarding this issue, which point to service users' own rudimentary understanding of the role of welfare. The latter has already been alluded to in Chapter Four.

The main argument to make here is that service users expect immediate social assistance to satisfy urgent needs and are not fussy about service quality. The first point to mention in this regard is that service users are desperate for social assistance to cover health and educational needs. To this extent, there are cases of dependency and indeed abuse.

> **MSA2**: Some people have made it their business to put their children on account of the MSA.

> **MSA13**: People want to take something material and palpable. That is a problem.

Nevertheless, organisations like Caritas emphasised the need to re-educate service users that the war mentality of urgent relief and cash handouts is no longer valid, even though this is making Caritas unpopular.

> **CAR1**: We have reached a stage where we are responsible for educating people about other things … the fast financial support we were giving has stopped so we are not popular any more.

The extent to which service users expect that it is the RWOs' duty to help them because of their religious identity also exists. Thus, the RWOs have wider social symbolism and status, which has already been alluded to in Chapter Four and will also form part of the next chapter.

At this stage, suffice to say that service users are a mixture of demanding and accepting individuals some of whom try to benefit as much as they can and some of whom benefit as much as they need to. But the role of service users in defining social welfare remains limited and this is illustrated more fully below.

Outcome measures: not poverty but morality

The outcome measures I shall describe here represent the main indicators that the social actors and RWOs themselves set as measures of their service impact. Thus, I consider the extent to which both service providers and service users perceive that their standards of human well-being are being upheld. I supplement these subjective perceptions with my own field observations. A critical aspect of the discussion will entail consideration of the extent to which the RWOs impact more profoundly on the wider society around them. A key conclusion is that the RWOs symbolise the internal cohesion and unity of their sectarian communities.

The overarching idea I shall put across is that human welfare is embodied in a deeply moral discourse of needs satisfaction, correct behaviour and social solidarity. At the heart of this lies the preservation of the family bond, which forms the basis of the good society. Crucially, for proponents of family care and a return to the traditional conceptualisation of social care, income poverty is considered much less a risk to child welfare than inadequate parental care.

> **MSA7**: The family is rich because the family is a unit and the parents are on good terms with each other even if they have no food.

It should be noted at this point that the problematic of family versus institutional care clearly remains an organising theme around which many of the indicators of social welfare revolve. While this problematic has already been explored extensively, reference will be made to it here within the actual discussion of the indicators. The problematic of social care itself raises questions about issues of correct moral behaviour and social solidarity, which also figure below as measures of social welfare.

The indicators of welfare that were referred to by service providers are listed as follows. Some are cited as polarities since this is how they were express by interviewees:

- happiness vs sadness;
- deviance vs moral rectitude and social integration;
- self-confidence;
- dignity, hope and security;
- self-sufficiency vs dependency;
- increase in income;
- religious identity;
- humanisation and solidarity.

Interviewees tended to make the following correlation: the higher the level of morality, social care and educational achievement, the higher the level of welfare.

Happiness vs sadness

Welfare as a psychological/emotional condition was used by RWOs to describe two situations: in the context of social care, it refers to the child who receives correct social care and in the context of poverty, it denotes the individual whose need(s) is(are) satisfied. Service users often described themselves or their children as happy and service providers also attributed this feeling to themselves when they helped others in need. The smile on the service user's face is the typical example referred to.

Street decorations and happy colours to denote a happy atmosphere as opposed to one of pity towards abandoned children was most often used at Dar Al Aytam where, nevertheless, the women who care for the children acknowledged that this is not always the case. At Urfan too, the same admission was made. This contrasts with Caritas and Emdad where family care is the norm. At the MSA, very clear recognition was made of the fact that institutional care harms children.

> **MSA1**: The children that are in social care institutions suffer from added problems. Sometimes health, sometimes psychological, sometimes educational....

> **DAR5**: It is just their state of mind ... the relationship between the carer and the child may not become very close because in the end they are strangers to each other. At home they may eat an olive but they would be happy because they are with their mother.

> **H10 (B1)**: Everyone went out happy: those who need help with hospital care, rations, financial sponsorship, educational scholarships....

Of course, the extent to which the state of happiness is a transient or superficial state of being depends on the impact of the service on the needs of the service users. Where service users have made advances in their educational achievements, there is a sense in which their state of happiness is more long term; indeed, access to education was given central attention by all research participants. Where the needs themselves are short term or of an urgent form, it is clear that eventually the service user will need further assistance if they are to deal with their problems in a profound way.

To this extent, this raises a fundamental question about how far institutional care deals with the deeper and more complicated emotional needs of children that were directly dependent on affection and a sense of belonging. MSA2 made it very clear that that there is a lack of affection and personal attention to children in the large social organisations even though their more superficial physiological needs are satisfied:

> **MSA2**: When I visited the large organisations, the children ate well and slept well but you feel there is sadness in their faces, whereas when I visited the ★★★ organisation, I found the girls running to the woman in charge of them to hug her.

The dilemma of institutional care goes hand in hand with the inevitable estrangement the child might start to feel towards their family. This led a social worker at one of the local development centres I visited to note the inevitable irony that institutional care solves the problem of essential material needs such as nutrition, shelter and education but it creates deeper psychological and emotional problems for the child, leading to the paradox that any happiness the child may feel in the social care institution is dampened by their sadness of having been uprooted from their family. Yet parents believed that their child would be brought up better in institutional care.

> **MSA10 [social worker]:** We solve the problem of basic needs and education only to create another of jealousy and resentment the child feels towards their family.

Deviance vs moral rectitude and social integration

Parents' dishonest or immoral behaviour, theft, crime, children spending their time on the streets, drug addiction, incorrect sexual behaviour, hostility – these are all the antitheses of human welfare, which service providers and service users argued that social service protects against. Parents were proud that their children have been given an education and kept off the streets just as RWOs argued that poverty and unsatisfied needs lead to deviance and sin. Thus, the ability of the individual to reintegrate into society as a normal human through marriage and employment were key indicators of their welfare.

Conversely, opponents of institutional care argued that children living in such organisations remain hostile and are prone to delinquency. To this extent, one social worker at the MSA drew attention to a study by the Save the Children Fund-UK, which looked at the impact of institutional care in Lebanon. The study concluded that three quarters of child delinquents in Lebanon had grown up in institutional care. The much-awaited study by UNICEF (in collaboration with the MSA), which is due to be launched, will also reveal important data about the state of children in care in Lebanon.

Indeed, the extent to which institutional care is encouraging family break-up and parental abandonment of children was remarked on by many middle-level managers and social workers at the MSA as well as some social care managers at the RWOs.

> **ANT1:** I ask myself if we are helping or harming.

Moreover, insistence by defenders of institutional care that they work hard to correct the family situation so that the child can return to their family or indeed that they never take a child into institutional care when there is a family member able to take care of the child was disproved by generalised admission at the MSA and RWOs that very few children actually return to their families, and most children do go home for weekends and holidays to visit their families while they are living in institutional care. I shall cite again figures provided by Dar Al Aytam, the largest institutional care organisation in Lebanon: only 8% of children returned to their families in 2002 and 85% of children went home either at weekends or on school holidays.

MSA3 diplomatically admitted that the rate of return was very low indeed. MSA1 shed serious doubt on the sustainability of social care through social institutions and argued that they are indeed doing more harm than good. MSA2 and MSA7 went to the extent of arguing that top management at the MSA does not think that the work of the ministry is being affected by the confusion surrounding the issue of poverty even though there are clear signs that children are leaking through the system, as shown in the continued presence of street children. A key issue in point is the lack of regular follow-up of the families whose children are going into care.

Self-confidence

Closely linked to happiness and social integration is the service user's ability to gain in self-confidence through the help of the organisation. Great emphasis was paid to this indicator, not just in reference to the children in care but also to the women, mothers and widows who made use of the literacy courses, vocational training, family allowances and moral support they accessed from both MSA local development centres and the RWOs. Again, the casualties were children in care.

> **DAR5**: From time to time they become introvert, otherwise they are confident and assertive.

> **CAR5**: With their family the child will be open and love life.

> **MSA11 (B1)**: I benefit a lot from the centre: my self-confidence, how I deal with others….

The significance of self-confidence is borne out further by the fact that service users tend to have low educational attainments and high levels of dependency: children, women, older people and disabled people who have traditionally depended on their male providers. Thus, the ability to become autonomous, develop their capacities and to integrate into society to lead normal lives are critical indicators.

At the Hizbullah RWOs, self-confidence is directly related to returning the human being to their original state of strength and leadership, as vice-gerent of God on earth.

H13 argued that the human being must not be weak or servile and it is only by satisfying essential human needs and teaching the human being to value themselves again that they can become strong again. Closely linked to the idea of giving value to the human being is the ability to revive their sense of dignity and hope.

Dignity, hope and security

Referred to mostly by the organisations with a more socially transformational agenda – Hizbullah and Caritas – preserving human dignity and honour are seen to be more important than any other physiological or short-term indicator of human welfare. For the Hizbullah organisations, their affiliation to a political movement of resistance is at the heart of their defence of human dignity. For Caritas, it is the ability of the service user to lead the way in finding the solution to their own problems and to thus take control of their own life through developmental projects.

Linked closely to reviving human dignity and honour is the possibility of giving weak and oppressed people hope and security. These ideas are most heavily stressed at Caritas and Emdad but also to a certain degree at one of the MSA local development centres and the Antonine Nuns.

> **H10 (B1)**: Before, the family may have been neglected but now it feels someone cares.

Service users at all of the RWOs expressed a sense of deep relief at the help they received at a time when their own family members cannot or do not want to help them. Where the service offered by the RWO is comprehensive and involves close follow-up of the family's progress, then it can indeed be said that the RWOs are fulfilling their adherence to the four key indicators of human welfare. This is particularly felt in the programmes for widows and their children as well as the income-generation projects.

The extent to which children in institutional care were seen to be gaining a sense of self-worth remained questionable. DAR9, a 20-year-old woman who had grown up in Dar Al Aytam and had no family, concluded our interview saying she was happy and looking forward to her future career but several comments she made during the interview and her very demeanour gave the impression of a highly reserved and rather solitary person.

Self-sufficiency vs dependency

The extent to which service users are able to gain autonomy and self-sufficiency through the use of the RWOs' services is the ultimate indicator of their welfare. But the results were mixed.

In the SALVE Programme for widows and children at Caritas, 210 families had already gained self-sufficiency, by earning their own income and being able to fend for themselves, since the start of the programme. I was able to visit two families of those still being helped by the programme. Both of the mothers were now in full-time employment with social security and had found their jobs through contacts that Caritas had with outside employers. One of the mothers actually worked at Caritas as a cleaner. The children of both women were all in secondary or further education with a view to becoming employed.

The Caritas micro-credit village projects I visited involved women who already had a certain level of self-sufficiency when they started on the projects since they were already depending on their husband's incomes. A major problem for the women remains finding a market for the products they want to sell.

At Emdad, the number of families whose situation improves sufficiently for them to stop receiving help from the organisation is very low: only around 10%–15% of families on the self-sufficiency programme are successful. I visited five such projects in south Lebanon. Only one family was fully self-sufficient.

At Dar Al Aytam, the mothers I met were not economically active and did not appear to have plans to be. They were waiting for their children to become economically active. However, I did meet two young girls who had benefited from the institutional care and family care programmes, both of whom were undergoing vocational training and looking to become productive individuals. The emphasis at Dar Al Aytam on developing capabilities of service users, be they disabled people, older people or children, is a key element in this regard.

Another way of expressing the idea of becoming autonomous is to become a 'productive' individual. This does not necessarily just mean becoming economically active, it also includes being an active member of society.

> **DAR8**: They are the only ones who gave me an opportunity to become a productive individual ... an active agent ... instead of just staying at home and being a burden on society....

At Urfan and the Antonine Nuns, the services provided are essentially educational and I was not able to ascertain beyond the comments made to me by employees and the parents of the children that children were able to become self-sufficient once they left the organisations.

Increase in income

Income plays an important role in the income-generation projects and the family care programmes that give family allowances. Indeed, for all of these programmes, assistance is withdrawn or modified once the family starts earning an income.

> **CAR5**: At least someone must start earning an income before we leave the family.

But in all the cases of family care it was stressed that income was only a minor element of welfare in comparison to the health, educational and awareness-raising services the families benefited from. This had implications for the understanding of welfare as a primarily moral issue.

Religious identity

Reviving spirituality and educating the service user about their religious identity is thus at the heart of the social exchange that occurs between service providers and service users.

At Emdad, it was often pointed out that 90% of service users became more religious through contact with the RWO. Indeed, the primary role of the organisation is to preserve the religion of service users, which means ensuring their correct moral behaviour although it was stressed that this never happens by force. Religious morality and spirituality are thus expressed as a way of developing service users' personality and allowing them to know themselves and their humanity. This resonates in the literature and has been commented on by Tyndale (2003). A similar situation is found at all the other RWOs where having a religion is a critical axis of correct moral behaviour.

> **DAR2**: Without religion, the person is nothing.

> **CAR1**: A person should not be a big man in their intellect and a dwarf in their spirituality so we work on all dimensions of the human being.

> **H2**: Feeding people is a means but the objectives are reviving the personality of the human being ... worshipping God correctly....

For the majority of service users, faith and prayer played a pivotal role in giving them a sense of solace and in appreciating the role of the RWO in their lives although they paid less attention to the influence of the organisation on their religious life and emphasised more the social assistance they are offered. This is not because religion is not important but rather because it is taken for granted. It is also more the concern of the RWO than the service user.

Social welfare is as much a matter of the service user being taught to continue worshipping God correctly as it is the fulfilment of a religious duty for the service providers who themselves believe that God will bless their work. Retribution in the afterlife is as important as the satisfaction of human needs in this life.

Humanisation and solidarity

This leads to the final issue, where social cohesion becomes itself an enactment of social welfare defined as the mere expression of human bonds. For some RWOs, such as Caritas and the Hizbullah organisations, it was very clear that improving social solidarity is both a key means and an outcome of social welfare. Likewise, at the MSA, some social workers lamented the fact that children going into institutional care were not able to enjoy this fundamental trait in Lebanese society, which is *takaaful*. The fundamental concern with preserving the family bond in the care of both children and older people merely echoes this.

Likewise, Caritas is now beginning to show preference for projects that depend on group solidarity as opposed to individual benefit. Social welfare as an expression of human unity and social integration rang very loudly although the reality of services sometimes gave conflicting reports.

The extent to which the RWOs are indeed impacting on society at large and improving social cohesion will be explored in the next chapter, which looks at the concept of solidarity and social cohesion in the Lebanese context. Suffice to give one indicator of social solidarity at this point. On the one hand, there is a sense in which RWOs like Emdad, Caritas and even Dar Al Aytam that run family care programmes successfully keep families united.

> **CAR7 (B2):** There is a sense in which the families that pass through them have a lot of solidarity.

Yet, in other programmes the case is different or at least it may not have been achieving its objectives totally. Al-Qard Al-Hassan focuses heavily on reviving social ties through borrowers financially sponsoring each other. This is symbolised by the Ishtirakat membership programme whereby any individual would contribute a monthly donation to the organisation as a means of saving money, which they could withdraw after three years. Likewise, when borrowers apply to the organisation, they need to provide insurance on their loans either by making a deposit of gold in the organisation against which they borrow money or by bringing a financial sponsor who will guarantee their loan.

I had the opportunity to speak with 16 borrowers at Al-Qard Al-Hassan. Twelve of them had borrowed money against a gold deposit since they had no one to guarantee their loan for them. Only four of them paid the monthly membership fee. The majority were concerned to satisfy an urgent need and did not seem to have a sense of being part of a solidarity fund. The deep economic recession in Lebanon is one of the main reasons they cited for not calling on financial assistance from family or friends.

I shall now attempt to provide an answer to the key thread running through the discussion: the extent to which the policies and welfare provision systems that are put in place by welfare organisations adequately define and respond to the object of their interventions.

Treating causes or symptoms of poverty

The final aim in this chapter is to look at the extent to which social care and micro-credit programmes treat the causes or symptoms of human impoverishment, based primarily on the case of the Lebanon, but also drawing on supplementary insights from some of the other countries that are discussed in this book. To a certain extent, I shall argue that the degree to which the causes of poverty are treated in the context of this research depends on how the social actors define the social problems they seek to solve. Nevertheless, the overarching claim I shall seek to illustrate is that the focus on social care means that the RWOs and the MSA are primarily involved in preventative intervention through health, education and social care services that deal indirectly with the problem of poverty and at best can only treat its symptoms or results. This does not preclude, though, the existence of programmes that do deal with the issue more directly.

Focus on poverty and reaching the poor

Responses were mixed with regard to the extent to which service providers and users thought their organisations were dealing directly with the issue of poverty or indeed reaching the poorest of the poor. This was hampered by three main issues:

* an emphasis on responding to human need, which competes directly with reducing poverty;
* the very construction of certain programmes, which by their nature exclude certain categories of the poor;
* qualifying the condition of poverty with other variables.

All interviewees agreed that only the government could reduce poverty by creating jobs. The RWOs providing social care services tended to argue that education and awareness raising dealt directly with the poor although they treated the problem itself of poverty in an indirect way. In that sense, not only are the RWOs educating Lebanon's future generations but they are also helping to reduce the burden of poverty for parents who can no longer afford to pay for their children's education.

DAR2 considered Dar Al Aytam to be much more sensitive to the poor since unlike other RWOs, none of Dar Al Aytam's services is fee-paying. It should be noted, however, that the services for older people at this particular RWO are all fee-paying and the children in the care of the organisation all attend public schools whereas other RWOs such as Emdad have their own private schools where poor children pay subsidised fees or are taught for free.

What was also noteworthy in welfare actors' conceptualisation of the role of poverty in policy was that the condition of poverty was qualified by other variables such as absence of the male breadwinner or the beneficiaries' sex, age and health status. Thus, none of the organisations has welfare programmes for unemployed (non-disabled) men except the micro-credit programme at Al-Qard Al-Hassan, which basically lends money to anyone who can pay the loan back.

While the RWOs do help service users find employment, the main social groups they focus on are the dependants of male breadwinners, meaning orphans, widows, older people and disabled people, or where the male breadwinner is terminally sick. Otherwise, they argue, they would have to cater for "three quarters of the

Lebanese population", which according to them are poor. This perception of widespread poverty in Lebanon is confirmed by a recent UN study categorising 28% of the Lebanese population as poor, and 8% as chronically poor (Laithy et al, 2008). As a result, the approach to poverty adopted by the RWOs tends to be palliative in most of the RWOs except in those that have income-generating projects. A final point is how need replaces poverty as the key unit of analysis, as has already been discussed previously.

There are thus reasons to question the extent to which the RWOs truly are addressing the issue of poverty or indeed reaching the poor and these can be better appreciated by looking at the way poverty is defined by social actors and how programmes are designed to reach those who really need to benefit from them.

Figure 5.1 (recently presented in Jawad, 2009) presents a taxonomy of the rationale underpinning the two main programmes that were researched for this book: social care and micro-credits. It suggests that from the outset, the make-up of such programmes limits their ability to directly target the issue of poverty. This is especially evident in the micro-credit programmes where the RWO's main concern that borrowers should pay back loans immediately excludes social groups that have no capital to use as collateral. In the case of Al-Qard Al-Hassan, H13 argued that the truly destitute are in need of direct services and thus have to seek recourse in an organisation such as Emdad.

At Caritas, there is a more mixed response but it is evident that not all beneficiaries of Caritas are truly among the poorest of the poor. The case of the village banks for women illustrates this. The following conversation highlights how service users are spread out along varying degrees of need whereby the most destitute have access to direct social assistance and those who experience sporadic financial hardship have access to micro-credit services.

Author: Were you in need of work? The extra income?

CAR4 (B1): No.

Author: So you had an income and you were comfortable anyway. You don't need the money to feed your children.

CAR4 (B1): No, not to that extent. There are cases ... with us to whom $200 really meant something, to open a small kiosk. But our work had already started so $200 helped us buy tights, for example.

Figure 5.1:Treating causes or symptoms of poverty: taxonomy of social care and micro-credit programmes

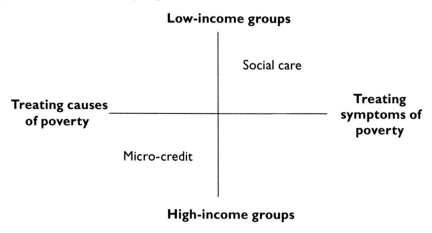

Treating causes or symptoms

There are three main themes that will be considered in this subsection:

- the extent to which social actors at the MSA and the RWOs believe they are treating the causes or symptoms of poverty;
- the propositions the RWOs and the MSA staff gave for the underlying solutions to the problem of poverty;
- social actors' perceptions of how far they are treating the causes or symptoms of poverty, which ultimately rests on how they define what social needs are.

With respect to the extent to which social actors thought they were treating the causes of poverty, the general view expressed was that the RWOs are primarily "relieving a burden off" service users. This is confirmed by their views that only the government has the resources and mandate to fully tackle the problem of poverty. Even some members of staff at the MSA thought that the MSA cannot deal with the problem of poverty alone since this is a problem that the whole government apparatus should address as a coordinated body.

As a ministry, the MSA's mandate is restricted to social care, which alone can only act as a form of preventative treatment for poverty or, as has already been argued above, can only deal with the issue indirectly. Moreover, it is the very ethos of work at the MSA to deal with social problems in an ad hoc and unplanned way. MSA12 described this as providing solutions to problems to individual cases as opposed to offering sweeping solutions such as providing real free education.

> **MSA13:** What I am doing isn't development. Health, education in a neighbourhood, that's a dimension of development. You do lightweight

things. So the problem recurs because the essential problem is still the same. We solve the problem not from its roots but as a problem.

> **MSA1**: Institutional care isn't sustainable in the middle and long terms because it is not treating the causes of the problem. It treats the reality of the problem as it is now....

However, critics of institutional care at the MSA and the RWOs that are oriented towards family care such as Caritas, Emdad, Urfan and to a certain extent the Antonine Nuns argue that such a system of social care causes more problems than it solves.

Yet as the taxonomy above illustrates, there are services such as micro-credit, the self-sufficiency programme and to a certain extent the widows/orphans programmes that deal more directly with the issues of impoverishment by promoting income generation, vocational training and job creation.

Thus, solutions to human impoverishment are depicted by service providers and users as being first and foremost about job creation, a task that only the government can take on board fully. Development is thus a major angle of this line of argument. This is most vividly expressed at Caritas, where development is described as the only way of dealing directly with the roots of social problems. The reason for this is because it entails service users reaching a level of autonomy and self-sufficiency, whereas social care maintains dependency.

> **MSA1**: But there should be next to it or above it or greater than it, policies that eliminate the problem and the demand for social care. But that isn't effective yet.... That's why the services are facing today the fact that there are no general policies working to limit poverty which are effective.

In another sense, the education and health services that are part of the social care services were also considered key facets of needs satisfaction. As H5 noted, the major problem that the Lebanese population suffers from is an inability to afford health and education services. ANT1, MSA3 and URF1 also voiced similar opinions; as such they considered that social care is responding to the key problems in society.

Thus, there is a strong sense in which social actors consider themselves to be indeed treating the causes of poverty depending on how they define what the essential social problem is in the first place. CAR3 went to the extent of refining the terms on which I had posed this question by saying that the main issue is to find out what people's real needs are and to respond to them. Some service users need development. Others need emergency relief aid. The issue is to find out the root needs and deal with them adequately.

Conclusion: needs reinterpretation and policy focus

The aim of this chapter has been to engage directly with the key issues involved in the formulation, implementation and evaluation of social programmes. The key question I have sought to answer is to what extent policy implementation adequately defines the object of its interventions and thus responds to the causes of human impoverishment as opposed to its symptoms. The underlying mechanism behind this aim has been to consider social welfare in Lebanon as a system of provision and a measure of outcomes. The chapter has thus focused on the interface of service delivery points where welfare providers and consumers met during the research for this book.

In answer to the question outlined above, I have attempted to show that human need, the social case and poverty are three core concepts directing the formulation of social interventions in Lebanon but they also serve to confuse the definition of the object of social policy. I have proposed new concepts such as *istid`aaf* that have emerged as significant alternatives and more comprehensive definitions of poverty. *Istid`aaf* adds political and structural connotations to poverty, which subsequently translates into the importance of social and political resistance as a basis on which to improve human welfare. However, I have noted that I was not able to research the concept beyond the definitions given to it by Islamic welfare actors.

The chapter has argued that needs interpretation is a source of deep contention in the policy-making process since the lack of clarity in defining the object of policies hampers the effective impact of services. The latter are sometimes ill-suited to certain problems. The example in point is how institutional care is presented as the remedy when the family's problem is income poverty and not childcare.

The MSA and RWOs have thus been depicted as grappling with important issues relating to how socially transformational the impact of services is. Among these, I have highlighted how the formulation of policy becomes torn between social care as a paternalistic and short-term solution to the symptoms of poverty in contrast to development as a more long-term solution promoting equal partnership and self-sufficiency. Likewise, I have explored the chasm regarding the advantages and disadvantages of family-based or institutionally based care. Social care has been depicted as creating needs deficits at the emotional and psychological levels, although it fills other nutritional, educational and healthcare deficits among children.

The service evaluation I have explored has represented the points of view of social actors and welfare organisations. I have supplemented these with my own observations.

In conclusion, I would argue that policies and programmes in Lebanon, certainly, although further research in the Middle East suggests a regional pattern, remain focused more on palliative services and a smaller number of service users who benefit from programmes providing solutions to their root problems. There is a need to review the way in which human needs are interpreted and how best to focus policy in the light of resource constraints. This is crucial if social policy in Lebanon is to deliver more than the palliative measure of "relieving a burden off society".

I have suggested that at the heart of human well-being lies an equally fundamental concern with social cohesion epitomised by the focus on social care and the unity of the family. This will indeed be the focus of the next chapter, where I shall demonstrate further how the focus on poverty is sidelined by concern with morality in the Lebanese welfare context.

SIX

Social solidarity: between power and morality

Introduction

The preceding two chapters have sought primarily to build an evaluative profile of who does welfare in Lebanon (and to a certain degree the three other Middle Eastern countries that are of interest in this book), how and why they do it and what they actually achieve. This chapter continues to build on this profile by engaging with the fifth of the main questions outlined in Chapter One:

- How does religious affiliation shape the conceptualisation of social cohesion and solidarity in the region?

This will add analytical insights to the overall configuration of social policy in the Middle East. Indeed, the analytical purpose of this chapter is to lay the more conceptual groundwork for the model of welfare that will be discussed in the next chapter. In this sense, the tone of the book changes in this chapter as it engages more directly in an analytical synthesis of the descriptions offered so far.

The primacy of social cohesion as a conceptual tool for the analysis of welfare in Western social policy is well established but its role in modern forms of social welfare in the Arab world remains poorly researched. Previous research I conducted in Lebanon (Jawad, 2002) considered the relevance of social exclusion and suggested that this particular concept was neither a reality nor of primary concern there. This led me to question, for the purposes of the present book, of what role social cohesion and solidarity played in social welfare in Lebanon and the extent to which social exclusion was indeed absent from the conceptual landscape of local welfare actors.

So far, I have argued that social solidarity in the Lebanese context appears to be a key motivator of social action although it is coloured by non-civic forms of association, namely family, clientelism, regional or religious. Likewise, concern with social cohesion as a moral bond in the Lebanese welfare context is epitomised by efforts to promote family unity in social care programmes, the concept of *takaaful* (financial sponsorship, social solidarity) in micro-credit programmes as well as the sustainability of the sects.

The title given to this chapter hints at how the above ideas are incorporated into an overall argument about the nature and role of social cohesion in Lebanon.

I shall present below four arguments that form the basis of the main conclusions made in this chapter.

First, social cohesion in Lebanon draws on two interlocking and mutually reinforcing discourses of social order: one predicated on morality and the other on power. This brings together religion and politics as forces that dominate the arena of the 'social', leading to the definitions of both social cohesion and social exclusion becoming reduced to specific forms of social behaviour, depending on the actors they refer to. Human agency thus comes out as the paramount explanatory tool for social processes and social outcomes, hence the emphasis by welfare RWOs on developing cognitive, physical and spiritual capabilities.

A key conclusion is proposed: concern with social cohesion in Lebanon is translated in a very specific way to mean two things: (a) solidarity shown by initiators of welfare, usually depicted as wealthy or powerful, towards those who are less fortunate, and (b) moral rectitude exercised by 'receivers' of welfare and, where possible, an improvement of their physical, spiritual and cognitive capabilities so that they can become autonomous and productive individuals. This also means that service users would become more adept at integrating into the established social order.

The welfare RWOs themselves act as key symbols if not guardians of this social order into which their beneficiaries are ultimately integrated. The RWOs occupy the centre of gravity of the social order, which they reproduce through their services.

Second, the concept of social reproduction as an analytical framework by which to understand social policy will be used to frame the analysis of social cohesion and illustrate how the RWOs researched contribute to the reproduction and maintenance of the social order within which they operate. This will also entail a definition of the 'social' as it emerged from the Lebanese context. Such a perspective follows Kabeer's (2004) analysis of social policy in the South, and the way forward, in her opinion, towards promoting this.

Framing the discussion of social cohesion in this way will allow theoretical development of the conceptualisation of social cohesion in this book and serve as a platform for Chapter Seven. The ultimate aim of this level of the argument is to bring to light the critical role of developing the human capabilities in the work of the RWOs and the way in which they can promote socioeconomic well-being.

Third, the difference between the social and human will be the organising axis of this chapter. The understanding of social cohesion that emerges from the Lebanese case takes seriously into account what it means to be human and it ties welfare very closely to this. This corroborates the arguments of other authors such as Kumar (2003), Muzzafar (2003) and Tyndale (2003), who consider the way in which a religious perspective redefines development. What I hope to show is that whereas concern with social cohesion in Western policy discourse has usually placed the highest emphasis on getting societal or market structures right, in the context of the Lebanon it is the human being, and 'getting human nature right', which is at the centre of the debate about welfare. In some respects this also echoes the welfare-oriented activities of faith groups in the Western context. Indeed, it finds similarity with the secular arguments put forward by key figures of social policy such as Tawney (1920) and Titmuss (1970), who sought to defend the dignity and value of the human being as the principal objectives of modernity and economic progress. What I will propose is that in the context of Lebanon, the definition of the 'social' must also take into account how moral education and spirituality affect human personality.

Fourth, the place of social cohesion in the policies of the service providers in Lebanon: is this a strategy, a policy outcome or a tool of rhetoric? Indeed, to what extent are specific social programmes effectively fostering social solidarity? This brings to bear the essential 'value' of social cohesion in social policy and asks to what exte t it is superseded by concerns with moral rectitude.

The chapter culminates with two analytical models, one representing the dynamics of social cohesion and one, derived from Kabeer (2004), which introduces the role of the sacred into the model of social reproduction. The chapter concludes with a consideration of the extent to which social welfare in Lebanon conforms to processes of *vertical integration* (Davis, 2001) and is predicated on moral practices of charity based on ascribed identity as opposed to legal mechanisms of citizenship rights and participation (Van Kersbergen, 1995). It thus brings to bear the extent to which the social order promulgated by the RWOs entrenches existing inequalities or opens the way to social change.

The chapter contains five sections. The first section explores the meaning of the social in the context of the Lebanon case study. Spiritual faith, a leitmotif of the book, is introduced into this definition of the social as a key variable in the analysis of social cohesion in Lebanon. In Chapter Four, I argued that the religion-based system of social welfare in Lebanon is itself predicated on particular power structures. Thus, the second section extends that argument by exploring more broadly how the social order in Lebanon is built upon two pillars: morality and power. Concern with human nature is intricately connected to the moral conceptualisation of social cohesion.

The third section completes this exploration of social cohesion by looking specifically at the concept of social exclusion and its relevance to the Lebanese context. The fourth section advances an analytical model based on the social reproduction framework by way of illustrating the way in which social cohesion works in Lebanon. The fifth section synthesises the argument by presenting key conclusions about the nature of social cohesion in Lebanon and its role in policy. The chapter then ends with some concluding thoughts.

Defining the 'social': factoring in the sacred

In accordance with other authors' arguments (Kabeer, 2000, 2004; Karshenas and Moghadam, 2006a) that devising social policies adapted to the context of Southern countries necessitates reconsideration of the meaning of the 'social' distinctly from its evolution in Western social policy, I shall offer here a brief definition of the 'social' as it emerges from the Lebanese case study. This definition has important implications for solidarity and social cohesion in Lebanon.

Kabeer (2004, pp 6-8) offers two definitions of the 'social' based on a review of the development policy discourse:

- the 'social' as distinct from the 'economic', where domains of social life not governed by the rational self-interest of economic behaviour preside, namely the family and the community;
- the 'social' as distinct from the 'individual', which reinforces the influence of social relationships and social institutions on individual actors.

Although Kabeer (2004) does not seek to propose an actual definition of the 'social' for countries of the South, what she does propose is the basis on which such definitions can be arrived at: this entails a citizen-based approach, which emphasises the role of social institutions and citizen rights. Kabeer (2004) also uses a model of social reproduction to explore the domain of social policy.

Kabeer's (2004, p 1) key concern is to advocate a view of the social and economic as intricately intertwined. She aptly recognises that this "has particular resonance for those areas of the developing world where economic life continues to be embedded within, and governed in important ways by, non-market relationships". The extent to which this assessment is borne out in the present Lebanese case study is noteworthy, although the conflation of the 'social' occurs with other domains not considered by authors such as Kabeer (2004).

In the context of Lebanon, I would propose a different approach to defining the 'social'. To this end, two competing views dominate. The first corresponds with Kabeer's (2004, p 5) usage of the 'welfarist' definition of the 'social': "relief of those who cannot help themselves". In Lebanon, this means that more positive definitions of the 'social' linked to a concern with social integration or social capital do not arise automatically although, as this chapter will subsequently show, prime concern with social care among the RWOs means that they are indeed concerned with the social integration of the child and their family. In any case, this 'welfarist' approach was advocated by all the service providers and users who took part in the research for this book.

Moreover, MSA staff and more secular members of the RWOs are eager to disassociate social affairs from religious worship and political activity. Here, the 'social' is a sphere of activity that is more concerned with needs satisfaction and the development of skills and capabilities.

> **MSA7**: Let the religious organisations go back to the mosques and churches and care for people religiously … their background is not social. It's government that should do the work, it has the background.

Yet the definition of the 'social' strictly as the domain of social relations, characterised by feelings of human compassion and fellowship, is also expressed by the more religious–minded welfare actors.

H1: Social life is full of feeling for others.

Indeed, this is where the human and the religious can no longer be delineated from one another and the 'social' becomes not only religious but also distinctly political. The conflation of the social with the political in the Lebanese context under the overarching banner of religion constitutes the second definition of the social that challenges Kabeer's (2004) argument but is reminiscent of Kumar (2003) and Tyndale (2003), as explained below.

All the RWOs recognise the foundational role that religion plays in their understanding and practice of social welfare. However, all reject any political interference in their social work even though they acknowledge that they are serving particular sects more than others. Chapter Four has already shown how the RWOs take special care of their contacts with elite families and prominent political figures in Lebanon. Indeed, all RWO participants are quick to denounce the culture of politicisation of social welfare, which merely serves the exploitation of the less fortunate and excludes those in real need. CAR3 argued forcefully that the underlying political structures and social institutions in Lebanon are such that the prospects for positive social change are grim.

Only Emdad and senior staff in charge of social policy at Hizbullah argue favourably for the fusion of their social and political work, which they see as ultimately aiming to serve society in the name of religion. In the case of the Hizbullah social welfare sphere, social work supports the political mission of resistance. The latter is indeed what binds the 'social' to the political: in a literal sense, Hizbullah and its constellation of organisations led a resistance movement against Israel; in a metaphorical sense, resistance against poverty and deprivation represent the more social dimension of Hizbullah's work. The concept of *istid`aaf* (oppression) unites the 'social' with the political and is a concept drawn directly from religious teachings.

H1: [The social and the political] are ... one entity ... the background is much larger...: it is religion. That is our platform ... politics should serve society ... the capitalist trend, or rather, the self–interest trend which is imported and is spreading all over the world, we are against that.

The example of the Hizbullah organisations is perhaps extreme and differs from the standard consideration of how religion can modify our understanding and treatment of social problems.

A range of authors such as Harcourt (2003), Kumar (2003), Muzzafar (2003), Tyndale (2003, 2006), Clarke and Jennings (2008) and Opielka (2008) argue strongly for factoring in the spiritual, moral and sacred dimensions of human life into the analysis of social problems. While none of the religious movements they describe were involved in armed conflict as Hizbullah is (although Monan Harb's chapter in Clarke and Jennings, 2008, does explore Hizbullah as a faith-based organisation), many of the measures taken by such movements as liberation Theology in Latin America, Gandhi's *gram seva* (village service) and Vinoba Bhave's land redistribution movement in India and Sarvodaya in Sri Lanka depended on 'awakening' oppressed people's sense of personal power and thus had important political impact on upturning practices of exploitation and social injustice (Kumar, 2003). Many senior personnel in Hizbullah will argue that Imam Musa Sadr (who mysteriously disappeared in Libya in 1979) is the spiritual father of the Shi'a revival in Lebanon. It is his legacy that Shi'a welfare organisations in Lebanon today seek to keep alive.

Away from Hizbullah's military role, what organisations such as Emdad effectively do is very much in line with the faith-based movements mentioned above. Indeed, Emdad is disassociated from Hizbullah's armed wing and does not have any direct involvement in military struggle. Other welfare wings of Hizbullah are devoted solely to taking care of the resistance fighters and their families.

In conclusion to this section, the understanding of the social that can be found in Lebanon is one that gives importance to two types of freedoms: political freedom of autonomy and social freedom from exploitation or deprivation. Religious identity and moral values take over social relations as everything becomes an act of worship and service to God. The social is thus substituted by the individual since welfare organisations are deeply concerned with preserving moral rectitude and using social welfare to promote adherence to human nature. The idea of reviving *fitra* (pure human nature) is a key correlate here. How these ideas effectively translate into the definitions of solidarity and social cohesion is addressed in the next sections.

Social cohesion: morality and power

Chapter Four began with a consideration of the initiatives that led social actors to engage in social action. It immediately became clear that one of the main initiatives behind social action was based on feelings of solidarity and compassion felt towards those who were less fortunate. Other factors motivated social actors to engage in social action such as political or sectarian interests. Thus, the initiative for social action was portrayed as emitting important signals of social cohesion. The discussion of social cohesion in this chapter completes the picture by adding new dimensions to the notion of social cohesion as a reciprocal process.

What should be noted here, though, is that social cohesion was not an obvious topic of discussion for interviewees in the research I conducted. Although the RWOs researched are fundamentally concerned with issues of social integration and social solidarity as essential strategies and measures of outcomes in their work, when prompted to comment on the nature of social ties they sought to preserve or indeed those that predominated in their society, their response was often a request for clarification of the question as if their work was not really impacting on social cohesion or indeed that the domain of social cohesion was not an obvious concern to them. This situation actually only reflected a semantic glitch and in that sense a particular way of thinking about social cohesion that will be revealed as this chapter unfolds.

I shall now outline the main principles on which the concept of social cohesion was finally articulated by social actors and corroborated by my fieldwork observations. Social cohesion is a moral concept fundamentally concerned with human nature and social order. It posits seven basic principles that are listed below according to the order in which they appear in the narrative that follows:

- The family (nuclear and extended) is the basic unit of society. Users of welfare thus tend to be individuals or families who have little or no family support.
- The closer an individual is to pure human nature, the more likely they are to want to preserve social ties since they would have greater capacity for compassion.
- Human nature is naturally inclined to worship God, and religion is the natural expression of human morality, but religion can also cause social segregation, especially if it becomes a tool of politics.
- To preserve the human being is to preserve the social order and is itself an act of religious worship, which pleases God. These key principles are illustrated below along the twin axes of morality and power.
- In Lebanon, citizenship and nationhood remain overshadowed by ties based on kinship, sectarianism and patronage, which contributes to a politically charged culture of social welfare that divides society more than it unites it.
- Social cohesion is a form of social insurance against deprivation through the mechanisms of social care and financial sponsorship, which is usually offered within the family, but since it is also dependent on moral behaviour and human instinct, high-income groups do not necessarily have higher levels of social cohesion.
- Social processes of inclusion and exclusion are explained more through agency than structure, whereby the actor determines their own position.

These key dimensions of the nature of social cohesion are embedded in the narrative that follows.

The power of morality: social cohesion as preservation of the social order

The primacy of moral values and emotional bonds as the core of human identity and the social order resonates loudly among the RWOs and the MSA. The power of moral values acts on two levels:

- their ability to sanction social relations and structure society through a matrix of correct and incorrect behaviours;
- the immense attention the RWOs pay to education and awareness raising as a means by which poor and deprived individuals or families can gain greater self-knowledge as well as a set of principles and capabilities that allow them to participate correctly in society and make successful life choices.

This view of social cohesion emphasises aspects such as the essential goodness of human nature and the intrinsic role of human compassion, religious education and worship, behaviour correction, and the family. It finds its policy expression most closely in the form of the social care programmes discussed in this book. Thus, social cohesion is directly linked to social reproduction and is most focused on maintaining social order. This automatically entails the prevention of deviance.

Social reproduction: the social care foundations of social cohesion

> **H2**: We are building a human being.

This section frames the connection between social cohesion and morality through the lens of one of the main policies addressed in this book: social care. Thus, it argues that social cohesion, be it of the family or the reintegration of the individual into society, is the central concern of social care programmes.

To this extent, social care is here presented as an essential tool of social reproduction, which works on three mutually reinforcing levels as described by Kabeer (2004, p 9):

- at the micro level: the reproduction of life, which is concerned with birth, childcare and care of the family;
- at the meso level: the reproduction of labour, which is concerned with human capabilities, human capital and physical labour;
- at the macro level: the reproduction of society, which acts on the ideological and social conditions that ensure the sustainability of the social order.

The RWOs are engaged on all three levels of social reproduction but at this point, I will magnify the micro level in order to demonstrate the key role that social care plays in sustaining the social order within which the RWOs are operating.

The relative advantages of family care and institutional care have been amply discussed in the previous chapter. It is useful to remember here that social care is presented by service providers as being fundamentally a problem of social cohesion in terms of both the family's natural position to carry out such a task and the role of welfare to ensure that the deprived person has their essential needs satisfied so that they can re-enter society and participate correctly. Crucially, social care is not a matter of economic status since rich families too can suffer from family breakdown or inadequate parenting due to problems of immoral behaviour.

Criticism of institutional care by some service providers rests on examples given of the fate of leavers of institutional care with allegations that the proportion of leavers who turn into delinquents is "three quarters" (MSA5, MSA7). The family, both extended and nuclear, is indeed at the heart of the social order envisaged by the RWOs.

Family: basic unit of society and mechanism of social protection

The family is the essential social unit of oriental society in both real and metaphorical terms. In the discourses of my interviewees, poverty was a phenomenon affecting families; and families were the most important social safety network in Lebanon, acting as channels of income distribution and social care. Yet, all the service users I came into contact with had either very weak family support or none at all.

Orphans receive prime attention in social care services because they have no families. Marriage is a crucial measure of welfare outcomes; marital breakdown a crucial indicator for social intervention. The social actors who tend to set up or fund welfare organisations are families but some RWOs, notably Dar Al Aytam, criticise family influence since, as DAR1 and DAR2 argued, this reduces the RWO's social credibility and rootedness to its local community. Even at a metaphorical level, filial sentiment between service users and service providers is very common, with a generalised view being that the emotional attachment that service providers and service users feel towards each other is stronger than that which service users feel towards their own families.

The sanctity of the family is thus self-evident and the power of the family unit overrides that of the MSA when it comes to institutional care. In effect, the MSA has no right to intervene in family affairs and a child can only be taken into institutional care if their parent personally makes an application.

However, a key issue is that family breakdown is on the increase, according to service providers, and this is especially marked by the large number of female-headed households, who made up 42% of the 35 social care cases I encountered during research. Furthermore, 21% of the 60 beneficiaries I met with were female heads of households. Economic pressures, parental irresponsibility and deviant behaviour were cited as the most important causes of family disintegration in Lebanon. Further, the policies of the MSA that favoured institutional care were accused of creating a moral culture of parental irresponsibility. Thus, the family structure is changing in Lebanon, as elsewhere in the region, either due to mothers working or due to the family breaking up.

MSA7: The MSA is breaking up Lebanon's families!

A final key issue is family size. Large families, a feature most attributed to Muslims, are seen by service providers as exacerbating the problem of poverty although children are encouraged by the RWOs they benefit from to work once they are old enough. This is a measure to supplement family income.

Nevertheless, a cohesive family, the repository of correct moral upbringing, forms the basis of the good society and guards against social disorder. Crucially, this means that high-income families do not necessarily have higher levels of cohesion since the latter are fundamentally dependent on moral behaviour and human instinct. Hence, the critical importance of preventing deviance and, indeed, sin.

Deviance: social cohesion as behaviour correction

Perhaps the single most important measure of human well-being referred to by welfare actors in Lebanon is deviance, which denotes immoral, dishonest, criminal or sexually incorrect behaviour. In the case of Emdad, it is another word for sin. According to interviewees, deviance categorically leads to the violation of human nature and the social order, both of which are sacred and have to comply with God's will.

Deviance thus engenders alienation from society and signifies socially dysfunctional individuals who are responsible for their own exit from society. Rich families can partake in immoral behaviour. But service providers acknowledge that in some cases key causes of deviance are in fact poverty and economic pressures.

> DAR6: We want to bring up a generation who will mix with society and not learn theft or crime when they leave us.

> H8: The major cause of crime in Lebanon or in oriental society is the disintegration of the family unit.

Preventing deviance is fundamentally a matter of preserving social cohesion built around correct human/religious behaviour, as Figure 6.1 illustrates.

Figure 6.1: Deviance, religion, preserving humanity and the social order

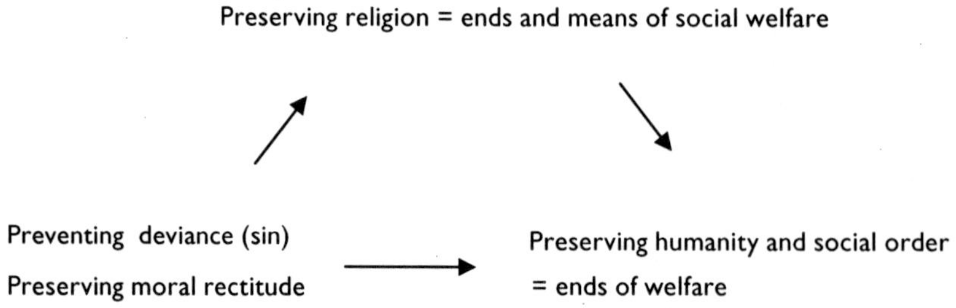

Preserving religion = ends and means of social welfare

Preventing deviance (sin)
Preserving moral rectitude

Preserving humanity and social order
= ends of welfare

H4: When we help them we are preserving them. We are keeping the family together. These families are also being tied to us and to religion and to Islam. They are not becoming deviant or being exploited by others.

The preoccupation with deviance signals a deep concern with spiritual matters and obedience to God. This locates concern with social cohesion squarely within the discourse of preserving human nature.

At this point, social cohesion is about enacting God's will on earth by preserving creation according to a natural order established by Him. Concern with social cohesion almost becomes suspended in this regard and superseded by the sole concern for moral rectitude and pleasing God. Humanity thus becomes an all-encompassing metaphysical space that all human beings are automatically ascribed to and, as such, discussion of inclusion and exclusion is rendered inconsequential.

Ensuring moral conduct is, from the perspectives of service providers, intrinsically about preserving the social order. Religion after all is a set of laws, in the words of H2, and the Qur'an is a social constitution, according to DAR10.

Service to God: social cohesion and the preservation of the sacred

The importance of human unity and emotional bonds of love and compassion that tie humankind together could not be understated, according to all interviewees. This formed the backbone of discussions with policy makers and middle-level staff at the organisations but it was difficult to see how far down the hierarchy of staff members and service users these noble ideas really travelled. Indeed, as Chapter Four has already pointed out, the extent to which any of the RWOs truly surpass the boundaries of sectarianism remains open to question.

Nevertheless, the RWOs generally make very strong arguments in favour of preserving human bonds and human compassion. In this sense, social cohesion does not aim to promote social justice as much as it aims to preserve human dignity and this is based on deep conviction of the sanctity of the human being, created by God. By extension, this means that society is sacred too. Thus, the stronger the sense of humanity, the stronger the love for society. H13, a manager at Emdad, expressed this by noting that the closer a person is to their *fitra* (human nature), the more likely they are to feel compassion for others. This view is shared by other organisations such as Caritas, as I have noted in Chapter Four, where interviewees argued that religious faith strengthened one's sense of humanity. This sacred view of human nature means that the human being is naturally inclined to worship God and religion is the natural expression of human morality.

The primacy of preserving human dignity as opposed to fighting for social justice gains substance from the intensely spiritual nature of the human bond that interviewees described. Since they are speaking from a religious perspective, their concern is to preserve the human being and therefore the social order as

God has intended them to be. Thus, according to the RWOs, once this is done, social justice will follow automatically.

Yet, the human bond is overshadowed by other more pronounced layers of human identity such as family, community or religious ties. In Chapter Four, I provided illustrations of how citizenship and nationhood are overshadowed in Lebanon by expressions of identity based on blood ties or patronage. I also discussed how human solidarity is undermined when I considered the motivations behind social action in Lebanon. In the case of religion, it was noted how this disrupted social cohesion when it was used as a political tool. These ideas are explored further in this chapter.

Staff members at Emdad often recited a saying of the prophet Mohamed, which echoed the varying degrees of strength characterising human ties. Human beings were, according to Islam, "either brothers in religion or peers in creation". According to all service providers, although their sense of duty would inevitably be automatically towards those sharing their own religion, the sharing of a basic human nature also makes it just as imperative to help those outside of their religion.

Takaaful: *an Islamic response to social welfare*

Takaaful is an Arabic concept with particular meaning in Islam, where it acts as the alternative to *tabanni*, which means (child) adoption, which is forbidden. *Takaaful* has been defined in previous chapters but it is useful to repeat here that it means taking responsibility for others either financially or through social support. It thus brings together an act of financial sponsorship with one of social solidarity.

The concept is most elaborated by RWOs not founded primarily on institutional care, and particularly Islamic organisations that run financial sponsorship programmes for orphans and micro-credit. According to H5, *takaaful* is the instinct behind social welfare, based not on a blood tie but on human fellowship and compassion. Social cohesion thus reinforces its meaning as social protection against deprivation.

The Christian RWOs tend to use the concept of solidarity and although they tie it to welfare actors also contributing financially to others who are in need, the concept of solidarity as such does not have anything intrinsic to its definition that includes financial contributions of some sort.

Nevertheless, there is a sense in which solidarity or *takaaful* appears to grip the moral imagination of social actors at the RWOs much more profoundly than the concept of social cohesion itself. Indeed, I have noted that in most cases, I was the one to prompt discussion of social ties.

MSA15 argued that *takaaful* is a key concept on which social policy in Lebanon could be built as it draws very clearly on the idea of human solidarity. Although the concept of *zakat* (obligatory tax in Islam) already exists and plays a key role in income distribution in Lebanon, it is the concept of *takaaful* that conveys more fully notions of social responsibility and the common good. *Takaaful* implies long-term sustainability as follows:

- it is founded on rules and systems of practice;
- it implies long-term financial commitment as opposed to random one-off payments;
- it recognises the existence of collective identity and the common good;
- collective identity is a source of strength and makes social transformation possible.

But the extent to which micro-credit and social care programmes founded on the idea of *takaaful* or solidarity are actually building this has mixed answers. At Al-Qard Al-Hassan, I met 16 borrowers only five of whom had a financial sponsor. The rest had used gold (usually jewellery) as collateral for their loans. Only five borrowers were paying monthly membership fees into a collective fund and only five borrowers had a sense of others benefiting from their contributions.

At Caritas, solidarity is a key issue in terms of encouraging the wealthy classes to care more for the poor and in terms of putting up an ethical stance in the face of globalisation. The women's village banks that were founded on the idea of group solidarity funds appear to draw on already existing social ties. Hence, membership is made up of friends and families, usually of the same sect, since one of the key criteria for joining the group is the trustworthiness of the individual to pay back loans. But CAR3 argued that the village funds had generated strong community collaboration, indeed that they had even encouraged sectarian mixing and the promotion of a sense of the common good in certain villages. I could not verify this though. Social care programmes were saving families from break-up, as one widow at Caritas noted:

> **CAR7(B2)**: The families that pass through them have a lot of solidarity … had it not been for them … people would divorce and leave….

Staff members at Emdad, Caritas and the Antonine Nuns emphasised that local society in Lebanon needs to be educated about the importance of solidarity since the social and structural conditions of the country are not favourable to the cultivation of such an attitude. This was expressed as a reconfirmation that *takaaful* acts as a crucial form of social insurance in a country where protection against risk can be a real luxury. Health insurance is the most important form of social insurance cited. Ninety-seven per cent of beneficiaries I met had no health insurance that would have been employment based. Thus, dependence was on family or social safety networks and God's blessing.

Caritas and Al-Qard Al-Hassan do seek to promote solidarity funds as a form of social insurance and Dar Al Aytam has collaborated with other commercial organisations to set up social insurance schemes for older people to replace the current system of indemnity payment upon retirement.

A key issue that staff members point to is that lack of social insurance is particularly a characteristic of the weak, marginalised and oppressed groups of society otherwise referred to in previous chapters as *mustad`afin* (from the root concept *istid`aaf*). This leads to the second main dimension of social cohesion, which posits social cohesion along a spectrum of power, and the dualities of strong versus weak.

The morality of power: social cohesion as resistance to marginalisation and oppression

In this subsection the notion of power is presented in two ways, based on the case of Lebanon. First, the rationale behind power is set out, which shows both negative and positive connotations in the usage service providers and users made of the term. This understanding is in the dichotomous sense of the strong against the weak, power as something linear and quantifiably accumulated. Second, the role of power in social cohesion in a particularly moral sense is discussed: this posits power as a positive strength, expressed as autonomy, dignity and self-worth. In this sense, there is a moral argument for empowering people. These qualities were presented by interviewees as intrinsic to human nature, which is sacred and exalted by God. Thus, social cohesion has to entail freedom from deprivation, exploitation and oppression if it is to preserve the essential value of every human being. The literature on 'positive' and 'negative' freedoms is quite useful here (Sen, 1999; Kabeer, 2004).

In essence, this section builds on the notion of welfare being predicated on the prevention of marginalisation and *istid`aaf* (oppression and weakness). Thus, it is most closely associated with the notion of developing capabilities, which is a key element of the social programmes discussed in this book. Power implies a particular kind of freedom and therefore particular moral commitments, hence the morality of power.

What this discussion ultimately works towards is the configuration of entitlements, systems of participation and rules of access to resources that make up the social order in Lebanon. Previous mention of how far social action in Lebanon has promoted social transformation or maintained the status quo will again be alluded to.

Strength, freedom, dignity

> **H13**: In all religions, the human being is God's vice-gerent on earth. It is wrong for this vice-gerent to be humiliated and lowly, he must be strong. How can we enable this poor person to fight? We have to strengthen him.

> **CAR3**: Solidarity means strength.

DAR11: The marginalised are weak ... the disabled whom no one sees ... we are replacing their weaknesses with strengths for them to be active, not to depend on the organisation.

Defending human dignity and self-worth is a leitmotif of the RWOs' understanding of human nature and the social order. The above citations demonstrate how power understood as human capability, moral strength and self-confidence intertwines with social cohesion by advocating a particular understanding of human nature.

The key source of power that the above citations refer to are human capabilities: physical, cognitive, spiritual and emotional. Developing human capabilities or 'strengthening' them not only increases self-esteem and self-worth but also allows the service user to become autonomous again, a valued and productive member of society. Sen (1999), in making the association between freedom and development, focuses on the importance of developing human capabilities as a means of expanding the narrower concept of human capital, not just for the individual involved but also for the market.

> The perspective of human capability focuses ... on the ability – the substantive freedom – of people to lead the lives they have reason to value and to enhance the real choices they have.... While economic prosperity helps people to have wider options and to lead more fulfilling lives, so do more education, better health care, finer medical attention, and other factors that causally influence the effective freedoms that people actually enjoy. These 'social developments' must directly count as 'developmental' since they help us lead longer, freer and more fruitful lives *in addition* to the role they have in promoting productivity or economic growth or individual incomes.... We must go *beyond* the notion of human capital.... The broadening that is needed is additional and inclusive, rather than ... an alternative.... (Sen, 1999, pp 293-6, emphasis in original)

Kabeer (2004) also points out how capabilities allow "positive" freedom. By equating weakness with marginalisation and designating the poor as oppressed (*istid`aaf*), interviewees reconfirmed the need to strengthen human dignity and human capabilities as the basis of a just social order. The concept of marginalisation will be dealt with in more detail in the next subsection. Here, it serves to illustrate the important role that power plays in social cohesion in Lebanon. As DAR1, an influential actor in the arena of social welfare in Lebanon and also a senior member at Dar Al Aytam, noted: "This is the age of power, not weakness".

For this particular RWO, as indeed for all the others, size and growth are the hallmarks of success and sustainability. DAR1 made the above statement as a way of asserting the self-sufficiency and autonomy of the RWO he works for. Independence from political interference is also another prized quality inherent in DAR1's statement above. This contrasts strongly with the impotence of government in the welfare sector that I have remarked on in earlier chapters.

The importance attributed to power manifests itself in two societal structures, outlined below, which nevertheless point to an imbalance in power relations between service users and service providers. It is at this point where the exercise of power through the RWOs acts as a channel of social reproduction that maintains the status quo. These two structures of social cohesion are paternalism and patronage.

Paternalism and patronage: social cohesion and social status

Both these societal structures act on the same basic logic: one actor acting on behalf of and in the interest of another, whereby the other is dependent or submissive. They entail vertical forms of integration, which Davis (2001) documents.

Structures of paternalism relate mostly to the relationship between service users and service providers. The citations mentioned in the previous subsection reflect a paternalistic relationship between service providers and service users, which finds its ultimate expression in the very ethos of social care whereby families who have lost their main breadwinner are taken under the wing of a welfare organisation. I would also argue that one of the main reasons for this is that the majority of service users are children and single mothers, that is to say, individuals who are from vulnerable social groups: not well educated and considered ignorant or simple by the welfare organisations.

Structures of patronage, on the other hand, characterise the relationship between the RWOs and their connections with prominent political figures who ensure the social credibility and status of the welfare RWO. This is what is known as *mahsuubiya*. On two different occasions, important figures attached to specific RWOs were referred to as "godfathers". Indeed, it was often pointed out by RWOs that to have political connections in Lebanon is crucial if an RWO is to survive. Dar Al Aytam is the only organisation to adamantly deny any connection with political figures although I have already suggested that this may not necessarily be true in reality.

Social cohesion in Lebanon is thus marked by social status. The importance of *wasta* (personal favours) and contacts also confirms that, to a certain extent, this is perhaps the single most important source of entitlements in Lebanon, which greatly undermines other forms, as explained below.

Charity or rights: social cohesion and citizenship

To a certain extent, charity – a voluntary act of benevolence – plays an important role in determining access to welfare services in view of the great influence that societal structures based on status and paternalism exercise in Lebanon. This situation is also common in other parts of the Middle East where paternal structures can be even stronger. This also undermines entitlement structures based on citizenship and rights.

But the role of charity is complicated by other issues inherent in the amalgam of discourses supporting various forms of sociopolitical membership. Moreover, there is a gap between the RWOs' stated objectives and what is actually taking place on the ground. In effect, an array of practices and identities covers the spectrum between citizenship and ascribed identities based on kinship, sectarian or community ties.

With reference to the extent to which welfare providers actually see themselves as promoting social welfare as an act of rights as opposed to charity, there is general consensus that they are acting out of religious duty to fellow humans. To this extent, they are serving God and, by the same token, acting in the interest of fellow humans who are in need. Thus, religious impetus provides a very real sense of obligation and duty to help those in need. Welfare is a right in this respect.

Indeed, it is often pointed out by service providers that service users consider it their right that welfare organisations help them. This suggests that a system of obligations is in place and although it cannot be enforced legally, the religious person feels accountable to God and would therefore provide a charitable service on that basis. Thus, there exists a sense of rights although not one tied to a notion of citizenship.

In any case, where rights were mentioned during the research, this tended to be a symbolic reference to basic human needs. Thus, poverty is a denial of basic human rights: family, identity, shelter, nutrition and primary education. Only staff at Dar Al Aytam and Caritas and the more secular members at the MSA made serious reference to human rights conventions and the need to educate the Lebanese population about citizenship.

CAR3 went further by saying that the very notion of development connoted movement beyond rudimentary charity towards civic education that bound social relations together through rights and obligations. Yet, according to MSA6, Lebanon still has a long way to go in terms of becoming a country governed by the rule of law since entitlements are still based on associations of kinship, community and patronage.

Ultimately, I would argue that this situation does not negate the notion of rules governing social relations from the point of view of religious organisations. H13 noted that *takaaful* was built on "rules and systems of practice". I was not able to verify the extent to which service users were aware of such rules. The way in which service users understand solidarity and social cohesion has been described earlier in this chapter.

Thus, although there may not be in Lebanon a real system of civic citizenship built around a nation-state, what exist are clear terms of political membership to a sect, community, religion or patron. Although there may not be a corresponding system of entitlements based on rights and obligations for which the citizen and the state are accountable to each other, there is a notion of human duty to help those in need, which is based on religious identity and for which human beings are accountable to God. Moreover, community identity is so strong around the RWOs that this creates an imperative to support them.

But political motives remain high behind welfare, which greatly distorts the promotion of entitlements based on merit and true need. The next segment concludes this section by taking a brief look at the point where political interference in religion takes on a semi-ethnic nature characterised by the geographical appropriation of welfare. Thus, intra-community cohesion becomes the other face of inter-community exclusion.

Sectarianism as geographical politics: social cohesion and social exclusion

The geographical divisions that reinforce sectarian identity in Lebanon are well known (Beydoun, 1994). What is noteworthy is how geographical politics interferes with social welfare. In previous chapters, I have commented on sectarianism and the extent to which the welfare organisations prefer to operate in geographical areas where the population is of the same sect or at least the same religion as the RWO. Indeed, it is even the case that some RWOs are denied access to or at least have to seek the permission of the organisations that dominate a particular area. One caveat in the argument put forth by Islamic RWOs is that the majority of the poor tend to be Muslims, which is why they are located in Muslim areas.

Regardless of this, geographical identity is very strong in Lebanon, as DAR2 and DAR11 affirmed when they discussed why Dar Al Aytam is an intrinsically Beirut-based organisation and finds it difficult to integrate well into other regions. Indeed, many staff members noted that they encouraged service users to return to their regions of origin so that they may develop them.

Social exclusion: what relevance?

This chapter began by questioning the relevance of social exclusion in the context of the Lebanon, prompted by previous research (Jawad, 2002). The present book takes into account a deeper exploration of the concept of social exclusion.

CAR3 at Caritas was the only member of staff to immediately define poverty as social exclusion:

> **CAR3**: You have to go to the edges in development. A woman who is culturally/educationally excluded, we try to help her culturally.

CAR3 hastened to add that this is her own personal definition, which she did not think was shared by her superiors. Indeed, her understanding of poverty was based on structural factors in opposition to the overriding view among interviewees, which was that poverty is a result of ignorance and bad personal management. CAR3 argued, however, that her view of social exclusion was not influenced by her extensive contact with international development agencies.

In contrast, the majority of interviewees described social exclusion as a rare event and when it did occur, it was the result of social actors' own doing. Primary examples were drug abuse victims, criminals and individuals engaged in deviant behaviour. But social exclusion was also understood as referring to very extreme cases of social actors who had no family at all, namely older people, but even they were few. Even homelessness, CAR3 argued, did not exist at the worst of times during the civil war due to family support.

> **H5**: The people we work with … are part of the local community. They are poor.

> **MSA8**: They [socially excluded people] have decided to go out of society. It is not society that has excluded them.

> **MSA3**: There are many reasons that cause the individual to go out of society.

> **DAR3**: The people we deal with have been shed from society, like *Braara*.[1]

There is indeed the idea that the poor and oppressed "have no one near them" (H1), that "no one sees the disabled" (DAR11) and the job of the RWO is to make these groups of people feel that there is "someone near them, holding their hand" (H1). Likewise, the wealthy classes who were considered to have no sense of social responsibility were described as being "far away from society" (H13) or "very rarely do they show interest" (CAR1). There was also recognition that sectarianism and political interference in social life in Lebanon was the real cause of social divisions, something that the RWOs argued they were far away from.

Thus, although the RWOs and the MSA have a powerful belief in social cohesion and solidarity, exercise an active attempt to enhance and reinforce them and perceive that many service users are socially dysfunctional people who have somehow moved out of society or are existing on its margins, the concept of social exclusion does not hold much sway among interviewees. Instead, they tend to speak of marginalisation, deviance, ignorance or backwardness as examples of social actors who in some way are at odds with the established moral order. The marginalised tend to have low levels of awareness and are far away from "civilisation". They often live in remote rural areas. Thus, marginalisation goes hand in hand with backwardness and ignorance.

> **H7**: They are not normal people. They are even afraid of people.… They have nothing to do with civilisation.

In conclusion to this section, therefore, there were three alternative understandings of social exclusion that do not fit into the main strand described above:

- the case of socially backward or ignorant groups, usually families living in very poor or remote rural areas, who were depicted as being almost subhuman;
- the case of social exclusion as sectarian segregation, which is primarily the result of political interference in Lebanese social life;
- the case of the wealthy classes not showing solidarity or concern with the plight of the poor.

This serves to reinforce the deeply moral definition of social cohesion and implies that social exclusion, strictly speaking, is due to actor-dependent and not structural forces such as engagement in drug taking. Strong family ties are the primary source of protection against social exclusion. The key characteristic about the nature of processes of inclusion and exclusion is that they are more a matter of agency.

Thus, the phenomenon remains the exception in Lebanon and not a useful framework for understanding deprivation. But what it does confirm is that social cohesion is firmly predicated on a discourse of power whereby the marginalised are weak, dependent and oppressed.

To be true to one's human nature entails preserving the moral order on which society rests. To become socially excluded is to violate that moral order, a process that dehumanises the social actor, hence the association of ignorance and backwardness with social exclusion by interviewees.

Social cohesion is fundamentally about being true to human nature. Social welfare is fundamentally about being a correct human being as opposed to correcting societal structures to enhance human well-being. Poverty is thus sidelined by morality.

Social cohesion and social reproduction: two models

This section synthesises the preceding discussion with the aid of two typological models: one illustrates the core argument on social cohesion and the other borrows from Kabeer's (2004) incorporation of ideas on social reproduction, which attempts to map out the way in which the 'social' component of social policy creates and sustains social actors and societal structures.

The cumulative effect of this is to lay the ground for the subsequent chapter, which engages directly with the more conceptually controversial framework of welfare regimes and how accurately such a framework allows us to understand the mechanics and dynamics of social welfare in the context of the Middle East.

The use of the social reproduction perspective in this chapter is partly a recognition of the controversial status that welfare regime theory still holds in the analysis of social policy in the South (Kabeer, 2004). But it is also a suitable conceptual framework for understanding social programmes where social care and developing human capabilities occupy major roles as is the case with the basic core of social work in the geographical region being discussed in this book.

Social cohesion: synthesis and model

When the notion of social cohesion was first discussed in Chapter Four, it was in the very specific function of solidarity that the more fortunate members of society in Lebanon expressed towards those less fortunate. I suggested that solidarity, although itself an act of redressing social injustice, did not actually change the core structures of society in Lebanon, which continue to be based on levels of social status.

The present chapter, through its more direct engagement with the concept of social cohesion has added flesh to the above argument, by showing how social cohesion works at the other end of the spectrum, among the "receivers" of welfare. It has also shown how through the twin structures of moral education and moral supremacy, service users have also contributed to the maintenance of the social order in Lebanon through the particular function of complying with the moral rules set by RWOs.

The profile of social cohesion has also been rendered more complex by the interplay of other discourses based on citizenship and rights as well as religious, community and human identity. The latter were much more pronounced than the former and emphasised the sanctity of human nature and the elevation of all human beings to a level where their dignity and self-worth had to be preserved if the social order was to conform to religious teachings.

To this extent, social cohesion has been shown to operate in Lebanon as different social ties, which are listed in Figure 6.2 in order of their actual importance during the fieldwork as opposed to their rhetorical value. The diagram illustrates the core arguments about the interplay between morality and power and suggests a key conclusion about the nature of social cohesion in Lebanon: concern with social cohesion is translated in a very specific way to mean two things:

- solidarity shown by the wealthy or powerful with those less fortunate;
- moral rectitude exercised by users of welfare and, where possible, an improvement of their physical and cognitive capabilities so that they can become autonomous and productive individuals in society.

This specific interpretation of social cohesion, I would argue, may explain why interviewees did not automatically see the relevance of my questions about social ties.

From a social care perspective, service users in the Lebanese case study are expected to conform to an established moral order and to show moral rectitude, broadly signifying correct moral values and behaviour in line with the established social order that the welfare organisations represented. But correct moral values underpin a correct general education and awareness raising about how to live one's life correctly and responsibly. Thus, moral values are a means of empowerment for the service users, who are often depicted by RWO staff in compassionate terms as simple people who have no one to turn to. But there is also a moral argument

Figure 6.2: Model of social cohesion: power of morality, morality of power

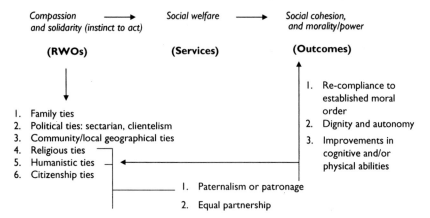

for power translated as autonomy and human self-worth, which fights against oppression and marginalisation.

Teaching morality is a source of power for the service provider who occupies the moral high ground and enjoys the trust and compliance of service users. To this extent, the moral order is not open to negotiation although service users are not coerced into accepting the religious teachings of the RWO. On the other hand, the organisation is merely applying religious laws and values in its work and, as such, if service users were to dispute it, they would be disputing religious teachings, something that they would not do. The typical example is the policy against smoking that Emdad introduced and social care beneficiaries had to conform to.

The social ties that are most likely to promote notions of equal partnership are those based on human ties, which are promoted by the religious discourse to the extent that this remains free of political influence. The Caritas women's village bank programmes and Caritas's general shift towards development as well as elements of the micro-credit programmes at Al-Qard Al-Hassan and one of the MSA centres I visited that was concerned with community development have the idea of service users leading decision-making processes as partners.

Social reproduction: synthesis and model

Kabeer (2004, p 9) proposes a model of social reproduction by way of delineating the domain of social policy and how the 'social' effectively interlocks with the economic. The notion of social reproduction is based on three levels, which feed into each other and maintain the social order:

- reproduction of life, based on birth, childcare and care of the family;
- reproduction of labour, which is based on building capacities, human capital and physical labour;

- reproduction of society, which is based on producing ideological and social conditions.

Through their social programmes, it could be argued that the RWOs impact on all three levels very clearly to produce the social order that has already been outlined above. At the lowest level, their intricate role in family and childcare through support of families who lose their main breadwinner, as well as their provision of institutional care services, show how influential they are at the micro level. The RWOs are even involved in providing family planning advice although it is the MSA local development centres who are most actively involved in reproductive health issues. This is because by the time the family arrives at the RWO for social assistance, the head of the household is usually a single mother (who may remarry).

The huge emphasis on education and awareness raising finds its natural expression in developing human capabilities, which underpins one of the key objectives of the RWOs. Developing physical, cognitive and spiritual capabilities is important in allowing beneficiaries not just to retrieve their self-esteem but also to become more productive individuals in society. In this sense, the RWOs are contributing to the improvement of human capital and, thus, the efficiency of the marketplace. The key factor that the RWOs want to stimulate here is human agency.

At the macro level, the RWOs play a pivotal role in reinforcing political and religious leadership in Lebanon as well as the supporting societal structures of charity and patronage and a geographical division of the sects in Lebanon. To the extent that their commitment to human unity and human rights remains rhetorical, then the founding social and ideological conditions in Lebanon stand to look very much the same in the near future.

But the factor that Kabeer's analysis (2004) misses out, indeed the factor that this chapter began with, is the sense of the sacred or spiritual. This requires another model that can take account of the internal spiritual experience of humanity at the micro level and provide a ceiling much higher than the macro level depicted in the initial conceptualisation by Kabeer (2004). Figure 6.3 illustrates this.

Figure 6.3 seeks to take into account, to the extent that this is feasible, the role of spiritual matters in the social order. This is depicted as an outer layer of spiritual life within which the basic structures of social reproduction are embedded. It takes into account the belief social actors had during my fieldwork of God's direct intervention in their daily lives and how seeking to please God through prayer and good deeds increased their chances of being blessed by Him.

The three levels of social reproduction thus directly feed into the wider metaphysical level, since they reinforce it and are sustained by it. The reproduction of labour could also include the development of spiritual capabilities. It is not surprising, then, that the RWOs (except perhaps Dar Al Aytam) pay a great deal of attention to the spiritual development of their employees and, when asked

Figure 6.3: Social reproduction: factoring in the sacred

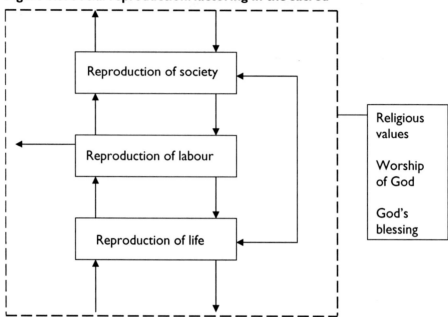

what the secret of their organisation's success is, they all unanimously cited God's blessing.

Conclusion: the place of social cohesion in policy

In highlighting the importance of social cohesion in the universe of social welfare in Lebanon, this chapter has brought to bear a key question, which constitutes the fifth line of questioning for this book outlined in Chapter One: where do social cohesion and solidarity lie in the work of the welfare RWOs, especially as they did not immediately perceive the significance of their role on social ties?

In conclusion, I shall summarise the main points this chapter has put forward by attempting to pin down the 'value' of social cohesion in policy making in Lebanon: is social cohesion a tool of rhetoric, a strategy or a policy outcome? This will lead to a final analysis of the extent to which social cohesion promotes a social order that maintains the status quo or allows progressive transformational change.

I have tried to show in this chapter that social cohesion qualifies on all three counts of policy making, as explained below.

Rhetoric

To a very large degree, the discourse of human solidarity during the fieldwork was constrained by its rhetorical value. Previous chapters have illustrated that sectarian divisions continue to operate very visibly in the RWOs and while all the RWOs had nationwide coverage and did offer services to beneficiaries not of their sect or religion, the reality remained one dominated by sectarian homogeneity at the level of service users, employees and donors. Even at the MSA local development centres, which were meant to be neutral arenas, the majority of employees and service users were of the dominant sect living in the vicinity of the centres.

Moreover, it is questionable to what extent each organisation truly promotes a sense of citizenship over and above sectarian identity among its beneficiaries. Perhaps the organisations that did not have their own schools, namely Dar Al Aytam, Caritas and the Antonine Nuns, were the ones most likely to succeed in this matter. Each organisation nevertheless had an obvious sectarian leaning in the kind of education it offered. Certainly, where employees are concerned, it is clear that a shared ideological or sectarian background is a key factor in the eligibility of the employee to work at the RWO.

However, the discourse of human solidarity is the only one that truly allows a level playing field for both service users and service providers in Lebanon. It provides the only vision of social cohesion that can indeed be based on equal partnership. But it still occupies the realm of the ideal and although there are welfare actors among the RWOs who do indeed adhere to this ethos, they are overpowered by the political culture at large. But the spiritual bonding that human unity implies is a very real force in the universe of social welfare in Lebanon. Religious conviction shows how social cohesion plays a key role as a strategy.

Strategy

In terms of social care, social cohesion has been demonstrated to be the basis of correct family upbringing, with many interviewees arguing that it was family breakdown that was causing deviance in society. Indeed, the whole ethos of social care programmes is built around helping children or families who have lost their main breadwinner to reintegrate into society as productive members. Micro-credit programmes too are founded on the idea of 'solidarity funds' and *takaaful* as a means by which collective identity could lead to a sense of common good and promote development. One of the key conclusions to be drawn is that it is precisely families who have weak or no family support that seek help from welfare organisations.

Social cohesion in the form of solidarity, which the powerful and wealthy have to muster in order to donate funds and provide their support for social welfare, has also been shown to be a key component of social welfare. To this extent, staff members at the RWOs lamented the fact that in Lebanon there is a heightened sense of individualism, which means that general members of the public "do not stand together" (CAR3). Thus, while all RWO staff argued that there is still a lot of goodness and generosity to be tapped into, the general public needs to be educated about the importance of solidarity and social responsibility. This is where RWO staff recognised that there are structural forces at play and social cohesion can only be solved by human agency.

Policy outcome

Both social care and micro-credit programmes rely on social cohesion as a key indicator of well-being, although they do this in different ways. Marriage, strong family bonds, active integration into the labour force as well as keeping away from deviant behaviour are the most important indicators of successful reintegration of service users into society. The micro-credit programmes too rely heavily on funding based on solidarity groups and membership fees. However, it has also been pointed out that the extent to which the RWOs are building solidarity in society has mixed results.

The ties of mutual obligation that bind the wealthy and the powerful to service users and deprived families are reduced to a basic regime of solidarity on the part of the former and moral rectitude on the part of the latter. However, this does not preclude the fact that service users do make gains in self-esteem and market-oriented capabilities, which allow them to exercise 'positive' freedom.

I have thus proposed seven key dimensions about the nature of social cohesion in Lebanon, which are based on moral concerns and the preservation of human nature:

- the family (nuclear and extended) is the basic unit of society;
- pure human nature has a greater capacity for compassion;
- human nature is naturally inclined to worship God, and religion is the natural expression of human morality;
- to preserve the human being is to preserve the social order;
- citizenship, nationhood and the rule of law are overshadowed by ties based on kinship, sectarianism and patronage;
- social cohesion is a form of social insurance against deprivation through the mechanisms of social care and financial sponsorship;
- processes of inclusion and exclusion are explained more through agency than structure.

Thus, consideration of social cohesion in this chapter has shown how concern with poverty is indeed sidelined by concern with morality and maintaining the status quo.

I have illustrated how social cohesion in Lebanon is still largely predicated on vertical social relations: actors want to help others whom they perceive to be less fortunate in some way. Thus, social welfare in Lebanon is not always socially transformational. In the case of the Shi'a sect, the initiative for social service has perhaps been more deeply socially transformational for the sect as a whole since it has gone hand in hand with political resistance to oppression of the whole sect. In this sense, social cohesion has been based on mass popular movements of resistance although this does not deny that the Hizbullah mother ship is a tightly guarded and tightly controlled management. In all the other cases, the initiative for social service remains an endeavour carried out by the elites.

To the extent that developing human capabilities can lead to transformational change, this is a process that takes time. Certainly, I was not able during my research to delve deeply into this. Sen's (1999) argument in favour of expanding the understanding of human capabilities beyond the notion of human capital provides a useful insight into the socially transformational impact of such a perspective.

> In looking for a fuller understanding of the role of human capabilities, we have to take note of: (1) their direct relevance to the well-being and freedom of people; (2) their indirect role through influencing social change; (3) their indirect role through influencing economic production. (Sen, 1999, p 297)

Further research in Lebanon (and in the rest of the region) needs to be undertaken in order to evaluate how far the focus on developing human capabilities as articulated so powerfully by organisations such as Dar Al Aytam fulfils Sen's (1999) vision. Certainly, all the RWOs believe fervently that their educational and health services contribute to positive social change, and the service users I spoke with appeared very satisfied with the educational help they were receiving for their children.

Nevertheless, I would argue that where political relations are concerned, social care and micro-credit programmes are still working at the micro level and the RWOs are sustaining a model of social reproduction that may not transform the existing social order significantly. The structures of patronage and paternalism look set to stay. Based on the preliminary research conducted in other countries in the region, this paternalistic attitude would appear to be prevalent.

I have thus argued in this chapter that power has an ability to sustain its occupation of the moral high ground. Power is also a basic tenet of human dignity and freedom. Thus, there was a moral argument among social actors in favour of allowing others to become more capable and more autonomous since morality itself was an overpowering justification for social intervention.

I encountered a critical conviction during the fieldwork that human life on earth must adhere to a spiritual order, and this forms the final key statement of this chapter and opens the way for the next.

I have tried to show that while RWOs are indeed working on the economic and social planes of material life through their social care and micro-credit programmes and even though they meander into murky political territory, what they are striving to keep real is a vision of human nature as sacred. This flows directly from a belief that human activity must be centred around doing what pleases God and living by His will. Factoring in the sacred is critical in understanding the dynamics of social welfare and social cohesion in Lebanon and how RWOs actively reproduce the moral order.

The next chapter synthesises the arguments put forward so far by exploring a model of Lebanese welfare that I call the 'social ethics–welfare particularism' model. Links will be drawn with social policy in the region as a whole in Chapter Eight.

Note

[1] *Braara* is an agricultural term that refers to superfluous or useless material in nature that is shed.

SEVEN

Social ethics and welfare particularism

Introduction: theoretical implications of the Lebanese case

The research on which this book is based set out to explore how religion intersects with social welfare and social cohesion, primarily in Lebanon, and draw preliminary comparisons with other countries of the Middle East, namely Egypt, Iran and Turkey. Thus, it is the main purpose of this chapter to synthesise the empirical analysis provided in the preceding three chapters by establishing some of the key dimensions of a potential welfare model for the region, which is based on the empirical evidence provided.

I now reassemble, through the tool of a Lebanese 'welfare model', the disparate parts of religious welfare mapped out in the preceding chapters. The latter 'unpacked' the world of religious welfare into its constitutive actors, moral values and bonds, rules of access and obligation, welfare-promoting strategies and services. This chapter will broaden the analysis by introducing other key dimensions of welfare in Lebanon (and the three other countries), most notably the systems of formal social protection and social insurance as well as other key state and non-state sectors such as health, education, the market and international development agencies. Thus, this chapter addresses the sixth and elements of the seventh main questions for this book, as outlined in Chapter One:

- Is there a model of social welfare for the region emanating from the Lebanese case?
- What are the theoretical and practical implications of the Lebanese case for the future prospects of social policy in the Middle East?

The welfare model discussed in this chapter is called 'social ethics–welfare particularism' (henceforth SEWP). It takes into account how social policy is formed in Lebanon as well as its subject content. It is argued here that the latter point is the more distinguishing feature of the model and is what demarcates it particulary from Western social policy. The chapter presents two broad arguments as follows.

First, it presents a configuration of religious welfare in Lebanon through the SEWP model, which shows the main welfare actors, their social exchanges (interactions) and the ties that bind them. It depicts how the welfare strategies and outcomes that exist in this country context diverge from mainstream thinking on social policy, giving rise to the need for new more locally relevant concepts. The main features of the SEWP model are highlighted and an explanation of the historical, cultural and political forces shaping it is provided. This incorporates a view on the distinguishing features of welfare in Egypt, Iran and Turkey, with consideration of how well the Lebanese example reflects the welfare settings of these other countries.

Second, the chapter then outlines the contribution that the SEWP model makes to the theoretical literature on international social policy, with particular reference to welfare regime theory. Thus, the discussion engages directly with the study of social policy in non-Western contexts and considers in particular the adaptability of existing concepts such as welfare regime, welfare mix and indeed welfare society for understanding the Middle Eastern context.

In essence, the chapter highlights the relevance of religious welfare in the region to the definitions of social welfare and social policy. This is supported by my claim that religious values and beliefs change the welfare priorities and strategies of social actors and, thus, fundamentally the nature and purpose of social policy. The juxtaposition of spirituality with concern for social insurance is an organising axis of the argument in this regard. Further, the SEWP model proposes that desperate socioeconomic circumstances in certain parts of the world (including the Middle East, of course), not to mention civil conflict, have given rise to a diverse array of welfare forces, leading to apparent contradictions in local policy settings. Finally, the model emphasises the distinction between state and society in the provision of welfare, arguing that while the role of the Lebanese government in social policy is mainly productivist or residual[1] (Gough, 2000; Kabeer, 2004), there is in contrast a very dynamic society-based welfare sector.

Effectively, the chapter offers a response to some of the conceptual gaps in the existing literature as well as suggestions of new angles that could trigger future research. But it has two possible limitations:

The first is that the chapter engages superficially with a politico-economic analysis of Middle Eastern welfare, partly due to the practical restrictions dictated on the length of this monograph. Such an effort would have entailed more detailed consideration than I shall offer of employment and income-based welfare patterns in Lebanon as well as the roles of both governmental and international actors in the country's social policy regime. It is helpful to note again that such data do not readily exist anyway, and at best would be incomplete (UN-ESCWA, 2005).

Nevertheless, the present sociocultural focus reflects the policy prioritisations of the religious RWOs that are discussed in this book. Likewise, it reflects an overall orientation here towards shifting the parameters of policy analysis so that it can render more accurately the welfare forces acting in Southern settings. Some reference will, however, be made to social expenditures by Middle Eastern governments and religious RWOs but I acknowledge that the SEWP model is a 'type' and merely a preliminary step towards more theoretically grounded work on social policy in the Islamic world.

A second possible limitation is that the chapter cannot engage with an in-depth historical analysis[2] of the welfare systems in Lebanon and the other countries studied, which would be necessary in order to conform with welfare regime theory. This historical discussion will need to be left to another piece of work on the region. However, for the case of Lebanon, the historical discussion includes an overview of some of the causal processes that have influenced Lebanese welfare, the sporadic outbreaks of war being among the most prominent. The mapping of religious welfare in Chapter Four also contributes a useful historicisation of welfare patterns in Lebanon. The benefits of typologies notwithstanding, the next section outlines the main dimensions of the SEWP model.

The Lebanese case: contradictions and hybridism

The configuration of social welfare presented here basically tells the story of what happens to those members of the Lebanese population (and to a large extent other populations around the Middle East) who have little or no access to formal or informal social protection measures. According to one of the most recent reliable estimates (Melki, 2000), no less than 50% of the Lebanese population are not covered by any formal social or health insurance scheme.[3]

In their 1997 household living conditions survey, the UNDP and MSA (1998, p 45) cited 58.2% of the population as not having health coverage, which, save for public sector employees, is the crux of social protection for the majority of the Lebanese population. In the early 2000s, the NSSF, the main government social insurance body, which covers private sector employees, had no official data on this subject but the view generally expressed was that only one third of the Lebanese population benefits from the NSSF. New public statements by the NSSF issued in 2008 confirmed that over half of the Lebanese population are indeed without health insurance coverage (Al-Manar satellite channel, 2008).

Of the 60 service users who were involved in the research for this book, none had health insurance, let alone any kind of formal social protection cover, except for a mere handful of service users who had managed to become attached to private sector occupational insurance schemes. This situation in itself has important implications for the task at hand and will be explored more fully as the chapter unfolds.

This argument here gradually builds the SEWP model based primarily on the Lebanese welfare case, depicting the main actors involved, the social exchanges that take place between them and the social ties that bind them. In order to structure this model, I shall follow some of the arguments presented by various authors (Ferrera, 1996; Gough, 1999; Davis, 2001) who have evaluated the applicability of the welfare regime approach to two different regions: Southern Europe (Greece, Italy, Portugal and Spain) and East/South Asia (Bangladesh, Indonesia, Malaysia, the Philippines, Singapore and Thailand).

The SEWP model will be discussed in relation to five key areas:

- welfare actors, exchanges and social ties;
- welfare strategies and outcomes;
- alternative programme equivalents of social protection;

- new welfare concepts (for the Middle East);
- main features of the SEWP model and a historical explanation.

As Davis (2001) argues in the case of Bangladesh, for each of the categories outlined, Lebanon and the region as a whole present a diverse array of actors and strategies that should be incorporated into the comparative social policy literature if this discipline is to accurately render the reality of welfare in non-Western settings.

Thus, the SEWP configuration of social welfare and social cohesion suggests two key conclusions about the type of welfare regime that may exist in Lebanon (and is supported by the cases of Egypt, Iran and Turkey): on the one hand, Lebanon shows similar characteristics to the model of Southern European welfare proposed by Ferrera (1996). Ferrera (1996) rejects Esping-Andersen's (1990) *conservative-corporatist* classification of Southern Europe in favour of emphasising the "dualism and polarization" of social benefits schemes there as well as the roles of the family, the Catholic Church and networks of clientelism and patronage. The latter are linked to dominant political parties and often mediated through national and local government. Echoing Italian social scientists, Ferrera (1996) thus refers to the *particularistic-clientelistic* model. In the case of Turkey, Bugra (2007) argues that the corporatist model describes well the situation there, although less attention is given in this model type to the role of Islamic welfare organisations in Turkey.

The second possible scenario presented about the Lebanese case is that it may be a contradictory and hybrid or indeed altogether different case, since unlike Ferrera's (1996) example, market-based social protection figures quite strongly in Lebanon. Likewise, the religious component of welfare that makes up the voluntary and community-based 'third sector', which remains under-addressed in the welfare regime literature, dominates the welfare sector in Lebanon (as well as the Arab region more generally). In this sense, I shall explore the implications of religion and sectarianism through the SEWP model.

The finer details of this typological discussion will be taken up subsequently when the full picture of SEWP is brought into view.

Welfare actors, exchanges and social ties

The purpose here is to highlight the main welfare actors in the Middle East, and depict them within their networks of mutual exchanges and social ties. By mutual exchanges I mean what social actors effectively give to each other through their social interaction such as political protection or social services.

Two illustrations (or models) are presented in this regard, the first depicting the actors and their exchanges, and the second showing the signals of social cohesion (and solidarity) the welfare actors emit. By the latter I mean the types of social ties actors effectively interact through. The two models highlight the positions of six key welfare providers in Lebanon, which can also be found in the other countries discussed in this book:

- the family unit;
- the RWO;
- political patrons;
- the market;
- the government;
- international institutions and development agencies.

This list roughly reflects the order of importance of each of these actors in Lebanon. I shall discuss each of them subsequently and show how they shape the SEWP model.

The family unit and the RWO are depicted as the two principal competing arenas of welfare provision and are placed at the centre of the models. Both, however, are closely buttressed by networks of political clientelism whereby preferential access to services and benefits is provided through *wasta* (personal intermediation). Social protection in this sense takes on an almost feudal form whereby the political patron has to bless all initiatives of social action occurring in his sect or political constituency.

The key issue to highlight is that the service user who eventually reaches a welfare organisation is someone who has little or no family support let alone protection from a political figure or party.

The family (nuclear and extended)

The nuclear family plays a more important role in social welfare than the extended family in Lebanon; however, the extended family still exists and is stronger in the more traditional communities. The crucial role played by the family in welfare echoes arguments made by many authors such as Ferrera (1996), Gough (2000), Davis (2001) and Kabeer (2004) who have engaged with analysis of social policy in countries of the South. Melki (2000), in his panoramic overview of the social security system in Lebanon, also makes a similar point, and the research I conducted confirmed the family to be not just the de facto safety net for social and economic disadvantage but also a key policy target for all of the RWOs in my research.

The logic of 'subsidiarity' that prevails in countries where the Catholic Church has had a long history in social welfare, exists in Lebanon too, as MSA senior and junior staff consistently repeated that the ministry had no right to intervene in family affairs except when the family broke down and was no longer a suitable structure for social care. Indeed, there was poignant irony in the fact that applications to place children into institutional care had to be made personally by the parents.

The nuclear family remains more cohesive than the extended family in Lebanon, although all interviewees noted that the increasing economic pressures on households as well as greater economic participation by female family members was resulting in a reduction of traditional social support. The civil war, CAR3 noted, had had such a positive impact on family solidarity, that even then, there was no homelessness in Lebanon. Cash remittances from family members living abroad were also a key feature of the welfare role of the family and one that was apparent among some of the families I met. In the 1980s, foreign remittances accounted for up to 25% of Gross National Product (GNP) (Choueiri, 1999).

Nevertheless, among the families I met during fieldwork, links with extended family or even siblings were very weak if not non-existent due to family feuds or generalised financial hardship. A particular recurring example was widows whose relations with their in-laws had deteriorated after the death of their husbands.

I was not able during the fieldwork to probe more deeply into the prevalence or impact of extended family support save for what service users mentioned about their extended family relations, which I have already noted above. The key point is that service users who sought help from RWOs tended to have very weak or no family support. Related to this is the prevalence of family-based small enterprises in the countries that form the discussion of this book. These enterprises constitute a major source of income and welfare for the families involved.

The RWO

Non-state welfare organisations (whether religious or not) form the other key locus of welfare provision in Lebanon and one which in the theoretical literature on social policy in the South is often mentioned but not researched (Deacon, 1997; Gough, 2000; Davis, 2001). Certainly, this book has sought to demystify Islamic welfare, which in comparison to Christian and Jewish welfare is less well known, at least in its modern forms.

The preceding chapters have sought to map out a thorough profile of RWOs in Lebanon and to illustrate how they have a near monopoly of the social care sector, not to mention their key role in income-maintenance and income-generation services. The average budget of the RWOs discussed in this book is not less than US$7 million (one reached US$12 million) and with strategic attachments to political figures or social institutions both in Lebanon and abroad, such organisations must occupy centre-stage in any analysis of social policy in the region.

Thus, religious organisations form an important basis of social authority and political legitimacy as well as commanding a significant pool of resources. This is not only true of the Middle East but also of other Western countries (Wuthnow, 1988). In Lebanon, as in Egypt, the government falls behind on all three factors.

I would like to draw attention to two key ways in which religious faith and identity reformulate the conceptualisation of social welfare and social policy in this regard. The first has to do with the locus of welfare itself. Religious organisations promulgate a discourse that shifts the locus of social action into popular society, thereby opposing welfare action as the prime responsibility of the state for two reasons: (a) the state is a political machine and welfare is a charitable altruistic activity and (b) because of the latter, human emotional bonding and solidarity can only occur when there is a spirit of volunteering between individuals. Interviewees argued that by allocating social welfare to the state, the very essence of welfare as human obligation was undermined. Indeed, state welfare encouraged apathy among the lay population.

The second key issue regarding how religion reformulates the conceptualisation of welfare and social policy is the corresponding emphasis placed on spiritual activities such as prayer, worship and receiving God's blessing and protection, as well as the ability to feel compassion for other human beings. As Figure 7.1, presented later in this chapter, shows, religious faith and identity occupy an overarching position in the world of welfare in Lebanon and the other countries discussed in this book, not only because they are the source of sectarian politics, but also because they inspire altruistic social action and earn the believer God's protection against misfortune.

Both RWO staff and service users believed that God protected them because they were acting in ways that pleased Him, either by praying or by helping others in need. Faith as a source of social protection and worldly fortune was a real issue for these social actors, which was a theme taken up right at the very start of this book. Yet this form of pure religiosity was marred by sectarian politics, especially in the case of Lebanon.

Political patrons

Wasta and political clientelism are a key feature of Middle Eastern (especially Arab) sociopolitical life (Cunningham and Sarayrah, 1993). Ironically, they play a key role in poverty reduction and income redistribution, which nevertheless escapes easy measurement (Jawad, 2002).

All interviewees who took part in this research recognised that patronage existed and influenced access to services and resources. This is not just the case for Lebanon but also applies to Egypt, Iran and Turkey. I have already argued that political interference impacts upon the purpose and outcomes of welfare services in Lebanon. The extent to which the social actors I met thought that political patronage was indispensable for access to services and resources varied. All the RWOs have strong links to prominent political figures or parties in Lebanon. Only Dar Al Aytam and the Antonine Nuns play down these political connections but the general view is that such connections make the work of RWOs easier in terms of resource appropriation and social standing.

Regarding service users, who are predominantly single mothers, children, adolescents, disabled people and older people, their political activism is not very pronounced, particularly at Caritas, Dar Al Aytam and the Antonine Nuns. However, at Al-Qard Al-Hassan, Emdad and Urfan, the most overtly political organisations, service users tend to be more inclined to express support for the particular political factions these RWOs are affiliated to. But the political activism of these service users is not an issue, rather their affiliation to the RWOs is a matter of ideological conviction. The extent to which the single mothers who are benefiting from the RWOs are regarded (by the RWOs) as bringing up the next generation of politically active supporters for the RWOs is not a subject I discussed with them but it is a plausible reality. In this respect, however, these RWOs are not unique and other welfare organisations in Lebanon develop specific political orientations in their service users. For example, DAR2 argued that politically active organisations set up their own schools in order to breed political allegiance to them from a very early age.

In his analysis of the welfare regimes of Southern Europe, Ferrera (1996) argues very strongly for putting political clientelism at the centre of his regime model. His analysis emphasises how personal contacts in the public sector can help Greek service users access public services faster, as well as how political parties in Italy and Spain co-opt government resources and services by staffing ministries with their own employees, thereby opening direct channels, through the apparatus of the state between their parties and their clients. This is concomitant with the reality of political interference in social welfare in Lebanon. Ferrera (1996) rests his case on the concept of *particularistic-clientelism*, which was already being used from the 1980s to designate the policy regime of Italy. This classification renders well the Lebanese situation too, where personal ties are very important, although it captures less well the religious dimension of welfare.

Moreover, Ferrera's (1996) analysis excludes the role played by the private sector in the provision of essential public and social services although he does allude to the important private–public mix in health services and hospitalisation in Southern Europe. This is also a characteristic of Lebanon. Here, however, there is more use of private sector insurance as a more reliable substitute for inefficient state schemes, this being the key factor in which perhaps the Lebanese case differs from the South European analysis forwarded by Ferrera (1996).

The market

There are 175,000 private sector employees who should otherwise be benefiting from the NSSF who have taken up private health coverage (Melki, 2000, p 196). Table B2 in Appendix B estimates that 8.7% of the Lebanese population have private insurance.

The service users who took part in this research clearly could not afford private insurance companies. However, the health and educational services they had access to were invariably offered by private not-for-profit schools and health clinics/hospitals that were either owned by the RWOs or had contracts with them to cater for service users. These same educational and health centres operated as private providers to other members of the population who had the capacity to pay.

Lebanon has long been oriented towards laissez-faire liberalism in its approach to public policy (Ghaleb, 2000; Issa, 2000; Melki, 2000). Melki (2000), in his analysis of the social security system in Lebanon, echoes a similar line of argument adopted by Ferrera (1996) when he notes the peculiar private–public mix that characterises the health system in Lebanon. This has effectively translated into the dependence of public health provision on private health providers just like the MSA depends totally on private social care organisations. The 2008 UNDP *Human Development Report* cites private health expenditure as a percentage of GDP in Lebanon to be 8.4% in 2004 (down from almost 10% in 2002) whereas public health expenditure as a percentage of GDP was 3.2%.

The most notable example of the way in which private healthcare is contracted out by the state is through the system of beds in private hospitals that are reserved for patients who qualify for public health insurance. Ghaleb (2000, p 111) notes that 75% of public health expenditure goes towards reimbursements for healthcare provided through the private sector. Thus, Melki (2000, p 192) notes: "The health sector in Lebanon is still … ruled by market forces and operates in an economic framework made up of buildings, goods, human resources, dominated by the private sector".

In the education sector too, the number of private schools, whether they be free or fee-paying, outweighs the number of public schools in Lebanon. Even the latter depend on some form of contribution from parents.

But the role of the free market is contradicted in Lebanon by state interventionism in other aspects of the provision of welfare, which leads Melki (2000) to describe Lebanon as a hybrid case showing strong traits of liberalism and corporatism. This also echoes the dualism and polarisation that Ferrera (1996) describes in Southern Europe's pensions and benefits schemes.

The government

The use of government social services and the role of the government generally in social welfare in Lebanon has already been highlighted in preceding chapters. Generally depicted by interviewees as over-politicised and starved of resources, it was cynically accepted that the state played a residual role in social welfare, which at best was to regulate and finance the social sector, and maintain minimum standards of service quality and equity. The RWOs preferred to retain their autonomy in the policy-making process.

The role of the Lebanese state in social welfare has been touched on by Ghaleb (2000), Issa (2000) and Melki (2000), who lament the lack of a long-term social vision across the ministries, including the MSA. I have also argued, based on my fieldwork, that a short-term social assistance orientation dominates the work of the MSA. However, it should also be remembered that the Paris III Conference, mentioned in Chapter Three, marked an important event, the fruits of which have yet to be borne completely.

But there is a contradiction in the involvement of state welfare in Lebanon, one that Melki (2000) points to in his consideration of the public–private mix in the health sector, which causes him to classify Lebanon in *corporatist* terms. But noting the strong liberal tendencies in certain programmes, Melki (2000) denotes Lebanon as a hybrid.

State social insurance schemes in Lebanon offer an illustrative example. Table B1 (in Appendix B) presents the full breakdown of formal social protection schemes in Lebanon, which I have qualified as 'insufficient' for the NSSF, 'generous' for the Public Sector Cooperative for Civil Servants and 'very generous' for military/security personnel. This contradiction in the extent to which the Lebanese government offers social coverage for the population also resembles the "dualism" that Ferrera (1996) speaks of in the social protection schemes that exist in Southern Europe: peaks of generosity for pensioners and public sector workers and hardly any coverage for the unemployed and youth. In Lebanon, the contradiction is clearly drawn between the public and private sectors in terms of social insurance coverage, making public sector employment quite attractive, as in Southern Europe.

Contribution-based social protection is indeed the system followed in Lebanon. The NSSF is a public institution affiliated to the Ministry of Employment. Similar situations exist in Egypt, Iran and Turkey. Occupational social insurance is also reminiscent of Ferrera's (1996) South European model, which is characterised by a high degree of fragmentation. In Southern Europe as in Lebanon, this situation demarcates public and private sector workers, with the highest preferential treatment offered to military personnel.

Table B2 (in Appendix B) shows the distribution of health insurance coverage (arguably the most important form of social protection in Lebanon), whereby military/security personnel followed by public sector workers are the two most highly insured sectors of the workforce: 15.2% and 13.1% respectively. In terms of social insurance coverage as a whole, around 26% of private sector employees (355,407 employees) and their families are registered at the NSSF, which entitles them to state health and social coverage (NSSF data, 2004). This figure does not actually reflect the total number of private sector employees who are entitled to benefit from state funds, since many such workers and their employers have taken up social insurance with private companies due to dissatisfaction with the inefficiency of the NSSF (Melki, 2000). Crucially, unemployment benefit is not a key feature of either contexts.

The following situation, which Ferrera (1996) describes for Mediterranean countries, could easily be applied to Lebanon:

> A person who is neither old nor invalid, who has no job, no contributory entitlements and no source of income is not 'covered' at all in Southern Europe. In Spain and Italy however, this person may obtain some sort of minimum benefit by local authorities.... If it is true that the South Europeans are all to some extent engaged in a collective 'four corner game',[4] for each ... family it is of vital importance that at least one member remain firmly anchored in the corner of *garantisimo*. (Ferrera, 1996, pp 20-1)

In another instance, both Lebanon and the Mediterranean countries show similar welfare traits to the extent that their health and education systems claim to be universal or at least are attempting to move in that direction. In Lebanon, universal primary education is enacted in law but not enforced. There are also significant cases of working street children and child illiteracy, as I encountered in my fieldwork.

Likewise, the health system in Lebanon is meant to be universal but a critical shortage of resources exacerbated by the huge destruction of the civil war and current wastage of public funds has seriously hampered the state's capacity to offer universal healthcare (Melki, 2000). Before 1975, there were 24 public hospitals in Lebanon representing 10% of the total hospital sector with a view to expanding the public sector share (Melki, 2000, p 194). But decisions about where to establish new hospitals and who to employ in them were, prior to 1975 as they are now, strongly influenced by political bias, leaving certain regions in Lebanon seriously under-serviced (Melki, 2000). The discussion of the role of the government cannot end, however, without recognition of the new developments that have begun to take place in the last couple of years in the Middle East. In Lebanon, Iran, Egypt and Turkey, new Ministries of Welfare either have emerged or are seeking to have more of a coordinating role that can harmonise the social welfare sector. The extent to which RWOs are part of the policy discussions that Ministries of Welfare are holding with the UN agencies is not fully known, although I have been informed by UNDP personnel in Cairo (personal communication, May 2008) that the director of a major Coptic welfare organisation is part of the high-level talks that are taking place there. This is a space to watch.

International institutions and development agencies

This set of actors was the least explored in my research although their presence was strongly felt particularly when I met with policy-level staff at the RWOs. The mainstream international development institutions, particularly the UN agencies, the World Bank, the IMF and the EU, play an intrinsic role in directing the public policy agenda in Lebanon. This translates into development aid, which in 2005 accounted for 1.1% of Lebanon's GDP, or US$243 million (UNDP, 2008). What is more alarming is that Lebanon's debt service is beginning to top 16% of GDP (UNDP, 2008).

As became evident during my fieldwork, the UNDP has been the main partner in poverty research and projects with the Ministries of Welfare in Lebanon and Egypt, with the EU playing a more important role in Turkey due to accession. At the level of the RWOs, I have already noted how the international arena is a key source of funding and policy making for Caritas, the Antonine Nuns and Emdad. The United States Agency for International Development (USAID) is the main donor of Caritas's women's village banks.

It is the Christian RWOs that are more likely to have greater exposure to Western actors and international development discourse than Islamic RWOs, which tend to have contact with their contacts in the Middle East. Figure 7.1 (model 1) provides a configuration of the positions and social exchanges of the actors discussed above. Figure 7.2 (model 2) concerns the social ties binding the

Figure 7.1: Model of Lebanese welfare 1: welfare actors and exchanges

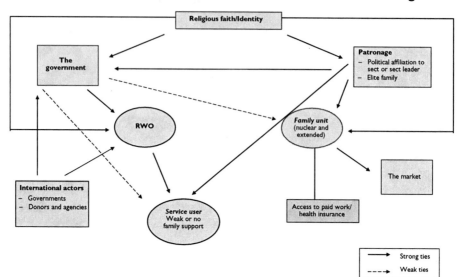

Figure 7.2: Model of Lebanese welfare 2: social ties and position of service user in relation to most immediately available sources of welfare

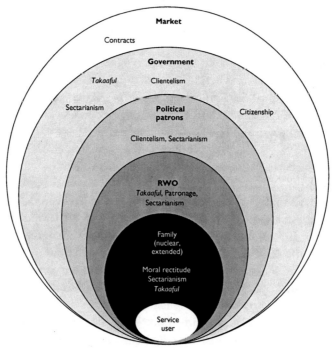

welfare actors or the signals of social cohesion that they emit. In this respect, the model illustrates the position of the service users in terms of their accessibility to providers of welfare services, with government and market services being the furthest away respectively.[5]

Welfare strategies and outcomes

The preceding chapters have highlighted several distinguishing features of Lebanese welfare that bring into question the focus of standard analyses of welfare regime theory concerning the strategies and outcome measures of welfare actors.

In terms of strategies, welfare in Lebanon is centred around health and education services, as opposed to income benefits. When one speaks of social protection in Lebanon, this automatically means health insurance except for the privileged minority of military personnel and public sector workers whose children also receive subsidised education. Moreover, the cash handouts that are offered by the RWOs represent only a symbolic gesture and a tactical one too, which gives an RWO a licence to visit the families it helps and slowly gain authority to incorporate them into its social programmes. This point was recurrently made to me by social care personnel.

The family allowances that the RWOs offered did not exceed the monthly US$20 per person at Emdad and US$50 per child at Caritas. This is much less than what families in the Palestinian Territories receive from *zakat* distributions, according to Johnson (2006), who reports that a family can receive around US$100 per month. In Lebanon, this type of family allowance is separate to the individual accounts that RWOs open for children in the orphan sponsorship programmes.

The importance of education is also reinforced by the very definition of poverty as ignorance, with many single mothers and orphans telling me that wealth meant education. Religious education is just as important as academic education in this regard. The sum total is self-knowledge and self-responsibility. I have shown in Chapter Five that the services offered by the RWOs were dominated by schools and vocational training centres, all of which act as private fee-paying institutions, but nevertheless accept poor children and children in the care of the RWO free of charge.

Thus, the way in which welfare is measured by the RWOs also contradicts standard welfare regime theory analysis, which focuses on stratification and political mobilisation. In Lebanon, as elsewhere in the world, poor communities can barely satisfy their most basic needs. The salutary effects this has on human welfare are not least measures in terms of the preservation of self-worth and human dignity. Gough (1999) and Davis (2001) make this point too. Likewise, correct moral behaviour is another key indicator of welfare inherent in the highly moral social order that exists in Lebanon and is buttressed by religion.

To this extent, the RWOs do not speak of welfare as such but of developing capabilities, satisfying needs or building self-sufficient individuals.

Alternative programme equivalents of social protection

Gough (1999) and Davis (2001) draw attention to the role of other strategies of welfare in countries of the South that do not normally exist in advanced capitalist economies but which alleviate the pressure on low-income families.

One key example that Davis (2001) refers to are the various food aid programmes in Bangladesh, which are provided by government as well as international donors and local RWOs. Poor families are given food in times of crises or as part of social programmes aimed at local development or social protection. Food aid in Bangladesh is thus accompanied by public works programmes or old-age pensions.

Among the RWOs I visited in the region, food and clothes distribution is a key feature of the sporadic social assistance the RWOs offer. This is especially evident during the month of Ramadan when rations are offered to poor families or meals are provided for the families benefiting from the RWOs. Food aid is, however, not tied to any particular social protection scheme but to acts of religious faith and solidarity.

Other significant equivalent strategies of social protection are micro-credit projects, orphan sponsorship (which is extremely important in Islamic welfare with an organisation such as Emdad running private accounts for each orphan child who has a financial sponsor) as well as obligatory Islamic charity known as *zakat* or *fitra*. Likewise, there are programmes for repairing the homes of poor families, finding marriage partners and providing marriage loans for leavers of social care.

Political mobilisation as a welfare outcome has resonance in an organisation like Emdad which is affiliated to Hizbullah where there is a clear agenda for resistance and the sociopolitical transformation of the Shi'a sect in Lebanon. To a certain extent, the Shi'a sect, after Musa Sadr, is now very active in social programmes aimed at the overall development of the regions where the Shi'as live. The tremendous progress the South of Lebanon has witnessed since the end of the civil war is a key illustration.

But again, such projects aimed at social transformation of poor regions or communities in Lebanon often occur under the banner of *development* or, as in the case of Hizbullah, political resistance against Israel. The language of social welfare and social policy rings low in such a context. Davis (2001) documents a highly similar situation in Bangladesh, reinforcing the need for conceptualising social policy differently in such contexts.

New welfare concepts: faith or social insurance

As this point of the argument draws to a close, the chapter will focus attention on the importance of using appropriate and context-relevant terminology to understand social welfare in Lebanon. A theme running through this book has been the way in which religious faith poses some critical re-evaluation of the role and purpose of social protection, which is at the heart of social policy in advanced capitalist democracies.

Protection from insecurity has inspired the conceptualisation of one of the major frameworks in development policy thinking, which has sought to be more sensitive to the reality of life in low-income contexts: the *sustainable livelihoods* approach (Kabeer, 2004). However, in analysing the significance of religion in the lives of the social actors involved in this research, I would argue that while faith could not fully compensate for the lack of food or income, social actors had a clear conviction that their religious faith helped them deal with their hardship better. Priorities were therefore changed.

Poverty, as in spiritual poverty or renunciation of worldly wants, did not figure very strongly among interviewees, as it does in some of the literature on religion and development (for example, Loy, 2003; Muzaffar, 2003; Swami, 2003; Tyndale, 2003). But the inverse of this was that economic hardship as a pre-ordained destiny was accepted by service users in my research although not given into. I have already commented that for all the policy makers interviewed, economic hardship was not accepted in any of their faiths.

I would argue that religious faith changes the welfare priorities and strategies of social actors in such a way that the definition and purpose of social policy is altered. Likewise, the importance of religion and the way in which it acts on the emotional and spiritual dimensions of human personality demands attention. Concepts such as *takaaful* and *fitra* would form key axes of understanding in this regard.

Likewise, the notion of social service, which in Chapter Four I have argued replaces the notion of social welfare as understood in the Western social policy experience, also bears significantly on the conceptualisation of social policy from the religious perspective. The importance of social service is commented on by Kumar (2003) in his analysis of Buddhism and Mahatma Gandhi's philosophy of *gram seva* (village service) to promote rural development in India.

Commentators on how religion provides useful insights for development work have tended to focus on two kinds of argument: (a) how various religious philosophies and traditions have important social teachings regarding ethical economic activity and social doctrines, for example the Christian *tithe* (Kliksberg, 2003), the Islamic *zakat* (Muzaffar, 2003) or the Buddhist interpretation of development as self-awakening (Loy, 2003); (b) qualitative changes in human values and behaviour such as increasing a sense of the spiritual or sacred through meditation and/or reducing greed through service to others (Kumar, 2003; Muzaffar, 2003; Swami, 2003). The final objective of both dimensions is to fulfil one's humanity, thereby showing solidarity with fellow humans and pleasing the divinity.

The world of welfare depicted in this book operates on both levels highlighted above: religion as social ethics and personal development. Similar indigenous experiences documented by Hope and Timmel (2003) in Kenya, Maoulidi (2003) in Tanzania and Martínez (2003) in Mexico, provide useful examples of the synergy between personal spiritual growth and group struggle against socioeconomic hardship.

But there is a real danger of religious welfare remaining an elitist activity, as argued in Chapter Four. Kabeer (2004) makes a similar point for certain religious movements in India. It is therefore important not to sentimentalise the world of religious welfare and to recognise, as Hope and Timmel (2003) argue, that material needs of shelter or good health come before spiritual faith for poor people.

Another danger inherent in religious welfare recalls that sectarianism and ethnic violence are the example par excellence of the ugly face of politicised religion. Likewise, the role of clientelism and *wasta* in the appropriation of resources and the co-option of the government apparatus require more attention in order to assess their impact on the quality of the services received.

In Lebanon, social welfare itself is overshadowed by concern with socioeconomic development, and the satisfaction of basic human needs is more of a concern than political mobilisation or social stratification outcomes.

A more direct engagement with concepts in the existing literature will be taken up in the next part of the discussion but it is useful to point out here that as a broad conceptual approach, the Lebanese case draws attention to the prevailing importance of sociocultural analyses for understanding social action. Bringing spirituality broadly defined into the fore of welfare analysis is an important endeavour in this regard.

Main features of the SEWP model and a historical explanation

To summarise the main argument here, I shall briefly outline again the main traits of the Lebanese case (many of which are also shared by Egypt and Turkey, while Iran differs in the dominance of the state over the para-state welfare organisations). I thus engage more specifically with how I have conceptualised the SEWP model. I will also offer a historical explanation for it. For this, I take a more politico-institutional perspective, which is reminiscent of Ferrera's (1996) analysis but will suggest that to a certain extent the problematic of social welfare in Lebanon is not merely an issue of underdevelopment but is also firmly hinged upon persistent cultural forces. In this respect, I challenge the cash–nexus approach advocated by Esping-Andersen (1990), which will aptly lead us to the second axis of debate in this chapter: the theoretical implications of the Lebanese case.

Characteristics of the Lebanese case (also shared by Egypt, Iran and Turkey)

The features of the Lebanese welfare model are outlined below. These have been alluded to as part of the general discussion on Lebanese social welfare throughout this book and are synthesised in this chapter. The key word describing social policy in the region is fragmentation: there are disparate sources of uncoordinated welfare, which leaves gaps and shortages in provision.

- political patronage and clientelism;
- religious welfare (with claims to universality but with a sectarian slant);
- strong family-based welfare: 'subsidiarity' principle;
- a peculiar public–private mix, particularly with regard to healthcare and hospitalisation;
- prioritisation of in-kind education and health services over cash benefits as well as the existence of functional equivalents to social protection such as micro-credit schemes and orphan sponsorship programmes;
- needs satisfaction, developing capabilities and moral rectitude as main welfare outcomes;
- a strong international influence and the presence of development aid agencies;
- significant state weakness in contrast to vibrant societal social action;
- a variety of sources of funding due to state lack of capacity;
- a 'productivist'/residual approach to social policy by the state: economic growth takes precedence over social policy;
- fragmented and dualistic occupational coverage (favouring public sector and military personnel) contradicted by theoretically universal healthcare and primary education.

The above characteristics are also shared by the other countries discussed in this book, although the case of Iran is slightly different due to the overbearing nature of the state through the para-state organisations such as Emdad. A key feature of the welfare regime of Egypt that is less apparent in Lebanon and Turkey is the commodity subsidies that the state provides. This is a massively controversial issue in Egypt that it inherited from the previous socialist era. The Egyptian state has tried many times to withdraw these subsidies but has been met with violent protests from the public.

The SEWP model draws attention to the way in which social policy is constructed as well as what its basic subject content is. I would also argue that the latter characteristic is the more distinguishing feature of the model since it represents the way in which the Lebanese case is qualitatively different from mainstream Western social policy. The two key concepts of social ethics and particularism are separate entities that try to capture the intensely humane and intensely political connotations of Lebanese policy discourse.

At the same time, both concepts draw meaning from each other: whereas particularism refers to a very individualistic and liberal culture of welfare provision which emphasies personal responsibility and work, the notion of social ethics concerns the fundamental preoccupation of Middle Eastern welfare with fulfilling basic human needs and preserving a correct moral order. This key concern with basic human issues reflects the overarching philosophy informing social welfare in Lebanon: social services are about getting human nature right more than they are about correcting societal structures or compensating for them. Only by getting human nature right, or going back to *fitra*, in the words of H13, can human solidarity be reactivated. Getting human nature right necessarily means reconnecting with God.

This primary focus by RWOs on human nature, on pleasing God through their work and on enabling service users to live a more holistic human experience through spiritual self-knowledge, emphasises that social welfare is a primarily personal experience in Lebanon. Hence, the particularism dimension of the model I am proposing. The individual consumption of health, educational and social services I have depicted in previous chapters illustrates this. But the particularism dimension also denotes the relations of clientelism and patronage, indeed the importance of the market and the private sector in social services. The preliminary research I have conducted in Egypt, Iran and Turkey did not provide clear indications of how far individuals were expected to take responsibility for their own welfare, but as these countries are all underlined by a basic Islamic philosophy, I would make an informed assumption that personal responsibility for one's own well-being is high on the agenda.

For our present purposes, the SEWP model magnifies these two distinguishing features of welfare in Lebanon, for which I offer the following historical explanation.

Historical explanation: a rudimentary welfare model?

Is the welfare system in Lebanon rudimentary, and if so, why? The historically weak position of the state in Lebanon and the lack of commitment to a long-term social agenda is a determining factor behind the inadequacy of state social coverage and public services in Lebanon today. The statement of the Lebanese delegation to the Copenhagen social development summit in 1995, cited in Chapter Two, illustrates the secondary role that social policy plays in economic policy in the country.

This has led commentators such as Ghaleb (2000) and Issa (2000) to differentiate between social spending and social investment in Lebanon as a parameter by to which to judge the long-term structural improvements that the Lebanese government undertakes. I have already argued in Chapter Four that there is a clear orientation to short-term social assistance at the MSA, as is corroborated by Issa (2000).

The subordination of social policy in Lebanon was further exacerbated by the Lebanese civil war, and subsequent confrontations between the Lebanese factions and between Hizbullah and Israel, all of which have not only intensified the social problems of impoverishment, physical disability, loss of life and sectarian division but also incapacitated the state apparatus for public service and real social engagement. According to commentators such as Issa (2000), and indeed some interviewees I met at the MSA, only in the era of President Chehab in late 1950s had there ever been real government commitment to social justice and progress.

The weakness of the state generally has been supplanted by the power of patronage and clientelism as well as other forms of society-based forces (of which religion is one of the most prominent) to ensure that some modicum of welfare provision is maintained. Thus, the prevailing political culture in the country, coupled with a diluted form of citizenship participation as a channel of social expression, contributes to the meagreness and inefficiency of public services and state social insurance measures. Yet the rudimentary character of state social policy stops at the public sector. Indeed, where the military sector is concerned, state social provisioning is very generous, as has already been illustrated.

The weakness of formal social insurance schemes in Lebanon is also reflected in the popularity of private insurance schemes among the middle classes. As Deacon (1997) argues, the impact of globalisation is directly to bear in this regard and the purchase of key social services poses a major threat to cross-class alliances and national citizenship solidarity, which are critical for the development of a common social vision.

There is, nevertheless, a very dynamic societal welfare sphere in Lebanon, which I have sought to convey in this book. In this respect, the repertoire of social services and policy regimes of this sector cannot be described as rudimentary since the RWOs are articulating very clear visions of social progress and development. These are built fundamentally on notions of basic human needs and basic moral conduct. This constitutes the 'human ethics' dimension of the welfare model I have proposed.

The health and education services these RWOs provide through schools, vocational training centres, universities, health clinics and hospitals as well as the greater involvement of some of them in infrastructural development and housing compete with the best services offered in the private sector.

The role of RWOs dates back centuries in Lebanon. Along with the residual role of government, this has led to the current situation where the market and charitable sectors dominate the sphere of social welfare.

In terms of cash benefits and income maintenance schemes, these RWOs are based on principles of solidarity and various types of affiliation: human solidarity is the ideal but sectarian affiliation is also pronounced. This brings to light how citizenship identity is poorly developed in Lebanon as a prime instigator of sociopolitical action.

The importance of identity politics is a determining force in understanding the evolution of these RWOs in the Lebanese social arena. All of the RWOs I reviewed except Dar Al Aytam and the Antonine Nuns were born during the Lebanese civil war, a period in which their sectarian bias was necessarily highly pronounced although perhaps not much more than in our present era. Identity politics highlights the important role of cultural forces in the provision and design of welfare services in Lebanon, of which religion is one very prominent actor.

Kabeer (2004, p 14), in her historical analysis of the birth of social policy in developed and developing country contexts, places at the heart of her comparison Polanyi's landmark 1944 work 'The Great Transformation', with its subsequent "spread of generalised commodity exchange" and social disembedding of institutions in Europe from the traditional formations of family, kinship, community and feudal ties. Esping-Andersen's (1990) typology also rests on Polanyi's analysis, hence the hinging of the welfare regime typology on 'decommodification' as the key measure of well-being (Esping-Andersen, 1990).

Taking the example of African states, Kabeer (2004) argues that in developing country contexts the advent of social policy, like the creation of the nation-state, was an artificial inheritance from colonial rulers, both of which merely served to entrench the existing structures of social relations in Africa, which were firmly rooted in family, kinship, clan and community relations. Relations of production thus remained firmly embedded within relations of reproduction whereby access to resources was built on ascribed identity and moral bonds as opposed to contracts or human rights. Destramau (2000) and Thompson (2000) describe similar situations in the Arab region.

The strong labour movement activity so deeply associated with the birth of social policy in advanced capitalist democracies contrasts with much lower levels of industrialisation and labour activism in Lebanon. In Thompson's (2000) documentation of the evolution of citizenship, gender and labour movements in Lebanon, the activism that was once vibrant in the independence era is now replaced by political co-optation and citizen apathy.

As mentioned in Chapter Two, Thompson (2000, p 72) argues that "the dream of a welfare state evaporated" when Lebanon gained independence in 1943. The French authorities of the mandate allied with the local elites and actively instituted a political system of "liberal paternalism" constituted of "mediated rule and gendered hierarchy of power" (Thompson, 2000, p 72). This directly undermined the political credibility of the Lebanese nation-state and the possibility of developing an equitable system of citizenship. I have not been able to research the extent to which French social policy has shaped welfare institutions in Lebanon although the highly moral basis of social cohesion and the occupation-based social insurance system may be hereditary from this.

The key point to note is that society in Lebanon, as in other parts of the South, is qualitatively different from those countries where social policy as we have come to know it has flourished. The way in which resource appropriation and distribution remains embedded in patronage, community and kinship-based social institutions is an even stronger argument for shifting the parameters of discussion on social policy.

My intention is not to suggest that there is a linear process of social progress on which populations can be pegged nor that Lebanon is synonymous with the whole of the Southern experience of social welfare; Polanyi's analysis simply serves to highlight the qualitatively different settings that international social policy is attempting to understand. Instead of contrasting the modern with the traditional in this book, I would advocate comparisons based on value systems. I am thus magnifying the faith-based value system of ascribed identity in the Lebanon as a contrast to the mainstream discourses based on citizenship or human rights.

The Lebanese welfare model is rudimentary if we consider the position of the state within it but where society actors are involved, I would argue quite the opposite.

Theoretical implications for the study of social policy in the Middle East

It is useful to begin by recognising the shortcomings and benefits of Esping-Andersen's (1990) welfare regime approach in light of the findings of the present research. Criticism of Esping-Andersen's work in the Western social policy literature is not new, in contrast to the development literature, where applying a welfare regime approach to the study of social policy in the South is a new endeavour which has been met with certain scepticism (see Kabeer, 2004, for example). The argument here considers the appropriateness of other existing concepts, namely welfare mix, welfare pluralism and welfare society. None of these concepts is new in the context of Western social policy either, but again, they are within development studies. The concept of social policy itself is put to question due its close association to social and political developments in Europe (Kabeer, 2004).

The sustainable livelihoods framework advocated by some development authors (for example, Kabeer, 2004) engaged in social policy analysis of Southern nations will not be considered since it falls outside of the remit of this book. The main aim in this chapter is to consider the structure of welfare provision and usage in Lebanon as it exists and not to advocate any particular policy orientation. This does not preclude the benefits of the sustainable livelihoods framework.

The argument supports the critiques made of Esping-Andersen's approach and its transferability to Southern contexts (as discussed in Ferrera, 1996; Bonoli, 1997; Gough, 2000; Davis, 2001; Arts and Gelissen, 2002; Kasza, 2002; Kabeer, 2004). But this does not deny the existence of policy regimes per se in low-income or Southern contexts (Kabeer, 2004). Conversely, I argue that it is important not to inflate the role of policy regimes in contexts where an amalgam of social actors is involved in determining the path of social development for many populations. In such settings there is a relatively higher degree of social, economic and political instability, leading to the necessity of reconsidering the nature and very viability of policy making.

This leads to an argument in support of the usefulness of the concept of social reproduction, advanced in the preceding chapter, to understand the work of the RWOs reviewed in this book. The concept takes into account the huge social care component of the RWOs' work as well as their preoccupation with maintaining the moral order. Consequently, economically oriented programmes of income generation, maintenance or redistribution are less pronounced.

Overall, I argue that there is a need to develop conceptual frameworks that can render more effectively the cultural, emotional and spiritual dimensions of welfare that religion highlights. I hope that the model I have proposed advances such research.

Which 'policy regime' approach?

Kabeer (2004) aptly argues that even though we may not support the transferability of Esping-Andersen's welfare regime classifications to Southern contexts, the analysis of policy regimes *tout court* is still possible and desirable.

> Policy regimes are clearly important ... because they represent the extent to which the state makes a purposive effort to ensure that different groups in society are protected from risks and insecurities in their environment. (Kabeer, 2004, p 34)

This book argues that while the above citation may indeed be true and useful for understanding the welfare sector in Lebanon, it is also crucial that we account for the role of societal actors and the emotional/spiritual dimension of welfare. At a time when international and domestic socioeconomic conditions are putting into question the survival of the welfare state as we have known it (Clarke, 2000), when social policy is being rethought in the light of new social paradigms (Lewis, 2000) and when arguments are being put forward to shift our focus from welfare states to welfare societies (Rodger, 2000), it seems that the Lebanese welfare setting like other similar settings does respond in concrete ways to critical questions being asked about the future of social policy. Not least because in Lebanon there are examples of social support networks that may provide useful insights for such questioning.

I should offer a clarification of what I refer to by regime at this point: I fully acknowledge that to speak of a welfare regime in the Esping-Andersen tradition is primarily to imply that a group of nation-states conform to a set of welfare characteristics. Clearly, I cannot make such a claim of my Lebanese welfare model, which is based on an isolated case study. My use of the concept of regime therefore lies primarily in its ability to render a sense of underlying norms and values adhered to by the social policy system in Lebanon. It is thus this latter meaning which I use to make claims about the dynamics of social welfare in Lebanon. However, this does not preclude the possibility of assessing how well Lebanon is represented by Esping-Andersen's typology and therefore engagement in an argument about the merits of his theoretical approach in a Southern context based on the Lebanese case.

The main shortcomings raised about Esping-Andersen's welfare regime theory have been alluded to in the literature review but I shall briefly recap here the main criticisms regarding the transferability of the concept to Southern contexts:

- Kabeer (2004) criticises the path-dependency dimension for assuming a false level of stability in the era of globalisation and structural adjustment programmes;
- Gough (1999) and Davis (2001) point to the way in which the welfare regime concept fails to highlight the importance of health, education and housing

programmes, which play a more important role in poor countries than do income-maintenance schemes;

- in terms of welfare outcomes, Gough (1999) and Davis (2001) also remark on the importance of needs satisfaction and self-sufficiency whereas Esping-Andersen's typology is built on decommodification;
- similarly, stratification outcomes overemphasise class-based social structures at the expense of gender, religious, ethnic and clientelistic outcomes (Ferrera, 1996; Davis, 2001);
- the typology does not account for the critical role of international development institutions without which policy analysis of social welfare in low-income settings would be very lacking (Gough, 1999; Davis, 2001).

The model of Lebanese welfare presented in this book responds in very direct ways to each of the shortcomings mentioned above. The 'third sector' that Esping-Andersen overlooks in his typology is indeed the key actor in Lebanon as it is in other low-income contexts such as Bangladesh, which Davis (2001) explores. Indeed, it is the government that is the marginal actor, as I have shown for Lebanon.

Moreover, there is a spiritual contentment factor and a sense of security in religious worship, which was evident among the service users I met during my research, which is very difficult to capture in a politico-economic analysis of social welfare. Likewise, the altruism, emotional bonding and human sentiment, which was very apparent in the policy discourses, although slightly tarnished by the sectarian slant, was very alive in the family contexts as well as relations between service providers and service users, with some of the service users becoming tearful as they spoke of the love and gratitude they felt for the social workers who assisted them.

Lewis (2000) and Rodger (2000) give importance to the role played by the emotions in reformulating the conceptualisation of social policy. Rodger (2000, p 10) advocates in this respect the concept of 'welfare society' as he questions the impact of "changing attitudes to caring and welfare" in advanced capitalist societies. He advocates an understanding of the welfare state that separates the state institutionally and conceptually from the domain of welfare in order for the concept to capture the roles of community, family and the voluntary sector in welfare. Interestingly, Rodger (2000) draws on the Dutch definition of welfare society:

> which is used as a description for the informal, private initiatives and charitable welfare institutions based on the confessional pillars ... of Dutch society.... The process of depillarisation ... which has characterised the Netherlands since the 1960s ... is easier to analyse if the distinction between welfare state and welfare society is retained. (Rodger, 2000, p 11)

Such an approach would appear to be quite fruitful for the context of Lebanon and indeed other country contexts where state resources and authority in the social sphere are undermined by societal forces. Alcock (2001) makes a similar comment with regard to Southern European contexts that rely more on the family, the RWO sector and the churches.

Such an approach would also be more in harmony with the concepts of welfare mix or welfare pluralism, which are being put forward to analyse not just advanced capitalist contexts but low-income settings too (Alcock, 2001). Alcock (2001) argues that even though welfare provision may no longer exclusively be the remit of the state, the latter continues to play a central role if only as regulator of standards or provider of subsidies. In effect, this is the situation in Lebanon, although we may even question the extent to which the state is a fair and effective moderator of standards. The exception in Lebanon remains certain public sector professions, which receive luxurious amounts of state protection and subsidisation, namely the military and security forces.

As a result of this shift in focus towards societal welfare actors in Lebanon, key issues are raised for the study of social policy in an international context:

- Society-based welfare provision and informal support networks are a key dimension of analysis, which problematise the policy-making process of social welfare.
- Ideology continues to play a key role in defining the scope and purpose of social welfare services as well as needs interpretation.
- Culture is also a key dimension of such an analysis, with important implications with regard to the role of the family.
- Developmental issues resulting from the role of international institutions in low-income settings must also be brought to the fore.
- Religion not only has spiritual implications for welfare but also a social and economic agenda that is responding to real problems in today's world.

Social reproduction and Lebanese welfare: prelude to social policy?

The concept of social reproduction has been discussed in Chapter Six, where I proposed that we consider religious RWOs as guardians of a moral order whose survival they ensure through their welfare services. My use of the concept of social policy here is based on the definition I advanced of it in Chapter Three. This drew attention to a definition of social policy as more than just a tool of public administration but as a legitimate institutional framework through which purposive social action is applied in the pursuit of positive social change. What I am suggesting here is that as a more rudimentary analytical framework, the concept of social reproduction could allow more complex development of social policy in Lebanon. The argument for this is as follows.

Kabeer (2004) offers a typological analysis of policy regimes in low-income countries based on the conceptual framework of "regimes of social reproduction". She characterises the framework as follows:

> (i) it assumes different institutional relations of reproduction and production; (ii) it defines different boundaries between public responsibility and private initiative; (iii) it generates different patterns of economic growth and human development. (Kabeer, 2004, p 21)

Social reproduction is a concept at the heart of the social sciences and the study of social policy (Spicker, 2000; Kabeer, 2004). Although it may give a false impression of clear patterns and stability in the social order (Spicker, 2000, pp 29-30), Kabeer's (2004) emphasis on the concept is precisely because it allows reconsideration of the meaning of the 'social', a critical point if social policy is to be formulated in a relevant way.

The usefulness of the concept of social reproduction is based on the crucial idea of how far relations of production and reproduction are really separated in settings like Lebanon where social ties based on ascribed identity such as family and community remain important. The preceding argument has sought to answer this question in the negative, although Lebanon is not as agrarian as some other parts of the world.

The extent to which the social and the economic can be separated has not been of similar concern in this book as it is in Kabeer's (2004) but certainly the interaction between the social and the religious/spiritual has. One important illustration of how all these spheres are nevertheless intertwined in the work of the welfare RWOs I researched is through the concept of developing human capabilities to promote needs satisfaction, agency and autonomy. Sen (1999) makes a strong argument in this direction, which I touched on in Chapter Six.

Thus, through the concept of social reproduction, Kabeer (2004) analyses development policies in various country contexts. Of pre-reform China, she (2004) quotes another author, as follows:

> [beginning of quotation] The creation of the material pre-requisites for building socialism in China was inseparable from the creation of the 'new socialist man' ... [end of quotation].... Governments in this part of the world generally embarked on the transformation of their societies without making a strong distinction between the 'economic' and the 'social' in their construction of policy. (Kabeer, 2004, p 25)

The fusion of the social with the economic in China was based on the socialist ideology of egalitarianism, which was part and parcel of the economic system.

Social reproduction captures the purposive intent of social actors to shape their environment as a moral/emotional social order. In post-war Lebanon, the work of social welfare RWOs that are acutely aware of how they are shaping their environments gains poignancy. As H2 at Emdad noted, "we are building the human being".

In this sense, the concept of social reproduction captures the immense emphasis on developing socioeconomic capabilities, spiritual self-knowledge and ideology, which are at the heart of the programmes offered by the RWOs. The interesting point about social reproduction is therefore that it does not necessarily imply the existence of formal state social policy but it could be a prelude to it. This is the situation in Lebanon.

A striking issue that was raised by the interviewees who took part in my research was the sheer inability to actually devise social policy. I have already looked at the Lebanese state's incapacity in this regard and I have also argued that the RWOs have a clear social agenda but the issue is: to what extent can this form the basis of social policy in Lebanon, not least when there is such poor coordination within the RWO sector?

Put together, all these factors would show that the concept's usefulness lies in its ability to illustrate how religious welfare in Lebanon is currently reconstructing the social parameters of post-war Lebanon, a process that needs to be harnessed if real engagement with the future of social development in Lebanon is to be achieved.

Conclusion: basic needs and moral order – primacy of the human being over societal structures

The purpose of this chapter has been to bring together the disparate parts of the profile of religious welfare that have formed the focus of the book so far in order to engage with a theoretical argument concerning the various conceptual approaches for understanding social policy in Southern settings. The chapter has contextualised this model within a modest historical overview of the politico-institutional and cultural forces shaping social welfare in Lebanon.

I have proposed a model of welfare based on the Lebanese case, which I have named social ethics–welfare particularism (SEWP). Based on this, I have argued that social policy making in Lebanon, as in other countries of the region, is predicated on fulfilling basic human needs and preserving a correct moral order in line with religious ethics. As such, welfare concerns preserving the correctness of human nature as opposed to reworking societal structures.

In formulating the welfare model, I have drawn on a wider array of factors working in the Lebanese welfare sphere, namely the system of formal social insurance as well as the role of other sectors such as public health and other actors such as international development institutions. Thus, I have gone beyond the strict parameters of religion in order to produce a Lebanese welfare 'type'. But I have acknowledged that in order for my model to qualify as a regime type, it must draw on other country-case experiences. This, however, does not preclude the possibility of assessing the merits of welfare regime theory to developing country contexts based on the Lebanese type.

I have also shown that the Lebanese case bears similar traits to the Southern European model advocated by Ferrera (1996) but that there are contradictions relating to the role of the state, which suggests that the Lebanese case may be a hybrid. I have highlighted the following main features of Lebanese welfare:

- political patronage and clientelism;
- religious welfare (with claims to universality but with a sectarian slant);
- strong family-based welfare: 'subsidiarity' principle;
- a peculiar public–private mix, particularly with regard to healthcare and hospitalisation;
- prioritisation of in-kind education and health services over cash benefits as well as existence of functional equivalents to social protection such as micro-credit schemes and orphan sponsorship programmes;
- needs satisfaction, developing capabilities and moral rectitude as main welfare outcomes;
- a strong international influence and the presence of development aid agencies;
- significant state weakness in contrast to vibrant societal social action;
- a variety of sources of funding due to state lack of capacity;
- a 'productivist'/residual approach to social policy by the state: economic growth takes precedence over social policy;
- fragmented and dualistic occupational coverage (favouring public sector and military personnel) contradicted by theoretically universal healthcare and primary education.

I have thus challenged the current literature on welfare regime theory, arguing that the Lebanese case responds to key critiques of the shortcomings of the welfare regime approach to reflect the reality of social welfare in Southern settings.

Similarly, I have proposed that the Lebanese model brings to the fore the important role of the emotional and spiritual dimensions of welfare as well as the critical role played by society in an era when state resources and authority are diminishing. I have thus argued that concepts like welfare mix, welfare society or welfare pluralism, although not new in Western social policy, may reflect better the diversity of welfare actors and strategies that operate in places like Lebanon.

The implications that the Lebanese welfare model has for the theoretical conceptualisation of social policy in the South are that factors such as ideology and culture should be taken into account as variables of analysis, indeed that the role of international development agencies must be considered and finally that religion is not only a source of emotional and spiritual influence but also bears profoundly on the socioeconomic dimensions of people's lives. Moreover, I have emphasised that the Lebanese case shows how society is a critical locus for social welfare.

In acknowledging that social policy itself may be a historically specific experience of advanced capitalist democracies, particularly in Europe, I have suggested that the study of social policy as we know it must take into account the qualitatively different social settings of Southern contexts in order to reflect their welfare activities more accurately. The concept of social reproduction may, in this sense, be more apt in understanding the work of RWOs that are primarily concerned with social care and social order as well as the development of human capabilities broadly defined.

In Lebanon, as in the rest of the region, the work of welfare organisations (especially the Islamic forms of almsgiving and social care services) is crucial for transforming the lives of large populations and must be harnessed if social development and civic harmony are to be promoted. That religious faith has specific implications for the welfare priorities and strategies used by social actors demands a shift of emphasis in social policy. The possibility that religious welfare may be an axis of more coherent social policy in the future in the Middle East has been suggested strongly in this chapter. This is the key idea I shall carry across to the next chapter, which will consider the practical possibilities and supportive arguments for a more formally recognised public role for religious welfare in the Middle East.

Notes

[1] Prioritisation of economic policy and economic growth over social policy.

[2] Table A3 in Appendix A on social expenditure in Lebanon goes back to 1997.

[3] Tables B1 and B2 in Appendix B provides a full breakdown of social insurance coverage in Lebanon.

[4] "Four corner society" is a term Ferrera (1996) borrows from the Spanish social policy literature, which suggests that there are four types of socioeconomic position in Southern Europe and, therefore, welfare entitlements that the population of Spain can have, *garantisimo* being the Italian equivalent of full state cover.

[5] In the narrative, the market preceded government due to the argument's logical progression. In model 2, market denotes specifically private health and insurance schemes not accessed through the RWOs.

EIGHT

What next for the Middle East? Re-reading history, re-visioning future possibilities of positive action

Introduction

Historical sociologists who have turned their attention to the major social phenomena of our times, such as religion, modernity and the creation of the welfare state, have opened up critical debates about the nature of "agency, power, structure, and modernity" (Orloff, 2005, p 224). Many such authors (see the volume edited by Adams et al, 2005, as a prime example) argue for the centrality of considering cultural and historical forces that have shaped the key institutions, processes, social relations and concepts of modernity. To this end, Orloff (2005) argues that social welfare programmes constitute political processes and bases for mobilisation. This is reminiscent of Clarke's (2004) treatment of Gramsci's concept of the "national popular" and the central role of culture in social policy analysis. Both Clarke (2004) and Orloff (2005) point to ways in which social policy entails a form of social regulation, which actively constructs social identities of gender, class, race and ethnicity. The Personal Responsibility and Work Opportunity Reconciliation Act (PRWORA) programme in the US is often cited as one such illustration (Clarke, 2004).

A central argument emerges here for taking culture seriously in the analysis of social processes, the welfare state included. According to Orloff (2005), this entails abandoning the weak utilitarian concepts that underpin current social policy thinking in favour of deeper analyses of the self, based on a cultural view of a much broader phenomenon denoted as social action. To a large degree, it is this intellectual orientation that has defined the subject matter of this book. Moreover, it is fair to argue that, regardless of all the political controversies surrounding social conservatism that religion throws up, the issues that a religious worldview prevents us from losing sight of are indeed the big moral questions that concern the very nature, existence and purpose of human life (and creation).

In stating that welfare states are an intrinsically Western political phenomenon, Orloff (2005, p 223) affirms that they "are only one possible institutional form for more widespread activities of reproduction". In this view, social policy is very much a tool of social control and social reproduction, one that can suppress dissent and revolution (ironically, not unlike the religious opiate) through measured provision of social welfare assistance. The beginnings of the "welfare" state are to be found in the security-oriented mentality of the inter-war years within Europe. At that point, welfare primarily denoted all non–military public expenditure (Orloff, 2005). It is crucial, then, to understand the historical and national factors shaping the welfare state. This is not far from Offer's (2006, p 5) account of the intellectual roots of British social policy where he argues (citing L.H. Lees):

> The welfare story is not a whiggish saga of progress toward the sunny land of egalitarian social citizenship. To the contrary it is a tale shaped by the shifting wind of particular economic and social worlds. History and politics give it shape, and culture gives it meaning.

Offer (2006) further situates Christian understandings of virtue and morality at the centre of post-war social welfare thinking, which many social policy historians have nevertheless chosen to ignore. Citing E. Norman, Offer (2006, pp 12-13) writes:

> For a long bleak interlude, historians are once more beginning to take religious issues in nineteenth century England seriously. For decades 'secular' historians have tended to regard the incidence of Christian belief, where they have come across it either in the lives of particular statesmen or in social groups, as a fringe cultural phenomenon, perhaps useful as a matter of social control. What they have not perceived as of importance in the modern world has not seemed to them, as noticed in the immediate past, as much more than the lingering evidence of a discarded order. When Morley, for example, wrote his famous biography of Gladstone, he could not as an atheist, bring himself to regard Gladstone's religious priorities as real priorities. The result, with an enduring legacy, was a depiction of Gladstone as a moralist (for atheists can understand moral priorities) rather than motivated by a religious view of the world.

It is easy to stand on the Middle Eastern terrain with a certain dose of myopia or historical amnesia and to despair at the prospects for progressive social policy in the region. This is why a central argument in this book and in the present chapter is to show how a dynamic historical perspective on social action in the Middle East is the surest way to dispel the myths that despair us, and to re-imagine new ways of advancing humanity. The central strategy of this book and the research on which it is based is in fact quite simple: what positive examples of social welfare are there in the Middle East and can we build on them? What are the implications of the preceding discussion for the future roles of religion and social policy in the Middle East? This is the subject matter of this chapter.

As Middle Eastern states feel the rising pressure of social and economic unrest within their populations and follow the lead of international development institutions like the World Bank and the UN-ESCWA in paying more serious attention to issues of social protection and social justice, is the role of religious groups conciliatory or hostile in this process?

There are some general lessons about religion and social policy that may be drawn from the vast array of experiences described in the preceding chapters. There are also some issues that are specific to the political, social and economic situation of the Middle East, which dictate particular considerations for future relations between religion and social policy. Although it is not the intention of this chapter to prescribe policy for the region, it is certainly possible to present a well-reasoned and well-researched argument for a possible future direction that governments and international actors in the region of the Middle East may pursue. This is what I intend to do in this chapter.

The structure of this chapter is as follows. First, it recaps on some of the key arguments made so far in this book about the role of religion in social policy in order to begin to formulate an argument for where social policy in the region might head. Second, it engages historically with social policy in the region as a whole, reviewing how scholars have analysed it, and shows that religious welfare continuously comes up as the missing link in studies of social action in the region. To a large extent, the empirical study of Lebanon provided in the preceding chapters fills this missing link and can therefore be seen as a prelude to the re-reading of the history of social policy in the Middle East. Although I have not made direct reference to social policy in Israel so far, there is evidence to suggest that Israel shares similar issues with the rest of its regional neighbours. Nation-building continues to preoccupy social policy in Israel (Shalev, 2007), leading to particular religious, ethnic, gender and class politics. Third, the argument consolidates the discussion by returning to the Lebanese case study and offering some tentative policy recommendations, based on the findings reported in this book on the Lebanese welfare setting. Fourth, I look again at the Middle East and offer tentative recommendations on what could be done to develop social policy in the region and where religious groups or religious values might figure in this. The chapter then ends with some concluding thoughts.

Defining some parameters for the relationship between religion and social policy

It is useful to begin with a recap of some of the key arguments and conclusions reached in Chapter Two and the supporting evidence reported in the preceding chapters.

For many authors, developing an agenda for social policy and social welfare in the lower-income countries is of primary concern as a response to the challenges facing state social provisioning as economic and political liberalisation take their toll on Southern nations (Deacon, 2000; Hong, 2000; Kabeer and Cook, 2000). It is not so much concern with religion that drives this book but the contribution religion makes to the social policy agenda in lower-income countries.

The previous chapters have sought to evaluate religious welfare not only for its religious content but as a system of social provision targeting socioeconomic goals. At the same time, the concern with religion has gone beyond those of mainstream social policy and development analysts in that I have addressed an under-researched area of enquiry that highlights the particularities of welfare practices in the South.

The resurgence in politically charged religious mobilisation worldwide has already received comment from a variety of authors already cited in the introduction to this book but the way in which religion can also inform social policy initiatives and issues of welfare away from the polemics of politics deserves, I have argued, more attention. This is especially the case for the contexts of lower-income countries where church organisations and Islamic welfare have traditionally occupied a central place. Although this book acknowledges that the social and political are not mutually exclusive, as is the case in Lebanon, I have sought to provide an analysis that accounts for both dynamics separately.

I have demonstrated that in Lebanon, religion is an important source of 'home-grown' solutions. Consequently, I have proposed that it may hold the key to sustainable measures of social action especially in view of the fact that religion holds powerful social and moral sway regardless of socioeconomic status. Religious welfare thus needs to be harnessed, I would argue, for the positive contribution it could make to the development of a constructive agenda for human progress and well-being. Lebanon is not alone in this regard. All over the Middle East, particularly in the Arab and Islamic worlds, *zakat* funds surpass state and development aid agency support in reaching vulnerable groups (Johnson, 2006; Roy, 2006). Islamic principles of social welfare that prioritise orphans and vulnerable groups who have lost their male breadwinner dominate the mentality of welfare thinking.

The moral impetus behind any form of economic and political action cannot be overlooked. As far back as 1980, Wilber and Jameson (1980) considered the import of religion to development in the Third World. They argued that the major social thinkers such as Emile Durkheim, Adam Smith, R.H. Tawney and Max Weber all lay emphasis on the moral basis of human prosperity and social action. According to Wilber and Jameson (1980), religion not only can provide a positive basis for development action, it is also a key factor in individual attitudes and behaviour and a key impetus for social mobilisation and resistance. In a similar vein, they critiqued secularisation, arguing that even secular states have committed major atrocities such as world wars, the Hiroshima bomb and Vietnam. There is after all a dark side to democracy. They conclude, therefore, that a religiously based society may not necessarily be more dangerous than a secular one.

Linked to this is the important distinction made in Chapter Two between the direct role of religion and clerics in policy making and the role of lay individuals who are influenced by religious values. Several authors point to the key role that voluntary religious organisations have played in developing democracy in the West, such as Skocpol (2000), who cites De Toqueville's observations of 19th-century

America, Demerath (2007b) and F. Powell (2007). Van Kersbergen (1995) argues that it was the special feature of Christian Democracy that it was led by lay Catholics. This political movement was able to bring out positive political and social changes not thanks to the Vatican social teachings, but "in spite of them". Demerath (2006) sees no harm in free political parties that have a religious base practising in a democracy as long as this does not entail actually establishing a religious state. What is clear though from all these arguments is that religious organisations have played an active role in the development of a healthy civil society (Skocpol, 2000). Moreover, religions, due to their transnational character, can lead to global forms of citizenship and civic engagement (Levitt, 2008). As Trigg (2007) argues, there is no real justification for the confinement of religion to the private sphere.

Therefore, a religious perspective on welfare should be considered as a value system on which social welfare can be pursued. As an inherently moral and ethical discourse, religious welfare merely reaffirms that all perspectives to social welfare bury within them certain ideological and normative convictions about the nature of the good society. If social policy is itself an intrinsically moral act (Spicker, 2000), then perhaps it is time that we faced such moral debates head on instead of shying away from them or stereotyping them.

A religious perspective on human welfare advances a holistic view of human needs and human nature, thus taking into account the importance of spiritual and emotional fulfilment. This necessarily expands the parameters of the debate on poverty since emotional and spiritual needs do not have to be dependent on socioeconomic status. To this end, Inglehart and Barker (2000) note that in societies that have achieved certain levels of economic security, individuals increasingly turn to spiritual and emotional concerns to fulfil their well-being. In this sense, spirituality is a subject that is gaining increasing attention in Western scholarship. It has certainly exercised a key influence on the social and economic decisions made by populations in poor and developing countries (Ver Beek, 2000).

Thus, it is important to note that the divide between the secular and the religious is itself quite thin, as Harcourt (2003) argues. Indeed, in more secular societies such as Europe and the US, Christian tradition continues to imbue the moral imaginary (Harcourt, 2003). As such, to take into consideration the role of religion or religiosity in daily living would contribute to a fuller and more balanced understanding of how human society functions. Finally, to end this section, it is useful to cite Wineburg (2001, pp 140-5) whose study of religious congregations in the US led to the identification of seven key assets that religious groups can offer social welfare:

- a mission to serve;
- a pools of volunteers;
- sacred space;
- an ability to raise funds;
- political strength;

- moral authority;
- creativity and experimentation.

If there can be an official faith-based initiative in the US to support federal-level social services, or there can be grants given in the UK to develop the capacities of faith groups to begin to take part in social welfare provision, are Islamic welfare organisations in the Middle East so different?

Overview of current analyses of social policy in the Middle East

The image of social policy in the Middle East that emerges from the main social policy texts currently available in the English language offers a view that we would expect to hear about social welfare in this region:

- The constant pressure of international intervention in the region since the deepening ties to European trade began in the 18th century has contributed to unequal wealth redistribution in the Middle East and the dominance of a consumerist urban elite over largely wageless peasants (Henry and Springborg, 2001).
- A statist political economy approach dominates the analysis of social policy in the region. Whether they are weak or coercive, all the states of the region are depicted as suffering from weak or non-existent democracy, which leads to misallocation of resources with most funds being spent on the military and being plagued by corruption and the embezzlement of public funds (Karshenas and Moghadam, 2006a).
- Social policy in the region is thus highly residual in nature, with the primary focus of governments on economic policy and economic growth (Karshenas and Moghadam, 2006a, 2006b).
- Equally, social policy is highly politicised in the region and is vulnerable to clientelist abuse as well as manipulation for political gain by political figures (Karshenas and Moghadam, 2006a, 2006b).
- The final goal of social policy is depicted by some of the main social policy observers of the region (Bayat, 2006; Karshenas and Moghadam, 2006a, 2006b) as being about welfare redistribution and the provision of basic needs. This is defined by the urgent developmental and survival needs of the populations in the region, which require less attention to social rights and freedom and more attention to basic needs such as housing, food, education and job creation.
- There is a general breakdown between state and society due to the failure of the democratic process. Poor populations have not organised politically and the main tension between state and society is expressed through the rise of Islamic social movements such as Hamas, the Muslim Brothers and Hizbullah seeking to solve social problems through Islam and at times offering a political alternative to the state.

- Islam is discussed at length in some of the books in terms of either a system of jurisprudence governing family law and gender relations or a doctrine for Islamic economics whereby the obligation of *zakat* (2.5% of assets) and the old practice of the *waqf* (religious endowments), which reached its height during the Ottoman Empire in the urban development of Istanbul, have played a key role in wealth redistribution and socioeconomic development (Dallal, 2004; Heyneman, 2004).

Thus, underpinning all of these works is an attempt to describe public policies that have failed or that have been successful in the Middle East. The body of knowledge that these works may be considered as representing of social policy in the Middle East is thus primarily descriptive in nature and offers a narrow view of contemporary social welfare in the Middle East, which rests on the conceptual framework of the Rentier state, a term coined in the 1970s as a result of the discovery of oil in Latin America and the Middle East and first used in 1990 to refer to social policy in the Middle East by Beblawi (1990), and more recently, referred to again by Karshenas and Moghadam (2006a) in their consultancy work for the UNRISD. I argued at the beginning of this book that the concept of the Rentier state is inadequate and it is hoped that the empirical evidence in this book has shown why.

Some policy implications for Lebanon

There are four key policy recommendations that I propose for the Lebanon, stemming from the research findings:

(1) Policy focus: Social care programmes need to redefine the object of their interventions by separating income poverty from the 'social case'. Family care needs to be supported as a viable social care programme, which cannot be substituted by institutional care. Credit programmes and income-generation projects need to target poor populations better and provide long-term solutions to income poverty as opposed to quick fixes of small loans.

(2) Structure of policy elaboration: Increasing coordination among NGOs and encouraging the role of the state as ultimate arbitrator in setting the agenda for social services would harmonise the social sector, promote better service standards and even ultimately promote nation-building. In order to achieve this, it is important to define the parameters of religious activity. Crucially, it is important to institute structures of accountability between service users and service providers and between the state and service providers.

(3) Religious welfare and post-war reconciliation: This research has shown that there are more similarities among the NGOs in Lebanon than they recognise. The sectarian structure of Lebanese politics is dividing the NGOs and the populations they serve, whereas religious welfare conceptualised as universal human experience could form the basis of viable social reconciliation in

post-war Lebanon. Welfare organisations have the capacity in Lebanon to pave the way for national reconciliation only if they can separate sectarian politics from their social work.

(4) *Citizenship education and legitimacy of social welfare:* It is important that the legitimacy of social policy be promoted through citizenship education. Only the state could harmonise such coordination among the NGOs by pronouncing a viable vision of the good society instead of adopting a palliative approach to the ills of market liberalism. Such ideas were already expressed by interviewees at some of the NGOs and the MSA during the fieldwork for this book.

The Middle East: a future for religious welfare?

What are the obstacles facing progressive development of social policy in the Middle East and what role can religion play in developing the social and political base for such progressive action?

I would argue that the primary problem in the region of the Middle East is political and to a lesser extent cultural. It is not economic because as a region, it is one of the wealthiest in the world, with GDP per capita reaching over US$25,000 in some of the Gulf states (UNDP, 2008). The primary problem in the region is also not social: societies in the region remain fairly tightly knit family units and problems of crime and corruption are very often a result of survival needs and oversized political bureaucracies. In terms of health and education, it is true that the region lags behind in terms of gender equality and participation but many women are increasingly entering the labour force due to economic necessity and higher levels of education.

The key obstacles facing the region are its undemocratic police states, the high levels of corruption, particularly in the public sector, which decades of economic and political malpractice have produced (Behdad, 2006; Roy, 2006) and the constant meddling of external international and regional political forces in the internal affairs of the region, including Lebanon. The resolution of the conflict with Israel is also part of the political impasse in the region. Military spending will continue as well as the constant problem of post-war reconstruction. Underpinning all of these forces is a cultural factor: a lack of self-reflexivity and critical thinking in the region, especially at public sector level. This is made even more complicated by the co-option of intellectuals along particular political lines as relations of patronage and feudalism continue to pervade society. Perhaps one possible positive effect of 9/11 is that Muslims have begun to feel the pressure for the need to ask themselves about who they are and why it is that they are perceived as socially regressive. Perhaps also the revival of interest in religion in the social sciences will allow deeper and more critical studies of the Muslim world to be carried out (Sutton and Vertigans, 2005).

So it seems that there is a tall order to social transformation before we can have effective social policy in the region. Does the Middle East need its own

Islamic reformation? I would argue that there are enough progressive-thinking Muslims around the world. Tripp (2006) argues that the Muslim world already had its reformation in the late 19th and early 20th century. The problem is they have very little scope for political activism in the region and are not willing to play the political game asked of them. Global political interference does not help internal self-critical thinking either.

The most pragmatic and accessible solution lies in RWOs. In spite of their traditional approach to family and the fact that they do not have sophisticated means of self-evaluation, religious groups exercise tremendous public influence and are having a direct impact on the lay population. They also have regional links that can help foster regional reconciliation. There also needs to be a more global reconciliation of inter-faith dialogue.

Clearly, many forces are at play, which is why I return to the simple pragmatic precept on which this whole book is based: let us give RWOs the scope to coordinate with each other, with government personnel and crucially with international development institutions in a framework that can provide a common agenda for social policy.

A final question remains: what if these religious groups are terrorist organisations? I will address the case of Hizbullah as this is the main Islamic social movement discussed in this book. I am not the first researcher to argue that Hizbullah is a legitimate political movement with elected lay deputies in the Lebanese government and a credible social mission spanning 30 years that has to be credited in some way for the social and economic development of the Shi'a community in Lebanon. Jaber (1997), Shadid (2001), Saad-Ghoreyeb (2002) and Harb (2006) have made this argument before me. Clark (2004) has produced further evidence from Egypt, Jordan and Yemen to show that Islamic welfare organisations are interested in just that, and moreover, that many of them are middle-class professional networks that are not primarily interested in poverty.

In the case of Hizbullah, if this organisation is to be accused of offering social welfare services in exchange for votes, then anyone who visits any of the other welfare organisations discussed in this book would find that, in Lebanon, the sectarian mentality pervades every dimension of society. Every welfare organisation has its political backing. With Hizbullah, part of the answer also lies in Islam itself: politics and religion work in mutual symbiosis (Saad-Ghoreyeb, 2002). It is impossible to separate Hizbullah's religious mission from its political identity. Likewise, it is virtually impossible to separate the political control Hizbullah has over particular geographical areas of Lebanon – from the southern suburb of Beirut southwards of the country – from its social welfare commitments. It is to a large extent inevitable that any Lebanese citizen living in these mainly Shi'a-populated areas and needing some sort of social or economic help will turn at one point or another to Hizbullah-affiliated organisations – as they may do to other Shi'a organisations.

But what we can distinguish between are the services Hizbullah offers to its military wing (the fighters, their families and the martyr-related social services) and the services it offers to the wider civilian population – the latter are what I have focused on in this book and which, I argue, deserve the legitimacy of the title 'social welfare services'. To this end, Emdad will indeed seek to instil 'correct' moral values in its beneficiaries, as all the welfare organisations do in Lebanon (which I have already demonstrated in this book) but it will not trade social services for political support of Hizbullah. Such is the logic of all of the Lebanese welfare organisations discussed in this book.

Some recent politically geared publications such as Berman and Laitin (2008) and to a certain extent Benthall and Bellion-Jourdan (2003) that include discussion of Hizbullah's social services provide no empirical evidence of direct contact with the social services provided by Hizbullah-affiliated organisations. It is difficult, from the perspective of this book, to find legitimate grounds for their arguments.

The questions that remain, as outlined in Chapter One, are as follows. Can governments and international development institutions find the political will to engage on an equal footing with religious groups and to see them as valid public actors? Can academic observers engage rationally with the contribution of RWOs to human well-being? The challenge for RWOs is to be able to put their message across in such a way that they are not misunderstood.

Conclusion

The main thrust of this chapter has been to consider some of the key lessons that can be deduced from the vast array of experiences described in the preceding chapters on the role of religion in social welfare. These experiences point to the positive role that religiously inspired groups have played in civil society across the world, including in the US and in Europe. A distinction has been drawn between clerics actively working in government writing government policy and lay social actors who are inspired by their religious ideals. The latter, I have argued, can contribute positively if they participate in a proper democratic system that gives them voice to organise.

The chapter has emphasised the importance of moral values for any political system to function effectively. Religion is a value system that can provide resources, moral authority and effective action at the local level for social welfare purposes. Religiously inspired public action has played a key role in developing a healthly civil society in many modern-day democracies.

Finally, the chapter has focused on policy recommendations for Lebanon and the Middle East. It has been acknowledged that there are major political obstacles in the region that impede effective social action at a time when these countries are not bereft of resources. There are also cultural obstacles that require Muslim societies, and Arab ones in particular, to re-vision their future in a critical manner and what aspirations they have for themselves.

Religious welfare has thus been presented as an immediate pragmatic solution for building bridges, healing souls and imaging a better future for the region.

Conclusion

As Gorski (2005, p 189) argues, the revival of interest in religion in the social sciences is due to a variety of historical and intellectual forces that have converged in the post-Cold War era:

- growing criticism of enlightenment thinking, the decline of modernism and materialist Marxism and the increasing post-modern awareness of the need to respond to multiculturalism;
- the increasing importance of cultural analysis in the social sciences;
- the emergence of a new generation of macro-sociologists whose political leanings have been formed after the fall of the Berlin Wall;
- a generalised revival of religious activism across the globe including the Western nations.

These are welcome developments as they facilitate the subject matter of this book. However, I would add further that in the case of Middle East social policy and of Islamic welfare, a focus on religion in public policy has been a long time coming. It is a gap that came to my mind some time before 9/11 as part of a simple awareness shared by many others that much more was going on in the Middle East than oil, repression of women and war. Indeed, it was/is the simple (or simplistic?) belief that we could still find new possibilities for positive social action in this region and that this could be based on the pragmatic premise of building on what already works.

This book thus marks a preliminary attempt to consider the role of religion in social welfare from the perspectives of local social actors in a Middle Eastern context. Drawing on the case of Lebanon and using supplementary evidence from Egypt, Iran and Turkey, it has embarked on the objective of exploring the dynamic characters of religious identity and values as these provide real solutions to real social problems. My underlying concern has been to understand how religious welfare is conceptualised, how it is applied in practice and what value it effectively holds as a basis for social policy in Lebanon and the wider Middle East region.

The primary objective of this book has been to describe and understand how welfare providers and users in Lebanon perceive religious welfare, employ it to achieve goals of human well-being and finally evaluate its impact on their lives. I have supplemented these subjective perceptions with my own fieldwork observations. The subsequent mapping of religious welfare I have produced has provided a platform on which I have synthesised the lay experience of religious welfare in Lebanon into a more abstract discussion aimed at contributing to the theoretical conceptualisation of social policy and human welfare in the Middle East.

In so doing, I have highlighted how a cultural perspective is extremely relevant to social policy analysis since, as the Lebanese case shows, human ethics is plural in nature and there is a qualitative diversity in human societies around the world that needs to be accounted for if policy analysis and making are to become more responsive to their target populations. I have supplemented this perspective of cultural relativism in the book with an analysis of the power structures and decision-making processes within which social policy and religious welfare are defined in Lebanon. To this extent, the book has responded to what I would regard as a prime concern in policy analysis, which is sensitivity to whose interests are ultimately represented in resource allocation and policy decisions within the public sphere.

Chapter Two set the scene for the general discussion in the book by reviewing what the five world faiths say about social welfare and how they have interacted with the formal apparatus of public policy to influence social welfare. The world faiths of Hinduism, Buddhism, Judaism, Christianity and Islam are all depicted as sharing fundamental universal values about solidarity, equality and justice. At the same time, they evolved dynamically with the environment around them. Thus, they have been influenced by the ideologies of capitalism and socialism, as much as they have shaped the development of social policy around the world. I have argued that while the clerical establishment may not write policy as such, religious groups are actively involved in setting the moral standards by which society lives and public policy is devised.

Chapter Three set the country context for the book by providing a social and political profile of Lebanon and the particular historical trajectory of social policy there. As the Middle East's most multi-faith country, Lebanon offers an insightful perspective on the politics/welfare/religion nexus. But this is also a country in deep political turmoil, where a historically weak state has paved the way for civil war, and for the dominance of religion in the social welfare sphere. The chapter argued that concern with the core issues of social policy such as poverty and social protection is a very recent phenomenon in Lebanon and has been spurred by the influence of international development agencies, primarily the World Bank and UN. Otherwise, social policy in Lebanon has been residual in nature, a characteristic in common with its Arab neighbours where the general policy focus on economic growth is seen as the driver of social progress. Historical accounts show that ever since the independence era, social welfare in Lebanon has been mediated by wealthy elites and religious leaders.

Chapter Four focused on the normative context within which social action is conceived in Lebanon in order to explore the philosophy from which social action draws meaning. This marks an attempt to begin at the beginning by locating religious welfare within its institutional discourses and moral contexts. The chapter drew profiles of the actors who initiate social action in Lebanon and the other three countries, what their motivations and objectives are and how they package their work. As such, I have unpacked the world of religious welfare through its underlying values and key welfare actors. I have proposed five types of welfare actors, namely the elite family, the religious order, the popular social movement, the para-state organisation and the international humanitarian organisation. The RWO sector has been depicted as being more powerful and dynamic than the over-politicised and under-resourced ministries, and in some cases more effective at relief than international humanitarian agencies.

The chapter made two main conclusions, one related to the role of welfare, the other to the nature of welfare. The conclusions suggest a paradox in the conceptualisation and use of welfare in Lebanon:

- The role of welfare is instrumental: if we consider the definitions and objectives attributed by social actors to what they do, then we find that social welfare is conceptualised instrumentally as an annex to political or personal ambitions.
- The nature of religious welfare is premised on spiritual faith as a counter-logic to social welfare based on social insurance. Here, social welfare has an intrinsic value that is built on notions of social service and human solidarity whereby social service is a human obligation and an act of worship.

Yet I have provided evidence of sectarianism among all of the organisations in Lebanon, which reinforces the conclusion made about the role of welfare. As a policy elaboration process, I have argued that social policy is dominated by religious and political elites who nevertheless enjoy moral authority. A generally poorly educated core of service users desperate for social assistance meant that channels of accountability were tenuous. This resulted in a rather paternalistic relationship between RWOs and beneficiaries.

The chapter argued that the conceptualisation of religious welfare constitutes a value system that makes a philosophical shift in social policy away from social insurance as statutory or contribution-based social protection to a notion of social protection based on God's blessing and religious faith. The chapter identified three modes of religious expression: spiritual faith, sectarian politics and religious practice. Each of these demonstrated the diversity of the RWOs I researched and how religion, broadly defined, impacted in different ways on welfare. The religious content of services was, I argued, more a matter of supply than demand and reflected the control the NGO sector had over the social agenda in Lebanon.

The argument then progressed in Chapter Five to consider the actual mechanics and dynamics of service delivery, consumption and evaluation. Here, I was concerned with how social policy makers in Lebanon conceptualised the object of their interventions, how they interpreted the needs of their target populations and, thus, how well they responded to them. Social welfare was explored in this chapter as a system of provision and a measure of outcome. The key question I sought to answer was how far policy treated the causes of human impoverishment or its symptoms.

For this purpose, the chapter engaged with definitions of the key concepts that have informed this book, namely human needs, poverty, social care and development, which were framed as key dilemmas of policy elaboration. The latter was predicated on the tension between long-term socioeconomic investment or development and short-term fixes of social care and relief assistance. Significant concepts that emerged during data collection were also considered, such as *istid`aaf*, which adds political and structural dimensions to the understanding of poverty.

The chapter considered social care and micro-credit programmes in detail and concluded that social action in Lebanon was working more on palliative in-kind services. Consequently, the very make-up of programmes impeded treatment of the causes of social problems and reaching the poorest of the poor. The focus on income poverty was itself blurred by concern with needs and an inadequate application of the eligibility criteria that was predicated on the social case. This led to institutional care acting as an inappropriate treatment for the problem of income poverty. Religious welfare organisations saw themselves as primarily relieving a burden off poor populations and argued that only government could solve the causes of poverty through job creation. Thus, the first main conclusion of the chapter was that the MSA in Lebanon and RWOs needed to review needs interpretation and policy focus, particularly in the area of social care.

The second main conclusion reached in Chapter Five related to how welfare was defined as a measure of outcome. A paramount preoccupation with preventing deviance and maintaining social integration through moral rectitude confirmed that morality and social cohesion were key elements of the social programmes offered by the RWOs. Indeed, such concern sometimes displaced the urgency of income poverty. Nevertheless, concern with developing capabilities and encouraging self-sufficiency were key measures of welfare for social actors, which demonstrated a progressive move towards positive social transformation.

Chapter Six took up this thread of the argument by focusing on the nature of social cohesion and solidarity in Lebanon, which I argued was based on the two logics of power and morality. Heavily focused on ascribed social ties based on family, the sect, patronage or regional community, social cohesion in Lebanon entailed mechanisms of vertical integration and a dualistic understanding of power as a linear resource that could be accumulated. Social cohesion thus took on particular definitions in Lebanon as (a) solidarity that welfare providers showed towards those less fortunate and (b) integration into the established social order by welfare users. Religious welfare organisations were thus depicted as reproducing and sustaining this hierarchical social order. Education and developing capabilities were key strategies in this regard.

The chapter concluded that in Lebanon (as in the rest of the literature on religious welfare), social welfare was more about getting human nature right through an emphasis on preventing deviance and fulfilling one's humanity than about modifying societal or market structures. Welfare actors considered that an individual's position within the social order depended on their own actions. Agency was thus more important than structure in understanding how processes of integration and exclusion worked. Indeed, the latter concept was shown to have little significance in the context of Lebanon due to the nature of social cohesion there.

Takaaful (solidarity) was also an important concept emerging during fieldwork. Solidarity was intricately related to an enactment of basic human nature and the natural emotional bond that ties all human beings through compassion. The place of social cohesion in policy existed on three levels:

- it has rhetorical value as human solidarity;
- it has strategic value as a means of promoting development, micro-credit and family care;
- it has an outcome value as a measure of morality and social integration.

The critical conclusion made in this chapter was that it was individuals with little or no family support who tended to seek help from RWOs.

Chapter Seven considered the theoretical ramifications of the Lebanese case for the study of social policy. It engaged with the existing literature on welfare regimes and social reproduction in order to determine how better to understand social policy in Lebanon. The Lebanese case was presented as having similar features to the Southern European model of welfare proposed by Ferrera (1996) where clientelism, religion, public–private mix in health services and dualism in benefits were prominent.

I proposed a model of welfare, based on the Lebanese case, which I denoted as the 'social ethics–welfare particularism' model. The chapter drew on a wider array of factors and actors in the welfare system in Lebanon in order to make this conclusion. Thus, it considered the system of social insurance, which is occupation based, and highlighted features of Lebanon that are also typical of many low-income contexts such as the focus on health and education services and the irrelevance of the measure of decommodification since basic needs are more important.

Indeed, human needs and morality are the sine qua non of religious welfare in Lebanon, which is why human ethics is at the heart of the welfare model I proposed. The particularistic aspect of the model reflects the importance of the private sphere, expressed in a variety ways: networks of clientelism and *wasta* through which resources and services are accessed, the importance of the market in service provision through fee-paying services, contracts with the RWOs for social care services and the primordial role of the personal human experience in faith and moral behaviour.

What value, then, can we draw from these conclusions in order to advance a constructive agenda for social policy that offers sustainable solutions to real social problems, which governments in the South could support without political interference, and which international development institutions could recognise as legitimate welfare action? I would argue that there is a need not only for clearer enunciation of social policies but also for delineation of a social vision *by* countries of the South. Kabeer (2004) suggests that this requires the redefinition of the social sphere altogether.

Religious welfare does not come with a ready-made blueprint for the treatment of socioeconomic ills or human well-being. Certainly, religious organisations are not the only welfare-oriented actors in lower-income countries. As H13 argued during our interview, there is no Islamic economics save for basic core principles on ethical economic conduct such as not charging interest and the importance of *zakat*. According to H13, religion only offers the basic structural parameters within which humanity is free to improvise. The sharing of ideas across ideologies, professions and indeed nations is thus not just possible but inevitable.

The important message that I want to put across here is that the religious worldview is precisely that: *a* worldview. In that sense, it has acted as a cultural axis and a *civilisational* force, in the words of many of my research participants. Islam in particular has had just that effect in the Arab world. Consequently, I have tried to render and scrutinise religious welfare in this book as a set of social policy measures concerned with human well-being in this life and not simply as a system of ritual worship in the scramble to heaven. The fact that many religious leaders and institutions in countries around the world are also closely connected to the ruling political establishments is a point of critical reflection for the nature and role of social policy (Harcourt, 2003).

Where I have discussed faith or spirituality, this has been in the context of analysing the experience of social welfare in Lebanon, how it is conceptualised, packaged, delivered and evaluated. As an inherently moral and ethical discourse, religious welfare merely reaffirms that all perspectives on social welfare bury within them certain ideological and normative convictions about the nature of the good society.

This also emphasises that culture must take a more central role in social policy analysis, indeed that cultural relativism, as Minogue (2002, p 130) argues, may well be the only "universal moral principle". Therefore, if social policy is an intrinsically moral act (Spicker, 2000) and development policy too is not immune to moral discourses of human well-being (Harcourt, 2003), then perhaps it is time that we faced such moral debates head on. In Chapter Eight, I argued that the social welfare state may be a cultural phenomenon of Western capitalist democracy and there may be other institutional forms, indeed other avenues for positive public action, that may be pursued in the region of the Middle East. Religious welfare offers a pragmatic solution in this respect. I have thus sought to provide a re-reading of the history of social policy in the Middle East, which I supplement directly with the empirical evidence supplied in this book. International development agencies can achieve a lot by inviting RWOs in the Middle East to the UN and World Bank offices to discuss their talents, their shortcomings and what role they play in shaping the future of the region.

To conclude, perhaps the first and the biggest challenge that this book is proposing is one related to our collective mindset on the role of religion in public life. To this end, it is important to remember that there also are progressive-minded Middle Easterners who would oppose religious involvement in the public sphere just as vehemently as any seasoned secular social policy thinker in the West might.

However, as Skocpol's (2000) historical review of the legacy left to US democracy by 19th-century religiously inspired voluntary action and social provision notes:

> Progressive-minded Americans, meanwhile, are shying away from religious or moral calls for social change, viewing them either as irrelevant, or inherently particularistic, or as socially and politically divisive. But this leaves Americans who want social justice lacking for arguments and institutional ties needed to energize broad majorities of fellow citizens on behalf of visions of fellowships and social justice ... no one has yet found any substitute for the democratic energy unleashed historically by the best in America's tradition of biblically inspired associationalism. Nor has anyone found a way to justify broad and inclusive social provision without appealing to moral ideals of community as well as the economic calculations of individuals. All Americans, therefore, have a strong stake in reconnecting with – and reinventing in new forms – the best traditions of religious and moral inspiration for democracy and generous social provision in our nation's history. Unless such reconciliations happen, it is hard to see what can stop the march of inequality and pure market individualism from undercutting American democracy and shared social provision for the future. (Skocpol, 2000, pp 47-8)

For those of us who know the Middle East well, the above is perhaps not very far off the mark. It has been the modest task of this book to begin to draw a picture of some of the best examples of associational life and social provision in the modern Middle East. For, the foundations of social policy everywhere in the world are religious, and it is to the foundations of religion in the Middle East that this book has turned in order to begin to imagine something new for the region, based on something that is already very old.

Bibliography[1]

A'al Mawdudi, Abdul (1976) *Human Rights in Islam*, The Islamic Foundation, Leicester.

Abdo, Nahla (2006) 'Muslim Family Law: Articulating Gender, Class and the State', in *Islam and the Everyday World: Public Policy Dilemmas*, Behdad, Sohrab and Nomani, Farhad (eds), Routledge, London, pp 88-112.

Adams, Julia, Clements, Elisabeth S. and Shola Orloff, Ann (eds) (2005) *Remaking Modernity: Politics, History and Sociology*, Duke University Press, Durham and London.

Adloff, Frank (2006) 'Religion and Social-Political Action: The Catholic Church, Catholic Charities and the American Welfare State', *International Review of Sociology*, vol 16 (1), pp 1-30.

Ahmad, Ziauddin (1991) *Islam, Poverty and Income Distribution*, The Islamic Foundation, Leicester.

Ahmed, Akbar and Donnan, Hastings (1994) 'Islam in the Age of Postmodernity', in *Islam, Globalisation and Postmodernity*, Ahmed, Akbar S. and Donnan, Hastings (eds), Routledge, London.

Alcock, Pete (2001) 'The Comparative Context', in *International Social Policy*, Alcock, Pete and Craig, Gary (eds), Palgrave, Houndsmill, pp 1-25.

Alcock, Pete and Scott, Duncan (2007) 'Voluntary and Community Sector Welfare', in *Understanding the Mixed Economy of Welfare*, Powell, Martin (ed), The Policy Press, Bristol, pp 83-106.

Aldridge, Alan (2000) *Religion in the Contemporary World: A Sociological Introduction*, Polity Press, Cambridge.

Aldridge, Alan (2007) *Religion in the Contemporary World: A Sociological Introduction* (2nd edition), Polity Press, Cambridge.

Al Zeera, Zahra (2001) *Wholeness and Holiness in Education: An Islamic Perspective*, International Institute of Islamic Thought, London.

Antoun, Richard T. and Hegland, Mary E. (eds) (1987) *Religious Resurgence: Contemporary Cases in Islam, Christianity and Judaism*, Syracuse University Press, New York.

Ariyaratne, A.T. (1980) 'The Role of Buddhist Monks in Development', *World Development*, vol 8 (7/8), pp 587-90.

Arksey, Hilary and Glendinning, Caroline (2007) 'Informal Welfare', in *Understanding the Mixed Economy of Welfare*, Powell, Martin (ed), The Policy Press, Bristol, pp 107-28.

---

[1]All translations are by the author. Arabic titles are accompanied by English translations in brackets.

Arts, Wil and Gelissen, John (2002) 'Three Worlds of Welfare Capitalism or More? A State-of-the-Art Report', *Journal of European Social Policy*, vol 12 (2), pp 137-58.

Ashencaen Crabtree, Sara, Hussein, Fatima and Spalek, Basia (2008) *Islam and Social Work: Debating Values, Transforming Practices*, The Policy Press, Bristol.

Assaf, Georges and El-Fil Rana (2000) 'Resolving the Issue of War Displacement in Lebanon', *Forced Migration Review*, vol 7, pp 31-3.

Atherton, John (ed) (1994) *Social Christianity: A Reader*, Society for Promoting Christian Knowledge (SPCK), London.

Ayubi, Nazih N. M. (1983) 'The Politics of Militant Islamic Movements in the Middle East', *Journal of International Affairs*, vol 36, pp 271-83.

Azer, Adel and Afifi, Elham (1992) *Social Support Systems for the Aged in Egypt*, United Nations University Press, Tokyo.

Baalbaki, Munir (2001) *Al-Mawrid: A Modern English–Arabic Dictionary 2001*, International Book Centre, Beirut.

Bacon, Derek (2006) 'Faith Based Organisations and Welfare Provisions in Northern Ireland and North America: Whose Agenda?', in *Landscapes of Voluntarism: New Spaces of Health, Welfare and Governance*, Milligan, Christine and Conradson, David (eds), The Policy Press, Bristol, pp 173-90.

Bainbridge, William Sims (2007) 'New Age Religion and Irreligion' in *The Sage Handbook of the Sociology of Religion*, Beckford, James and Demerath, N.J. III (eds), Sage Publications, London, pp 248-66.

Balchin, Cassandra (2003) 'With Her Feet on the Ground: Women, Religion and Development in Muslim Communities', *Development*, vol 46 (4), pp 39-49.

Barrientos, Armando (2004) 'Latin America: Towards a Liberal-Informed Welfare Regime', in *Insecurity and Welfare Regimes in Asia, Africa and Latin America: Social Policy in a Development Context*, Gough, Ian and Wood, Geoff (eds) with Barrientos, Armando, Beval, Phillipa, Davis, Peter and Room, Graham, Cambridge University Press, Cambridge, pp 88-120.

Bassam, Tibi (2001) *Islam between Culture and Politics*, Palgrave, in association with the Weatherhead Center for International Affairs, Harvard University, Basingstoke.

Bauberot, Jean (2007) 'Existe-T-il, Une Religion Civile Republicaine?', in *French Politics, Culture and Society*, vol 25 (2), pp 1-18.

Bayat, Asef (2006) 'The Political Economy of Social Policy in Egypt', in *Social Policy in the Middle East: Economic, Political and Gender Dynamics*, Karshenas, Massoud and Moghadam, Valentine M. (eds), United Nations Research Institute for Social Development, Palgrave Macmillan, Basingstoke, pp 135-55.

Bayat, Mangol (1980) 'Islam in Pahlavi and Post-Pahlavi Iran: A Cultural Revolution?', in *Islam and Development: Religion and Sociopolitical Change*, Esposito, John L. (ed), Syracuse University Press, New York, pp 87-106.

Bayley, Michael (1989) *Welfare – A Moral Issue? A Christian Perspective*, Diocese of Sheffield Social Responsibility Committee, Sheffield.

Bebbington, Anthony (1994) 'Theory and Practice in Indigenous Agriculture: Knowledge, Agency and Organization', in *Rethinking Social Development: Theory, Research and Practice*, Booth, David (ed), Longman, London.

Beblawi, Hazem (1990) 'The Rentier State in the Arab World', in *The Arab State*, Luciani, Giacomo (ed), Routledge, London.

Beckford, James A. (1989) *Religion in Advanced Industrial Society*, Routledge, London.

Beckford, James, A. and Demerath, N.J. III (2007) 'Introduction', in *The Sage Handbook of the Sociology of Religion*, in Beckford, James and Demerath, N.J. III (eds), Sage Publications, London, pp 1–16.

Beckford, James, A. and Richardson, James, T. (2007) 'Religion and Regulation', in *The Sage Handbook of the Sociology of Religion*, in Beckford, James and Demerath, N.J. III (eds), Sage Publications, London, pp 396–418.

Behdad, Sorab (2006) 'Islam, Revivalism and Public Policy', in *Islam and the Everyday World: Public Policy Dilemmas*, Behdad, Sohrab and Nomani, Farhad (eds), Routledge, London, pp 1–37.

Behdad, Sohrab and Nomani, Farhad (eds) (2006) *Islam and the Everyday World: Public Policy Dilemmas*, Routledge, London.

Bellah, Robert N. (1970) *Beyond Belief: Essays on Religion in a Post-Traditional World*, HarperCollins, London and New York.

Ben Romdhane, Mahmoud (2006) 'Social Policy and Development in Tunisia since Independence: A Political Perspective', in *Social Policy in the Middle East: Economic, Political and Gender Dynamics*, Karshenas, Massoud and Moghadam, Valentine M. (eds), United Nations Research Institute for Social Development, Palgrave Macmillan, Basingstoke, pp 31–77.

Benthall, Jonathan and Bellion-Jourdan, Jerome (2003) *The Charitable Crescent: Politics of Aid in the Muslim World*, I.B. Taurus, London.

Berger, Peter L. (2001) 'Reflections on the Sociology of Religion', *Sociology of Religion*, vol 62 (4), pp 443–54.

Berman, Eli and Laitin, David D. (2008) *Religion, Terrorism and Public Goods: Testing the Club Model*, Working Paper 13725, NBER Working Paper Series, National Bureau of Economic Research, Cambridge, MA, accessed 15/09/08 at www.nber.org/papers/w13725

Bevan, Phillipa (2004a) 'Conceptualising In/Security Regimes', in *Insecurity and Welfare Regimes in Asian, Africa and Latin America: Social Policy in a Development Context*, Gough, Ian and Wood, Geoff (eds), with Barrientos, Armando, Beval, Phillipa, Davis, Peter and Room, Graham, Cambridge University Press, Cambridge, pp 88–120.

Bevan, Phillipa (2004b) 'The Dynamics of Africa's In/Security Regimes', in *Insecurity and Welfare Regimes in Asian, Africa and Latin America: Social Policy in a Development Context*, Gough, Ian and Wood, Geoff (eds), with Barrientos, Armando, Beval, Phillipa, Davis, Peter and Room, Graham, Cambridge University Press, Cambridge, pp 202–54.

Beydoun, Ahmad (1994a) 'Images du Corps, Esprit de Corps et Démocratie', in *Du Privé au Public, Espaces et Valeurs du Politique au Proche-Orient*, Cermoc, Beirut.

Beydoun, Ahmad (1994b) 'L'Identité des Libanais', in *Le Liban aujourd'hui*, Kiwan, Fadia (ed), Cermoc, Cnrs Éditions, Paris.

Beyhum, Nabil (1994) 'Les Démarcations au Liban d'Hier à Aujourd'hui' in *Le Liban aujourd'hui*, Kiwan, Fadia (ed), Cermoc, Cnrs Éditions, Paris.

Blaikie, Norman (2000) *Designing Social Research: The Logic of Anticipation*, Polity Press, Cambridge.

Blair, Tony (2008) 'Faith and Globalisation', in *Faith and Life in Britain*, Blair, Tony, Thompson, Mark, Williams, Dr Rowan, Hague, William, Neuberger, Rabbi Julia and Murphy-O'Connor, Cardinal Cormac (eds), Matthew James Publishing, Chelmsford, pp 9-20.

Bonne, Emmanuel (1995) *Vie Publique, Patronage et Clientèle: Rafic Hariri à Saïda*, Iremam, Cnrs – Université d'Aix-en-Provence, France.

Bonoli, Giuliano (1997) 'Classifying Welfare Regimes: A two-dimension approach' *Journal of Social Policy*, vol 26(3), pp 351-72.

Boratav, Korkut and Ozugurlu, Metin (2006) 'Social Policies and Distribution Dynamics in Turkey: 1923–2002', in *Social Policy in the Middle East: Economic, Political and Gender Dynamics*, Karshenas, Massoud and Moghadam, Valentine M. (eds), United Nations Research Institute for Social Development, Palgrave Macmillan, Basingstoke, pp 156-89.

Bornstein, Erica (2002) 'Developing Faith: Theologies of Economic Development in Zimbabwe', *Journal of Religion in Africa*, vol 32 (1), pp 4-31.

Bowen, Donna Lee (2004a) 'Islamic Law and the Position of Women', in *Islam and Social Policy*, Heyneman, Stephen P. (ed), Vanderbilt University Press, Nashville, TN, pp 44-117.

Bowen, Donna Lee (2004b) 'Islamic Law and Family Planning', in *Islam and Social Policy*, Heyneman, Stephen P. (ed), Vanderbilt University Press, Nashville, TN, pp 118-55.

Brazier, David (2001) *The New Buddhism*, Palgrave, New York.

Bruce, Steve (1998) *Conservative Protestant Politics*, Oxford University Press, Oxford.

Bruneau, Thomas C. (1980) 'The Catholic Church and Development in Latin America: The Role of Basic Christian Communities', *World Development*, vol 8 (7/8), pp 535-44.

Bugra, Ayse (2007) 'Poverty and Citizenship: An Overview of the Social-Policy Environment in Republican Turkey', *International Journal of Middle Eastern Studies*, vol 39, pp 33-52.

Bugra, Ayse and Adar, Sinem (2008) 'Social Policy Change in Countries Without Mature Welfare States: The Case of Turkey', *New Perspectives on Turkey*, vol 38, pp 83-106.

Bullis, Ronald K. (1996) *Spirituality in Social Work and Practice*, Taylor and Francis, London.

Busapapathumrong, Pattamaporn (2005) 'Welfare Philosophy in Buddhism', *The Journal of the Royal Institute of Thailand*, vol 30 (2), pp 516-20.

Byrne, David (1999) *Social Exclusion*, Open University Press, Buckingham and Philadelphia, PA.

Casanova, José (2001) 'Religion, the New Millennium, and Globalization' in *Sociology of Religion*, vol 62 (4), pp 415-41.

Casanova, José (2008) 'Public Religions Revisited', in *Religion: Beyond A Concept*, de Vries, Hent (ed), Fordham University Press, New York, pp 101-19.

Castles, Francis G. (1994) 'On Religion and Public Policy: Does Catholicism Make a Difference?', *European Journal of Political Research*, vol 25, pp 19-40.

Chan, Chak-Kwan and Lap-Yan, Kung (2000) 'Christian Welfare Ideologies: The Basis of Human Welfare', *Social Thought*, vol 19 (4), pp 53-73.

Chau, Ruby C.M. and Kam Yu, Wai (2005) 'Is Welfare un-Asian?', in *East Asian Welfare Regimes in Transition: From Confucianism to Globalisation*, Walker, Alan (ed), The Policy Press, Bristol, pp 21-48.

Chiu, Sammy and Wong, Victor (2005) 'Hong Kong: from familialistic to Confucian Welfare' in *East Asian Welfare Regimes in Transition: From Confucianism to Globalisation*, Walker, Alan (ed), The Policy Press, Bristol, pp 73-94.

Choueiri, Youssef (1993) 'Introduction', in *State and Society in Lebanon and Syria*, Choueiri, Youssef (ed), University of Exeter Press, Exeter.

Choueiri, Youssef (1999) 'Lebanon', in *The Middle East and North Africa 2000, Europa Regional Surveys of the World*, Mcintyre, Philip et al (eds), Europa Publications, London.

Clark, Janine A. (2004) *Islam, Charity and Activism: Middle Class Networks and Social Welfare in Egypt, Jordan and Yemen*, Indiana University Press, Bloomington, IN.

Clarke, Gerard and Jennings, Michael (2008) 'Introduction', in *Development, Civil Society and Faith Based Organisations: Bridging the Sacred and the Secular*, Clarke, Gerard and Jennings, Michael (eds), Palgrave Macmillan, Basingstoke, pp 1-16.

Clarke, John (2000) 'A World of Difference? Globalization and the Study of Social Policy', in *Rethinking Social Policy*, Lewis, Gail, Gerwitz, Sharon and Clarke, John (eds), Open University and Sage Publications, London, Thousand Oaks, CA, and New Delhi.

Clarke, John (2004) *Changing Welfare, Changing States: New Directions in Social Policy*, Sage Publications, London.

Collins, Randall (2007) 'The Classical Tradition in Sociology of Religion', in *The Sage Handbook of the Sociology of Religion*, Beckford, James and Demerath, N.J. III (eds), Sage Publications, London, pp 19-38.

Conradson, David (2006) 'Values, Practices and Strategic Divestment: Christian Social Service Organisations in New Zealand', in *Landscapes of Voluntarism: New Spaces of Health, Welfare and Governance*, Milligan, Christine and Conradson, David (eds), The Policy Press, Bristol, pp 153-72.

Corm, Georges (1998) 'Reconstructing Lebanon's Economy', in *Economic Challenges Facing Middle Eastern and North African Countries*, Shafik, Nemat (ed), Macmillan, London.

Cornwall, Andrea and Gaventa, John (2000) 'From Users and Choosers to Makers and Shapers – Repositioning Participation in Social Policy', *IDS Bulletin*, vol 31(4), pp 50-9.

Cowen, Michael and Shenton, Robert (1995) 'The Invention of Development', in *Power of Development*, Crush, Jonathan (ed), Routledge, London.

Cowen, Michael and Shenton, Robert (1996) *Doctrines of Development*, Routledge, London.and New York.

Crecelius, Daniel (1980) 'The Course of Secularization in Modern Egypt', in *Islam and Development: Religion and Sociopolitical Change*, Esposito, John L. (ed), Syracuse University Press, New York, pp 49-70.

Creevey, Lucy (1980) 'Religious Attitudes and Development in Dakar, Senegal', *World Development*, vol 8 (7/8), pp 503-12.

Cristi, Marcela and Dawson, Lorne L. (2007) 'Civil Religion in America and in Global Context', in *The Sage Handbook of the Sociology of Religion*, Beckford, James and Demerath, N.J. III (eds), Sage Publications, London, pp 267-92.

Crush, Jonathan (1995) 'Imagining Development', in *Power of Development*, Crush, Jonathan (ed), Routledge, London.

Cummings, John Thomas, Askari, Hossein and Mustafa, Ahmad (1980) 'Islam and Modern Economic Change', in *Islam and Development: Religion and Sociopolitical Change*, Esposito, John L. (ed), Syracuse University Press, New York, pp 25-47.

Cunningham, Hugh (1998) 'Introduction', in *Charity, Philanthropy and Reform: From the 1690s to 1850*, Cunningham, Hugh and Innes, Joanna (eds), Macmillan, Basingstoke, pp 1-14.

Cunningham, Robert and Sarayrah, Yasin (1993) *Wasta, The Hidden Force in Middle Eastern Society*, Praeger, London.

Dah, Abdallah and Hijazi, Hussein (1997) *Tawzee' Addakhel, Namat Al-infaak wa Thaahira, Al Fukr fi Lubnan* [Income Redistribution, Patterns of Expenditure and Poverty in Lebanon], Lebanese Centre for Policy Studies, Beirut.

Daily Star (2004), accessed 15/08/04 at www.dailystar.co.lb

Dallal, Ahmad (2004) 'The Islamic Institution of Waqf: A Historical Overview', in *Islam and Social Policy*, Heyneman, Stephen P. (ed), Vanderbilt University Press, Nashville, TM, pp 13-43.

Davie, Grace (2001) 'Global Civil Religion: A European Perspective', *Sociology of Religion*, vol 62 (4), pp 455-73.

Davis, Eric (1987) 'Religion Against the State: A Political Economy of Religious Radicalism in Egypt and Israel', in *Religious Resurgence: Contemporary Cases in Islam, Christianity and Judaism*, Antoun, Richard T. and Hegland, Mary E. (eds), Syracuse University Press, New York, pp 145-65.

Davis, Francis, Paulhus, Elizabeth and Bradstock, Andrew (2008) *Moral, but no Compass: Government, Church and the Future of Welfare. A Report for the Church of England commissioned by the Rt. Rev Stephen Lowe, Bishop for Urban Life and Faith*, Matthew James Publishing, Chelmsford.

Davis, Peter (2001) 'Rethinking the Welfare Regime Approach: The Case of Bangladesh', *Global Social Policy*, vol 1 (1), pp 79-107.

Davis, Peter (2004) 'Rethinking the Welfare Regime Approach in the Context of Bangladesh', in *Insecurity and Welfare Regimes in Asia, Africa and Latin America: Social Policy in a Development Context* Gough, Ian and Wood, Geoff (eds), with Barrientos, Armando, Beval, Phillipa, Davis, Peter and Room, Graham, Cambridge University Press, Cambridge, pp 255-86.

Davis, Uri (1997) *Citizenship and the State: A Comparative Study of Citizenship Legislation in Israel, Jordan, Palestine, Syria and Lebanon*, Ithaca Press, Reading.

Deacon, Bob (2000) 'Globalisation: A Threat to Equitable Social Provision?', in *Social Policy Review 12*, Dean, Hartley, Sykes, Robert and Woods, Roberta (eds), Social Policy Association and University of Newcastle, Newcastle.

Deacon, Bob with Hulse, Michelle and Stubbs, Paul (1997) *Global Social Policy*, Sage Publications, Thousand Oaks, CA, and London.

Dean, Hartley (2001) 'Poverty and Citizenship: Moral Repertoires and Welfare Regimes', in *Poverty Reduction: What Role for the State in Today's Globalized Economy?*, Wilson, Francis, Kanji, Nazneen and Braathen, Einar (eds), Zed Books, London, pp 54-73.

Dean, Hartley (2006) *Social Policy*, Polity Press, Cambridge.

Dean, Hartley and Khan, Zafar (1997) 'Muslim Perspectives on Welfare', *Journal of Social Policy*, vol 26 (2), pp 193-209.

Deeb, Marius (1988) 'Shi'a Movements in Lebanon: Their Formation, Ideology, Social Basis and Links with Iran and Syria', *Third World Quarterly*, vol 10 (2), pp 683-98.

Deegan, Heather (1993) *The Middle East and Problems of Democracy*, Open University Press, Buckingham and Philadelphia, PA.

De Haan, Arjan (1998) 'Social Exclusion: An Alternative Concept for the Study of Deprivation?', *IDS Bulletin*, vol 29 (1).

Delibas, Kayhan (2009) 'Conceptualizing Islamic Movements: The Case of Turkey', *International Political Science Review*, vol 30 (1), pp 89-103.

Demerath, N.J. III (2007a) 'Secularization and Sacrilization Deconstructed and Reconstructed', in *The Sage Handbook of the Sociology of Religion*, Beckford, James and Demerath, N. J. III (eds), Sage Publications, London, pp 57-80.

Demerath, N.J. III (2007b) 'Religion and the State: Violence and Human Rights', in *The Sage Handbook of the Sociology of Religion*, Beckford, James and Demerath, N.J. III (eds), Sage Publications, London, pp 381-95.

Denoeux, Guilain (1993) *Urban Unrest in the Middle East, A Comparative Study of Informal Networks in Egypt, Iran and Lebanon*, State University of New York Press, Albany, NY.

Department for International Development (2000) 'Realising Human Rights for Poor People', accessed 09/12/00 at www.dfid.gov.uk/public/what/pdf/tsphuman.pdf

Destramau, Blandine (2000) 'Poverty, Exclusion and the Changing Role of the State in the Middle East', in *Social Policy Review 12*, Dean, Hartley, Sykes, Robert and Woods, Roberta (eds), Social Policy Association and University of Newcastle, Newcastle.

Destramau, Blandine (2001) 'Poverty, Discourse and State Power: A Case Study of Morocco', in *Poverty Reduction: What Role for the State in Today's Globalized Economy?*, Wilson, Francis, Kanji, Nazneen and Braathen, Einar (eds), Zed Books, London.

Devereux, Stephen and Cook, Sarah (2000) 'Does Social Policy Meet Social Needs?', *IDS Bulletin*, vol 31 (4), pp 63-73.

Donnison, David (1989) *Policies for a Just Society*, Macmillan, Basingstoke.

Donovan, Mark (2003) 'The Italian State: No Longer Catholic, No Longer Christian', in *Church and State in Contemporary Europe: The Chimera of Neutrality*, Madeley, John T.S. and Enyedi, Zsolt (eds), Frank Cass, London.and Portland, OR, pp 94-115.

Economist, The (2002a) 'Faith-based Institutions: Compassionate Conservatism?', 16 February.

Economist, The (2002b) 'Mormon Welfare Schemes: Bishop's Move', 16 February.

Edwards, Michael (1994) 'Rethinking Social Development: The Search for Relevance', in *Rethinking Social Development: Theory, Research and Practice*, Booth, David (ed), Longman, London.

El-Amine, Adnan (1994) 'Hétérogénéité de l'Enseignement et Déqualification du Travail Éducatif', in *Le Liban aujourd'hui*, Kiwan, Fadia (ed), Cermoc, Cnrs Éditions, Paris.

El-Bizri, Dalal (1994) 'La Parole Islamiste de la Langue Libanaise', in *Le Liban Aujourd'hui*, Kiwan, Fadia (ed), Cermoc, Cnrs Éditions, Paris.

El-Bizri, Dalal (1995) *L'Ombre et Son Double: Femmes Islamistes, Libanaises et Modernes*, Cermoc, Beirut.

El-Ghonemy, Riad (1998) *Affluence and Poverty in the Middle East*, Routledge, London.

El-Khazen, Farid (1993) 'The Making and Unmaking of Lebanon's Political Elites from Independence to Ta'if', *The Beirut Review*, 6, pp 53-64.

El-Khazen, Farid (1994) 'Une Place pour le Liban: la Marginalisation de l'État dans un Espace Régional Réduit', in *Le Liban Aujourd'hui*, Kiwan, Fadia (ed), Cermoc, Cnrs Éditions, Paris.

Ellor, James, Netting, Ellen F. and Thibault, Jane M. (1999) *Religious and Spiritual Aspects of Human Service Practice*, University of South Carolina Press, Columbia, SC.

El-Mernissi, Fatima (1988) 'Democracy as Moral Imagination', in *Women in the Arab World*, Toubia, Nahid (ed), Zed Books, London.

Ennaji, Moha (2006) 'Social Policy in Morocco: History, Politics and Social Development', in *Social Policy in the Middle East: Economic, Political and Gender Dynamics*, Karshenas, Massoud and Moghadam, Valentine, M. (eds), United Nations Research Institute for Social Development and Palgrave Macmillan, Basingstoke, pp 109-34.

Enyedi, Zsolt (2003) 'Conclusion: Emerging Issues in the Study of Church–State Relations', in *Church and State in Contemporary Europe: The Chimera of Neutrality*, Madeley, John T. S. and Enyedi, Zsolt (eds), Frank Cass, London and Portland, OR, pp 216-31.

Ernst, Carl W. (2004) *Rethinking Islam in the Contemporary World*, Edinburgh University Press, Edinburgh.

Escobar, Arturo (1995) *Encountering Development, The Making and Unmaking of the Third World*, Princeton University Press, NJ.

Esping-Andersen, Gosta (1990) *The Three Worlds of Welfare Capitalism*, Polity Press, Cambridge.

Esping-Andersen, Gosta (1999) *Social Foundations of Post-Industrial Economies*, Oxford University Press, Oxford and New York.

Esposito, John L. (1980) 'Introduction', in *Islam and Development: Religion and Sociopolitical Change*, Esposito, John L. (ed), Syracuse University Press, New York, pp ix-xix.

Esposito, John L. (2000) 'Islam and Secularism in the Middle East', in *Islam and Secularism in the Middle East*, Esposito, John L. and Tamimi, Azzam (eds), Hurst and Company, London.

Esposito, John and Mogahed, Dalia (2007) 'Battle for Muslims' Hearts and Minds: The Road Not (Yet) Taken', *Middle Eastern Policy*, vol XIV (1), pp 27-41.

Evans, Martin (1998) 'Behind the Rhetoric: The Institutional Basis of Social Exclusion', *IDS Bulletin*, vol 29 (1), pp 42-9.

Faour, Muhammad A. (2007) 'Religion, Demography and Politics in Lebanon', *Middle Eastern Studies*, vol 43 (6), pp 909-21.

Farnsley, Arthur E. II (2007) 'Faith Based Initiatives', in *The Sage Handbook of the Sociology of Religion*, Beckford, James and Demerath, N.J. III (eds), Sage Publications, London, pp 345-56.

Fehler, Timothy (1999) *Poor Relief and Protestantism: The Evolution of Social Welfare in Sixteenth Century Emden*, Ashgate, Aldershot.

Ferguson, James (1994) *The Anti-Politics Machine: 'Development', Depoliticization and Bureaucratic Power in Lesotho*, University of Minnesota Press, London and Minneapolis, MN.

Ferrera, Maurizio (1996) 'The "Southern Model" of Welfare in Social Europe', *Journal of European Social Policy*, vol 6 (1), pp 17-37.

Fighali, Kamal (1997) *Al-Tahjeer Fi Lubnan: Stratijiyaat Al-Awda Wal Enmaa* [Displacement in Lebanon: Strategies for Return of Development], Lebanese Centre for Policy Studies, Beirut.

Figueroa, Adolfo, Altamarino, Teofilio and Sulmont, Denis (1996) *Social Exclusion and Inequality in Peru*, ILO, Geneva.

Findlay, Allan (1994) *The Arab World*, Routledge, London.

Fischer, Clare B. (2001) 'Work and its Discontents: Two Cases of Contemporary Religious Response to Unemployment', in *Religion and Social Policy*, Nesbitt, Paula D. (ed), Altamira Press, Oxford, pp 146-63.

Fisk, Robert (2001) *Pity The Nation: Lebanon at War*, Oxford University Press, Oxford.

Fitzpatrick, Tony (2001) *Welfare Theory: An Introduction*, Palgrave, Basingstoke.

Fitzpatrick, Tony (2008) *Applied Ethics and Social Problems: Moral Questions of Birth, Society and Death*, The Policy Press, Bristol.

Fitzpatrick, Tony, Kwon, Huck-Ju, Manning, Nick, Midgley, James and Pascall, Gillian (eds) (2006) *International Encyclopedia of Social Policy*, Routledge, Oxford.

Fix, Birgit and Fix, Elisabeth (2002) 'From Charity to Client-Oriented Social Service Production: A Social Profile of Religious Welfare Associations in Western European Comparison', *European Journal of Social Work*, vol 5 (1), pp 55-62.

Francis, Paul (2002) 'Social Capital, Civil Society and Social Exclusion', in *Development Theory and Practice: Critical Perspectives*, Kothari, Uma and Minogue, Martin (eds), Palgrave, Basingstoke, pp 71-91.

Fraser, Nancy (1997) *Justice Interruptus*, Routledge, London. and New York.

Fraser, Paul (2005) 'Charles Taylor's Catholicism', *Contemporary Political Theory*, vol 4, pp 231-52.

Freston, Paul (2007) 'Evangelicalism and Fundamentalism: The Politics of Global Popular Protestantism', in *The Sage Handbook of the Sociology of Religion*, Beckford, James and Demerath, N.J. III (eds), Sage Publications, London, pp 205-26.

Furfey, Paul Hanly (1948) 'The Churches and Social Problems', *The Annals of the American Academy of Political and Social Science*, vol 256 (1), pp 101-9.

Gaventa, John (1998) 'Poverty, Participation and Social Exclusion in North and South', *IDS Bulletin*, vol 29 (1), pp 23-30.

Gellner, Ernest (1991) *Muslim Society*, Cambridge University Press, Cambridge.

Gethin, Rupert (1998) *The Foundations of Buddhism*, Oxford University Press, Oxford.

Ghaleb, Joey (2000) 'Al Infaak Al Ijtimaa`I mukaabel Al Estethmar Al Ijtima`I' [Social Expenditure versus Social Investment], in *Al Muwaazana wal Tanmiya-l-Ijtimaa`iya Fi Lubnan* [*The Budget and Social Development in Lebanon*], Lebanese Centre for Policy Studies, Beirut.

Giddens, Anthony (1992) 'Introduction' in Weber, Max, *The Protestant Work Ethic and the Spirit of Capitalism* (revised edn), Routledge, London and New York.

Giddens, Anthony (2000) *The Third Way and its Critics*, Polity Press, Cambridge.

Gilliat-Ray, Sophie (2003) 'Nursing, Professionalism and Spirituality', *Journal of Contemporary Religion*, vol 18 (3), pp 225-64.

Glazer, Nathan (1988) *The Limits of Social Policy*, Harvard University Press, Cambridge, MA.

Goody, Jack (2003) 'Religion and Development: Some Comparative Considerations', *Development*, vol 46 (4), pp 64-7.

Gorski, Philip, S. (2000) 'Historicizing the Secularization Debate: Church, State and Society in Late Medieval and Early Modern Europe', *American Sociological Review*, vol 65 (1), pp 138-67.

Gorski, Philip S. (2005) 'The Return of the Repressed: Religion and the Political Unconscious of Historical Sociology', in *Remaking Modernity: Politics, History and Sociology*, Adams, Julia, Clements, Elisabeth S. and Shola Orloff, Ann (eds), Duke University Press, Durham and London, pp 161-89.

Gough, Ian (1999) *Welfare Regimes: On Adapting the Framework to Developing Countries*, Working Paper, Bath: Institute for International Policy, accessed 20/02/03 at www.bath.ac.uk/ifipa/GSP/wpl.pdf

Gough, Ian (2000) *Welfare Regimes in East Asia*, Working Paper, Bath: Department of Social and Policy Sciences, University of Bath, accessed 20/02/03 at www. bath.ac/uk/ifipa/GSP/wpl.pdf

Gough, Ian (2004) 'Welfare Regimes in a Development Context: A Global and Regional Analysis', in *Insecurity and Welfare Regimes in Asia, Africa and Latin America: Social Policy in a Development Context*, Gough, Ian and Wood, Geoff (eds), with Barrientos, Armando, Beval, Phillipa, Davis, Peter and Room, Graham, Cambridge University Press, Cambridge, pp 15-48.

Gough, Ian and Olofsson, Gunnar (1999) 'Introduction: New Thinking on Exclusion and Integration', in *Capitalism and Social Cohesion*, Gough, Ian and Olofsson, Gunnar (eds), Macmillan, Basingstoke.

Gough, Ian and Wood, Geoff (eds) with Barrientos, Armando, Beval, Phillipa, Davis, Peter and Room, Graham (2004) *Insecurity and Welfare Regimes in Asia, Africa and Latin America: Social Policy in a Development Context*, Cambridge University Press, Cambridge, pp 15-48.

Goulet, Denis (1980) 'Development Experts: The One-Eyed Giants', *World Development*, vol 8 (7/8), pp 481-90.

Green, Maia (2002) 'Social Development: Issues and Approaches', in *Development Theory and Practice: Critical Perspectives*, Kothari, Uma and Minogue, Martin (eds), Palgrave, Basingstoke, pp 52-70.

Grettenberger, Susan E., Bartkowski, John P. and Smith, Steven R. (2006) 'Evaluating the Effectiveness of Faith-Based Welfare Agencies: Methodological Challenges and Possibilities', *Journal of Religion and Spirituality in Social Work*, vol 25 (3/4), pp 223-40.

Grillo, R.D. (1997) 'Discourses of Development: The View from Anthropology', in *Discourses of Development, Anthropological Perspectives*, Grillo, R.D. and Stirrat, R.L. (eds), Berg, Oxford and New York.

Guardian, The (2004) 'Wise and Wonderful?', 17 March, accessed 15/09/08 at www.guardianunlimited.co.uk

Gwynne, Paul (2009) *World Religions in Practice: A Comparative Introduction*, Blackwell, Oxford.

Haddad, Antouan (1996) *Al Fakr Fi Lubnan [Poverty in Lebanon]*, ESCWA, New York.

Haddad, Simon (2001) 'A Survey of Maronite Christian Socio-Political Attitudes in Postwar Lebanon', *Islam and Christian-Muslim Relations*, vol 12 (4), pp 465-79.

Hagopian, Elaine (1989) 'From Maronite Hegemony to Maronite Militancy: The Creation and Disintegration of Lebanon', *Third World Quarterly*, vol 11 (4), pp 101-17.

Hall, Anthony and Midgley, James (2004) *Social Policy for Development*, Sage Publications, London.

Hall, Stuart, Held, David and McGrew, Tony (eds) (1992) *Modernity and its Futures*, Polity Press in association with the Open University, Cambridge.

Hamilton, Malcolm B. (1998) *Sociology and the World's Religions*, Macmillan, Basingstoke.

Hancock, Ralph C. (1988) 'Religion and the Limits of Limited Government', *The Review of Politics*, vol 50 (4), pp 682-703.

Hanley, David (1994) 'Introduction: Christian Democracy as a Political Phenomenon', in *Christian Democracy in Europe: A Comparative Perspective*, Hanley, David (ed), Pinter, London, pp 1-11.

Hannoyer, Jean (1994) 'Présentation', in *Du Privé au Public, Espaces et Valeurs du Politique au Proche-Orient*, Cermoc, Beirut.

Harb, Imad (1999) 'Lebanon, Syria and the Middle East Process: Reconstructing Viable Economies', in *The Political Economy of the Middle East Peace Process*, Wright, J. W. (ed), Routledge, London

Harb, Mona (2008) 'Faith Based Organisations as Effective Development Partners? Hezbollah and Post War Reconstruction in Lebanon', in *Development, Civil Society and Faith Based Organisations: Bridging the Sacred and the Secular*, Clarke, Gerard and Jennings, Michael (eds), Palgrave Macmillan, Basingstoke, pp 214-39.

Harb El-Kak, Mona (1996) *Politiques Urbaines dans la Banlieue-Sud de Beyrouth*, Cermoc, Beyrouth.

Harb El-Kak, Mona (2000) 'Towards a Regionally Balanced Development', in *UNDP Conference on Linking Economic Growth and Social Development*, 11-13 January 2000, UNDP, Beirut.

Harcourt, Wendy (2003) 'Editorial: Clearing the Path for Collective Compassion', *Development*, vol 46 (4), pp 3-5.

Hardie, John B. and Algar, Hamid (2000) 'Introduction' in Qubt, Sayyid *Social Justice in Islam* (revised edn), Islamic Publications International, Oneonta, New York.

Hariba, Abdul Halim (1997) 'Al Daman Al Ijtimayi wa Ilakatahu bil tanmiya' [Social Security and its Relationship to Development], in *Abaad no 6, May*, Lebanese Centre for Policy Studies, Beirut.

Harik, Iliya (1990) 'The Origins of the Arab State System', in *The Arab State*, Luciani, Giacomo (ed), Routledge, London.

Harik, Iliya (1992) 'Privatization: The Issue, the Prospects, and the Fears', in *Privatization and Liberalization in the Middle East*, Harik, Iliya and Sullivan, Denis J. (eds), Indiana University Press, Bloomington, IN, pp 1-23.

Harik, Judith (1994) *The Public and Social Services of the Lebanese Militias*, Papers on Lebanon No 14, Centre for Lebanese Studies, Oxford.

Harris, Margaret, Halfpenny, Peter and Rochester, Collin (2003) 'A Social Policy Role for Faith-Based Organisations? Lessons from the UK Jewish Voluntary Sector', *Journal of Social Policy*, vol 32 (1), pp 93-112.

Harris, William (2007) 'Crisis in the Levant: Lebanon at Risk', *Mediterranean Quarterly*, vol 18 (2), pp 37-60.

Harvey, Peter (1990) *An Introduction to Buddhism: Teaching, History and Practices*, Cambridge University Press, Cambridge.

Hashim, Iman (1999) 'Reconciling Islam and Feminism', *Gender and Development*, vol 7(1), pp 7-14.

Haynes, Jeff (1993) *Religion in Third World Politics*, Open University Press, Buckingham.

Haynes, Jeff (2003) 'Religious Fundamentalism and Politics', in *Major World Religions: From their Origins to the Present*, Ridgeon, Lloyd (ed), Routledge, Curzon, London, pp 324-70.

Hearn, Julie (2002) 'The "Invisible" NGO: US Evangelical Missions in Kenya', *Journal of Religion in Africa*, vol 32 (1), pp 32-60.

Hechter, Michael (2004) 'From Class to Culture', *American Journal of Sociology*, vol 110 (2), pp 400-45.

Hefner, Robert W. (2001) 'Public Islam and the Problem of Democratization', *Sociology of Religion*, vol 62 (4), pp 491-514.

Hegland, Mary Elaine (1987a) 'Introduction', in *Religious Resurgence: Contemporary Cases in Islam, Christianity and Judaism*, Antoun, Richard T. and Hegland, Mary E. (eds), Syracuse University Press, New York, pp 1-11.

Hegland, Mary Elaine (1987b) 'Islamic Revival or Political and Cultural Revolution? An Iranian Case Study', in *Religious Resurgence: Contemporary Cases in Islam, Christianity and Judaism*, Antoun, Richard T. and Hegland, Mary E. (eds), Syracuse University Press, New York, pp 194-215.

Hegland, Mary Elaine (1987c) 'Conclusion: Religious Resurgence in Today's World – A Refuge From Dislocation and Anomie or Enablement for Change?', in *Religious Resurgence: Contemporary Cases in Islam, Christianity and Judaism*, Antoun, Richard T. and Hegland, Mary E. (eds), Syracuse University Press, New York, pp 233-51.

Henkel, Heiko and Stirrat, Roderick (2001) 'Participation as Spiritual Duty; Empowerment as Secular Subjection', in *Participation: The New Tyranny?*, Cooke, Bill and Kothari, Uma (eds), Zed Books, London and New York, pp 168-82.

Henry, Clement M. and Springborg, Robert (2001) *Globalization and the Politics of Development in the Middle East*, Cambridge University Press, Cambridge.

Heyneman, Stephen P. (2004) 'Introduction', in *Islam and Social Policy*, Heyneman, Stephen P. (ed), Vanderbilt University Press, Nashville, TN, pp 1-13.

Higgins, Joan (1981) *States of Welfare: Comparative Analysis in Social Policy*, Basil Blackwell and Martin Robertson, Oxford.

Hill, Michael (1997) *Understanding Social Policy*, Blackwell, Oxford.

Hill, Michael (2006) *Social Policy in the Modern World: A Comparative Text*, Blackwell, Oxford.

Hobart, Mark (1993) 'Introduction: The Growth of Ignorance?', in *An Anthropological Critique of Development: The Growth of Ignorance*, Routledge, London.

Hogan, Trevor (2005) 'The Use of Failure: Christian Socialism as a Nomadic City of the Gift Economy', *Thesis Eleven*, 80, pp 74-93.

Hollinger, Franz, Haller, Max and Valle-Hollinger, Adriana (2007) 'Christian Religion, Society and the State in the Modern World', *Innovation*, vol 20 (2), pp 133-57.

Hong, Zhou (2000) 'Decomposing Welfare: A Methodological Discourse on Welfare States with Lessons for China', *IDS Bulletin*, vol 31 (4), pp 42-9.

Hoogvelt, Ankie (1997) *Globalisation and the Post Colonial World*, Macmillan, Basingstoke.

Hope, Anne and Timmel, Sally (2003) 'A Kenyan Experience for Faith-Based Transformative Action', *Development*, vol 46 (4), pp 93-9.

Hornsby-Smith, Michael (1999) 'The Catholic Church and Social Policy in Europe', in *Welfare and Culture in Europe*, Chamberlayne, Prue, Cooper, Andrew, Freeman, Richard and Rustin, Michael (eds), Jessica Kingsley Publishers, London, pp 172-89.

Hovland, Ingie (2008) 'Who's Afraid of Religion? Tension Between "Mission" and "Development" in the Norwegian Mission Society', in *Development, Civil Society and Faith Based Organisations: Bridging the Sacred and the Secular*, Clarke, Gerard and Jennings, Michael (eds), Palgrave Macmillan, Basingstoke, pp 171-86.

Hruby, Suzanne (1982) 'The Church in Poland and its Political Influence', *Journal of International Affairs*, vol 36, pp 317-28.

Hudson, Michael C. (1980) 'Islam and Political Development', in *Islam and Development: Religion and Sociopolitical Change*, Esposito, John L. (ed), Syracuse University Press, New York, pp 1-23.

Iannaccone, Laurence R., Finke, Roger and Stark, Rodney (1997) 'Deregulating the Church: The Economics of Church and State', *Economic Inquiry*, vol XXXV, pp 350-64.

ILO (International Labour Organization) (2003) 'Key Indicators of the Labour Market – Lebanon', accessed 15/08/04 at www.ilo.org/public/english/employment/gems/eeo/download/lebanon.pdf

Inglehart, Ronald and Barker, Wayne E. (2000) 'Modernization, Cultural Change and the Persistence of Traditional Values', *American Sociological Review*, vol 65 (1), pp 19-51.

Innes, Joanna (1998) 'State, Church and Voluntarism in European Welfare 1690–1850', in *Charity, Philanthropy and Reform: From the 1690s to 1850*, Cunningham, Hugh and Innes, Joanna (eds), Macmillan, Basingstoke, pp 15-65.

Introvigne, Massimo (2004) 'The Future of New Religions', *Futures*, vol 36, pp 979-90.

Ion, Jacques (1995) 'L'Exclusion, Une Problématique Francaise?', *Lien Social et Politique*, vol 34, pp 63-9.

Isin, Engin and Üstündăg, Ebru (2008) 'Wills, Deeds, Acts: Women's Civic Gift-giving in Ottoman Istanbul' in *Gender, Place and Culture*, vol 15(5), pp 519-32.

Ismael, Jacqueline S. and Ismael, Tareq Y. (1995) 'Cultural Perspectives on Social Welfare in the Emergence of Modern Arab Social Thought', *The Muslim World*, vol 85 (1-2), pp 82-106.

Issa, Najib (1994) 'Les Structures Économiques et le Conflit au Liban', in *Le Liban aujourd'hui*, Kiwan, Fadia (ed), Cermoc, Cnrs Éditions, Paris.

Issa, Najib (2000) 'Al Muwazana wal Kita` Al Khaas (Wizarat Al Shu-un Al Ijtimaa`iya)' [Distribution of Social Expenditure] (The Ministry of Social Affairs)], in *Al Muwaazana wal Tanmiya-l-Ijtimaa`iya Fi Lubnan* [*The Budget and Social Development in Lebanon*, Lebanese Centre for Policy Studies, Beirut.

Jaber, Hala (1997) *Hizbolla: Born With a Vengeance*, Columbia University Press, New York.

Jackson, Cecile (1999) 'Social Exclusion and Gender: Does One Size Fit All?', *European Journal of Development Research*, vol 11 (1), pp 125-46.

Jawad, Rana (2002) 'A Profile of Social Welfare in Lebanon: Assessing the Implications for Social Development Policy', *Global Social Policy*, vol 2 (3), pp 319-42.

Jawad, Rana (2006) 'Lebanon', in *International Encyclopedia of Social Policy, Volume 2*, Fitzpatrick, Tony, Kwon, Huck-Ju, Manning, Nick, Midgley, James and Pascall, Gillian (eds), Routledge, Oxford.

Jawad, Rana (2008) 'Possibilities of Positive Social Action in the Middle East: A Re-Reading of the History of Social Policy in the Region', *Global Social Policy*, vol 8 (2), pp 267-80.

Jawad, Rana (2009) 'Religion and Social Welfare in Lebanon: Treating the Causes or Symptoms of Poverty?', *Journal of Social Policy*, vol 38(1), pp 141-56.

Jennings, Michael and Clarke, Gerard (2008) 'Conclusion', in *Development, Civil Society and Faith Based Organisations: Bridging the Sacred and the Secular*, Clarke, Gerard and Jennings, Michael (eds), Palgrave Macmillan, Basingstoke, pp 260-74.

Johnson, Penny (1997) *Palestinian Women: A Status Report. Social Support, Gender and Social Policy*, Women's Studies Programme, Birzeit University, Birzeit, Palestine.

Johnson, Penny (2006) 'Palestine', in *International Encyclopedia of Social Policy, Volume 2*, Fitzpatrick, Tony, Kwon, Huck-Ju, Manning, Nick, Midgley, James and Pascall, Gillian (eds), Routledge, Oxford, pp 969-74.

Jones, Ben and Lauterbach, Karen (2005) 'Conference Report: Bringing Religion Back In: Religious Institutions and Politics in Africa', *Journal of Religion in Africa*, vol 35 (2), pp 239-43.

Jones, Charles B. (2000) 'Buddhism and Marxism in Taiwan: Lin Qiuwu's Religious Socialism and its Legacy in Modern Times', *Journal of Global Buddhism*, vol 1, pp 82-111.

Jones, Toby (2003) 'Seeking a "Social Contract" for Saudi Arabia', *Middle East Report*, no 228, pp 42-8.

Jordan, Bill (1996) *A Theory of Poverty and Social Exclusion*, Polity Press, Cambridge.

Kabeer, Naila (2000) 'Social Exclusion, Poverty and Discrimination', in *IDS Bulletin*, vol 31 (4), pp 83-97.

Kabeer, Naila (2004) 'Re-visioning "the Social": Towards a Citizen-Centred Social Policy for the Poor in Poor Countries', IDS Working Paper, IDS, Brighton, accessed 23/02/04 at http://server.ntd.co.uk/ids/bookshop/details.asp?id=791

Kabeer, Naila and Cook, Sarah (2000) 'Editorial Introduction: Re-Visioning Social Policy in the South: Challenges and Concepts', *IDS Bulletin*, vol 31 (4), pp 1-10.

Kahl, Sigrun (2005) 'The Religious Roots of Modern Poverty Policy: Catholic, Lutheran, and Reformed Protestant Traditions Compared', *European Journal of Sociology*, vol XLVI (I), pp 91-126.

Karshenas, Massoud and Moghadam, Valentine M. (2006a) 'Social Policy in the Middle East: Introduction and Overview', in *Social Policy in the Middle East: Economic, Political and Gender Dynamics*, Karshenas, Massoud and Moghadam, Valentine M. (eds), United Nations Research Institute for Social Development and Palgrave Macmillan, Basingstoke, pp 1-30.

Karshenas, Massoud and Moghadam, Valentine M. (eds) (2006b) *Social Policy in the Middle East: Economic, Political and Gender Dynamics*, United Nations Research Institute for Social Development and Palgrave Macmillan, Basingstoke.

Kasza, Gregory J. (2002) 'The Illusion of Welfare "Regimes"', *Journal of Social Policy*, vol 31 (2), pp 271-87.

Kedourie, Elie (1994) *Democracy and Arab Political Culture*, Frank Cass, London.

Khalidi, Walid (1991) 'State and Society in Lebanon', in *State and Society in Lebanon*, Fawaz, Leila (ed), Centre for Lebanese Studies and Tufts University, Oxford.

Khalidi-Beyhum, Ramla (1999) *Poverty Reduction Policies in Jordan and Lebanon: An Overview*, Eradicating Poverty Series No 10, Economic and Social Commission for Western Asia, United Nations, New York.

Khalili, Laleh (2007) 'Understanding Islam in Politics', *Social Movement Studies: Journal of Social, Cultural and Political Protest*, vol 6 (1), pp 105-10.

Khashan, Hilal (1992) *Inside the Lebanese Confessional Mind*, University Press of America, Maryland, MD.

Kiwan, Fadia (1994) 'Forces Politiques Nouvelles, Système Politique Ancien', in *Le Liban Aujourd'hui*, Kiwan, Fadia (ed), Cermoc, Cnrs Éditions, Paris.

Kliksberg, Bernardo (2003) 'Facing the Inequalities of Development: Some Lessons from Judaism and Christianity', *Development*, vol 46 (4), pp 57-63.

Klostermaier, Klaus K (1994) *A Survey of Hinduism* (2nd edition), State University of New York Press, New York.

Kothari, Uma and Minogue, Martin (2002) 'Critical Perspectives on Development: An Introduction', in *Development Theory and Practice: Critical Perspectives*, Kothari, Uma and Minogue, Martin (eds), Palgrave, Basingstoke, pp 1-15.

Kumar, Satish (2003) 'Development and Religion: Cultivating a Sense of the Sacred', *Development*, vol 46 (4), pp 15-21.

Laithy, Heba, Abu-Ismail, Khalid and Hamdan, Kamal (2008) *Poverty, Growth and Income Distribution in Lebanon*, Country Study No 13, International Poverty Centre, Brazilian Institute of Applied Economic Research (IPEA) and the Bureau for Development Policy, UNDP, Brazil.

Land, Hilary (1998) 'Altruism, Reciprocity and Obligation', in *The Student's Companion to Social Policy*, Alcock, Pete, Erskine, Angus and May, Margaret (eds), Blackwell, Oxford, pp 49-54.

Latouche, Serge (1997) 'Standard of Living', in *The Development Dictionary*, Zed Books, London and New Jersey, NJ.

LaTowsky, Robert J. (1997) *Egypt's NGO Sector: A Briefing Paper*, Education for Development Occasional Papers Series I, No 4, University of Reading, Reading.

Layachi, Azzedine (2006) 'Algeria: Crisis, Transition and Social Policy Outcomes', in *Social Policy in the Middle East: Economic, Political and Gender Dynamics*, Karshenas, Massoud and Moghadam, Valentine M. (eds), United Nations Research Institute for Social Development and Palgrave Macmillan, Basingstoke, pp 78-108.

Lebanon Ministry of Finance (2004) *Budget Proposal 2004*, Lebanon Ministry of Finance, Beirut.

Leege, David C. (1988) 'Catholics and the Civic Order: Parish Participation, Politics and Civic Participation', *The Review of Politics*, vol 50 (4), pp 704-36.

Levinas, Emmanuel and Guwy, France (2008) 'What no one else can do in my place: A Conversation with Emmanuel Levinas', in *Religion: Beyond a Concept*, de Vries, Hent (ed), Fordham University Press, New York, pp 297-310.

Levitt, Peggy (2008) 'Religion as a Path to Civic Engagement', *Ethnic and Racial Studies*, vol 31 (4), pp 766-91.

Lewis, Gail (2000) 'Introduction', in *Rethinking Social Policy*, Lewis, Gail, Gewirtz, Sharon and Clarke, John (eds), Open University and Sage Publications, London, Thousand Oaks, CA, and New Delhi.

Lewis, Jane (1999) 'Voluntary and Informal Welfare', in *British Social Welfare in the Twentieth Century*, Page, Robert M. and Silburn, Richard (eds), Macmillan, Basingstoke, pp 249-70.

Lifshitz, Joseph Isaac (2007) 'Welfare, Property and Charity in Jewish Thought', *Social Science and Modern Society*, vol 44 (2), pp 71-8.

Ling, Trevor (1980) 'Buddhist Values and Development Problems: A Case Study of Sri Lanka', *World Development*, vol 8 (7/8), pp 577-86.

Loewe, Markus (2000) 'Protecting the Old in a Young Economy: Old Age Insurance in the West Bank and Gaza Strip', *International Social Security Review*, vol 53 (3), pp 59-83.

Loewe, Markus (2004) 'New Avenues to be Opened for Social Protection in the Arab World: The Case of Egypt', *International Journal of Social Welfare*, vol 13, pp 3-14.

Long, Norman (1992) 'From Paradigm Lost to Paradigm Regained? The Case for an Actor-Oriented Sociology of Development', in *Battlefields of Knowledge: The Interlocking of Theory and Practice in Social Research and Development*, Long, Norman and Long, Ann (eds), Routledge, London.

Loy, David R. (2003) 'The Poverty of Development: Buddhist Reflections', in *Development*, vol 6 (4), pp 7-14.

Luciani, Giacomo (1990a) 'Introduction', in *The Arab State*, Luciani, Giacomo (ed), Routledge, London.

Luciani, Giacomo (1990b) 'Allocation vs. Production States: A Theoretical Framework', in *The Arab State*, Luciani, Giacomo (ed), Routledge, London, pp 65-84.

Luciani, Giacomo and Salamé, Ghassan (1990) 'The Politics of Arab Integration', in *The Arab State*, Luciani, Giacomo (ed), Routledge, London, pp 394-419.

Luckmann, Thomas (1967) *The Invisible Religion: The Problem of Religion in Modern Society*, Collier-Macmillan, London.

Mac Ginty, Roger (2007) 'Reconstructing Post-War Lebanon: A Challenge to the Liberal Peace?', *Conflict, Security and Development*, vol 7 (3), pp 457-82.

Macarov, David (1995) *Social Welfare: Structure and Practice*, Sage Publications, Thousand Oaks, CA, London and New Delhi.

Macmillan, Rob and Townsend, Alan (2006) 'A "New Institutional Fix"? The "Community Turn" and the Changing Role of the Voluntary Sector', in *Landscapes of Voluntarism: New Spaces of Health, Welfare and Governance*, Milligan, Christine and Conradson, David (eds), The Policy Press, Bristol, pp 15-32.

Madeley, John (1991) 'Politics and Religion in Western Europe', in *Politics and Religion in the Modern World*, Moyser, George (ed), Routledge, London.

Madeley, John T.S. (2003a) 'European Liberal Democracy and the Principle of State Religious Neutrality', in *Church and State in Contemporary Europe: The Chimera of Neutrality*, Madeley, John T.S. and Enyedi, Zsolt (eds), Frank Cass, London and Portland, OR, pp 1-22.

Madeley, John T.S. (2003b) 'A Framework for the Comparative Analysis of Church–State Relations in Europe', in *Church and State in Contemporary Europe: The Chimera of Neutrality*, Madeley, John T.S. and Enyedi, Zsolt (eds), Frank Cass, London and Portland, OR, pp 23-49.

Madeley, John T.S. and Enyedi, Zsolt (eds) (2003) *Church and State in Contemporary Europe: The Chimera of Neutrality*, Frank Cass, London and Portland, OR.

Maheshvarananda, Dada (2003) 'Revolutionary Consciousness: Development as Transformation', *Development*, vol 46 (4), pp 74-8.

Makris, G. P. (2007) *Islam in the Middle East: A Living Tradition*, Blackwell, Oxford.

Manji, Firoze and O'Coill, Carl (2002) 'The Missionary Position: NGOs and Development in Africa', *International Affairs*, vol 78 (3), pp 567-83.

Maoulidi, Salma (2003) 'The Sahiba Sisters Foundation in Tanzania: Meeting Organizational and Community Needs', *Development*, vol 46 (4), pp 85-92.

Martin, J. Paul, Chau, Jason and Patel, Shruti (2007) 'Religions and International Poverty Alleviation: The Pluses and Minuses', *Journal of International Affairs*, vol 61 (1), pp 69-92.

Martínez, Socorro M. (2003) 'Women's Leadership in Mexico: Education for Social Change at the Grassroots', *Development*, vol 46 (4), pp 79-84.

Marzouk, Mohsen (1997) 'The Associative Phenomenon in the Arab World: Engine of Democratisation or Witness to the Crisis', in *NGOs, States and Donors, Too Close for Comfort?*, Edwards, Michael and Hulme, David (eds), Macmillan, London.

Mauduro, Otto (2001) 'Globalization, Social Policy, and Christianity at the Dawn of the New Millennium: Some Reflections from a Latin American Emigrant Perspective', in *Religion and Social Policy*, Nesbitt, Paula D. (ed), Altamira Press, Oxford, pp 3-14.

Mavrogordatos, George Th. (2003) 'Orthodoxy and Nationalism in the Greek Case', in *Church and State in Contemporary Europe: The Chimera of Neutrality*, Madeley, John T.S. and Enyedi, Zsolt (eds), Frank Cass, London and Portland, OR, pp 116-35.

Mawdudi, Abul A'la (1993) *Human Rights in Islam*, The Islamic Foundation, Leicester.

Maxwell, Simon (1998) 'Comparisons, Convergence and Connections: Development Studies in North and South', *IDS Bulletin*, vol 29 (1).

May, Margaret (1998) 'The Role of Comparative Study', in *The Student's Companion to Social Policy*, Alcock, Peter (ed), Blackwell, Oxford.

Mayer, Victoria (2008) 'Crafting a New Conservative Consensus on Welfare Reform: Redefining Citizenship, Social Provision, and the Public/Private Divide', *Social Politics: International Studies in Gender, State and Society*, vol 15 (2), pp 154-81.

Mehden, Fred R. von der (1980) 'Religion and Development in South-East Asia: A Comparative Study', *World Development*, vol 8 (7/8), pp 545-54.

Mehdizadeh, Nerjes and Scott, Gill (2008) 'Educated Mothers in Iran: Work, Welfare and Childcare', Paper presented at the 42nd Social Policy Association Annual Conference, University of Edinburgh, 23-25 June.

Mehmet, Ozay (1990) *Islamic Identity and Development: Studies from the Islamic Periphery*, Routledge, London.

Melki, Roger (2000) 'La Protection Sociale au Liban: Entre Réflexe d'Assurance et Logique d'Assurance', in *Linking Economic Growth and Social Development*, UNDP, Beirut.

Melville, Rose and McDonald, Catherine (2006) '"Faith-based" Organisations and Contemporary Welfare', *Australian Journal of Social Issues*, vol 41 (1), pp 69-85.

Merkel, Wolfgang (2002) 'Social Justice and the Three Worlds of Welfare Capitalism', *European Journal of Sociology*, vol 43 (1), pp 59-91.

Messara, Antoine (1991) 'The Hostage State in the Modern International System', in *State and Society in Lebanon*, Fawaz, Leila (ed), Centre for Lebanese Studies and Tufts University, Oxford.

Messara, Antoine (1995) 'Civil Society against the War System: The Lebanese Case', in *Toward Civil Society in the Middle East: A Primer*, Schwedler, Julian (ed), Lynne Rienner Publishers, London.

Messkoub, Mahmood (2006) 'Constitutionalism, Modernization and Islamization: The Political Economy of Social Policy in Iran', in *Social Policy in the Middle East: Economic, Political and Gender Dynamics*, Karshenas, Massoud and Moghadam, Valentine M. (eds), United Nations Research Institute for Social Development and Palgrave Macmillan, Basingstoke, pp 190-220.

Midgley, James (1990a) 'Review Article: Religion, Politics and Social Policy: The Case of the New Christian Right', *Journal of Social Policy*, vol 19 (3), pp 430-1.

Midgley, James (1990b) 'Rescuing the Good Samaritan: An Exposition and a Defence of the Samaritan Principle in the Welfare State', *Journal of Social Policy*, vol 19 (3), pp 281-98.

Midgley, James (1995) *Social Development: The Developmental Perspective in Social Welfare*, Sage Publications, London.

Midgley, James (1997) *Social Welfare in Global Context*, Sage Publications, Thousand Oaks, CA, London and New Delhi.

Midwinter, Eric (1994) *The Development of Social Welfare in Britain*, Open University Press, Buckingham.

Migdal, Joel (1988) *Strong Societies and Weak States*, Princeton University Press, Princeton, NJ.

Milligan, Christine and Conradson, David (2006) 'Contemporary Landscapes of Welfare: The "Voluntary Turn"?', in *Landscapes of Voluntarism: New Spaces of Health, Welfare and Governance*, Milligan, Christine and Conradson, David (eds), The Policy Press, Bristol, pp 1-14.

Milligan, Christine and Fyfe, Nicholas R (2006) 'Renewal or Relocation? Social Welfare, Voluntarism and the City', in *Landscapes of Voluntarism: New Spaces of Health, Welfare and Governance*, Milligan, Christine and Conradson, David (eds), The Policy Press, Bristol, pp 33-52.

Ministry of Finance (2004) *2004 Budget Proposal*, Ministry of Finance, Lebanon.

Minkenberg, Michael (2003) 'The Policy Impact of Church–State Relations: Family Policy and Abortion in Britain, France and Germany', in *Church and State in Contemporary Europe: The Chimera of Neutrality*, Madeley, John T. S. and Enyedi, Zsolt (eds), Frank Cass, London and Portland, OR, pp 194-215.

Minogue, Martin (2002) 'Power to the People? Good Governance and the Reshaping of the State', in *Development Theory and Practice: Critical Perspectives*, Kothari, Uma and Minogue, Martin (eds), Palgrave, Basingstoke, pp 117-35.

Mitsuo, Nakamura (2001) 'Introduction', in *Islam and Civil Society in Southeast Asia*, Mitsuo, Nakamura, Siddique, Sharon and Bajunid, Omar Farouk (eds), Institute of Southeast Asian Studies, Pasir Panjang, Singapore.

Moghadam, Valentine (2006a) 'Materialist Policies versus Women's Economic Citizenship? Gendered Social Policy in Iran' in *Gender and Social Policy in a Global Context*, Shahra Razavi and Shireen Hassim (eds), UNRISD Social Policy in Development Context Series, Palgrave Macmillan, London.

Moghadam, Valentine M. (2006b) 'Gender and Social Policy: Family Law and Women's Economic Citizenship in the Middle East', in *Social Policy in the Middle East: Economic, Political and Gender Dynamics*, Karshenas, Massoud and Moghadam, Valentine M. (eds), United Nations Research Institute for Social Development and Palgrave Macmillan, Basingstoke, pp 221-53.

Monsma, Stephen V. (2006) 'The Effectiveness of Faith-Based Welfare to Work Progams: A Story of Specialization', *Journal of Religion and Spirituality in Social Work*, vol 25 (3-4), pp 175-96.

Montgomery, Tommie Sue (1982) 'Cross and Rifle: Revolution and the Church in El Salvador and Nicaragua', *Journal of International Affairs*, vol 36, pp 209-21.

Moore, Mick (2000) 'States, Social Policies and Globalisations: Arguing on the Right Terrain?', *IDS Bulletin*, vol 31 (4), pp 21-31.

Mortensen, Nils (1999) 'Mapping System Integration and Social Integration', in *Capitalism and Social Cohesion*, Gough, Ian and Olofsson, Gunnar (eds), Macmillan, Basingstoke.

Mouzelis, Nicos (1999) 'Differentiation and Marginalization in Late Modernity', in *Capitalism and Social Cohesion*, Gough, Ian and Olofsson, Gunnar (eds), Macmillan, Basingstoke.

Moyser, George (1991) 'Politics and Religion in the Modern World: An Overview', in *Politics and Religion in the Modern World*, Moyser, George (ed), Routledge, London.

MSA (Ministry of Social Affairs of Lebanon) (2006) *Social Action Plan*, Internal report, Beirut: Lebanon.

MSA and UNDP (United Nations Development Programme) (2006) *Comparative Mapping of Living Conditions between 1995 and 2004*, MSA and UNDP, Beirut.

MSA and UNDP (2007) *Poverty, Growth and Income Distribution in Lebanon*, MSA and UNDP, Beirut.

Mulgan, Geoff and Landry, Charles (1995) *The Other Invisible Hand: Remaking Charity for the 21st Century*, Demos, London.

Multi-Faith Centre (2007) *Religions in the UK Directory 2007–2010*, Weller, Paul (ed), researched by Paul Weller, Michel Wolfe and Eileen Fry, The Multi-Faith Centre at the University of Derby.

Muzaffar, Chandra (2003) 'The Global Rich and the Global Poor: Seeking the Middle Path', *Development*, vol 46 (4), pp 29-34.

Nash, Manning (1980) 'Islam in Iran: Turmoil, Transformation or Transcendence?', *World Development*, vol 8 (7/8), pp 555-62.

Nasr, Marlene (1996) *Al-Ghurabaa'* [*The Strangers*], Buhuth Ijtima'iya [Social Research Studies] No 20, Dar Al Saqi, London.

Nauphal, Naila (1996) 'Nationalism, Repatriation and Post-War Reconciliation in Lebanon', in *ASEN Bulletin*, No 11, Wolfson College, University of Oxford, Oxford.

Nehme, Adib (1997a) 'Siyasat al-amn alijtimai wal thahiriya fi i'adat tawzi' altharwa fi Lubnan' [Policies for Social Security in Wealth Redistribution in Lebanon] in *Abaad*, No 6, Lebanese Centre for Policy Studies, Beirut.

Nehme, Adib (1997b) 'A Profile of Sustainable Human Development in Lebanon', accessed 13/09/99 at www.undp.org.lb/undp/HDR97.htm

Nepstad, Sharon Erickson and Williams, Rhys, H (2007) 'Religion in Rebellion, Resistance and Social Movements', in *The Sage Handbook of the Sociology of Religion*, Beckford, James and Demerath, N.J. III (eds), Sage Publications, London, pp 419-37.

Nesbitt, Paula D. (ed) (2001a) *Religion and Social Policy*, Altamira Press, Oxford.

Nesbitt, Paula D. (2001b) 'Introduction – Religion and Social Policy: Fresh Concepts and Historical Patterns', in *Religion and Social Policy*, Nesbitt, Paula D. (ed), Altamira Press, Oxford, , pp ix-xiii.

Nesbitt, Paula D. (2001c) 'The Future of Religious Pluralism and Social Policy: Reflections from Lambeth and Beyond', in *Religion and Social Policy*, Nesbitt, Paula D. (ed), Altamira Press, Oxford, pp 244-62.

Neuberger, Rabbi Julia (2008) 'Faith, Morality, Giving Time to Others', in *Faith and Life in Britain*, Blair, Tony, Thompson, Mark, Williams, Rowan, Hague, William, Neuberger, Rabbi Julia and Murphy-O'Connor, Cardinal Cormac (eds), Matthew James Publishing, Chelmsford, pp 65-80.

Nienhaus, Volker (2006) 'Zakat, Taxes and Public Finance in Islam', in *Islam and the Everyday World: Public Policy Dilemmas*, Behdad, Sohrab and Nomani, Farhad (eds), Routledge, London, pp 193-223.

Nomani, Farhad (2006) 'The Dilemma of Riba-Free Banking in Islamic Public Policy', in *Islam and the Everyday World: Public Policy Dilemmas*, Behdad, Sohrab and Nomani, Farhad (eds), Routledge, London, pp 193-223.

Novak, David (1992) *Jewish Social Ethics*, Oxford University Press, Oxford.

O'Brien, David, Wilkes, Joanna, de Haan, Arjan and Maxwell, Simon (1997) *Poverty and Social Exclusion in North and South*, IDS Working Paper No 55, IDS, Brighton.

Offer, John (2006) *An Intellectual History of British Social Policy: Idealism versus Non-Idealism*, The Policy Press, Bristol.

Opielka, Michael (2008) 'Christian Foundations of the Welfare State: Strong Cultural Values in Comparative Perspective', in *Culture and the Welfare State: Values and Social Policy in Comparative Perspective*, van Oorschot, Wim, Opielka, Michael and Pfau-Effinger, Birgit (eds), Edward Elgar, Cheltenham, pp 89-116.

Orloff, Ann S. (2005) 'Social Provision and Regulation: Theories of States, Social Policies and Modernity', in *Remaking Modernity: Politics, History and Sociology*, Adams, Julia, Clements, Elisabeth S. and Orloff, Ann S, (eds), Duke University Press, Durham and London, pp 190-224.

Ortiz, Isabel (2007) *Social Policy*, UNDESA Policy Notes, United Nations Department for Economic and Social Affairs (UNDESA), New York, accessed 15/09/08 at http://ssrn.com/abstract=1001486

Page, Robert M. and Silburn, Richard (eds) (1999) *British Social Welfare in the Twentieth Century*, Macmillan, Basingstoke.

Paugam, Serge (1996a) 'Pauvreté et exclusion', in *L'Exclusion: L'État des Savoirs*, Paugam, Serge (ed), La Découverte, Paris.

Paugam, Serge (1996b) 'Introduction: La Constitution d'un Paradigm', in *L'Exclusion: L'État des Savoirs*, Paugam, Serge (ed), La Découverte, Paris.

Paugam, Serge (1996c) 'Conclusion: Les Sciences Sociales Face à l'Exclusion', in *L'Exclusion: L'État des Savoirs*, Paugam, Serge (ed), La Découverte, Paris.

Pemberton, Alec (1990) 'Rescuing the Good Samaritan: An Exposition and a Defence of the Samaritan Principle in the Welfare State', *Journal of Social Policy*, vol 19 (3), pp 281-98.

Perret, Bernard and Roustang, Guy (1993) *L'Économie Contre la Société*, Collection Esprit/Seuil, Paris.

Perry, Glenn E. (1991) 'The Islamic World: Egypt and Iran', in *Politics and Religion in the Modern World*, Moyser, George (ed), Routledge, London.

Pfau-Effinger, Birgit (2004) 'Culture and Welfare State Policies: Reflections on a Complex Interrelation', *Journal of Social Policy*, vol 34 (1), pp 3-20.

Pfau-Effinger, Birgit (2008) 'The Culture of the Welfare State: Historical and theoretical arguments' in *Culture and the Welfare State: Values and Social Policy in Comparative Perspective*, van Oorschot, Wim, Opielka, Michael and Pfau-Effinger, Birgit (eds), Edward Elgar, Cheltenham, pp 1-28.

Phares, Walid (1995) *Lebanese Christian Nationalism: The Rise and Fall of an Ethnic Resistance*, Lynne Rienner Publishers, London.

Pierson, Christopher (1998) *Beyond the Welfare State: The New Political Economy of Welfare*, Polity Press, Cambridge.

Pieterse, Nederveen (2001) *Development Theory: Deconstructions/Reconstructions*, Sage Publications, London.

Pin-Fat, Véronique (2000) '(Im)possible Universalism: Reading Human Rights in World Politics', *Review of International Studies*, vol 26 (4), pp 557-73.

Piscatori, James P. (1980) 'The Roles of Islam in Saudi Arabia's Political Development', in *Islam and Development: Religion and Sociopolitical Change*, Esposito, John L. (ed), Syracuse University Press, New York, pp 123-38.

Powell, Fred (1995) 'Citizenship and Social Exclusion', *Administration*, vol 43 (3), pp 22-35.

Powell, Frederick (2007) *The Politics of Civil Society: Neoliberalism or Social Left?*, The Policy Press, Bristol.

Powell, Martin (2007) 'The Mixed Economy of Welfare and the Social Division of Welfare', in *Understanding the Mixed Economy of Welfare*, Powell, Martin (ed), The Policy Press, Bristol, pp 1-22.

Prochaska, Frank K. (1980) *Women and Philanthropy in 19th Century England*, Clarendon Press, Oxford.

Prochaska Frank K. (1988) *The Voluntary Impulse: Philanthropy in Modern Britain*, Faber and Faber, London.

Qubt, Sayyid (1953) *Social Justice in Islam*, Islamic Publications International, Oneonta, New York.

Rafi, M. and Chowdhury, A.M.R. (2000) 'Human Rights and Religious Backlash: The Experience of a Bangladeshi NGO', *Development in Practice*, vol 10 (1), pp 19-30.

Ragab, Ibrahim A. (1980) 'Islam and Development', *World Development*, vol 8 (7/8), pp 513-22.

Rahnema, Majid (1997) 'Poverty', in *The Development Dictionary*, Sachs, Wolfgang (ed), Zed Books, London and New Jersey, NJ.

Ramadan, Tariq (2001) *Islam, the West and the Challenges of Modernity*, The Islamic Foundation, Leicester.

Raouff Ezzat, Heba (2000) 'Secularism, The State and The Social Bond: the Withering Away of the Family', in *Islam and Secularism in the Middle East*, Esposito, John L. and Tamimi, Azzam (eds), Hurst and Company, London.

Renders, Marleen (2002) 'An Ambiguous Adventure: Muslim Organisations and the Discourse of "Development" in Senegal', *Journal of Religion in Africa*, vol 32 (1), pp 61-82.

Richan, Willard C. (1988) *Beyond Altruism: Social Welfare Policy in American Society*, Hawthorn Press, New York and London.

Richards, Glyn (ed) (1985) *A Sourcebook of Modern Hinduism*, Curzon Press, Richmond.

Ridgeon, Lloyd (2003) *Major World Religions: From their Origins to the Present*, Routledge, London.

Richardson, Gail (2004) 'Islamic Law and Zakat: Waqf Resources in Pakistan', in *Islam and Social Policy*, Heyneman, Stephen P. (ed), Vanderbilt University Press, Nashville, TN, pp 156-80.

Rizk, Hanna (1955) 'Social Services Available for Families in Egypt', *Marriage and Family Living*, vol 17 (3), pp 212-16.

Robbins, Thomas and Lucas, Phillip Charles (2007) 'From "Cults" to New Religious Movements: Coherence, Definition, and Conceptual Framing in the Study of New Religious Movements' in *The Sage Handbook of the Sociology of Religion*, Beckford, James and Demerath, N.J. III (eds), Sage Publications, London, pp 227-47.

Roberts, Michael J. D. (1998) 'Head versus Heart? Voluntary Associations and Charity Organizations in England c.1700–1850, in *Charity, Philanthropy and Reform: From the 1690s to 1850*, Cunningham, Hugh and Innes, Joanna (eds), Macmillan, Basingstoke, pp 66-86.

Rodger, John J. (2000) *From a Welfare State to a Welfare Society: The Changing Context of Social Policy in a Postmodern Era*, Macmillan, London.

Romain, Jonathan A. (1991) *Faith and Practice: A Guide to Reform Judaism Today*, Reform Synagogues of Great Britain (RSGB), London.

Room, Graham (2004) 'Multi-Tiered International Welfare Systems', in *Insecurity and Welfare Regimes in Asia, Africa and Latin America: Social Policy in a Development Context*, Gough, Ian and Wood, Geoff (eds), with Barrientos, Armando, Beval, Phillipa, Davis, Peter and Room, Graham, Cambridge University Press, Cambridge, pp 287-311.

Roy, Arun (2006) 'Iraq', in *International Encyclopedia of Social Policy, Volume 2*, Fitzpatrick, Tony, Kwon, Huck-Ju, Manning, Nick, Midgley, James and Pascall, Gillian (eds), Routledge, Oxford, pp 687-9.

Saad-Ghoreyeb, Amal (2002) *Inside Hizbullah: Politics and Religion*, Pluto Press, London.

Saadah, Sofia (1993) 'Greater Lebanon: The Formation of a Caste System?', in *State and Society in Lebanon and Syria*, Choueiri, Youssef (ed), University of Exeter Press, Exeter.

Sabri, Sarah (2005) 'The Social Aid and Assistance Programme of the Government of Egypt: A Critical Review', *Environment and Urbanization*, vol 17 (2), pp 27-42.

Saeidi, Ali A. (2002) 'Dislocation of the State and the Emergence of Factional Politics in Post Revolutionary Iran', *Political Geography*, vol 21, pp 525-46.

Saeidi, Ali A. (2004) 'The Accountability of Para-Governmental Organizations (Bonyads): The Case of Iranian Foundations', *Iranian Studies*, vol 37 (3), pp 479-98.

Sahlins, Marshall (1997) 'The Original Affluent Society', in *The Post-Development Reader*, Rahnema, Majid and Bawtree, Victoria (eds), Zed Books, London.

Salam, Nawaf (1994) 'Individu et Citoyen au Liban', in *Le Liban Aujourd'hui*, Kiwan, Fadia (ed) Cermoc, Cnrs Éditions, Paris.

Salamé, Ghassan (1990) 'Strong and Weak States: A Qualified Return to the *Muqaddimah*', in *The Arab State*, Luciani, Giacomo (ed), Routledge, London, pp 29-64.

Salamé, Ghassan (1991) 'Unity, Reform and Independence', in *State and Society in Lebanon*, Fawaz, Leila (ed), Centre for Lebanese Studies and Tufts University, Oxford.

Salamey, Imad and Pearson, Frederic (2007) 'Hezbollah: A Proletarian Party with an Islamic Manifesto – A Sociopolitical Analysis of Islamist Populism in Lebanon and the Middle East', *Small Wars and Insurgencies*, vol 18 (3), pp 416-38.

Salibi, Kamal (1988) *A House of Many Mansions: The History of Lebanon Reconsidered*, University of California Press, Berkeley, Los Angeles, CA, and London.

Schnapper, Dominique (1996) 'Intégration et Exclusion dans les Sociétés Modernes', in *L'Exclusion: L'État des Savoirs*, Paugam, Serge (ed), La Découverte, Paris.

Schwarzmantel, John (1994) *The State in Contemporary Society: An Introduction*, Harvester Wheatsheaf, New York, London, Toronto, Sydney, Tokyo and Singapore.

Sen, Amartya (1999) *Development as Freedom*, Oxford University Press, Oxford and New York.

Shadid, Anthony (2001) *Legacy of the Prophet: Despots, Democrats and the New Politics of Islam*, Westview Press, Colorado.

Shalaq, Al-Fadl (1993) 'Concepts of Nation and State with Special Reference to the Sunnis in Lebanon', in *State and Society in Lebanon and Syria*, Choueiri, Youssef (ed), University of Exeter Press, Exeter.

Shalev, Michael (2007) 'The Welfare State Consensus in Israel: Placing Class Politics in Context', in *Social Justice, Legitimacy and the Welfare State*, Mau, Steffen and Veghte, Benjamin (eds), Ashgate, Aldershot, pp 193-216.

Sharot, Stephen (2007) 'Judaism in Israel: Public Religion, Neo-Traditionalism, Messianism, and Ethno-Religious Conflict', in *The Sage Handbook of the Sociology of Religion*, Beckford, James and Demerath, N.J. III (eds), Sage Publications, London, pp 670-96.

Sherr, Michael E. and Straughan, Hope H. (2005) 'Volunteerism, Social Work and the Church: A Historic Overview and Look into the Future', *Social Work and Christianity*, vol 32 (2), pp 97-115.

Silburn, Richard (1999) 'Introduction', in *British Social Welfare in the Twentieth Century*, Page, Robert M. and Silburn, Richard (eds), Macmillan, Basingstoke, pp 1-30.

Silver, Hilary (1995) 'Reconceptualizing Social Disadvantage: Three Paradigms of Social Exclusion', in *Social Exclusion: Rhetoric, Reality and Responses*, Rodgers, Gerry, Gore, Charles G. and Figueiredo, Jose B. (eds), ILO, Geneva.

Singerman, Diane (2006) 'Restoring the Family to Civil Society: Lessons from Egypt', *Journal of Middle Eastern Studies*, vol 2 (1), pp 1-32.

Skocpol, Theda (2000) 'Religion, Civil Society and Social Provision in the U.S.', in *Who Will Provide? The Changing Role of Religion in American Social Welfare*, Bane, Mary J., Coffin, Brent and Thiemann, Ronald (eds), Westview Press, Boulder, CO, pp 21-50.

Slaiby, Ghassan (1994) 'Les Actions Collectives de Résistance Civile à la Guerre', in *Le Liban Aujourd'hui*, Kiwan, Fadia (ed), Cermoc, Cnrs Éditions, Paris.

Sleiman, Issam (1994) 'Équilibre interconfessionel et Équilibre Institutionnel au Liban', in *Le Liban Aujourd'hui*, Kiwan, Fadia (ed), Cermoc, Cnrs Éditions, Paris.

Smart, Ninian (1987) 'Three Forms of Religious Convergence', in *Religious Resurgence: Contemporary Cases in Islam, Christianity and Judaism*, Antoun, Richard T. and Hegland, Mary E. (eds), Syracuse University Press, New York, pp 223-32.

Smith, Christian (1996) 'Correcting a Curious Neglect, or Bringing Religion Back In', in *Disruptive Religion: The Force of Faith in Social-Movement Activism*, Smith, Christian (ed), Routledge, New York and London, pp 1-25.

Soroush, Abdolkarim (2002) *Reason, Freedom and Democracy in Islam: Essential Writings of Abdolkarim Soroush*, Sadiri, Mahmoud and Sadiri, Ahmad (edited and translated), Oxford University Press, Oxford.

Spalek, Basia and Imtoual, Alia (eds) (2008) *Religion, Spirituality and the Social Sciences: Challenging Marginalisation*, The Policy Press, Bristol.

Spargo, John (1909) *The Spiritual Significance of Modern Socialism*, Arthur F. Bird, London.

Spicker, Paul (2000) *The Welfare State: A General Theory*, Sage Publications, London.

Stark, Rodney (2005) *The Victory of Reason: How Christianity Led to Freedom, Capitalism, and Western Success*, Random House, New York.

Sullivan, Antony T. (2008) 'Wars and Rumours of War: The Levantine Tinderbox', *Middle East Policy*, vol XV (1), pp 125-32.

Sutton, Philip W. and Vertigans, Stephen (2005) *Resurgent Islam: A Sociological Approach*, Polity Press, Cambridge.

Swami, Agnivesh (2003) 'A Spiritual Vision for the Dialogue for Religions', *Development*, vol 46 (4), pp 35-8.

Taft Morris, Cynthia and Adelman, Irma (1980) 'The Religious Factor in Economic Development', *World Development*, vol 8 (7/8), pp 491-502.

Tal, Nachman (2005) *Radical Islam in Egypt and Jordan*, Sussex Academic Press, Brighton.

Tamimi, Azzam (2000) 'The Origins of Arab Secularism', in *Islam and Secularism in the Middle East*, Esposito, John L. and Tamimi, Azzam (eds), Hurst and Company, London.

Tangenberg, Kathleen (2004) 'Spirituality and Faith Based Social Services: Exploring Provider Values, Beliefs and Practices', *Journal of Religion and Spirituality in Social Work*, vol 23 (3), pp 3-23.

Tawney, Richard H. (1920) *The Sickness of an Acquisitive Society*, Fabian Society, London.

Tekeli, Sirin and Devrim-Bouvard, Nukte (1996) 'Turkish Women and the Welfare Party: An Interview with Sirin Tekeli', *Middle East Report*, *vol* 199, pp 28-9.

Thomas, George M. (2001) 'Religions in Global Civil Society', *Sociology of Religion*, vol 62 (4), pp 491-514.

Thomas, Scott (2007) 'Outwitting the Developed Countries? Existential Insecurity and the Global Resurgence of Religion', *Journal of International Affairs*, vol 61 (1), pp 21-47.

Thompson, Elisabeth (2000) *Colonial Citizens: Republican Rights, Paternal Privilege and Gender in French Syria and Lebanon*, Columbia University Press, New York.

Tinker, Claire (2006) 'Islamophobia, Social Cohesion and Autonomy: Challenging the Arguments against State Funded Muslim Schools in Britain', *Muslim Education Quarterly*, vol 23 (1), pp 4-19.

Titmuss, Richard (1970) *The Gift Relationship: From Human Blood to Social Policy*, George Allen & Unwin, London.

Titmuss, Richard M. (1976) *Commitment to Welfare*, George Allen & Unwin, London.

Tomalin, Emma (2008) 'Faiths and Development', in Desai, Vandana and Potter, Robert (eds), Hodder Arnols, London.

Traboulsi, Omar with the collaboration of Ramadan, Bassam and Shaha, Riza (2001) *Mapping and Review of Lebanese NGOs*, Internal Report, World Bank, Beirut.

Trigg, Roger (1998) *Rationality and Religion: Does Faith Need Reason?*, Blackwell, Oxford.

Trigg, Roger (2007) *Religion in Public Life: Must Faith Be Privatized?*, Oxford University Press, Oxford.

Tripp, Charles (2006) *Islam and the Moral Economy: The Challenges of Capitalism*, Cambridge University Press, Cambridge.

Tripp, Linda (1999) 'Gender and Development from a Christian Perspective: Experience from World Vision', *Gender and Development*, vol 7 (1), pp 62-8.

Tucker, Vincent (1996) 'Introduction: A Cultural Perspective on Development', *European Journal of Development Research*, vol 8 (1), pp 1-21.

Turner, Harold W. (1980) 'African Independent Churches and Economic Development', *World Development*, vol 8 (7/8), pp 523-34.

Tyndale, Wendy (2000) 'Faith and Economics in "Development": A Bridge Across the Chasm?', *Development in Practice*, vol 10 (1), pp 9-18.

Tyndale, Wendy (2003) 'Idealism and Practicality: The Role of Religion in Development', *Development*, vol 46 (4), pp 22-7.

Tyndale, Wendy R. (2006) 'Some Final Reflections', in *Visions of Development: Faith Based Initiatives*, Tyndale, Wendy R. (ed), Ashgate, Basingstoke, pp 153-78.

Underwood, Carol (2004) 'Islam and Health Policy: A Study of the Islamic Republic of Iran', in *Islam and Social Policy*, Heyneman, Stephen P. (ed), Vanderbilt University Press, Nashville, TN, pp 181-206.

UNDP (United Nations Development Programme) (2002) *Arab Human Development Report*, United Nations Publications, New York, accessed 12/07/02 at www.undp/ahdr/org

UNDP (2004) *Cultural Liberty in Today's Diverse World*, UNDP, New York.

UNDP (2005) *Arab Human Development Report*, United Nations Publications, New York, accessed 15/09/08 at http://204.200.211.31/contents/file/ArabHumanDevelopRep2005En.pdf

UNDP (2008) *Fighting Climate Change: Human Solidarity in a Divided World*, Human Development Report, United Nations Publications, New York, accessed 9/10/08 at http://hdrstats.undp.org/countries/data_sheets/cty_ds_LBN.html

UNDP and Institute of National Planning, Egypt (2008) *Egypt Human Development Report 2008: Egypt's Social Contract: The Role of Civil Society*, United Nations Publications, New York.

UNDP and MSA (Ministry of Social Affairs) (1998) *Mapping of Living Conditions in Lebanon*, Beirut, Lebanon.

UN-ESCWA (United Nations Economic and Social Commission for Western Africa) (2004) *Central Issues Related to Social Policies: Comparative Study and Guidelines for the Formulation of Social Policies in the ESCWA Region*, Social Policy Series No 9, United Nations, New York.

UN-ESCWA (2005) *Towards Integrated Social Policies in Arab Countries: Framework and Comparative Analysis*, United Nations, New York, accessed 15/9/08 at www.escwa.un.org/sp-readings/Final%20Towards%20Integrated%20Social%20Polic y%20in%20Arab%20Region-En.pdf

Valins, Oliver (2006) 'The Difference of Voluntarism: The Place of Voluntary Sector Care Homes for Older Jewish People in the United Kingdom', in *Landscapes of Voluntarism: New Spaces of Health, Welfare and Governance*, Milligan, Christine and Conradson, David (eds), The Policy Press, Bristol, pp 135-52.

Van Kersbergen, Kees (1995) *Social Capitalism: A Study of Christian Democracy and the Welfare State*, Routledge, London and New York.

Van Kersbergen, Kees and Manow, Philip (eds) (2009) *Religion, Class Coalitions and Welfare States*, Cambridge University Press, Cambridge.

Van Oorschot, Wim, Opielka, Michael and Pfau-Effinger, Birgit (2008) 'The Culture of the Welfare State: Historical and Theoretical Arguments', in *Culture and the Welfare State: Values and Social Policy in Comparative Perspective*, van Oorschot, Wim, Opielka, Michael and Pfau-Effinger, Birgit (eds), Edward Elgar, Cheltenham.

Ver Beek, Kurt A. (2000) 'Spirituality: A Development Taboo', *Development in Practice*, vol 10 (1), pp 31-43.

Voll, John O. (1987) 'Islamic Renewal and the "Failure of the West"', in *Religious Resurgence: Contemporary Cases in Islam, Christianity and Judaism*, Antoun, Richard T. and Hegland, Mary E. (eds), Syracuse University Press, New York, pp 127-44.

Von der Mehden, Fred R. (1980) 'Islamic Resurgence in Malaysia', in *Islam and Development: Religion and Sociopolitical Change*, Esposito, John L. (ed), Syracuse University Press, New York, pp163-80.

Walker, Alan and Wong, Chack-kie (2005) 'Introduction: East Asian Welfare Regimes', in *East Asian Welfare Regimes in Transition: From Confucianism to Globalisation*, Walker, Alan and Wong, Chack-kie (eds), The Policy Press, Bristol, pp 3-20.

Walker, Robert (1995) 'The Dynamics of Poverty and Social Exclusion', in *Beyond the Threshold: The Measurement and Analysis of Social Exclusion*, Room, Graham (ed), The Policy Press, Bristol.

Weber, Max (1930) *The Protestant Work Ethic and the Spirit of Capitalism*, Routledge, London and New York.

Weiss, Holger (2002) 'Reorganising Social Welfare among Muslims: Islamic Voluntarism and Other Forms of Communal Support in Northern Ghana', *Journal of Religion in Africa*, vol 32 (1), pp 83-109.

Whelan, Robert (1996) *The Corrosion of Charity*, IEA Health and Welfare Unit, London.

Wickham, Carrie Rosefsky (2002) *Mobilizing Islam*, Columbia University Press, New York.

Wiktorowics, Q. (2004) *Islamic Activism: A Social Movement Theory Approach*, Indiana University Press, Indianapolis, IN.

Wilber, Charles K. and Jameson, Kenneth P. (1980) 'Religious Values and Social Limits to Development', *World Development*, vol 8 (7/8), pp 467-80.

Williamson, Sabrina A. and Hodges, Vanessa G. (2006) 'It Kind of Made Me Feel Important: Client Reflections on Faith-Based Social Services', *Journal of Religion and Spirituality in Social Work*, vol 25 (2), pp 43-57.

Wineburg, Bob (2001) *A Limited Partnership: The Politics of Religion, Welfare and Social Service*, Columbia University Press, New York.

Wolfe, Marshall (1995) 'Globalization and Social Exclusion: Some Paradoxes', in *Social Exclusion: Rhetoric, Reality and Responses*, Rodgers, Gerry, Gore, Charles G. and Figueiredo, Jose B. (eds), ILO, Geneva.

Wolfinger, Nicholas H. (2002) 'On Writing Fieldnotes: Collection Strategies and Background Expectancies', *Qualitative Research*, vol 2 (1), pp 85-95.

Wood, Geoff (2004) 'Informal Security Regimes: The Strength of Relationship', in *Insecurity and Welfare Regimes in Asia, Africa and Latin America: Social Policy in a Development Context*, Gough, Ian and Wood, Geoff (eds), with Barrientos, Armando, Beval, Phillipa, Davis, Peter and Room, Graham, Cambridge University Press, Cambridge, pp 49-87.

Wood, Geoff and Gough, Ian (2004) 'Conclusion: Rethinking Social Policy in Development Contexts', in *Insecurity and Welfare Regimes in Asia, Africa and Latin America: Social Policy in a Development Context*, Gough, Ian and Wood, Geoff (eds), with Barrientos, Armando, Beval, Phillipa, Davis, Peter and Room, Graham, Cambridge University Press, Cambridge, pp 312-26.

World Bank (2004) *World Development Report 2004: Making Services Work for Poor People*, World Bank and Oxford University Press, Washington, DC.

World Bank (2008) *Lebanon Data at-a-Glance*, World Bank, New York, accessed 9/10/08 at http://devdata.worldbank.org/AAG/lbn_aag

Wuthnow, Robert (1987) 'Indices of Religious Resurgence in the United States', in *Religious Resurgence: Contemporary Cases in Islam, Christianity and Judaism*, Antoun, Richard T. and Hegland, Mary E. (eds), Syracuse University Press, New York, pp 15-33.

Wuthnow, Robert (1988) *The Restructuring of American Religion: Society and Faith since World War II*, Princeton University Press, Princeton, NJ.

Xiberras, Martine (1994) *Les Théories de l'Exclusion*, Méridiens Klincksieck, Paris.

Zadek, Simon (1993) 'The Practice of Buddhist Economics?', *American Journal of Economics and Sociology*, vol 52 (4), pp 433-45.

Zahl, Mari-Anne, Dyrud Furman, Leola, Benson, Perry W. and Canda, Edward R. (2007) 'Religion and Spirituality in Social Work Practice and Education in a Cross-Cultural Context: Findings from a Norwegian and UK Study', *European Journal of Social Work*, vol 10 (3), pp 295-317.

Zrinščak, Siniša (2006) 'Religion' in *International Encyclopedia of Social Policy, Volume 2*, Fitzpatrick, Tony, Kwon, Huck-Ju, Manning, Nick, Midgley, James and Pascall, Gillian (eds), Routledge, Oxford, pp 1131-4.

Zubaida, Sami (1992) 'Islam, the State and Democracy: Contrasting Conceptions of Society in Egypt', *Middle East Report*, vol 179, pp 2-10.

Appendix A: Lebanon country profile

Table A1: Basic data

Indicator (year and source)	Value
Population (2007)[a]	4.1 million
Urban population (2007)[a]	87%
Population aged under 15 (2005)[b]	28.6%
Population aged 65 and above (2005)[b]	7.2%
Surface area (km sq)[c]	10,000 km sq
Human Development Index rank (2005)[b]	88
Human Poverty Index rank (2005)[b]	14
Adult literacy (2002)[c]	86.5%
Youth literacy (1990)[c]	92.1%
Maternal mortality (per 100,000 live births) (2005)[b]	150
Infant mortality (per 1,000 live births) (2005)[b]	27
GNI (2007)[a]	US$23.7 billion
GNI/capita (2007)[a]	US$5,770
Female economic participation (2005)[b]	32.4%
Unemployment (1997)[d]	8.6%
External debt (2004)[e]	US$40 billion
Total debt service as % of GDP (2005)[b]	16.1%
ODA assistance as % of GDP (2005)[b]	1.1%

Sources:

[a] World Bank (2008)

[b] UNDP (2008)

[c] UNDP (2004)

[d] ILO (2003)

[e] World Bank (2004)

Table A2: Public expenditure as % of GDP: key development indicators (2002)

Type of public expenditure	As % of GDP
Education	2.6
Health	3.2
Military	4.5
Debt service	16.1

Source: UNDP (2008)

Table A3: Share of social expenditure as % of GDP and Budget after debt servicing

Budget year	Social expenditure as % of GDP	Social expenditure as % of Budget (after debt servicing)
1997	5.63	20.03
1998	6.21	21.3
1999	6.94	20.52
2000	7.85	22.7
2001	8.51	21.6
2002	7.92	22.47
2003	8.09	25.71
2004	8.2	24.93

Source: Ministry of Finance (2004)

Appendix B: Social protection institutions and coverage

Table B1: Formal social protection institutions (with note on level of generosity)

Social protection institution	Categories of beneficiaries	Services
National Social Security Fund (*insufficient*)	Private sector employees Employees and retired personnel of public institutions not subject to the civil service Private school teachers Public transportation drivers and owners of taxis Employees and employers of the bakery sector Newspaper sellers University students	Family allowances (20% for the spouse and 11% for each child – must be >75%) Sickness and maternity indemnities (90% of hospitalisation costs, 80% for medical consultations and medications) End of service indemnities Injuries at work and sickness due to work (exists in law but not applied) Old-age pension (replacing end of service indemnity) still under discussion
Public Sector Cooperative for Civil Servants (*generous*)	Public sector employees within the civil service	Indemnities for hospitalisation and medical consultations (for the employee, 90% of hospitalisation costs, 75% of medical consultations costs, medication and dental treatment; 75% for the spouse and 50% for the children) School grants (75% of children's school fees – excludes university studies – up to five children) Social assistance (marriage, death, birth) Indemnity pay for end of service or retirement (not linked to the public sector cooperative for civil servants)
Social Protection for Non-Civil Sectors (*very generous*)	All military forces: Army Internal Security Forces National Security State Security Customs Police	Hospitalisation costs and medical consultations (100% for soldiers, 75% for their spouses and children, 50% for other members of their families) School grants (75% of school education, 50% of university education) Social assistance (marriage, death, birth) Indemnity pay for end of service or retirement (not linked to the public sector cooperative for civil servants)

Source: Melki, (2000, p 191)

Table B2: Health coverage by type of insurance

Type of insurance	% of population covered
Public sector insurance	13.1
National Social Security Fund	15.2
Private insurance	8.7
Insurance by employer	1.9
Mixed insurance	2.9
No insurance	58.2

Source: UNDP and MSA (1998, p 45), citing Lebanese Central Administration for Statistics

Index

Page references for notes are followed by n